SKELMERSDALE

FICTION RESERVE STOCK

AUTHOR

CLASS
AFSF

TITLE
CYBERSEX

CYBERSEX

Cybersex

Edited by
RICHARD GLYN JONES

RAVEN BOOKS
London

Robinson Publishing Ltd
7 Kensington Church Court
London W8 4SP

First published in the UK by Raven Books, an imprint of Robinson
Publishing Ltd, 1996

06852751

A copy of the British Library Cataloguing in Publication data is
available from the British Library

ISBN 1-85487-447-0

Printed and bound in the EC

10 9 8 7 6 5 4 3 2 1

CONTENTS

ACKNOWLEDGEMENTS

For their help, advice and encouragement, my thanks to Brian W. Aldiss, Mark Crean, John Clute, Maxim Jakubowski, Virginia Kidd, Sam J. Lundwall, David Pringle, Will Self, Susanna J. Sturgis and Ian Watson, and to the following for permission to publish or reprint these stories:

"The Time Disease" by Martin Amis, first published in *Granta*, from *Einstein's Monsters* (London: Jonathan Cape, 1987), copyright © 1987 by Martin Amis, reprinted by permission of Random House UK Ltd and the author's agent, Peters Fraser and Dunlop.

"Kiss Booties Night-Night" by Storm Constantine, first published in this collection, copyright © 1996 by Storm Constantine, published by permission of the author.

"[Learning About] Machine Sex" by Candas Jane Dorsey, first published in *Machine Sex . . . and Other Stories* (Canada: Tesseract (Porcépic) Books, 1988), copyright © 1988 by Candas Jane Dorsey, reprinted by permission of the author.

"Bettina's Bet" by L. Timmel Duchamp, first published in *Asimov's Science Fiction*, January 1996, copyright © 1995 by L. Timmel Duchamp, reprinted by permission of the author.

"Closer" by Greg Egan, first published in *Eidolon 9*, Winter 1992, copyright © 1992 by Greg Egan, reprinted by permission of the author.

"Catman" by Harlan Ellison, first published in *Final Stage: the Ultimate Science Fiction Anthology*, ed. Edward L. Ferman and Barry N. Malzberg (New York: Charterhouse Books, Inc., 1974), copyright © 1974 by Harlan Ellison, reprinted by arrangement with, and permission of, the author and the author's agent, Richard Curtis Associates, Inc., New York, USA. All rights reserved.

"Love Story in Three Acts" by David Gerrold, first published in *Nova 1*, ed. Harry Harrison (New York: Delacorte Press, 1970), copyright © 1970 by David Gerrold, reprinted by permission of the author and the author's agent, Richard Curtis Associates, Inc.

"More Than the Sum of His Parts" by Joe Haldeman, first published in *Playboy*, March 1993, copyright © 1993 by Joe Haldeman, reprinted by permission of the author.

"Bots: a Love Story and a Dream" by Michael Hemmingson, first published in *Puck 11*, 1995, copyright © 1995 by Brian C. Clark/Permeable Press, reprinted by permission of Permeable Press.

"Points of View" by Kathe Koja, first published in *Asimov's Science Fiction*, October 1989, copyright © 1989 by Kathe Koja, reprinted by permission of the author's agent, Russell Galen.

"Borovsky's Hollow Woman" by Nancy Kress and Jeff Duntemann, first published in *Omni*, October 1983, copyright © 1983 by Nancy Kress and Jeff Duntemann, reprinted by permission of Writers' House, Inc.

"A Coney Island of the Mind" by Maureen F. McHugh, first published in *Asimov's Science Fiction*, February 1993, copyright © 1993 by Maureen F. McHugh, reprinted by permission of the author.

"Love and Sex Among the Invertebrates" by Pat Murphy, first published in *Alien Sex*, ed. Ellen Datlow (New York: Dutton, 1990), copyright © 1990 by Pat Murphy, reprinted by permission of the author and the author's agent, Jean V. Naggar Literary Agency.

"Artificially Induced Dub Syndrome" by Jeff Noon, first published in *Technopagan*, ed. Elaine Palmer (London: Pulp Faction, 1995), copyright © 1995 by Jeff Noon, reprinted by permission of Pulp Faction and the author's agent, Michelle Kass.

"Day Million" by Frederik Pohl, first published in *Rogue*, February 1966, copyright © 1966 by Frederik Pohl, reprinted by permission of the Carnell Literary Agency.

"Randy Karl Tucker, or, The Education of a Moldie-Lover" by Rudy Rucker (an episode from his forthcoming novel *Freeware*), first published in this collection, copyright © 1995 by Rudy Rucker, published by permission of the author.

Foreword by Will Self, copyright © Will Self 1996.

"Profit and Lust" by Will Self, first published in *The Observer*, 15 October 1995, copyright © 1995 by *The Observer*, reprinted by permission of Guardian Newspapers Ltd.

"The Girl Who Was Plugged In" by James Tiptree, Jr [Alice Sheldon], first published in *New Dimensions 3*, ed. Robert Silverberg (New York: Signet, 1974), copyright © 1973 by James Tiptree, Jr, reprinted by permission of the author's Estate and the Estate's agent, Virginia Kidd.

"Memories of the Body" by Lisa Tuttle, first published in *Interzone* 22, Winter 1987–8, copyright © 1987 by Lisa Tuttle, reprinted by permission of the author.

"Pairpuppets" by Manuel Van Loggem, first published in Holland in 1974, English translation by the author first published in *The Best from the Rest of the World: European Science Fiction*, ed. Donald A. Wollheim (New York: Doubleday, 1976), copyright © 1974 by Manuel Van Loggem, reprinted by permission of the author.

"The Big Space Fuck" by Kurt Vonnegut, Jr, first published in *Again, Dangerous Visions*, ed. Harlan Ellison (New York: Doubleday, 1972), copyright © 1972 by Kurt Vonnegut, Jr, reprinted by permission of Donald C. Farber, Attorney for Mr Vonnegut.

"Custom-Built Girl" by Ian Watson (an episode from his unpublished novel *The Woman Machine*), first published in this collection, copyright © 1976, 1996 by Ian Watson, published by permission of the author.

"All My Darling Daughters" by Connie Willis, first published in *Fire Watch* (New York: Bluejay Books, 1985), copyright © 1984 by Connie Willis, reprinted by permission of the author.

"It's Very Clean" by Gene Wolfe, first published in *Generation*, ed. David Gerrold (New York: Dell, 1972), copyright © 1972 by Gene Wolfe, reprinted by permission of the author and the author's agent, Virginia Kidd.

"Starcrossed" by George Zebrowski, first published in *Eros in Orbit*, ed. Joseph Elder (New York: Trident Press, 1973), copyright © 1973 by George Zebrowski, reprinted by permission of the author and the author's agent, Richard Curtis Associates, Inc.

Foreword

As a thirteen-year-old teenager in the mid-seventies, I consumed science fiction and fantasy in large, indiscriminate chunks, somewhat like a calf being fed a bale of hay. I couldn't for certain have said why it was that I did so, why it was – precisely – that I liked the genres, but I did. I would go to the library and select six books purely on the basis that they were on a publisher's science fiction list, then go home and chomp through them, tucked up under the bed covers in a slew of biscuit crumbs and adolescent secretions.

The possibilist worlds of science fiction were actually not so bad a place to learn something about the real, adult world that was coming my way. Projected on to canvases measured in parsecs were the more emotionally parochial concerns of the writers. Thus I came to appreciate – at some level – that Robert Heinlein had something of an aversion to representative democracy; that J. G. Ballard, while nominally classed as a science fiction writer, was in fact no respecter of space or time; and that Frank Herbert had a thing for the bedouin.

There was one aspect of the books and stories that I read which puzzled me, given that my main preoccupation at the time was that I would die without having engaged in a penetrative sexual act with another life form (aged thirteen, more or less *any* life form would have done!), and that was the way sex was written about. I couldn't, for example, understand why it was that the Savage had such an aversion to the Brave New World. I myself would have settled happily for the Central Hatcheries, the personality conditioning and the cult Our Ford, if I could have had the soma and the group sex. Damn it all! Even Winston Smith got laid in 1984. Robert Heinlein's expansive space operas may have been tendentious exercises in allegory, but the salient facts, for me, were those of mutated life, happily coupling in endless permutations.

I fell out of my science fiction phase sometime around then, shocked when I realized that the *Dune* trilogy was in fact depicting events not dissimilar to those going down in the contemporary Middle East, rather than the distant future of deep space. It was my loss. Had I been able to read some of these narratives with more discrimination, I would have realized that the real *primum mobile* of the genre was not an unabashed belief in the advancement of technology (and its concomitant impact on human society), but the rather more problematic question of what impact that technology would have on the human psyche itself. Sexually inexperienced, taken in by space opera, and the Spirit of the Age, I was unable to fully appreciate the parallel investigation being conducted within the genre, a mapping of what J. G. Ballard has termed "inner space".

Of course, from the vantage of the mid-nineties much of the futurism of twenty and thirty years ago looks sloppy, if not to say absurd. But what is more remarkable is that some of it is still so much more acute (by which I mean more believable) than what is currently being produced. Imagining the future seems to have been – on the whole – better in the past than it is now! (By the same token Concorde is still the only supersonic passenger aircraft in the world, twenty-five years after its maiden flight.)

In matters sexual the particular time frame of the last thirty years also presents us with a titivating paradox. Writing in the white-hot lust of the promiscuous sixties (and their aftermath), many science fiction and fantasy writers were able to document the psychic and practical impact of changes in sexual mores which were yet to become institutionalized, or even widely understood.

It's a perspective that is drawn out very effectively in this anthology by the arrangement of the stories in their chronological order of imagining, beginning with my flippant view of the very near future (only a hop, a skip and a grunt away), and ending with Frederik Pohl's spirited, wry rendition of matters sexual a hundred millennia from now.

Pohl's story, written in the sixties, exhibits both one of the best methods for taking a reader into the future (making the present appear arbitrary, even absurd) and one of the enduring, valuable perceptions that the genre has allowed for. "Genital organs," Pohl's shadowy narrator tells us, "feel nothing. Neither do hands, nor breasts, nor lips; they are only receptors accepting and transmitting impulses. It is the brain that feels; it is the interpretation of these impulses that makes agony or orgasm."

And it is within the liminal, the millimetric gap between those receptors and that feeling brain that all the technological impact upon our sense of ourselves as sexual beings can occur. Technologies concerned with the biology of reproduction are, of course, enormously influential; but while their mechanics may be placed outside and either anterior or posterior to the sexual act itself, the way they affect our erotic perception is implicit in this selfsame gap.

Pohl envisions a future of virtual sex, from the standpoint of the sixties, with as much credibility as Candas Jane Dorsey, who was writing some twenty years later. Both writers are preoccupied with the idea that the creation of artificial intelligence will allow for virtual loving, but while Pohl advocates cultural–temporal relativism, holding that our own preoccupation with sexual embodiment is not a limiting constraint, Dorsey is more dystopic, recoiling from the prospect, and making her protagonist, the creator of the perfect virtual sex programme, herself a sexually vulnerable, if not to say sexually abused woman.

Harlan Ellison's "Catman" is one of those stories I read aged thirteen and couldn't quite get to grips with. I couldn't understand why the thief would pass up on all that fab free-fall sex with the delicious Joice, in order to stick his wingwang in a two-mile-long hunk of metal. Now, of course, I see that Ellison was attempting to do many things with this story: recast the Oedipus myth, investigate the relations between autonomy and desire; and most importantly identify that sharp declivity wherein the forbidden points up the erotic.

Mind you, while I couldn't grasp the thematic content of the story, even at that age I appreciated that Ellison knew how to write a good fuck when he wanted to. There may not be much in the way of straightforwardly arousing writing in this anthology, but for my money the human sex scene in "Catman" still hits the G-spot.

A persistent theme for writers marrying matters sexual to matters machine, has been the creation – if not manufacture – of idealized sexual partners. Thus Lisa Tuttle in "Memories of the Body" breathes life into a sort of Stepford Wives psychodrama. Here, as in Ellison's "Catman", the ultimate taboo is to have sex with a machine, but the machines are at least far more personable. So personable, indeed, that they are able to engage in quite subtle, metaphysical discussions concerning their predicament. But really, Tuttle's tale is as much about the timeless and pernicious question of what it means to sexually possess another, as it is about cybernetics. The "faxes" (human replicants) of the protagonist and her lover's former spouses, are really the ultimate incarnation of Readers' Wives, acting out ancient strategies of possession through controlled abandonment.

The same Othello-vision – in a more fantastical way – applies to the fictional topography mapped by Ian Watson in the excerpt from his notorious novel, published here under the title "Custom-Built Girl". Watson's word-painting may be of a distant future, when humans are "grown" to certain sexual specifications, but the eerily empathetic personality of his eponymous heroine plugs us back into a grand tradition of literature that pits the naïve against the decadent. In her benighted progress, Jade seems to reprise the venal voyaging of Georges Bataille's characters in *Blue of Noon* and *Story of the Eye*, or Pauline Réage's anonymous love-object in *The Story of O*. And in creating a setting for his characters, Watson borrows the furniture of Surrealism, with its banjaxed anachronism, to create a picture of a future that I feel would not have seemed anomalous or unbelievable to Kafka.

Another, important tendency represented in this anthology would also have gone straight over the head (or glans!) of my thirteen-year-old self, and this is the extent to which women science fiction and science fantasy writers have made the fertile ground of future sex their own. It is not without accident that James Tiptree, Jr (the *nom de plume* of Alice Sheldon) was one of the originators of the sub-genre which came to be known as Cyber-Punk. Tiptree's story "The Girl Who Was Plugged In", while being one of the earliest imaginings of the extreme attenuation that technology may make possible between brain and receptor, is also one of the most chilling and coherent.

Feminist writers, while not reacting with knee-jerk antipathy to the prospect of an exponential increase in polymorphous perversity, none the less seem to have sicked on early that where there is greater sexual control at a remove, there is also a greater possibility of sexual exploitation. But then, had I really grasped at thirteen what lay ahead for me, for you, for us all, I might well have simply pulled the covers back over my head, grabbed hold of whatever book-bound alternative world was to hand, and struggled to remain Peter Pan-like, within it forever.

Will Self

INTRODUCTION

Richard Glyn Jones

As humans and machines grow ever closer, it is the sexual aspects of the merger that are making the news. Can you commit adultery on the Internet?, asks the London *Observer* under the headline KISS OF THE CYBER WOMAN. It seems that you can. Meanwhile, an electronic contraceptive will shortly become available which will flash a green light when it is safe to have sex. Safe in the sense of avoiding pregnancy rather than avoiding AIDS, that is. Eventually, it is inevitable that we'll *merge* with computers, predicts Clive Sinclair, who invented the pocket calculator and went on to build computers. He doesn't like the idea much.

This seems like a good moment to pause and take stock of how far such things have progressed in the last few years, and to ponder the implications of what might be around the corner. That we should turn for the most part to writers of science fiction to do so will not surprise devotees of the genre, for these issues were being explored there long before they grabbed the attention of the media pundits. Artificial intelligence, robots indistinguishable from humans, minds and bodies electronically linked . . . these (and many other things) have been familiar elements in the SF universe for decades, and writers and readers have long passed the gosh–wow stage of simple amazement at such technological wizardry to engage in more intelligent debate about its possible implications, and its morality. And, since the late 1960s, when it became possible to write freely about sexual matters in the SF magazines, much of the debate has focused sharply on issues of sex, love and the very nature of identity.

The stories that follow form part of this debate, and readers in search of pornographic thrills should be warned at the outset that they won't find much of that here. Many of the stories *are* sexually explicit, of course, but that is not the main concern. Rather, they contemplate the sexual future in a variety of ways, from Will Self's wry stroll into the next century to Greg Egan's searching exploration of a future relationship, taking that particular line of inquiry about as far as it will logically go – and then we're off into space, with all problems *that* might bring. The stories are arranged in the order in which they are supposed to happen, from the state-of-the-art present to the remote future.

I have taken a broad view of what the 'cyber' part of the title means (we all know what sex is, I take it), using it not just in its current vague form meaning 'something to do with computers' but more in its original sense, which derives from Norbert Wiener's *cybernetics*: the study of all systems that show some degree of self-determination, whether they be machines, computers or indeed human beings. Cybersex in this context is therefore sex that depends to a greater or lesser extent on technology.

The sexual possibilities of machines have been interesting to people ever since there have been machines, from the flogging and masturbatory devices of Georgian times to the latest electronic gadgets from Japan. With the revolution in home computing of the 1980s and the rapid current spread of the Internet the possibilities have suddenly and dramatically increased, and already the Internet is prowled by stalkers, purveyors of child porn and other unwelcome visitors. Technology is moving more rapidly than anyone could have foreseen – even the SF writers mostly failed to anticipate the trend towards miniaturization and the sheer *speed* at which things would become not only possible but affordable – and every change inevitably has a sexual dimension. The home video revolution was driven largely by the sudden realization that it was possible to watch porn in the comfort of one's own home (plus a few cartoons for the kids), and it was several years before laws relating to videos were introduced to try and control the situation. Too late. Meanwhile, technology has marched on regardless, and continues to do so; Virtual Reality is now a reality, and even more interesting things are no doubt in the pipeline. It's easy to feel overwhelmed, to want to pause and get to grips with *this* before even starting to contemplate *that*, but it isn't going to stop.

The stories in *Cybersex*, by some of the best writers to have considered the subject in the last thirty years or so, look at some of these possibilities. I hope that reading them will prove a stimulating, even an enlightening experience, because the sexual future is almost upon us.

Damn, it's here.

Richard Glyn Jones

PROFIT AND LUST
Will Self

The elegantly wasted fiction of Will Self – the novel My Idea of Fun *and the stories collected in* The Quantity Theory of Insanity *and* Grey Area *– is concerned with drugs, madness and strange fantasy, and it is often wildly funny. These, together with a recent collection of non-fiction,* Junk Mail, *have earned him a reputation as one of England's hottest young writers. "Profit and Lust", a so-far-uncollected piece, takes us on a stroll into the sexual future, and serves admirably as a taster for what is to follow . . .*

Last week, in a bid for pop-scientific stardom, I took Professor Hawking's remarks about the possibility of time travel to heart. My reasoning was – like that of all great pop scientists – incredibly straightforward. If time travel is possible then the best way to access it will surely be by utilizing those natural drives which concentrate on the link between the present and the future, and its annihilation. Put simply: the sexual drive.

For sex is always either about procreation, or not about procreation. It tantalizes with this binary opposition and in so doing draws our attention inexorably to the future-that-is-in-the-present, and the past that is eaten up in the ecstasy of now. Therefore, in order to travel to the future, some sort of mechanical gizmo that linked orgasm to time seemed to be in order.

Rummaging behind my bed, I came up with some 15 vibrators left there by unsatisfied former lovers. I wired all of them together using hanks of frayed telephone extension cord, plugged them into various of my orifi, and then plugged the socket into the phone.

Finally – and I think this is the little twist of lateral reasoning that will guarantee me my place in the history of engineering alongside Watt, Faraday and Ann Summers – I dialled the number of another dissatisfied former lover, who had moved east, to a time zone well ahead of ours, in order to escape my febrile gropings.

She picked up the phone, I started panting, and – bingo! – I found myself yanked forward into the future. About 55 years into the future to be precise.

I won't tire you with all the details of my sojourn in the next millennium, suffice it to say that while here I've gathered a considerable amount of information on what most concerns us all. Namely, the future of sex and gender. The salient facts I have set out below, in the form of a sort of Innovations catalogue.

Yes, when you arrive in 2050, shagged by the passing of the years, these are some of the sexual realities you will be facing.

Ret-Gel™

I was much interested during my future trip to see people of all ages, genders and orientations spraying themselves – in public – with what appeared to be some kind of deep heat embrocation in aerosol form. Emblazoned on the side of the can was the trademark Ret-Gel.

Standing in the queue for films, at cafés, at the opera, even walking down the street, they would stop, expose the afflicted portion and give it a good, long blast of this stuff. What was most intriguing about this was that the portion was usually genital rather than muscular. I bearded one of these sprayers, explained my status as a time traveller (this didn't faze her at all; apparently the future is as cluttered with travellers from the past as today's Carnaby Street is with Dutch teenagers having their hair turned into limp dreadlocks) and asked what the spray was.

Ret-Gel was, it transpired, short for 'Retroactive Jealousy'. And the spray the aerosol contained was a specially formulated treatment which would banish the effects of this pernicious condition – albeit only for a short, tingling period.

Some sage once said that those who fail to learn from their sexual history are condemned to repeat it, and repeat it, and repeat it again. The next millennium is marked by this phenomenon at the level of the collective unconscious. If you thought the late 20th century was bad as far as serial monogamy goes – just you wait.

In 2050 most periodicals consist of only a few pages of editorial or listings and a great wodge of lonely hearts ads. In this Kingdom of Blind Dating most people consider themselves virtually celibate unless they contract for a new relationship – with all the trimmings – about once a week.

Naturally this strange quasi-marital status brings with it both advantages and disadvantages. The disadvantages are that no one becomes bored with their partner. Relationships are over long before anyone has heard the anecdote about the Triumph Dolomite and four pints of Old Peculier once – let alone twice.

The downside is the almost crippling sense of retroactive jealousy with which everyone is imbued. Your great love – of the moment – has contained within her/him the impress of a myriad lovers. The only solution to this gut-twirling feeling, this hard bone of emotionality stuck in the proverbial gullet, is Ret-Gel. Apply it frequently, and the disturbing sensation that you are lying, not with a human being, but with some ancient monument which has been recreationally scaled by a multitude, will evaporate.

The trouble is that Ret-Gel only works for a limited time. Applications need to be longer and longer, more and more frequent. Eventually, even these hyper-serial monogamists of the future are driven to embrace procreation, albeit in a somewhat bizarre way.

Foetal Gap

Strolling through the centre of London in 2050 I noticed that few changes appeared to have been wrought by the millennium. Same oiled bikers, wearing ridged and knobbled rubbers and leathers, astride their 5cc mopeds in Soho Square. Same epicene television people wafting down Wardour Street (although in Brewer Street they were no longer selling GHB, only W3, a new drug which makes you feel as if you're having sex in Acton). Same Cantonese gamblers, hunched in their windcheaters under the gateway to the East in Gerrard Street. But when I reached Covent Garden I saw something new, something arresting.

The lettering on the sign was the same, and the overall interior design of the emporium was just as I remembered it, but the sign said Foetal Gap, and the clothes hanging on the racks were ridiculously small – Action Man size. I went in and accosted the manager. He was effusive and enthusiastic, only too eager to tell me all about this strange, futuristic redoubt of the trendy.

"You see, parents nowadays don't want to wait for parturition itself to ensure that their progeny are decked out in the latest threads. We here at Foetal Gap are dedicated to ensuring that your baby won't be dowdy, won't feel – how can I put it – sartorially challenged at birth.

"All the clothes you see on the racks are the correct sizes for foetuses in the second and third trimesters of pregnancy. We have bib 'n' braces, baseball caps, T-shirts and sun dresses, all specially styled for the womb in textures that show up well on ultrasound. And we offer a comprehensive service. Come in and purchase 3,000 Ecus' worth of our fab gear, and we'll provide – absolutely free of charge – the services of a top micro-surgeon. The womb of the expectant mother will be opened up in one of our customised changing booth-cum-operating theatres and her foetus will be clad in the birthing costume of her choice."

"But surely," I asked this epigone of the epidural, "the foetus must find this radical interference rather traumatic?"

"Not at all," he grinned. "In our experience Gap-clad newborns are far more contented than those delivered, as it were, in a state of nature. As long, that is, as they're provided with a full-length mirror soon after birth."

I still wasn't convinced. When I explained my status as a time traveller the manager rolled his eyes, but he was prepared to let me see a fitting in progress (as we talked, a young mother who was heavily *enceinte* passed us, cooing over a pair of woolly tights Thumbelina would have been lost in). However, I declined when he started extolling the virtues of washed denim placenta bags.

The Innuendo Converter

I headed up Long Acre with not just my head but my whole body shaking. I felt like a Spanish fly that had eaten another Spanish fly. How, I wondered, could sex be sexy any longer, in a world of such strident revelation, where every hidden and dark portion of the body had become the stuff of side show?

For, as we all know, the erotic depends on having something left to reveal. And we British, with our genitals for the best part of the year dry-docked in Damart, are past-masters and mistresses of the skewed comment, the titivating remark. We are used to conjuring eroticism out of the most unpromising of materials, such is the stuff of our national obsession: sexual innuendo. How, in 2050, could anyone say: "She's got a lovely bunch of coconuts," and expect to refer to anything but the fruit of the palm?

I didn't have to wonder for long, because in the window of a computer store I was passing I saw a device about the size of a computerised notebook. Emblazoned on the plastic cover were the words: "Macintosh Innuendo Converter". I headed inside and the saleswoman readily answered my enquiry.

"Yes, this is our standard innuendo converter. One of the best on the market, I think. It carries more than 250,000 explicit sexual statements in its memory (500 megabytes), and there's plenty of . . ." she broke off and fiddled with the keyboard for a second before proceeding ". . . RAM as well. Which means that within six seconds the converter will provide you with anything up to 30 double entendres, as it were . . ." she broke off again to consult the gadget, ". . . at your fingertips".

She demonstrated the converter to me with great aplomb, but really it was alarmingly simple. You keyed in expressions of the form: "Would you like to come back to my place for a screw?", punched "enter" and within the allotted six seconds were presented with:

"Would you like to come up and see my etchings?"
"You look Greek – mind if I return the Elgin Marbles?"
"Can I lose my ball on your crazy golf course?"
"If you promise not to wiener I'll give you my schnitzel . . ."

And many, many more too prurient and puerile to mention. I was rather taken by the thing and began to fiddle enthusiastically, punching its buttons and twiddling its toggles with abandon, and finding out in the process more than 297 allusions for intercrural sex, until the saleswoman became agitated and said: "Look, stop playing with that as if it were an extension of your cock. Either pay up or piss off." Truly this was a brave new world of direct statement.

"There's one thing that bothers me," I told her. "I can see the converter provides a myriad of innuendos given a direct statement, but what if you do the reverse?"

"No," she cried, "you mustn't – the programme can't handle it!" But it was too late. I had plugged the seemingly innocuous expression "handy shandy" into the converter and now it was emitting a series of high-pitched peeps and pips, like the speaking clock faking an orgasm. I felt the converter grow hotter and hotter and hotter as it laboured to convert the innuendo back into plain demotic, but it was no good. I dropped it and ran into the street.

My whirl was a head as I ran back towards where I had left my vibraphone (catchy name for a time machine made out of a telephone and 15 vibrators, eh?). I'd always found the late 20th century problematic enough to live in as far as sex and gender issues were concerned, but the 21st century looked even grimmer. Quite clearly the pernicious, polymorphous perversity of my own era had run its course, to be replaced with a kind of outrageous dullness.

I found the vibraphone where I had left it, hidden in the lingerie department of Peter Jones. I lined up the vibrators, plugged in the phone and dialled the number of an old pilot light in New York. Nothing happened. *Nada. Rien de tout.* In a frenzy I cranked the settings on the vibrators still higher and dialled points west. Nothing, not a flicker or a twinge of chrono-tripping. I knew I was irremediably stuck when the sales assistant popped up from behind the counter and said: "Have you any idea what an utter tosser you look?"

So, I'm condemned to remain here in the future, fiddling with my fake phalli. The best I can offer is to try to send you back some more dispatches the same way I sent this one: by fax. Because, after all, the faxes are, at least, a rich source of innuendo: long, white and coming – as they do – almost instantly.

BOTS:
A LOVE STORY AND
A DREAM

Michael Hemmingson

"Bots", a story set very much in the sexual present, is the work of a young novelist, playwright and poet whose reputation is now spreading beyond his native California. Michael Hemmingson is also the author of the novel The Naughty Yard *(1994) and* Stories Jam Packed With Sex and Violence, *published last year by the splendidly named Cyberpsychos Press.*

Dreaming of Kyoko

And sometimes I dream of Kyoko; these are the kinds of dreams I like. Kyoko reverie: I see her naked, see her clothed, see her standing on a hill, slight breeze tousling her hair; she's in her shorts, maybe in one of her flowerprint neo-hippie skirts. The dream shifts to her in skirt, sitting behind one of her computers and writing scripts for bots, simple or complex designs in Fortran or C, hair over her face, fingers moving fast over keyboard, these bots I like to think of as her children without a father. I know now I can never be a father to a bot. I dream of Kyoko naked behind her computer; and when I open my eyes, I see my dream Kyoko is not in this dream – Kyoko is here, in her room. She is sitting behind her computer – in a T-shirt and pink panties – and peering into one of her CPUs. I ask her what she's doing, it's three a.m., come back to bed, and when she looks at me, it's like I'm a stranger: the intangible lack of regard, as if to say who is this guy in my bedroom, in my bed, in my home? Who is he to talk to me? She turns back to the screen for a moment, then glances my way again, now smiling, recognition having returned to her small dark eyes like a hard drive booted up and ready to play. She says in her strained accent: "Oh, nothing, doing nothing." She stands up, comes back to me, returns to her bed, pulls the sheets away, slides her smooth skin against mine, purrs a bit, sits on top of me, looking down, hair in her face, then lies next to me, one muscular leg sheathed over my stomach, her three computers still on, our bodies aglow in techno-illuminance from the computers' green and blue background screens. Kyoko moves up to kiss me, her black hair falling over my face, a cascade of oriental dreamscape as taut and precise as haiku, and I grab her, pull at her panties, glad that this is all real, no bots between us.

Digitally Clean

In the shower I still dream of her, sleep in my eyes, her scent on me like spring's new lilacs spread on a floor – and I'm rolling in them, these petals, I'm rolling around in Kyoko – I have Kyoko all over me. I rub Kyoko into me, her essences invade my skin like a computer virus: I am an accessible system with no security zones. I open my eyes, see that I am touching myself, I am erect, here in the shower, soap all over my body – not the lilacs that I dreamed were Kyoko. I feel ridiculous. I don't need this dream – Kyoko is not a sacrosanct icon – she's in the other room. I need to wake up.

She's behind one of her computers when I come out. She's wearing a halter and shorts. She types quickly at her keyboard. There is a large paperweight on the desk; I have always liked that paperweight. I see scrolling text – don't know what it is, don't care. My mind is in the lower brain, beguiled with abject intentions, the animal in the technological sprawl. I still have my erection and, yes, it hurts. Never has it hurt before and this scares me, makes me think of new possibilities. I lie on the bed, naked and still wet from the shower, and call to her. She smiles when she sees my erection. She says: "Let me finish," staying at her computer for another ten minutes which seem, to my mind and my tumescence, like ten eternities in the termite pit, lost to dream all the dreams I fear, the dream of her, this image of my lover ensnared forever behind the computer. And when I strain to see what she is writing, I see that it is a script for another bot.

Stepping away from the dream, Kyoko comes to me, purring again. She steps out of her shorts, climbs on top of me again; and I feel her, feel that she is wet. I wonder whether her excitement is due to me or to her bots. She uses one hand to guide me carefully into her, making that small high-pitched sound she always makes whenever our connections are successful, her other hand at my face, two fingers into my mouth, these fingers that have been busy at the keyboard. I can almost taste her bots. I close my eyes for a moment, bogged in the sensation of her body on mine, feeling her amiable interior, and when I open my eyes, I see that her eyes are now closed. One of her computers beeps but neither of us pays any attention. I feel a moment of triumph: it is one of those rare times when I am more important than her machines. She moves slow at first, shaking her head a bit, letting her hair fall over her face. She bends down, brushing her hair over my visage. I reach for her halter, pull it down, hands over small, pert breasts, dark nipples erect under my gaze. At first use my palms, then taking each nipple between thumb and forefinger, tease them to expand like mushrooms from the wet earth. Her breasts pulsate. I feel the blood flowing through, hot and fast, and I know, yes, yes, my Kyoko is beyond the dream and the machine, she is real. Kyoko gyrates faster, her pelvis slamming into mine. Her breath heavier, she mumbles Japanese words I do not understand, these words I often hear in and out of the presumption that has become my life. Kyoko opens her eyes, shrieking, crying a bit as she always does, her eyes dismal, slicing into me, hacking into my wraith borders.

The Stranger

I feel like an outcast, at times, when Kyoko's friends, all Japanese, are around, or when she talks to friends or family on the phone. Besides a few key phrases, I don't understand Japanese; I have never been to Japan, my travel limited to Europe, North Africa. Kyoko has tried to teach me more words, sentences, phrases, passages that I could use and discern; I don't want to learn them – I have always been a lousy student. But I do always wonder what it is she's saying. Sometimes on the phone she'll look over at me during her conversation and smile, laugh, wink; and I wonder if she might be talking to her friends about me. I know when I hear my name in the middle of that alien tongue that I'm the subject, but I wonder if she disguises her references to me in her language. I start to feel like I'm gathering a new file and data fork of complexes. I am ready for anything global. I would ask her to speak English more; but her English is limited, and I have to strain as it is to comprehend her words and sentences in her strong accent. I like the expression she gets when she's speaking English and stumbles on a word. When she can't find the linguistic symbol in my language for what she wants to say, she may interject something Japanese, or something else, maybe in the diction of computers. For all I know, she may not be speaking Japanese and could be forming the verbal equivalent of COBOL or Unix. When she gets upset because she can't find the words, I want to hold her – and sometimes I do – and tell her it's okay, that I know what she means (whether I do or not). I wonder if we ever really need to speak.

In my sophomore year, I had a Moroccan roommate who spoke very little English; we conversed in French. He started hanging around with a Korean girl. She didn't speak English well, nor did she speak French. It was amusing to watch these two attempt a conversation in English, a language neither had a clue about. Their language was the language of smiling, eye contact, touching, and sex, brought down to the most common, most natural method of semiotics.

"We have the rhetoric of fucking," my roommate told me. I envied him for it.

Kyoko's girlfriends are always giggling, shy, and they never look me in the face. Kyoko was once this way herself, when we met, and often still is; but she has become used to me, has become bold. She once said: "Each day I learn more and more to be American."

I have discovered since being with her that the timidity of Asian women is attractive. Before, I had preferred women to be open, in charge, never afraid to say what they want to say or do.

"They say I lucky," Kyoko tells me, "because I have American boyfriend."

I have noticed that many of her girlfriends, most of them quite pretty, do not have male companions.

"They too want American boys," Kyoko tells me, "but boys hard to find."

She giggles and says: "All the white boys are with white girls."

I have noticed since being with her that I seldom see Asian women with Asian men on campus, at least not in any intimate fashion. Our university has a large Asian population.

I have also perceived of myself how I have become more and more sexually aware of the Asian females here. I find myself attracted to a good number of them. But when I look at them, I know I am merely trying to find the elements of Kyoko they may have.

I ask her why I don't see the Asian girls with the Asian boys.

She laughs and says: "Why would one be in America and date boy of the same race when that is all we do back home?"

"What?"

"The men of my race ugly," she says.[1]

"You don't really mean that," I say.

"I mean that," she says, nodding, hair falling into her eyes. "I come here, I want variety, I want . . . the different. This why I come U.S. for school. To get way Japan, get way crowds, from men I find so . . . *repulsive?* That a word? I saw that word. Ugly men. I come U.S. and say myself me I will find nice American white-boy boyfriend to be with and what joy now, now I have one."

And she smiles and kisses me and I feel myself starting to slip back into the dream.

"So that why you no see them with Asian boys," Kyoko says, "we all us want Anglo-Saxon men!"

She adds: "And Asian men bad lovers."

I tell her that those comments almost sound racist.

She laughs: "How I be racist against my own race? What I talk of is preference."

Her hair falls into my face more, she leans against me, touching me; and I know I am lost to our dream.

"Once I slept with a black," she tells me; but I kiss her to stop her from revealing any more. I do not want to know. I am jealous of anyone who has ever had her before me. Only now, as I come to terms with this feeling, do I know how much of a stranger I am in her world.

IRC

Computers brought us together. I had seen Kyoko a number of times in several of the campus labs. I didn't pay much attention, thought she was attractive: I liked her neo-hippie attire and the black choker she often wore around her neck. I thought she was haughty, noticing how when several guys tried to talk to her she either ignored them or only looked briefly their way and gave a half-smile. I didn't know until later, of course, that she was just too shy to interact. The guys would give up when she'd return to her computer, stoic. Several times I glanced at her screen and saw a lot of scrolling numbers and symbols. Once I saw her hooked into the Usenet News Server, replying to a post. She was on a science group, and it wasn't until later that I remembered the group and went searching its bandwidth for information on her. As it stood, we were the only two people who were often in the lab. I was working on stories and a novel. I had no idea what she was doing. When it came time for the lab to close at eleven at night, we were usually the only two there. We would nod when seeing one another, having now become familiar faces. Of course, during the day the labs were often full. I was also in the lab a great deal because I didn't, and don't, own a computer; and I refused to go back to my typewriter when all these machines were available. I began to play around more in the Usenet, using gophers to retrieve files and programs, and finally went to Computer Services to open up my own account so I could have e-mail. It was inevitable. As Kyoko and I were in the lab at the same time more often, I began to take note of her. Several times, I caught her looking at me from the terminal, and when I returned the glance, she'd go a bit red and quickly act busy with whatever task she was doing. I was involved with someone else at the time so I didn't give much thought to other possibilities of attraction.[2]

Later, Hunting around the net more, I discovered IRC: Internet Relay Chat, a zone in cyberspace that connects thousands of people on various channels to talk in real time. I began to talk to people far away, and people on campus, people in the next city, people at the universities and at home. I began to notice one girl in particular from my school who went by the name of Culla on channels like #vampires and #bondage and #darkrealm and #erotica. She had what I thought were friends who followed her and gave her operator status; but they were actually her bots –

short for robots, little (or big) programs that do a variety of tasks at your command. I talked with her some, but she jumped from channel to channel, describing in virtual terms what she was doing to people – drinking their blood, tying them up, having strange sexual encounters. Her spelling and grammar were bad. I was particularly interested one day as she talked of how she hated men and was going to become a lesbian, although she'd still be a vampire with men. Another user in a different country asked me if I knew her, knew where she was on campus. I told him no – how could I? He showed me the commands that revealed her location:

/whois Culla /trace Culla

When I did this, I saw her e-mail account. This user also told me how to "finger" her, which would give me more information.

/ctcp finger Culla

What I located was a computer right across from me, where the Japanese girl was sitting.

She saw me staring at her and hid behind her screen.

"Culla?" I said.

I heard her make a sound. She tried harder to hide. I saw her virtual persona vanish from the IRC realm:

***signoff: Culla (bad link?)

I told her the nickname I was using: AvanTpOp.

She quickly gathered her stuff, placing it all messily in her knapsack, and ran out of the computer lab, face very red.

I felt bad. But I was damn curious. I remembered the science group I saw her posting to. I pulled that group out from the net news server and checked for any articles that had the same e-mail address. I found one, and her name: Kyoko Murakami.

I didn't see her in a lab again until several days later. When she saw me, she hunched, tried to hide again. I sat at the computer next to her.

"I'm sorry if I embarrassed you the other day," I said.

She looked away. She was shaking.

"Really," I said, "I don't know much about that, and someone told me how to use the command to show me where you were. I didn't mean to blurt out like that."

Slowly, she turned to me, uncertain.

"What you want?" she asked.

"Just to say I'm sorry, I mean you left so fast, and . . ."

"It all game," she laughed nervously, hitting the screen with a hand, "all that I write I don't mean. I just . . . play there when I am bored. Culla really not me, just play-fun-game me."

"Oh I know that," I said.

She smiled.

I asked her what she spent so much time working on in the lab. She said it was math stuff, physics, programming, posting on news groups, talking on IRC, and: "Sometime testing new bots."

"Bots," I said, "I keep hearing about them but I don't know what they are."

"You no bot?" she said. "Have no bot I mean?"

"No."

"Some are very very simple," she said, "and some not. You want, sometime I give you bot script."

"Sure."

"Other bot very complex, I don't use on IRC, bot collects information I need."

I nodded. We went back to our computers, but she soon got up and left. She didn't say good-bye. Leaving so hastily, she seemed nervous again.

I didn't see her for several days.

Since I had her e-mail address, I sent her a note to say hi and that I was looking forward to getting the bot she promised.

I saw her at the commons the next week. I asked if I could join her. She was hesitant, but nodded.

"Get my e-mail?" I asked.

She nodded again.

I nodded.

"Give you bot soon," she said.

We started going out a week after that.

While I do not fully understand the concept of bots, I like to think about them. On the net, they can act like people. They can react to certain phrases, and sometimes even hold a small conversation with you and others. Kyoko likes to write bots. I don't know how to compile or program, so I may never understand. I once looked on Kyoko's screen as she went to get something to eat; she was typing in a word processing program, the file called CATA-LOGUE: BOTS. I saw this:

File kyokobot3.2.tar.Z is my complete and fully-functional C bot. Features include access levels, various ON PUBLIC equivalents including singing song lyrics, configurable action kicks, band evasion using helper bots, full help files sent out using a sub-bot so as not to lag the main bot.

I dreamt that night of bots. I dreamt that I was a fully functional C programmer sitting behind a Sun SparcStation, and I was writing a massive bot that I would launch into cyberspace to do my bidding. I added to this bot everything I had ever written that was on disk – all my stories, my various novels and parts of novels, my poetry, my essays, all that encompassed my experience and philosophy. This bot would draw from these writings to converse with people, react to their words, answer their questions. In this dream I saw myself dead and my bot still out there in the electronic universe. I knew that I had programmed my bot to move from channel to channel, server to server – gathering more information, learning all that it could, stealing disk space off various sites to house the information that it gathered – and to draw off it as much as it drew off my writings. Although I was physically dead, I was still alive in cyberspace, for my bot was me. It knew what I knew, it had my work, and therefore I lived on in a new dimension. I woke from this dream absolutely fascinated, Kyoko asleep next to me, her computers on as always. I didn't know if what I dreamt was technically possible; I liked the aesthetics of it. If I had a bot that housed everything that was me – if I could some way download all that was in my mind into the script of this bot – and the bot was able to live infinitely in the cyberrealm, then I would never die. I would indeed be immortal.

When I told Kyoko my idea of this, she gave me a strange look, smiled, shook her head, and went back to her keyboard and screen.

Homing Bots

"Not bot like on the IRC," Kyoko told me, "but sort of bot because it perform task."

What she called her homing bots were programs she'd written that went into cyberspace to collect data from various sites and news groups. Anything containing certain key words or phrases was accumulated by these bots and brought back to her account for perusal.

"So you actually send them, uh, out there into the system, they're not in your computer, they go out and, return home?"

"Yes."

"So would it be possible for, say, someone to catch this bot, like a fish in net, put a virus inside it, so that when it came back to you, the virus would attack your computer?"

She thought about this.

"Theoretical, it possible," she nodded, "but why anyone want to do that?"

Serenade in C

Kyoko and I go out. I am realizing that we go out less and less, and our time together is either in the computer lab or at her apartment. She doesn't like to come to my apartment because, she says, I don't have a computer there, and she needs to be by her computers at all times. I am in competition with C and Fortran and Unix. We go out to eat, and I ask if she'd like to see a movie. She says no. I can tell her mind is on computers, on applications and shell archives. We go to the beach and walk near the surf. The sky is clear. I put my arm around her. She moves in close, I smell her hair, her skin, and I'm happy to be here. We don't speak. She seems distant. We kiss, touch; she doesn't want to make love on the beach. She says: "Not in public . . ."

We are alone in the computer lab at school and it's late and she has her hand on my knee and we start to kiss and we look around. Yes, alone, and it is late, the lab will close in an hour. She says: "I want be dangerous," and she pulls her panties out from under her skirt, she gets into my lap, she opens my jeans, taking me out, sliding me in, her skirt covering us, moving slowly, her arms around my neck, my face in her breasts (she's wearing a white blouse); and I tell myself to come quickly, we have to be quick, what if someone walks in, a student or a security guard or maybe even the damn system administrator, we have to be quick, dozens of lone computers around us watching. And I thrust into Kyoko fast, hard. She looks at me surprised, closes here yes, that high-pitched sound coming out of her again; and I know I am drifting back into the dream, that I am a bot having a dream of being human and excitable. But when we are done, and I leave the lab to go to the bathroom, I start to lose the dream, I become aware of the cold air around me, I become aware of the wetness in my crotch, of the fact that I think I am losing my humanity. I almost didn't go back to the lab, I don't want to see those computers, I don't want to see Kyoko, but I go back, and she's there, typing away, and she stops, she smiles, she says she hasn't even put her underwear back on, they're in her purse. She says: "I can feel you coming out of me and it make me feel good. I want to run and I don't know why." We walk to her apartment when the lab closes, holding onto each other maybe more because of the cold night air than anything. We don't say a word. When we get to her place, we go to the bedroom, she goes to her three computers, checking each one, gathering her information. She curses in my language: "Those assholes! They killed my bots!" I lie on her bed and say: "What?" She says: "Nothing." She plays around with her computers more, then comes to me, lifting her skirt to show me she has no underwear, her pubes thick and dark. I stare at the ceiling. She kisses me and I do not respond. "Turn your computers off," I whisper. She says: "What say?" I shake my head. She says: "What wrong? Are you mad at me?" We talk no more, falling asleep like that, dreamless and cold like the implements that guide our life.

Bot Wars

When I wake up I see that she has left our dream of peace and sex and she's maniacal. She's cursing, in Japanese and English and maybe something else, running back and forth among her three computers.

"Assholes have sent out warbots to kill my bots!"

I don't understand. She's on the verge of screaming. I get up, grab her, asking her to tell me what the hell is going on.

She explains about these people she has been having a war with on the IRC, people with their own bots.

"Our bots have been fighting each other."

"Why didn't you tell me about this?" I say, thinking of CNN news coverage on bot wars.

She shrugs and says: "It all game, it not real, why tell?"

I think of clandestine battles in another universe far from our own.

"I don't get it," I say, "what did they do?"

"Dress, dress," she says, "we must go campus fast!"

We both hastily dress. I run to keep up with her. We go to one of the labs, the closest one, and she sits behind a machine and logs into her account. She tries to get on IRC and I see this:

GHOSTS ARE NOT ALLOWED ON IRC

She makes a small sound, hitting her fist on the keyboard.
"What is that?"
"Banned me from server," she says, "I try another."
She types: /server
The same message appears. She tries again. The same appears. She screams this time, balling her fist and sticking it in her mouth. People give us looks.

I grab her arm, take her out of the lab. She's jumpy, looking around, eyes wide.

"Don't understand," she says, "why they do this me? I think of way of getting them, I will!"

"Tell me what the hell this is all about," I say, pinching her flesh.

She looks surprised, then frightened. I have never been harsh with her.

I let go. I say: "Kyoko?"

She moves to me. "These people on sex channels," she says, "I don't know how war started, I tell them they are idiots and now they begin war. They make warbots to kill my bots, and now they disconnect me. I find another way, but I not understand why these people want to be evil so much. It not real, why do they be so serious?"

"What people?" I say, feeling the need to protect her, to harm anyone who might bother her.

"Who knows," she says, "all over, everywhere, around the world, people. Bad people. One named Danny . . ."

I wonder what she was doing playing on sex channels when she has me.

Warbots

I become worried – Kyoko doesn't answer her phone, though I know she has to be there. I go to her apartment; I knock. I hear her inside. She won't answer the door. I knock harder. She finally opens up. She looks terrible. Her hair is messy, unwashed, her face red, eyes puffed. I know she has been crying. She stand there, staring at me.

"Let me in," I say.

She steps aside.

I move to hold her, kiss her, and she pushes me away.

"What have I done?" I ask.

She shakes her head, looking down. "Sorry," she says, "it not you. I think I am losing my mind."[3]

"What?"

"They did like what you say once. They capture homing bot and put virus in it."

She takes me to her room to show me. I see something I have never seen: her three computers are not on.

"What happened?"

"When I access homing bot," she says weakly, "the virus let loose and crash hard drives. All three, they networked. I can get fixed, restore data, but I – I –"

And she screams, hitting the bedroom wall.

I grab onto her, she thrashes in my grip. She kicks at me, bites me, finally settles down.

"Give me pain," she whispers.

We stare at each other.

"Make me feel alive," she says, "I not know if I alive anymore. Hurt me, tell me I real . . ."

A Posthuman Turn

. . . the reader learns for the first time that human beings make love to their machines because they cannot make love to other human beings.

Lance Olsen

It is only after our interlude of violence – something I cannot come to terms with, something I would choose to believe does not happen between us – that Kyoko talks to me and tells me the truth, the past, or what fragile thing we would believe to be memory. When she came to the States last year, she knew no one. She'd been on IRC in Japan before, but this was the first time she'd used it in English. Her entire "social life," she tells me, was centered around IRC. "I spend many many hours on it," she says, "never really knowing what outside world was there." Her eyes water a bit; and she hastily, in jumbled English, relays to me the events of those she knew on IRC, and those she met in real life. There was Julie, a girl at the school, who conversed with her boyfriend on the computer system because it was free and she couldn't afford to call him in Kentucky. His name was Erich, and he proclaimed himself an "IRC god". Kyoko met Julie in real life and they became friends. Kyoko began to talk to Erich a lot, when Julie wasn't logged in. It was from Erich that the interior world of the computer became more real, that Kyoko learned of the flesh and blood behind the names that popped up on her screen. There was Danny, Erich's friend, who was often despondent about having failed as a musician and who hid his failures in a bong and marijuana and his Amiga computer. There was Charlotte who lived in the next city and who Erich had reportedly twice talked out of committing suicide over her depression about the death of a boy she loved. And there was Slime, a self-labeled maniacal hard-drinking poet and friend of Erich's that Julie was often afraid was a bad influence on him. The more she talked with Erich, the more he opened up; he told her things that Julie didn't know. Erich was unemployed, lived with his mother whom he didn't get along with, and was in a constant battle with his bisexuality. He confessed to Kyoko that he was afraid he would slip back to homosexuality and leave Julie behind – he was afraid of hurting her. After Julie and Erich had met on IRC, they began to exchange letters, photographs, called each other on the phone, and then she went out to Kentucky to see him. She told Kyoko it was love at first sight; she told Kyoko she wanted to marry him. But Julie didn't know about his other sexual conduct, and Erich had asked her not to mention it to Julie. Kyoko agreed, flabbergasted by it all. Not experienced with differences among people other than those she knew in Japan, she didn't understand how a man could desire to make love to both sexes. Eventually the long distance romance waned; Julie met someone else on campus and called it off with Erich. Kyoko, from her understanding of the talks she'd had with him, thought he'd be relieved. His reaction was quite the opposite – he constantly asked Kyoko what Julie was doing with this other man. Kyoko didn't know. Erich accused her of helping Julie out. Then Erich disappeared from the IRC. After two weeks Kyoko thought it strange he never logged on. She found out from others that Erich had committed suicide. Kyoko couldn't believe he did this over Julie, there must have been more. She wondered about his life. Then

Danny began to attack her. He was convinced that it was Kyoko's fault that Erich had killed himself – he believed Kyoko had told Julie the secrets Erich had confided in her and had talked Julie into breaking up with Erich. Danny had operator status, and began to "kill" her off the servers so Kyoko couldn't use IRC. Kyoko couldn't understand how someone far away and whom she'd never met face to face could hate her so.

"It stopped for while," she says, "but lately Danny has started up again, and got many others on IRC after me, telling lies. He make warbots to kill my bots, and now he sent virus into my system and ruined my data . . ."

Extremities Outside The Flesh

But I cannot get away from what we do in those brief moments, before she confesses, what she asks me to do.

"Slap me," Kyoko says.

I just look at her.

She's crying and says: *"Slap me, wake me up, show me I am real!"*

I don't. I back away.

She attacks, biting and scratching again, and I slap her, I hit her; blood comes from her mouth.

"Do anything to me to make me hurt . . ."

The Moment of Death

Hence the academic grappling with his computer . . . memorizing everything in an effort to escape the final outcome, to delay the day of reckoning of death and that other – fatal – moment of reckoning . . . forming an endless feedback loop with the machine.

Jean Baudrillard

And it is there, the two of us lying on the floor still breathing hard, bleeding and bruised, her story now done, that Kyoko's eyes widen, she shrieks something in Japanese, she jumps, picks up the large paperweight on her desk and smashes it into the screen of one of her computers. The screen caves in – sparks. Kyoko cries out, turns to the next, smashes that screen. I move to her, fast, frightened, push her away from the computers. She raises the paperweight, ready to hit me. I cover myself. She stops. We both breathe hard, tears run down her face. She slams the paperweight on one of the keyboards, then goes to the bed, tears at the sheets. She is not aware of me, absent in the elapsed, forfeited to the automaton, lost in the life she could not have in the flesh, the electronic actuality that escaped from the cyberorb and infested her palpable life. I am inconsequential as of this moment, I am like a piece of hardware – outdated, obsolete, discarded, the dream losing its edge—

"Hurt me," she said, "make me wake up from this."

Last and Final Dream

Where I go into the computer lab on campus with a baseball bat and, with a battle cry much like Kyoko's, I begin to smash every computer there. With each one I destroy, I feel relieved, I feel the chains removed, feel more like a human being. Smash, crash, *boom* – I laugh and dance as I take the final blow at my would-be killers. So much is possible, so much is true, and even when the campus police come and cart me away and I spit in their faces and tell them there's nothing they can do because this is just a dream and soon I'll wake up, they get pissed, one hits me in the gut, I begin to vomit, they drag me into a car and take me to the station, somewhere in the heart of the school. Where I'll wake up I don't know, but as long as this mirage, now without my Kyoko, continues, I will continue to kick and shriek and demand my humanity back.

In Unix, no one can hear you scream.

Notes

1 I did ask her once if she ever read Marguerite Duras' *The Lover*. She told me she saw the movie. She also brought up the matter of how we always seek the different. ("The French girl in story did not want French man," she said, "but Asian lover; often French men go to Japan looking for Asian woman to have sex with.") It later made me think of Duras' work, how the Asian male lover is often prominent, as in the cult classic, *Hiroshima, Mon Amour*. According to Duras, and from some opinions I have read and heard, the male Asian is a good lover hard to

match. Of course, these opinions could be biased, since I heard them from Asian men. The Arab man will say Arabs are the best lovers, the German man will say German, the black man will say black, the Texan will say only men from Texas are the best. Preference is always the key factor, as Kyoko pointed out to me. Kyoko and I have experienced harsh looks from Asian men when they see us together, and she has told me some of them have angrily asked her why she is with me, a white American. "Really," she says, "they are upset because they ask me out once and I say no."

2   It was another one of those things that never last long. Her name was Candice, and she worked at a coffeehouse. She dressed grunge and loved the blues and everything was going pretty good for a while. A couple of good weeks of fun. But like many relationships, the excitement of the new fades fast and you realize you really don't care for being intimate with this person any more and that, in effect, you fail to fall into the dream with them; you get bored with being awake.

3   When I think of it, it now reminds me of the actress Solvieg Donmartin who goes insane with her addiction to a technological gadget of recorded dreams, in Wim Wenders' 1992 film, *Until the End of the World*.

[LEARNING ABOUT] MACHINE SEX

Candas Jane Dorsey

Candas Jane Dorsey is one of Canada's leading writers of speculative fiction, and is a co-owner of Tesseract Books, Canada's only specialist SF publisher. She has also published journalism, drama and four volumes of poetry, and co-edited an anthology of Canadian SF. "Machine Sex", from her collection of the same name, offers a female take on some of the subject-matter of Cyberpunk in a story that has acquired something of the status of a modern classic. The protagonist also features in the novel Hardwired Angel, *written in collaboration with Nora Abercrombie.*

A naked woman working at a computer. Which attracts you most? It was a measure of Whitman that, as he entered the room, his eyes went first to the unfolded machine gleaming small and awkward in the light of the long-armed desk lamp; he'd seen the woman before.

Angel was the woman. Thin and pale-skinned, with dark nipples and black pubic hair, and her face hidden by a dark unkempt mane of long hair as she leaned over her work.

A woman complete with her work. It was a measure of Angel that she never acted naked, even when she was. Perhaps especially when she was.

So she has a new board, thought Whitman, and felt his guts stir the way they stirred when he first contemplated taking her to bed. That was a long time ago. And she knew it, felt without turning her head the desire, and behind the screen of her straight dark hair, uncombed and tumbled in front of her eyes, she smiled her anger down.

"Where have you been?" he asked, and she shook her hair back, leaned backward to ease her tense neck.

"What is that thing?" he went on insistently, and Angel turned her face to him, half-scowling. The board on the desk had thin irregular wings spreading from a small central module. Her fingers didn't slow their keyboard dance.

"None of your business," she said.

She saved the input, and he watched her fold the board into a smaller and smaller rectangle. Finally she shook her hair back from her face.

"I've got the option on your bioware," he said.

"Pay as you go," she said. "New house rule."

And found herself on her ass on the floor from his reflexive, furious blow. And his hand in her hair, pulling her up and against the wall. Hard. Astonishing her with how quickly she could hurt how much. Then she hurt too much to analyze it.

"You are a bitch," he said.

"So what?" she said. "When I was nicer, you were still an asshole."

Her head back against the wall, crack. Ouch.

Breathless, Angel: "Once more and you never see this bioware." And Whitman slowly draws breath, draws back, and looks at her the way she knew he always felt.

"Get out," she said. "I'll bring it to Kozyk's office when it's ready."

So he went. She slumped back in the chair, and tears began to blur her vision, but hate cleared them up fast enough, as she unfolded the board again, so that despite the pain she hardly missed a moment of programming time.

Assault only a distraction now, betrayal only a detail: Angel was on a roll. She had her revenge well in hand, though it took a subtle mind to recognize it.

Again: "I have the option on any of your bioware." This time, in the office, Whitman wore the nostalgic denims he now affected, and Angel her street-silks and leather.

"This is mine, but I made one for you." She pulled it out of the bag. Where her board looked jerry-built, this one was sleek. Her board looked interesting; this one packaged. "I made it before you sold our company," she said. "I put my best into it. You may as well have it. I suppose you own the option anyway, eh?"

She stood. Whitman was unconsciously restless before her.

"When you pay me for this," she said, "make it in MannComp stock." She tossed him the board. "But be careful. If you take it apart wrong, you'll break it. Then you'll have to ask me to fix it, and from now on, my tech rate goes up."

As she walked by him, he reached for her, hooked one arm around her waist. She looked at him, totally expressionless. "Max," she said, "it's like I told you last night. From now on, if you want it, you pay. Just like everyone else." He let her go. She pulled the soft dirty white silk shirt on over the black leather jacket. The complete rebel now.

"It's a little going away present. When you're a big shot in MannComp, remember that I made it. And that you couldn't even take it apart right. I guarantee."

He wasn't going to watch her leave. He was already studying the board. Hardly listening, either.

"Call it the Mannboard," she said. "It gets big if you stroke it." She shut the door quietly behind herself.

It would be easier if this were a story about sex, or about machines. It is true that the subject is Angel, a woman who builds computers like they have never been built before outside the human skull. Angel, like everyone else, comes from somewhere and goes somewhere else. She lives in that linear and binary universe. However, like everyone else, she lives concurrently in another universe less simple. Trivalent, quadrivalent, multivalent. World without end, with no amen. And so, on.

They say a hacker's burned out before he's twenty-one. Note the pronoun: he. Not many young women in that heady realm of the chip.

Before Angel was twenty-one – long before – she had taken the cybernetic chip out of a Wm Kuhns fantasy and patented it; she had written the program for the self-taught AI the Bronfmanns had bought and used to gain world prominence for their MannComp lapboard; somewhere in there, she'd lost innocence, and when her clever additions to that AI turned it into something the military wanted, she dropped out of sight in Toronto and went back to Rocky Mountain House, Alberta, on a Greyhound bus.

It was while she was thinking about something else – cash, and how to get some – that she had looked out of the bus window in Winnipeg into the display window of a sex shop. Garter belts, sleazy magazines on cheap coated paper with dayglo orange stickers over the genitals of bored sex kings and queens, a variety of ornamental vibrators. She had too many memories of Max to take it lightly, though she heard the laughter of the roughnecks in the back of the bus as they topped each others' dirty jokes, and thought perhaps their humour was worth emulating. If only she could.

She passed her twentieth birthday in a hotel in Regina, where she stopped to take a shower and tap into the phone lines, checking for pursuit. Armed with the money she got through automatic transfer from a dummy account in Medicine Hat, she rode the bus the rest of the way ignoring the rolling of beer bottles under the seats, the acrid stink of the on-board toilet. She was thinking about sex.

As the bus roared across the long flat prairie she kept one hand on the roll of bills in her pocket, but with the other she made the first notes on the program that would eventually make her famous.

She made the notes on an antique NEC lapboard which had been her aunt's, in old-fashioned BASIC – all the machine would support – but she unravelled it and knitted it into that artificial trivalent language when she got to the place at Rocky and plugged the idea into her Mannboard. She had it written in a little over four hours on-time, but that counted an hour and a half she took to write a new loop into the AI. (She would patent that loop later the same year and put the royalties into a blind trust for her brother, Brian, brain-damaged from birth. He was in Michener Centre in Red Deer, not educable; no one at Bronfmann knew about her family, and she kept it that way.)

She called it Machine Sex; working title.

Working title for a life; born in Innisfail General Hospital, father a rodeo cowboy who raised rodeo horses, did enough mixed farming out near Caroline to build his young second wife a big log house facing the mountain view. The first baby came within a year, ending her mother's tenure as teller at the local bank. Her aunt was a programmer for the University of Lethbridge, chemical molecular model analysis on the University of Calgary mainframe through a modem link.

From her aunt she learned BASIC, Pascal, COBOL and C; in school she played the usual turtle games on the Apple IIe; when she was fourteen she took a bus to Toronto, changed her name to Angel, affected a punk hairstyle and the insolent all-white costume of that year's youth, and eventually walked into Northern Systems, the company struggling most successfully with bionics at the time, with the perfected biochip, grinning at the proper young men in their grey three-piece suits as they tried to find a bug in it anywhere. For the first million she let them open it up; for the next five she told them how she did it. Eighteen years old by the phony records she'd cooked on her arrival in Toronto, she was free to negotiate her own contracts.

But no one got her away from Northern until Bronfmann bought Northern lock, stock and climate-controlled workshop. She had been sleeping with Northern's boy-wonder president by then for about a year, had yet to have an orgasm though she'd learned a lot about kinky sex toys. Figured she'd been screwed by him for the last time when he sold the company without telling her; spent the next two weeks doing a lot of drugs and having a lot of cheap sex in the degenerate punk underground; came up with the AI education program.

Came up indeed, came swaggering into Ted Kozyk's office, president of Bronfmann's MannComp subsidiary, with that jury-rigged Mannboard tied into two black-box add-ons no bigger than a bar of soap, and said, "Watch this."

Took out the power supply first, wiped the memory, plugged into a wall outlet and turned it on.

The bootstrap greeting sounded a lot like Goo.

"Okay," she said, "it's ready."

"Ready for what?"

"Anything you want," she said. By then he knew her, knew her rep, knew that the sweaty-smelling, disheveled, anorectic-looking waif in the filthy, oversized silk shirt (the rebels had affected natural fabrics the year she left home, and she always did after that, even later when the silk was cleaner, more upmarket, and black instead of white) had something. Two weeks ago he'd bought a company on the strength of that something, and the board Whitman had brought him just yesterday, even without the software to run on it, had been enough to convince him he'd been right.

He sat down to work, and hours later he was playing Go with an AI he'd taught to talk back, play games, and predict horse races and the stock market.

He sat back, flicked the power switch and pulled the plug, and stared at her.

"Congratulations," she said.

"What for?" he said; "you're the genius."

"No, congratulations, you just murdered your first baby," she said, and plugged it back in. "Want to try for two?"

"Goo," said the deck. "Dada."

It was her little joke. It was never a feature on the MannComp A-One they sold across every MannComp counter in the world.

But now she's all grown up, she's sitting in a log house near Rocky Mountain house, watching the late summer sunset from the big front windows, while the computer runs Machine Sex to its logical conclusion, orgasm.

She had her first orgasm at nineteen. According to her false identity, she was twenty-three. Her lover was a delegate to MannComp's annual sales convention; she picked him up after the speech she gave on the ethics of selling AIs to high school students in Thailand. Or whatever, she didn't care. Kozyk used to write her speeches but she usually changed them to suit her mood. This night she'd been circumspect, only a few expletives, enough to amuse the younger sales representatives and reassure the older ones.

The one she chose was smooth in his approach and she thought, well, we'll see. They went up to the suite MannComp provided, all mod cons and king-size bed, and as she undressed she looked at him and thought, he's ambitious, this boy, better not give him an inch.

He surprised her in bed. Ambitious maybe, but he paid a lot of attention to detail.

After he spread her across the universe in a way she had never felt before, he turned to her and said, "That was pretty good, eh, baby?" and smiled a smooth little grin. "Sure," she said, "it was okay," and was glad she hadn't said more while she was out in the ozone.

By then she thought she was over what Whitman had done to her. And after all, it had been simple enough, what he did. Back in that loft she had in Hull, upstairs of a shop, where she covered the windows with opaque mylar and worked night and day in that twilight. That night as she worked he stood behind her, hands on her shoulders, massaging her into further tenseness.

"Hey, Max, you know I don't like it when people look over my shoulder when I'm working."

"Sorry, baby." He moved away, and she felt her shoulders relax just to have his hands fall away.

"Come on to bed," he said. "You know you can pick that up whenever."

She had to admit he was being pleasant tonight. Maybe he too was tired of the constant scrapping, disguised as jokes, that wore at her nerves so much. All his efforts to make her stop working, slow her down so he could stay up. The sharp edges that couldn't be disguised. Her bravado made her answer in the same vein, but in the mornings, when he was gone to Northern, she paced and muttered to herself, reworking the previous day until it was done with, enough that she could go on. And after all what was missing? She had no idea how to debug it.

Tonight he'd even made some dinner, and touched her kindly. Should she be grateful? Maybe the conversations, such as they were, where she tried to work it out, had just made it worse—.

"Ah, shit," she said, and pushed the board away. "You're right, I'm too tired for this. *Demain*." She was learning French in her spare time.

He began with hugging her, and stroking the long line along her back, something he knew she liked, like a cat likes it, arches its back at the end of the stroke. He knew she got turned on by it. And she did. When they had sex at her house he was without the paraphernalia he preferred, but he seemed to manage, buoyed up by some mood she couldn't share; nor could she share his release.

Afterwards, she lay beside him, tense and dissatisfied in the big bed, not admitting it, or she'd have to admit she didn't know what would help. He seemed to be okay, stretched, relaxed and smiling.

"Had a big day," he said.

"Yeah?"

"Big deal went through."

"Yeah?"

"Yeah, I sold the company."

"You what?" Reflexively moving herself so that none of her body touched his.

"Northern. I put it to Bronfmann. Megabucks."

"Are you joking?" but she saw he was not. "You didn't, I didn't . . . Northern's *our* company."

"My company. I started it."

"I made it big for you."

"Oh, and I paid you well for every bit of that."

She got up. He was smiling a little, trying on the little-boy grin. No, baby, she thought, not tonight.

"Well," she said, "I know for sure that this is my bed. Get out of it."

"Now, I knew you might take this badly. But it really was the best thing. The R&D costs were killing us. Bronfmann can eat them for breakfast."

R&D costs meant her. "Maybe. Your clothes are here." She tossed them on the bed, went into the other room.

As well as sex, she hadn't figured out betrayal yet either; on the street, she thought, people fucked you over openly, not in secret.

This, even as she said it to herself, she recognized as romantic and certainly not based on experience. She was street-wise in every way but one: Max had been her first lover.

She unfolded the new board. It had taken her some time to figure out how to make it expand like that, to fit the program it was going to run. This idea of shaping the hardware to the software had been with her since she made the biochip, and thus made it possible and much more interesting than the other way around. But making the hardware to fit her new idea had involved a great deal of study and technique, and so far she had had limited success.

This reminded her again of sex, and, she supposed, relationships, although it seemed to her that before sex everything had been on surfaces, very easy. Now she had sex, she had had Max, and now she had no way to realize the results of any of that. Especially now, when Northern had just vanished into Bronfmann's computer empire, putting her in the position again of having to prove herself. What had Max used to make Bronfmann take the bait? She knew very clearly: Angel, the Northern Angel, would now become the MannComp Angel. The rest of the bait would have been the AI; she was making more of it every day, but couldn't yet bring it together. Could it be done at all? Bronfmann had paid high for an affirmative answer.

Certainly this time the bioware was working together. She began to smile a little to herself, almost unaware of it, as she saw how she could interconnect the loops to make a solid net to support the program's full and growing weight. Because, of course, it would have to learn as it went along – that was basic.

Angel as metaphor; she had to laugh at herself when she woke from programming hours later, Max still sleeping in her bed, ignoring her eviction notice. He'll have to get up to piss anyway, she thought; that's when I'll get him out. She went herself to the bathroom in the half-dawn light, stretching her cramped back muscles and thinking remotely, well, I got some satisfaction out of last night after all: the beginnings of the idea that might break this impasse. While it's still inside my head, this one is mine. How can I keep it that way?

New fiscal controls, she thought grimly. New contracts, now that Northern doesn't exist any more. Max can't have this, whatever it turns into, for my dowry to MannComp.

When she put on her white silks – leather jacket underneath, against the skin as street fashion would have it – she hardly knew herself what she would do. The little board went into her bag with the boxes of pills the pharmaceutical tailor had made for her. If there was nothing there to suit, she'd buy something new. In the end, she left Max sleeping in her bed; so what? she thought as she reached the highway. The first ride she hitched took her to Toronto, not without a little tariff, but she no longer gave a damn about any of that.

By then the drugs in her system had lifted her out of a body that could be betrayed, and she didn't return to it for two weeks, two weeks of floating in a soup of disjointed noise, and always the program running, unfolding, running again, unfolding inside her relentless mind. She kept it running to drown anything she might remember about trust or the dream of happiness.

When she came home two weeks later, on a hot day in summer with the Ottawa Valley humidity unbearable and her body tired, sore and bruised, and very dirty, she stepped out of her filthy silks in a room messy with Whitman's continued inhabitation; furious, she popped a system cleanser and unfolded the board on her desk. When he came back in she was there, naked, angry, working.

A naked woman working at a computer. What good were cover-ups? Watching Max after she took the new AI up to Kozyk, she was only triumphant because she'd done something Max could never do, however much he might be able to sell her out. Watching them fit it to the bioboard, the strange unfolding machine she had made to fit the ideas only she could have, she began to be afraid. The system cleanser she'd taken made the clarity inescapable. Over the next few months, as she kept adding clever loops and twists, she watched their glee and she looked at what telephone numbers were in the top ten on their modem memories and she began to realize that it was not only business and science that would pay high for a truly thinking machine.

She knew that ten years before there had been Pentagon programmers working to model predatory behaviour in AIs using Prolog and its like. That was old hat. None of them, however, knew what they needed to know to write for her bioware yet. No one but Angel could do that. So, by the end of her nineteenth year, that made Angel one of the most soughtafter, endangered ex-anorectics on the block.

She went to conferences and talked about the ethics of selling AIs to teenagers in Nepal. Or something. And took a smooth salesman to bed, and thought all the time about when they were going to make their approach. It would be Whitman again, not Kozyk, she thought; Ted wouldn't get his hands dirty, while Max was born with grime under his nails.

She thought also about metaphors. How, even in the new street slang which she could speak as easily as her native tongue, being screwed, knocked, fucked over, jossed, dragged all meant the same thing: hurt to the core. And this was what people sought out, what they spent their time seeking in pick-up joints, to the beat of bad old headbanger bands, that nostalgia shit. Now, as well as the biochip, Max, the AI breakthrough, and all the tailored drugs she could eat, she'd had orgasm too.

Well, she supposed it passed the time.

What interested her intellectually about orgasm was not the lovely illusion of transcendence it brought, but the absolute binary predictability of it. When you learn what to do to the nerve endings, and they are in a receptive state, the program runs like kismet. Warm boot. She'd known a hacker once who'd altered his bootstrap messages to read "warm pussy". She knew where most hackers were at; they played with their computers more than they played with themselves. She was the same, otherwise why would it have taken a pretty-boy salesman in a three-piece to show her the simple answer? All the others, just like trying to use an old MS-DOS disc to boot up one of her Mann lapboards with crystal RO/RAM.

Angel forgets she's only twenty. Genius is uneven. There's no substitute for time, that relentless shaper of understanding. Etc. Etc. Angel paces with the knowledge that everything is a phase, even this. Life is hard and then you die, and so on. And so, on.

One day it occurred to her that she could simply run away.

This should have seemed elementary but to Angel it was a revelation. She spent her life fatalistically; her only successful escape had been from the people she loved. Her lovely, crazy grandfather; her generous and slightly avaricious aunt; and her beloved imbecile brother: they were buried deep in a carefully forgotten past. But she kept coming back to Whitman, to Kozyk and Bronfmann, as if she liked them.

As if, like a shocked dog in a learned helplessness experiment, she could not believe that the cage had a door, and the door was open.

She went out the door. For old times' sake, it was the bus she chose; the steamy chill of an air-conditioned Greyhound hadn't changed at all. Bottles – pop and beer – rolling under the seats and the stench of chemicals filling the air whenever someone sneaked down to smoke a cigarette or a reef in the toilet. Did anyone ever use it to piss in? She liked the triple seat near the back, but the combined smells forced her to the front, behind the driver, where she was joined, across the country, by an endless succession of old women, immaculate in their fortrels, who started conversations and shared peppermints and gum.

She didn't get stoned once.

The country unrolled strangely: sex shop in Winnipeg, bank machine in Regina, and hours of programming alternating with polite responses to the old women, until eventually she arrived, creased and exhausted, in Rocky Mountain House.

Rocky Mountain House: a comfortable model of a small town, from which no self-respecting hacker should originate. But these days, the world a net of wire and wireless, it doesn't matter where you are, as long as you have the information people want. Luckily for Angel's secret past, however, this was not a place she would be expected to live – or to go – or to come from.

An atavism she hadn't controlled had brought her this far. A rented car took her the rest of the way to the ranch. She thought only to look around, but when she found the tenants packing for a month's holiday, she couldn't resist the opportunity. She carried her leather satchel into their crocheted, frilled guest room – it had been her room fifteen years before – with a remote kind of satisfaction.

That night, she slept like the dead – except for some dreams. But there was nothing she could do about them.

Lightning and thunder. I should stop now, she thought, wary of power surges through the new board which she was charging as she worked. She saved her file, unplugged the power, stood, stretched, and walked to the window to look at the mountains.

The storm illuminated the closer slopes erratically, the rain hid the distances. She felt some heaviness lift. The cool wind through the window refreshed her. She heard the program stop, and turned off the machine. Sliding out the back-up capsule, she smiled her angry smile unconsciously. When I get back to the Ottawa Valley, she thought, where weather never comes from the west like it's supposed to, I'll make those fuckers eat this.

Out in the corrals where the tenants kept their rodeo horses, there was animal noise, and she turned off the light to go and look out the side window. A young man was leaning his weight against the reins-length pull of a rearing, terrified horse. Angel watched as flashes of lightning strobed the hackneyed scene. This was where she came from. She remembered her father in the same struggle. And her mother at this window with her, both of them watching the man. Her mother's anger she never understood until now. Her father's abandonment of all that was in the house, including her brother, Brian, inert and restless in his oversized crib.

Angel walked back through the house, furnished now in the kitschy western style of every trailer and bungalow in this country-side. She was lucky to stay, invited on a generous impulse, while all but their son were away. She felt vaguely guilty at her implicit criticism.

Angel invited the young rancher into the house not only because this is what her mother and her grandmother would have done.

Even Angel's great-grandmother, whose father kept the stopping house, which meant she kept the travellers fed, even her spirit infused in Angel the unwilling act. She watched him almost sullenly as he left his rain gear in the wide porch.

He was big, sitting in the big farm kitchen. His hair was wet, and he swore almost as much as she did. He told her how he had put a trailer on the north forty, and lived there now, instead of in the little room where she'd been invited to sleep. He told her about the stock he'd accumulated riding the rodeo. They drank Glenfiddich. She told him her father had been a rodeo cowboy. He told her about his university degree in agriculture. She told him she'd never been to university. They drank more whiskey and he told her he couldn't drink that other rot gut any more since he tasted real Scotch. He invited her to see his computer. She went with him across the yard and through the trees in the rain, her bag over her shoulder, board hidden in it, and he showed her his computer. It turned out to be the first machine she designed for Northern – archaic now, compared with the one she'd just invented.

Fair is fair, she thought drunkenly, and she pulled out her board and unfolded it.

"You showed me yours, I'll show you mine," she said.

He liked the board. He was amazed that she had made it. They finished the Scotch.

"I like you," she said. "Let me show you something. You can be the first." And she ran Machine Sex for him.

He was the first to see it: before Whitman and Kozyk who bought it to sell to people who already have had and done everything; before David and Johnathon, the Hardware Twins in MannComp's Gulf Islands shop, who made the touchpad devices necessary to run it properly; before a world market hungry for the kind of glossy degradation Machine Sex could give them bought it in droves from a hastily created – MannComp-subsidiary – numbered company. She ran it for him with just the automouse on her board, and a description of what it would do when the hardware was upgraded to fit.

It was very simple, really. If orgasm was binary, it could be programmed. Feed back the sensation through one or more touchpads to program the body. The other thing she knew about human sex was that it was as much cortical as genital, or more so:

touch is optional for the turn-on. Also easy, then, to produce cortical stimuli by programmed input. The rest was a cosmetic elaboration of the premise.

At first it did turn him on, then off, then it made his blood run cold. She was pleased by that: her work had chilled her too.

"You can't market that thing!" he said.

"Why not. It's a fucking good program. Hey, get it? Fucking good."

"It's not real."

"Of course it isn't. So what?"

"So, people don't need that kind of stuff to get turned on."

She told him about people. More people that he'd known were in the world. People who made her those designer drugs, given in return for favors she never granted until after Whitman sold her like a used car. People like Whitman, teaching her about sexual equipment while dealing with the Pentagon and CSIS to sell them Angel's sharp angry mind, as if she'd work on killing others as eagerly as she was trying to kill herself. People who would hire a woman on the street, as they had her during that two-week nightmare almost a year before, and use her as casually as their own hand, without giving a damn.

"One night," she said, "just to see, I told all the johns I was fourteen. I was skinny enough, even then, to get away with it. And they all loved it. Every single one gave me a bonus, and took me anyway."

The whiskey fog was wearing a little thin. More time had passed than she thought, and more had been said than she had intended. She went to her bag, rummaged, but she'd left her drugs in Toronto, some dim idea at that time that she should clean up her act. All that had happened was that she had spent the days so tight with rage that she couldn't eat, and she'd already cured herself of that once; for the record, she thought, she'd rather be stoned.

"Do you have any more booze?" she said, and he went to look. She followed him around his kitchen.

"Furthermore," she said, "I rolled every one of them that I could, and all but one had pictures of his kids in his wallet, and all of them were teenagers. Boys and girls together. And their saintly dads out fucking someone who looked just like them. Just like them."

Luckily, he had another bottle. Not quite the same quality, but she wasn't fussy.

"So I figure," she finished, "that they don't care who they fuck. Why not the computer in the den? Or the office system at lunch hour?"

"It's not like that," he said. "It's nothing like that. People deserve better." He had the neck of the bottle in his big hand, was seriously, carefully pouring himself another shot. He gestured with both bottle and glass. "People deserve to have – love."

"Love?"

"Yeah, love. You think I'm stupid, you think I watched too much TV as a kid, but I know it's out there. Somewhere. Other people think so too. Don't you? Didn't you, even if you won't admit it now, fall in love with that guy Max at first? You never said what he did at the beginning, how he talked you into being his lover. Something must have happened. Well, that's what I mean: love."

"Let me tell you about love. Love is a guy who talks real smooth taking me out to the woods and telling me he just loves my smile. And then taking me home and putting me in leather handcuffs so he can come. And if I hurt he likes it, because he likes it to hurt a little and he thinks I must like it like he does. And if I moan he thinks I'm coming. And if I cry he thinks it's love. And so do I. Until one evening – not too long after my *last* birthday, as I recall – he tells me that he has sold me to another company. And this only after he fucks me one last time. Even though I don't belong to him any more. After all, he had the option on all my bioware."

"All that is just politics." He was sharp, she had to grant him that.

"Politics," she said, "give me a break. Was it politics made Max able to sell me with the stock: hardware, software, liveware?"

"I've met guys like that. Women too. You have to understand that it wasn't personal to him, it was just politics." Also stubborn. "Sure, you were naive, but you weren't wrong. You just didn't understand company politics."

"Oh, sure I did. I always have. Why do you think I changed my name? Why do you think I dress in natural fibres and go through all the rest of this bullshit? I know how to set up power blocs. Except in mine there is only one party – me. And that's the way it's going to stay. Me against them from now on."

"It's not always like that. There are assholes in the world, and there are other people too. Everyone around here still remembers your grandfather, even though he's been retired in Camrose for fifteen years. They still talk about the way he and his wife used to waltz at the Legion Hall. What about him? There are more people like him than there are Whitmans."

"Charlotte doesn't waltz much since her stroke."

"That's a cheap shot. You can't get away with cheap shots. Speaking of shots, have another."

"Don't mind if I do. Okay, I give you Eric and Charlotte. But one half-happy ending doesn't balance out the people who go through their lives with their teeth clenched, trying to make it come out the same as a True Romance comic, and always wondering what's missing. They read those bodice-ripper novels, and make that do for the love you believe in so naively." Call her naive, would he? Two could play at that game. "That's why they'll all go crazy for Machine Sex. So simple. So linear. So fast. So uncomplicated."

"You underestimate people's ability to be happy. People are better at loving than you think."

"You think so? Wait until you have your own little piece of land and some sweetheart takes you out in the trees on a moonlit night and gives you head until you think your heart will break. So you marry her and have some kids. She furnishes the trailer in a five-room sale grouping. You have to quit drinking Glenfiddich because she hates it when you talk too loud. She gets an allowance every month and crochets a cozy for the TV. You work all day out in the rain and all evening in the back room making the books balance on the outdated computer. After the kids come she gains weight and sells real estate if you're lucky. If not she makes things out of recycled bleach bottles and hangs them in the yard. Pretty soon she wears a nightgown to bed and turns her back when you slip in after a hard night at the keyboard. So you take up drinking again and teach the kids about the rodeo. And find some square-dancing chick who gives you head out behind the bleachers one night in Trochu, so sweet you think your heart will break. What you gonna do then, mountain man?"

"Okay, we can tell stories until the sun comes up. Which won't be too long, look at the time; but no matter how many stories you tell, you can't make me forget about that thing." He pointed to the computer with loathing.

"It's just a machine."

"You know what I mean. That thing in it. And besides, I'm gay. Your little scenario wouldn't work."

She laughed and laughed. "So that's why you haven't made a pass at me yet," she said archly, knowing that it wasn't that simple, and he grinned. She wondered coldly how gay he was, but she was tired, so tired of proving power. His virtue was safe with her; so, she thought suddenly, strangely, was hers with him. It was unsettling, and comforting at once.

"Maybe," he said. "Or maybe I'm just a liar like you think everyone is. Eh? You think everyone strings everyone else a line? Crap. Who has the time for that shit?"

Perhaps they were drinking beer now. Or was it vodka? She found it hard to tell after a while.

"You know what I mean," she said. "You should know. The sweet young thing who has AIDS and doesn't tell you. Or me. I'm lucky so far. Are you? Or who sucks you for your money. Or josses you 'cause he's into denim and Nordic looks."

"Okay, okay. I give up. Everybody's a creep but you and me."

"And I'm not so sure about you."

"Likewise, I'm sure. Have another. So, if you're so pure, what about the ethics of it?"

"What *about* the ethics of it?" she asked. "Do you think I went through all that sex without paying attention? I had nothing else to do but watch other people come. I saw that old cult movie, where the aliens feed on heroin addiction and orgasm, and the woman's not allowed orgasm so she has to OD on smack. Orgasm's more decadent than shooting heroin? I can't buy that, but there's something about a world that sells it over and over again. Sells the thought of pleasure as a commodity, sells the getting of it as if it were the getting of wisdom. And all these times I told you about, I saw other people get it through me. Even when someone finally made me come, it was just a feather in his cap, an accomplishment, nothing personal. Like you said. All I was was a program, they plugged into me and went through the motions and got their result. Nobody cares if the AI finds fulfilment running their damned data analyses. Nobody thinks about depressed and angry Mannboard ROMs. They just think about getting theirs.

"So why not get mine?" She was pacing now, angry, leaning that thin body as if the wind were against her. "Let me be the one who runs the program."

"But you won't be there. You told me how you were going to hide out, all that spy stuff."

She leaned against the wall, smiling a new smile she thought of as predatory. And maybe it was. "Oh, yes," she said. "I'll be there the first time. When Max and Kozyk run this thing and it turns them on. I'll be there. That's all I care to see."

He put his big hands on the wall on either side of her and leaned in. He smelled of sweat and liquor and his face was earnest with intoxication.

"I'll tell you something," he said. "As long as there's the real thing, it won't sell. They'll never buy it."

Angel thought so too. Secretly, because she wouldn't give him the satisfaction of agreement, she too thought they would not go that low. *That's right*, she told herself, *trying to sell it is all right – because they will never buy it*.

But they did.

A woman and a computer. Which attracts you most? Now you don't have to choose. Angel has made the choice irrelevant.

In Kozyk's office, he and Max go over the ad campaign. They've already tested the program themselves quite a lot; Angel knows this because it's company gossip, heard over the cubicle walls in the washrooms. The two men are so absorbed that they don't notice her arrival.

"Why is a woman better than a sheep? Because sheep can't cook. Why is a woman better than a Mannboard? Because you haven't bought your sensory add-on." Max laughs.

"And what's better than a man?" Angel says; they jump slightly. "Why, your MannComp touchpads, with two-way input. I bet you'll be able to have them personally fitted."

"Good idea," says Kozyk, and Whitman makes a note on his lapboard. Angel, still stunned though she's had weeks to get used to this, looks at them, then reaches across the desk and picks up her prototype board. "This one's mine," she says. "You play with yourselves and your touchpads all you want."

"Well, you wrote it, baby," said Max. "If you can't come with your own program . . ."

Kozyk hiccoughs a short laugh before he shakes his head. "Shut up, Whitman," he says. "You're talking to a very rich and famous woman."

Whitman looks up from the simulations of his advertising storyboards, smiling a little, anticipating his joke. "Yeah. It's just too bad she finally burned herself out with this one. They always did say it gives you brain-damage."

But Angel hadn't waited for the punch-line. She was gone.

THE TIME DISEASE

Martin Amis

One of the brightest stars of contemporary fiction, Martin Amis has frequently employed SF themes (sometimes mockingly) in his work, from Dead Babies *(1975), which is set in a near-future where the protagonist works in an abortion factory, to* Time's Arrow *(1991), where the twentieth century happens in reverse, with all the grim ironies that that implies. The stories collected in* Einstein's Monsters *(1987) depict shattered future worlds of various kinds, including this one; a technological near-future where all is far from well . . .*

Twenty-twenty, and the *time* disease is epidemic. In my credit-group, anyway. And yours too, friend, unless I miss my guess. Nobody thinks about anything else any more. Nobody even pretends to think about anything else any more. Oh yeah, except the sky, of course. The poor sky . . . It's a thing. It's a situation. We all think about *time*, catching *time*, coming down with *time*. *I'm* still okay, I think, for the time being.

I took out my handmirror. Everybody carries at least one handmirror now. On the zip trains you see whole carloads jack-knifed over in taut scrutiny of their hairlines and eye-sockets. The anxiety is as electric as the twanging cable above our heads. They say more people are laid low by *time*-anxiety than by *time* itself. But only *time* is fatal. It's a problem, we agree, a definite feature. How can you change the subject when there's only one subject? People don't want to talk about the sky. They don't want to talk about the sky, and I don't blame them.

I took out my handmirror and gave myself a ten-second scan:

lower gumline, left eyelash count. I felt so heartened that I moved carefully into the kitchen and cracked out a beer. I ate a *hero*, and a *ham salad*. I lit another cigarette. I activated the TV and keyed myself in to the Therapy Channel. I watched a seventy-year-old documentary about a road-widening scheme in a place called Orpington, over in England there . . . Boredom is meant to be highly prophylactic when it comes to *time*. We are all advised to experience as much boredom as we possibly can. To bore somebody is said to be even more sanative than to be bored oneself. That's why we're always raising our voices in company and going on and on about anything that enters our heads. Me I go on about *time* the whole time: a reckless habit. Listen to me. I'm at it again.

The outercom sounded. I switched from Therapy to Intake. No visual. "Who is it?" I asked the TV. The TV told me. I sighed, and put the call on a half-minute hold. Soothing music. Boring music . . . Okay – you want to hear my theory? Now some say that *time* was caused by congestion, air plague, city life (and city life is the only kind of life there is these days). Others say that *time* was a result of the first nuclear conflicts (limited theatre, Persia v. Pakistan, Zaire v. Nigeria, and so on, no really big deal or anything: they took the heat and the light, and we took the cold and the dark; it helped fuck the sky, that factor) and more particularly of the saturation TV coverage that followed: all day the screen writhed with flesh, flesh dying or living in a queer state of age. Still others say that *time* was an evolutionary consequence of humankind's ventures into space (they shouldn't have gone out there, what with things so rocky back home). *Food*, pornography, the cancer cure . . . Me I think it was the twentieth century that did it. The twentieth century was all it took.

"Hi there, Happy," I said. "What's new?"

". . . Lou?" her voice said warily. "Lou, I don't feel so good."

"That's not new. That's old."

"I don't feel so good. I think it's really happening this time."

"Oh, sure."

Now this was Happy Farraday. That's right: the TV star. *The* Happy Farraday. Oh, we go way back, Happy and me.

"Let's take a look at you," I said. "Come on, Happy, give me a visual on this."

The screen remained blank, its dead cells seeming to squirm or hover. On impulse I switched from Intake to Daydrama. There was

Happy, full face to camera, vividly doing her thing. I switched back. Still no visual. I said,

"I just checked you out on the other channel. You're in superb shape. What's your factor?"

"It's here," said her voice. "It's *time*."

TV stars are especially prone to *time*-anxiety – to *time* too, it has to be said. Why? Well I think we're looking at an occupational hazard. It's a thing. True, the work could hardly be more boring. Not many people know this, but all the characters in the Armchair, Daydrama and Proscenium channels now write their own lines. It's a new gimmick, intended to promote formlessness, to combat sequentiality, and so on: the target-research gurus have established that this goes down a lot better with the homebound. Besides, all the writing talent is in game-conception or mass-therapy, doing soothe stuff for the non-employed and other sections of the populace that are winding down from being functional. There are fortunes to be made in the leisure and assuagement industries. The standout writers are like those teenage billionaires in the early days of the chip revolution. On the other hand, making money – like reading and writing, come to that – dangerously increases your *time*-anxiety levels. Obviously. The more money you have, the more time you have to worry about *time*. It's a thing. Happy Farraday is top credit, and she also bears the weight of TV fame (where millions know you or think they do), that collective sympathy, identification and concern which, I suspect, seriously depletes your *time*-resistance. I've started to keep a kind of file on this. I'm beginning to think of it as reciprocity syndrome, one of the new –

Where was I? Yeah. On the line with Happy here. My mind has a tendency to wander. Indulge me. It helps, *time*-wise.

"Okay. You want to tell me what symptoms you got?" She told me. "Call a doctor," I joked. "Look, give me a break. This is – what? The second time this year? The third?"

"It's different this time."

"It's the new role, Happy. That's all it is." In her new series on Daydrama, Happy was playing the stock part of a glamorous forty-year-old with a bad case of *time*-anxiety. And it was getting to her – of course it was. "You know where I place the blame? On your talent! As an actress you're just too damn good. Greg Buzhardt and I were –"

"Save it, Lou," she said. "Don't bore me out. It's real. It's *time*."

"I know what you're going to do. I know what you're going to do. You're going to ask me to drive over."

"I'll pay."

"It's not the money, Happy, it's the time."

"Take the dollar lane."

"Wow," I said. "You're, you must be kind of serious this time."

So I stood on the shoulder, waiting for Roy to bring up my Horsefly from the stacks. Well, Happy is an old friend and one of my biggest clients, also an ex-wife of mine, and I had to do the right thing. For a while out there I wasn't sure what time it was supposed to be or whether I had a day or night situation on my hands – but then I saw the faint tremors and pulsings of the sun, up in the east. The heavy green light sieved down through the ripped and tattered troposphere, its fissures as many-eyed as silk or pantyhose, with a liquid quality too, churning, changing. Green light: let's go . . . I had a bad scare myself the other week, a very bad scare. I was in bed with Danuta and we were going to have a crack at making love. Okay, a dumb move – but it was her birthday, and we'd been doing a lot of tranquillizers that night. I don't happen to believe that love-making is quite as risky as some people say. To hear some people talk, you'd think that sex was a suicide pact. To hold hands is to put your life on the line. "Look a the *time*-fatality figures among the underclasses," I tell them. They screw like there's no tomorrow, and do they come down with *time*? No, it's us high-credit characters who are really at risk. Like me and Danuta. Like Happy. Like you . . . Anyway, we were lying on the bed together, as I say, semi-nude, and talking about the possibility of maybe getting into the right frame of mind for a little of the old pre-foreplay – when all of a sudden I felt a rosy glow break out on me like sweat. There was this clogged inner heat, a heavy heat, with something limitless in it, right in the crux of my being. Well, I panicked. You always tell yourself you're going to be brave, dignified, stoical. I ran wailing into the bathroom. I yanked out the triple mirror; the automatic scanlight came on with a crackle. I opened my eyes and stared. There I stood, waiting. Yes, I was clear, I was safe. I broke down and wept with relief. After a while Danuta helped me back into bed. We didn't try to make love or anything. No *way*. I felt too damn good. I lay there dabbing my eyes, so happy, so grateful – my old self again.

"You screw much, Roy?"

"– Sir?"

"You screw much, Roy?"

"Some. I guess."

Roy was an earnest young earner of the stooped, mustachioed variety. He seemed to have burdensome responsibilities; he even wore his cartridge belt like some kind of hernia strap or spinal support. This was the B-credit look, the buffer-class look. Pretty soon, they project, society will be equally divided into three sections. Section B will devote itself entirely to defending section A from section C. I'm section A. I'm glad I have Roy and his boys on my side.

"Where you driving to today, sir?" he asked as he handed me my car card.

"Over the hills and far away, Roy. I'm going to see Happy Farraday. Any message?"

Roy looked troubled. "Sir," he said, "you got to tell her about Duncan. The new guy at the condo. He has an alcohol thing. Happy Farraday doesn't know about it yet. Duncan, he sets fire to stuff, with his problem there."

"His problem, Roy? That's harsh, Roy."

"Well okay. I don't want to do any kind of value thing here. Maybe it was, like when he was a kid or something. But Duncan has an alcohol situation there. That's the truth of it, Mr Goldfader. And Happy Farraday doesn't know about it yet. You got to warn her. You got to warn her, sir – right now, before it's too late."

I gazed into Roy's handsome, imploring, deeply stupid face. The hot eyes, the tremulous cheeks, the mustache. Jesus Christ, what difference do these guys think a *mustache* is going to make to anything? For the hundredth time I said to him, "Roy, it's all made up. It's just TV, Roy. She writes that stuff herself. It isn't real."

"Now I don't know about none of that," he said, his hand splayed in quiet propitiation. "But I'd feel better in my mind if you'd warn her about Duncan's factor there."

Roy paused. With some difficulty he bent to dab at an oilstain on his superwashable blue pants. He straightened up with a long wheeze. Being young, Roy was, of course, incredibly fat – for reasons of *time*. We both stood there and gazed at the sky, at the spillages, the running colours, at the great chemical betrayals . . .

"It's bad today," said Roy. "Sir? Mr Goldfader? Is it true what they say, that Happy Farraday's coming down with *time*?"

Traffic was light and I was over at Happy's before I knew it. Traffic
is a problem, as everybody keeps on saying. It's okay, though, if you
use the more expensive lanes. We have a five-lane system here in our
county: free, nickel, dime, quarter and dollar (nothing, five, ten,
twenty-five or a hundred dollars a mile) – but of course the free lane
is non-operational right now, a gridlock, a caravan, a linear
breakers' yard of slumped and frazzled heaps, dead rolling-stock
that never rolls. They're going to have a situation there with the
nickel lane too, pretty soon. The thing about driving anywhere is,
it's so unbelievably boring. Here's another plus: since the ban on
rearview mirrors, there's not much scope for any *time*-anxiety.
They had to take the mirrors away, yes sir. They got my support on
that. The concentration-loss was a real feature, you know, driving
along and checking out your crow's-feet and hairline, all at the same
time. There used to be a party atmosphere out on the thruway, in
the cheap lanes where mobility is low or minimal. People would get
out of their cars and horse around. Maybe it still goes on, for all I
know. The dividing barriers are higher now, with the new Boredom
Drive, and you can't really tell what gives. I *did* see something
interesting, though. I couldn't help it. During the long wait at the
security intersect, where even the dollar lane gets loused up by all
the towtrucks and ambulances – and by the great fleets of copbikes
and squadcars – I saw three *runners*, three *time* punks, loping
steadily across the disused freightlane, up on the East Viaduct.
There they were, as plain as day: shorts, sweatshirts, *running*-shoes.
The stacked cars all sounded their horns, a low furious bellow from
the old beasts in their stalls. A few dozen cops appeared with
bullhorns and tried to talk them down – but they just gestured and
ran defiantly on. They're sick in the head, these punks, though I
guess there's a kind of logic in it somewhere. They do vitamins, you
know. Yeah. They work out and screw around; they have their
nihilistic marathons. I saw one close down at the studios last week.
A security guard found her *running* along the old outer track. They
asked her some questions and then let her go. She was about thirty,
I guess. She looked in terrible shape.

  And so I drove on, without incident. But even through the treated
glass of the windshield I could see and sense the atrocious lancings
and poppings in the ruined sky. It gets to you. Stare at the blazing
noon of a high-watt bulb for ten or fifteen minutes – then shut your
eyes, real tight and sudden. That's what the sky looks like. You

know, we pity it, or at least I do. I look at the sky and I just think
. . . *ow*. Whew. Oh, the sky, the poor *sky*.

Happy Farraday had left a priority clearance for me at Realty HQ,
so I didn't have to hang around that long. To tell you the truth, I was
scandalized by how lax and perfunctory the security people were
becoming. It's always like this, after a quiet few weeks. Then there's
another shitstorm from section C, and all the writs start flying
around again. In the cubicle I put my clothes back on and dried my
hair. While they okayed my urinalysis and X-ray congruence tests,
I watched TV in the commissary. I sat down, delicately, gingerly
(you know how it is, after a strip search), and took three clippings
out of my wallet. These are for the file. What do you think?

Item 1, from the news page of *Screen Week*:

In a series of repeated experiments at the Valley Chemistry
Workshop, Science Student Edwin Navasky has "proven"
that hot water freezes faster than cold. Said Edwin, "We did
the test four times." Added Student Advisor Joy Broadener:
"It's a feature. We're real baffled."

Item 2, from the facts section of *Armchair Guide*:

Candidate Day McGwire took out a spot on Channel 29
Monday last. Her purpose: to deny persistent but unfounded
rumors that she suffered from heart trouble. Sadly, she was
unable to appear. The reason: her sudden hospitalization with
a cardiac problem.

Item 3, from the update column of *Television*:

Meteorological Pilot Lars Christer reported another sighting
of "The Thing Up There" during a routine low-level flight.
The location: 10,000 feet above Lake Baltimore. His description: "It was kind of oval, with a kind of a black circle in the
center." The phenomenon is believed to be a cumulus or spore
formation. Christer's reaction: "I don't know what to make
of it. It's a thing."

"Goldfader," roared the tannoy, scattering my thoughts. The
caddycart was ready at the gate. In the west now the nuked heavens
looked especially hellish and distraught, with a throbbing, peeled-

eyeball effect on the low horizon – bloodshot, conjunctivitic. Pink eye. The Thing Up There, I sometimes suspect, it might look like an eye, flecked with painful tears, staring, incensed . . . Using my cane I walked cautiously around the back of Happy's bungalow. Her twenty-year-old daughter Sunny was lying naked on a lounger, soaking up the haze. She made no move to cover herself as I limped poolside. Little Sunny here wants me to represent her someday, and I guess she was showing me the goods. Well, it's like they say: if you've got it, flaunt it.

"Hi, Lou," she said sleepily. "Take a drink. Go ahead. It's five o'clock."

I looked at Sunny critically as I edged past her to the bar. The kid was a real centrefold, no question. Now don't misunderstand me here. I say *centrefold*, but of course pornography hasn't really kept pace with *time*. At first they tried filling the magazines and mature cable channels with new-look women, like Sunny, but it didn't work out. *Time* has effectively killed pornography, except as an underground blood sport, or a punk thing. *Time* has killed much else. Here's an interesting topic-sentence. Now that masturbation is the only form of sex that doesn't carry a government health warning, what do we think about when we're doing it there, what is *left* for us to think about? Me, I'm not saying. Christ, are *you*? What images slide, what spectres flit . . . what happens to these thoughts as they hover and mass, up there in the blasted, the totalled, up there in the fucked sky?

"Come on, Sunny. Where's you robe?"

As I fixed myself a vodka-context and sucked warily on a *pretzel*, I noticed Sunny's bald patch gently gleaming in the mist. I sighed.

"You like my dome?" she asked, without turning. "Relax, it's artificial." She sat up straight now and looked at me coyly. She smiled. Yeah, she'd had her teeth gimmicked too – by some cowboy snaggle-artist down in the Valley, no doubt. I poled myself poolside again and took a good slow scan. The flab and pallor were real all right, but the stretch-marks seemed cosmetic: too symmetrical, too pronounced.

"Now you listen to me, kid," I began. "Here are the realities. To scudbathe, to flop out all day by the pool with a bottle or two, to take on a little weight around the middle there – that's good for a girl. I mean you got to keep in shape. But this mutton routine, Sunny, it's for the punks. No oldjob ever got on my books and no oldjob ever will. Here are the reasons. Number one –" And I gave young Sunny a long talking-to out there, a real piece of my mind. I had her in the boredom corner and I wasn't letting her out. I went on and on at her – on and on and on and on. Me, I almost checked out myself, as boredom edged towards despair (the way boredom will), gazing into the voided pool, the reflected skyscape, and the busy static, in the sediment of sable rain.

"Yeah, well," I said, winding up. "Anyway. What's the thing? You look great."

She laughed, coughed and spat. "Forget it, Lou," she said croakily. "I only do it for fun."

"I'm glad to hear that, Sunny. Now where's your mother?"

"Two days."

"Uh?"

"In her room. In her room two days. She's serious this time."

"Oh, sure."

I rebrimmed my drink and went inside. The only point of light in the hallway came from the mirror's sleepless scanlamp. I looked myself over as I limped by. The heavy boredom and light stress of the seven-hour drive had done me good. I was fine, fine. "Happy?" I said, and knocked.

"Is that you, Lou?" The voice was strong and clear – and it was quick, too. Direct, alert. "I'll unlatch the door but don't come in right away."

"Sure," I said. I took a pull of booze and groped around for a chair. But then I heard the click and Happy's brisk "Okay" . . .

Now I have to tell you that two things puzzled me here. First, the voice; second, the alacrity. Usually when she's in this state you can hardly hear the woman, and it takes an hour or more for her to get to the door and back into bed again. Yeah, I thought, she must have been waiting with her fingers poised on the handle. There's nothing wrong with Happy. The lady is fine, fine.

So in I went. She had the long black nets up over the sack – streaming, glistening, a cot for the devil's progeny. I moved through the gloom to the bedside chair and sat myself down with a grunt. A familiar chair. A familiar vigil.

"Mind if I don't smoke?" I asked her. "It's not the lungburn. I just get tuckered out lighting the damn things all the time. Understand what I mean?"

No answer.

"How are you feeling, Happy?"

No answer.

"Now listen, kid. You got to quit this nonsense. I know it's problematic with the new role and everything, but – do I have to tell you again what happened to Day Montague? Do I, Happy? Do I? You're forty years old. You look fantastic. Let me tell you what Greg Buzhardt said to me when he saw the outtakes last week. He said, "Style. Class. Presence. Sincerity. Look at the ratings. Look at the profiles. Happy Farraday is the woman of men's dreams." That's what he said. "Happy Farraday is the –"

"*Lou.*"

The voice came from behind me. I swivelled, and felt the twinge of tendons in my neck. Happy stood in a channel of bathroom light and also in the softer channel or haze of her slip of silk. She stood there as vivid as health itself, as graphic as youth, with her own light sources, the eyes, the mouth, the hair, the dips and curves of the flaring throat. The silk fell to her feet, and the glass fell from my hand, and something else dropped or plunged inside my chest.

"Oh Christ," I said. "Happy, I'm sorry."

I remember what the sky was like, when the sky was young – its shawls and fleeces, its bears and whales, its cusps and clefts. A sky of grey, a sky of blue, a sky of spice. But now the sky has gone, and we face different heavens. Some vital casing has left our lives. Up there, now, I think, a kind of turnaround occurs. *Time*-fear collects up there and comes back to us in the form of *time*. It's the sky, the sky, it's the fucking *sky*. If enough people believe that a thing is real or happening, then it seems that the thing must happen, must go for real. Against all odds and expectation, these are magical times we're living in: proletarian magic. Grey magic!

Now that it's over, now that I'm home and on the mend, with Danuta back for good and Happy gone for ever, I think I can talk it all out and tell you the real story. I'm sitting on the cramped verandah with a blanket on my lap. Before me through the restraining bars the sunset sprawls in its polluted pomp, full of genies, cloaked ghosts, crimson demons of the middle sky. Red light: let's stop – let's end it. The Thing Up There, it may not be God, of course. It may be the Devil. Pretty soon, Danuta will call me in for my *broth*. Then a nap, and an hour of TV maybe. The Therapy Channel. I'm really into early nights . . . This afternoon I went walking, out on the shoulder. I don't know why. I don't think I'll do it again. On my return Roy appeared and helped me into the lift. He then asked me shyly,

"Happy Farraday – she okay now, sir?"

"Okay?" I said. "Okay? What do you mean, *okay*? You never read a news page, Roy?"

"When she had to leave for Australia there. I wondered if she's okay. It'll be better for her, I guess. She was in a situation, with Duncan. It was a thing there."

"That's just TV, for Christ's sake. They wrote her out," I said, and felt an abrupt, leaden calm. "She's not in Australia, Roy. She's in heaven."

"– Sir?"

"She's *dead*, God damn it."

"Now I don't know about none of that," he said, with one fat palm raised. "All it is is, I just hope she's okay, over in Australia there."

Happy is in heaven, or I hope she is. I hope she's not in hell. Hell is the evening sky and I surely hope she's not up there. Ah, how to bear it? It's a thing. No, it really is.

I admit right now that I panicked back there, in the bungalow bedroom with the chute of light, the altered woman, and my own being so quickly stretched by fragility and fear. I shouted a lot. *Lie Down! Call Trattman! Put on your robe!* That kind of thing. "Come on, Lou. Be realistic," she said. "Look at me." And I looked. Yeah. Her skin had that shiny telltale succulence, all over. Her hair – which a week ago, God damn it, lay as thin and colourless as my own – was humming with body and glow. And the mouth, Christ . . . lips all full and wet, and an animal tongue, like a heart, not Happy's, the tongue of another woman, bigger, greedier, younger. Younger. Classic *time*. Oh, classic.

She had me go over and lie down on the bed with her there, to give comfort, to give some sense of final safety. I was in a ticklish state of nerves, as you'd imagine. *Time* isn't infectious (we do know *that* about *time*) but sickness in any form won't draw a body nearer and I wanted all my distance. *Stay out*, it says. Then I saw – I saw it in her breasts, high but heavy, their little points tender, detailed, *time*-inflamed; and the smell, the smell of deep memory, tidal, submarine . . . I knew the kind of comfort she wanted. Yes and *time* often takes them this way, I thought, in my slow and stately terror. You've come this far: go further, I told myself. Go closer, nearer, closer. Do it for her, for her and for old times' sake. I stirred, ready to let her have all that head and hand could give, until I too felt the fever in my lines of heat, the swell and smell of youth and death. This is suicide, I thought, and I don't care . . . At one point, during the last hours, just before dawn, I got to my feet and crept to the window and looked up at the aching, the hurting sky; I felt myself grey and softly twanging for a moment, like a coathanger left to shimmer on the pole, with Happy there behind me, alone in her bed and her hot death. "Honey," I said out loud, and went to join her. I like it, I thought, and gave a sudden nod. What do I like? I like the love. This is suicide and I don't care.

I was in terrible shape, mind you, for the next couple of months, really beat to shit, out of it, just out of it. I would wake at seven and leap out of the sack. I suffered energy attacks. Right off my *food*, I craved thick meat and thick wine. I couldn't watch any therapy. After barely a half-hour of some home-carpentry show or marathon darts contest I'd be pacing the room with frenzy in my bitten fingertips. I put Danuta at risk too, on several occasions. I even threw a pass in on little Sunny Farraday, who moved in here for a time after the cremation. Danuta divorced me. She even moved out. But she's back now. She's a good kid, Danuta – she helped me through. The whole thing is behind me now, and I think (knock on wood) that I'm more or less my old self again.

Pretty soon I'll rap on the window with my cane and have Danuta fetch me another blanket. Later, she'll help me inside for my *broth*. Then a nap, and an hour of TV maybe. The Therapy Channel. I'm happy for the time being, and willingly face the vivid torment, the boiling acne of the dying sky. When the sky is dead, will they give us a new one? Today my answering service left a strange message: I have to call a number in Sydney, over in Australia there. I'll do it tomorrow. Or the next day. Yeah. I can't make the effort right now. To reach for my stick, to lift it, to rap the glass, to say *Danuta* – even that takes steep ascents of time. All things happen so slowly now. I have a new feature with my back. I broke a tooth last week on a piece of *toast*. Jesus, how I hate bending and stairs. The sky hangs above me in shredded webs, in bloody tatters. It's a big relief, and I'm grateful. I'm okay, I'm good, good. For the time being, at any rate, I show no signs of coming down with *time*.

ARTIFICIALLY INDUCED DUB SYNDROME

Jeff Noon

If The Stone Roses and Happy Mondays grabbed the headlines when in the late 1980s Manchester suddenly became the place to be, Jeff Noon is proving to be a more enduring talent. His novels Pollen *and* Vurt, *originally published by a small local press, delighted local readers but are now gaining much wider recognition, and he is fast becoming one of the most engaging writers of the 90s. "Artificially Induced Dub Syndrome" is his first fictional excursion outside Manchester.*

Rising upwards from Manchester, England, sickening from the dislocation changes, sucking our way into the dreamspace of Amirrorca, to land at the Donald Duck runway, five seconds later.

Like . . . uhh . . . whooooosh, man! . . . Like . . . uhh . . . shit! . . . Where in the head am I? . . . Captain can you help me, please?

"We hope you all enjoyed the trip, and please fly with World Psyche again, y'hear? We sure do appreciate your custom."

And then the mad scramble for the exit node. Into Neutral.

This was mine and Jodie's first ever trip to the UD of A, so you can guess we were suffering. I was getting my head round it, you know, second by second, if only to impress Krunch, but poor Jodie . . . man, she was screaming down the Art Deco corridors. Chillingly good interface, by the way; these Americans really knew how to make a dream live. I mean, the place looked more than real. Maybe this is why Jodie was suffering so; she was used to the old

English Fantasy, with it's cheap and nasty "Singland welcomes careful dreamers" design, where all the edges are fuzzy and the people feel like warmed-up cheese. Still, the girl wasn't helping our mission any, waving her arms around like that, and shouting abuse at the other refugees as they streamed through Neutral, towards the border controls. A pack of splicehounds had now locked onto Jodie's main scent; I could hear them snarling and pounding their cages, eager to rip flesh from some errant smuggler.

Okay, the UDA Immigration Authorities had splicehounds on their side; we had Krunch-Factor 9 on ours. The big Dogman slapped Jodie around the face, once or twice – claws sheathed, naturally – and then pushed her towards the customs post. She ran a smoky pathway between the sniffer beams of the splicers and the icy stares of the loaded guardsmen. No fire-sirens. Krunch himself cleared the customs like a well-heeled business-exec, firmly on his hind legs for the disguise. Now the pair of them are staring at me from the safe side of the dream. Nice of them that, considering that I was the cargo-carrier! One false move passing through the barrier, I was spliced-up meat and gravy on a pair of slobbering jaws. Man, this was gonna be one dangerous gig.

Let me introduce the band . . .

Jodie Ace was the singer and the lyricist. One gorgeous half-cast shadow of a girl, a little strung-up on being down, but with a voice of dewy mist, I swear, and a pair of smoky eyes that could read the contents of your mind from the distance of a kiss. And then turn all your secrets into a song . . .

I made a step towards the barrier that marked the end of Neutrality. Beyond that point, Amirrorca. Freedom's dance. The splicehounds started to growl.

Jodie was the song and I was the music, with the buzz-name of Lemon Deuce. I could turn myself into the drums and the violin, the acoustic and electric guitars, the piano and the trumpet, the ocarina and the Tibetan nose flute; shit, man, I could turn my body into anything that made a noise, but best of all I liked to turn myself into the double bass. This was my Mingus Demon, my deep down throb of bliss. Yeah, I was a Dub sufferer. I had the music virus swimming my cells. What else could I do with my illness, but allow some of its symptoms to add rhythm and lead to Jodie's soulfulness? We called our business Ace and the Deuce, purveyors of the finest illegal dance music.

Another step forwards. I was almost level with the first splicehound now. The rabid beast was making a thick bass grumble, like he'd sniffed out the aroma of Mingus on my skin. Stay cool. One of the borderguards had his hand ready on the cage release. Don't look at the guard! Look forwards. There's Krunch, just a few small steps away. He's waiting for me in Amirrorca. The bastard's grinning at me!

Krunch-Factor 9 was the wild card in the hand, our latest management. Krunch was halfdog and halfman, but with the dog-half in denial, full to the shaved-off cheekfur with promises of mega-dosh. On a good day he could almost pass for human.

All those promises that I'd followed, upwards and dreamwards, downwards and along, across the line, between the sights of robodogs and marksmen. Another step forwards. Any second now, expecting the sirens to start, the jaws to shut, the bullets to explode . . .

Krunch hired a Mustang Detonate from the dreamport's courtesy counter, and within fifteen minutes we were speeding away from Newer York City, northwards, through a neat array of suburbs. I was in the back with Jodie, trying my best to calm her down. Krunch was upfront and driving. Outside, the American Dream flashed by like a series of movie sets; a kid on a bike throwing newspapers onto front porches, an old soldier manicuring his lawn, a young golf-widow pushing the dog and walking the pram. And take a look at that giant, yellow W! Shit, the Americans couldn't even dream unless it contained burgers! The burbs petered out into a mess of shanty towns, where scrawny youths chased after a screaming piglet. The dream getting nastier. Some ruffian banged on the Mustang's window as we nudged around a pile of dream-trash. Krunch gave him the old canine one claw gesture and then accelerated; I could hear the kid screaming as we shot out of the sprawl. Open country. Sparse was the traffic, likewise the conversation. I was still seething from the gauntlet. "Play us some tune, Lemon Boy," Krunch finally growled at me. Canine and English.

"What about the cops?" I asked.

"You be seeing Boogie Cops, yes?" Krunch snarled. "Me not seeing no cops. Not at all! Road belongs to the swift."

"You didn't exactly help, Krunch, back there at the border."

"You not need any help."

"You helped Jodie."

"You got through good, no? Those cheap splicerhounds! Jesus Dog! Lemon Boy, your music be too deeply ridden for finding. Come on! Me thinking Jodie want to sing, yes? Calm her down some?"

From the look of her, the last thing on Jodie's mind was singing. She was pressing herself into the upholstery, sweat pouring from her brow. What else could I do but start some viral bass and drums in my veins? Mingus Demon and the Moon Demon, making my weak, thin body emit a dubbed-up version of Bass Spacer. It needed Jodie's sweet and smoking vocals, but the shadowgirl kept her mouth and her mind closed.

Krunch was tapping out the rhythm on the steering wheel, howling along quite tunelessly, until a honking siren added its treble pitch to by body's bass, and then Jodie started on a wailing scream.

Boogie Cops! Keepers of the Stillness. Man, those bastards were sure nimble for danceophobes!

The Authorities were scared of rhythm, you see, like they were scared of sex between the species. Man, those Authorities were neuters; they were scared of their own dried-up apertures! The brain-dead nano-fucks! Which is a laugh, because the Authorities were all for Vurt in the early days. Vurt was the name of an organic technology that allowed humans to walk, as though real, through the landscape of dreams. Above the real world called England, the Authorities created a vurtual world called United Singland; above the real world called America, a vurtual world called the United Dreams of America. The various dreams eventually joined hands, and all around the surface of Planet Earth floated Planet Vurt. Lots of Earthlings actually wanted to become Vurtlings; they wanted to live in their dreams forever. Access was strictly controlled, of course, via tollbooths and border controls, and a rising scale of fares; the deeper the dream, the higher the price. The Authorities were cleaning up! Until it all started to go wrong, and the dream-disease imported itself into reality.

It started in Manchester, of course, the thinnest membrane. You can imagine the Town Hall's despair as the first cases of Dub Sickness came to light. They'd always had a limp dick for music anyway, what with its "liberating effect upon the young", but this was a square's nightmare, because music was now a viral intruder.

I mean, music was actually penetrating the people. Seven per cent of the World's population was infected. And you're listening to the story of one of the first. We had all these demon players inside us, virus musicians from heaven that we could call up at anytime. Jesus Jagger, those early days . . . did we make the people dance, or what?! Even worse for the Authorities, the fact that the Dub virus could be passed on through sex. They called it the new VD for propaganda purposes. (Vurtual Dynamics, don't you know?)

Against a disease from an unknown dream, what chance of a cure? All the Authorities managed was to introduce the Laws of Stillness, a vicious edict that ruled against the pursuit of moving your body (in Reality or Vurtuality) to the measures of a repetitive beat; the Laws of Purity, which outlawed sex with a sufferer; and the Laws of Quarantine, a rather sweet name for the rounding up and imprisonment of all known sufferers. And one by one the nations fell, until this time that I'm telling about, when the Earth and its dream became quite unmoving and morose. To administer these pathetic measures, pray welcome the Stillness Enforcement League. To outlaw dancers the world and the dream over, otherwise known as the Boogie Cops . . .

I closed down the Mingus and the Moon demons, as a cop-car pulled us over to the road's edge. Two seconds later, a Boogie she-cop was banging on the driver's window. "Is anything the matter, officeress?" Krunch politely asked, with an immaculate human voice, all of a sudden. Man, that Krunch could play any game!

"The matter," the Boogie Cop replied, "is that we've picked up some illegal bass and drums being played on the dreamway."

"Officeress, does it look like we've got a drum kit in the vehicle? We have no interest in music. Unless it be the kind produced by rubbing your back legs together."

"Listen, bud . . . I've had a bad day."

"Please, we're an innocent trio of Mancunian enginemologists, heading on to Connect'n'cut for a convention on the mating habits of the robo-beetle. These remarkable creatures attract partners by rubbing their back legs together, thus producing a lusty, melodious song. Here are our papers . . . I think you'll find them all in order."

"What's wrong with her? The Boogie Cop was looking at Jodie.

"She's dream-lagged from the flight," Krunch replied, cool as dog-fuck.

The cop gazed at Jodie for a full ten seconds, then turned back to Krunch: "You wouldn't be a dogman, by any chance?"

"Officeress, please! How dare you? Dogmen are the scum of rabid DNA. I just haven't had a shave for a few weeks. That's all."

"Well . . . in Connect'n'cut . . ."

"Yes?"

"I recommend you buy some shaving tablets."

And then we were free, and riding. Open country. Krunch Factor 9 coming up trumps against one easy Boogie Cop! Maybe this trip wasn't such a bad idea, after all. Even Jodie seemed to be more at ease: she'd stopped shaking by now, and looking down at her shadowy face, I even caught a trace of love being stroked through my mind.

Or maybe not, as the case may be . . .

Things had never been easy between us. It wasn't just musical differences (although Jodie's insistence upon me releasing ancient Motown Demons sometimes riled); neither was it the singer against the band, because I was happy up in the DJ box – the last thing I needed was fame, what with the Boogies after my blood. It wasn't even that her Shadow allowed her access to my vilest thoughts . . .

Let me tell the truth . . .

After the Dubness invaded, I went right off women. I know some of the sufferers rejoiced in spreading the virus; they called it turning the world into music, pure music. But I was reticent and confused. Maybe I had an inkling about what the Dub would lead to, even then. I was gigging at a club called Jungle Jingles, a dingy hole in Unchester, Singland. Sure it was against the law, but the Boogies had a hard time policing the labyrinthine backstreets of Singland. Listen good: if the people want to dance, the people shall dance. Here and there in the dream you could find these tawdry palaces, whose managers were keen on the outlaw-dosh. After the gig, this young girl barged her way into the dressing room. I wasn't used to being harangued, the truth be known. "I suppose you're after my rhythm patterns?" My innocent question, to which the girl whispered in a breath of smoke, "I'm after your sperm."

It felt like my mind was being caressed by the fingers of a shadow.

That night I ended up in her bed, and we made a kind of love, I suppose: Jodie wanted everything but I was playing it safe. Our kisses floated like thought bubbles above trails of smoke from her skin. And after the kisses, this girl called Jodie Ace sang a lonesome song to me. Despite the virus running in beats through my body, this was a new song, and a new loving song. I tried to play along with my internal rhythm, but the beats came out all wrong . . . until Jodie gathered every drift of smoke from the room, blowing this dark cloud into my head. All the thoughts of a sad, young, constantly-searching girl seeping through me, and then . . .

Shiver song!

I was playing along with a new beat, a liquid rhythm. A demon musician called up from my dying cells. "Did you like that, Lemon?" Jodie asked. "It's called You Are, You Are."

"Whose beautiful song is that?" I pleaded.

"It's your song now, but originally Curtis sang it."

"Ian Curtis? The Joyful Divisionist?"

"Curtis Mayfield, silly! You call yourself a sufferer, but you've never played the Mayfield Demon before?"

"How did you do that new song for me?"

"Oh, you know . . . a little touch of Shadow. I just worked something loose for you. Now, won't you please give me the gift?"

Jodie really wanted to tune into the music direct, that constant searching, but still I refused to go all the way. For some slippery reason, I didn't want to reproduce the dream. Here, truly, begins the uneasiness between us.

But that was the origin of Ace and the Deuce, the smoke and dub of outlaw dance. And up and down the imagined Singland, again and again Ace and the Deuce fed the secret beat to eager, wet minds, making the people madly dance, making a secret joy in the darkness. Jodie and I, we made a dance of our own after the gigs, falling in love with each other and the illegal nature of our crimes against stillness. It was a chaste love, of course, and sometimes Jodie would scream at me, for denying her the ultimate access to music. But I was strong, I was safely-sexual. The intuitive knowledge inside, that this internal music would kill the sufferer eventually.

But how I loved those early days of our career, plying our illegal wares, easily finding a bass-path to dub out the cops. We were always on the run, of course; always only one small dancing step ahead of the Boogie Cops, but this escaping only fuelled my desire.

Ace and the Deuce released a record called Bass Spacer, a dream
the law-breakers could swallow with pride.

Man, how they swallowed! That debut tune made it to number
five in the outlaw charts and we were on some kind of dangerous
roll I guess, because this is when Krunch-Factor 9 came visiting.
We were playing the DFEX club in Unchester. Jodie was down on
the imaginary stage, singing her soul out:

> Stop your running of the human race.
>> Lick your lips at the cut and paste.
>> Make a Curtis Mayfield kind of pace;
>> Leave some space for the bass.

This is when I made my human-bass solo, up in the DJ booth,
feeding multiple dream-beats to the dancers. Ultra-low frequen-
cies sweeping out of my brain-amp. I called up the demon viruses
of Mingus and Moon and Davis and Hendrix. And a little touch
of Mayfield, just to please the singer. I was feeling like the
Dreamiest Jockey of all-time, and the crowd was revelling in this
trancing output of my body, dancing fit to burst against the laws.
This is when Krunch-Factor 9 burst into the booth, in such a hurry
that his sleeked-down whiskers sprung into life on his shaven
cheeks.

"You the buzz, my friend!" he snarled above the music. "You
be suffering from the dub-sickness, yes?"

"Yeah, I suffer . . ." Hesitant, you know, but I could tell that the
dogman had sniffed out with his wet nose that I was plugged in
direct to the music.

"Maybe I squeeze some mega-dosh out of you, yes?" Krunch
was gazing down at Jodie's lovely shape on the stage as he growled
this out. "You like this idea, Mister DJ Boy?"

Well, I wasn't too sure, but the next morning Jodie and I met up
with the Dogman over a Full English Breakfast at the Cafe de
Mush. Whilst dribbling bacon fat down his chin he regaled us with
stories of "certain sub-dreams" within the United Dreamscape of
America, and how they were "dancing ultra-good" over there:
"They be dancing free!"

Jodie was dead set against it at first, mainly because of her
Shadow's natural hatred of the Dogs.

"Me not no dog!" Krunch whimpered in response: "Me a man.
Me pure." Smoothing his cut-to-the-quick claws along his cheeks

the same time, pathetically hoping to hide the stubble of his fur.

"They kill you for dancing in Amirrorca," Jodie said. "Everybody knows that."

"Everybody forgetting the Originals, yes?" Krunch replied: "The Original Peoples of Amirrorca, they be one autonomous zone. They make the dancing free and easy. Big dosh! Mega Dosh! Why, they let Dub sufferers play free in that zone. Originals love the sufferers! You two following me?"

Following . . .

Upwards and dreamwards and downwards and along, until we were driving through the snow-layered forests of Connect'n'cut, a sparse realm of lonely log-cabins and broken-down tractors. The further we got from Newer York City, the fuzzier the interface became. Until the trees were shedding leaves like fragments of information. We turned one final, icy bend in the Mustang. The Original's borderline was just ahead of us, and beyond its shimmering curtain of frosty air the forest disappeared into mist. Maybe Jodie started to feel at home then, I don't know, but her shadow was quivering with a new love for that smokiness beyond the borderline. I was feeling my bass notes throb.

"Almost home, my people!" Krunch announced with a bark, like he was howling down all the laws of stillness. "Fucking dosh-bound!"

Maybe we could, at last, make this dream come true?

A bunch of people were gathered around the entry point, brandishing placards and shouting out fiery slogans: Originals go home! Vurth belongs to Earth! No more Unreservations! Kill the Twindians dead! Stop the evil rhythm! No more dancing! No more music disease! That stupid kind of stuff.

Jodie started to whimper over the shadow between us: Krunch unsheathed his claws to full-on mastiff mode.

Maybe not such an easy dream . . .

Can you imagine America's surprise when it first ventured into the dreamworld of Amirrorca; to find a people already living in the Vurt? America thought it was uncovering an untold continent; in fact it was invading a homeland. These natives of the dream called themselves the Original People. America called them the Red Twindians, and declared war on them, repeating the history of oppression. Until it was discovered that the Originals actually controlled access to the dreamworld; without the Originals,

America could not dream. America had to compromise. The Originals were allowed to remain in their homeland, but only within a few autonomous zones, known as the Unreservations. Of course the Originals used this autonomy to their own advantage, granting passage to all the desires that America deemed criminal, of which there were plenty, but dancing to repetitive music was the worst. America was shit-scared of the dancing virus. All the bad things came to be associated with Original Amirrorca. Which made for bad-ass press.

Krunch was now forcing a pathway through the protesters, waving his sharpened dog-claws around like a wicked promise. I was doing my best to keep up with him, dragged down as I was with Jodie's newly-awakened reluctance, and the scrabbling blows of the protest line. "Traitor to Earth!" one of them called me. "Twindian lover! Traitor, traitor, traitor!" I pulled Jodie along through the storm, reaching Krunch at the gateway. The Dogman was arguing with the border guard, demanding free passage to the Unreservation. The guard was shaking his heavy head and slow-speaking in alien syllables. "Me not make snout not tale of this talking," the Krunch barked, total-dog. "What you hearing, Deuce Boy?"

This was the first Original I had ever seen, and his crimson skin and his yellow eyes, and the array of silvery feathers tied to his long, midnight blue hair . . . these attributes burned a hole in my soul. I couldn't explain why.

"I'm hearing patterns, Krunch . . ."

"Deuce baby, you be playing some tune to him, yes?"

All around I could hear the traitor-calls, but still, I played . . .

I called up some ancient demons; I called up the drumming virus from Afreaka, and the Cajun virus from Loose'n'easiana; I even called up the reggae bass virus from Jam-maker. I dug deep down, to play a primal tune. The Original cracked his deep creases into the semblance of a smile, and then plucked one of the silvery feathers from his hair. He offered it to me. I didn't know what to do. "Him wanting you to swallow it," Krunch whispered.

So I swallowed, and so did Jodie and the Krunch; each of us, in turn, tickling the back of our throats with the offering feather.

And then dissolving . . . through the gateway to danceland . . .

Three hours later, man, I'm telling you. A multiverse of terpsichorians were outlaw-pounding the snows of dreamland into slush. Jodie was down on the stage between the Tumtum trees, singing with such beauty that even the Jubjub birds in the branches were beating their wings in time. And, for the very first time, I was on stage with the singer, playing the instruments of my sickness. I was free at last, to express my love. A kiss from my cells, and the people were dancing; Dub was welcomed here. I felt strong and viral, strong and virile, even. Especially when Bass Spacer came on-line. I turned the dream into joy-flesh and wantonness.

Five hours later, all but danced-out and glimmering, my brain's amp-lights turned to embers, I'm ready for my bed. I'm ready, at last and fuelled-up; enough dancing lust within me to want to pass on the Dub virus. But Jodie wasn't there. Jodie wasn't in my bed. I walk along pastel corridors. Another hotel door. Jodie wasn't there. Another bad dream. Jodie wasn't there. Another wisp of smoke. Another door. And there I find my once upon a time beauty, pouring her misty body all over Krunch's bristling fur.

Jesus of the Dream, how far have I got to go?

I make my lonely way towards my bedroom. I fall into a troubled sleep, into which a scarlet native comes ranting. The moniker is Moonkeeper. I'm the dumbfuck drummer of the tribe. You played well, tonight, my mate. Take this feather as your payment.

Taking a silvery, scarlet feather from the greasy braids of a chief. Let me show you the sights . . .

Following the Original down into a deeper land, a dream within a dream, where dancing was nothing unnatural, where dancing was gold. Moonkeeper telling me that he used to be called Keep Moon, in the real world, raging drummer with The Whom. (I think he was losing the plot a little.) And that Keep Moon had died ages and ages ago, and that his dreaming soul had been reborn to this Vurtdom called Beat Heaven. "So this is how the Moon Demon managed to get inside my cells?" I asked. My mate, I fed my drums into your body, the native replied. We wanted to get back to Earth, natch. We wanted to party again. Yeah, we're your disease and proud of it. How come you're not into shagging? Shagging's beautiful. Don't you want to pass on the gift? Can't you understand our yearning?

Of course I understand; Beat Heaven . . . the dream of drumming . . .

I saw Hendrix there, playing with bright fire; I saw Joplin and

Morrison there, singing with blue flowers. It was like the cheapest hippy death-dream, until I saw Curtis and Holly and Miller, making music out of forgiveness. I saw Mingus thrumming at the triple bass. I saw the Moon, and the Moon was pounding on the skin of the sky . . .

And then awakening. My corrugated face in a hotel mirror, you know, looking like a nightmare. What was real anymore? What was unreal? It was like I was caught halfway between. But the silver and red feather was still in my hands. Something, somewhere, must have been real. And a noise in my brain, nothing at all like music; altogether like a summons. A banging on my door . . .

People screaming down the corridors; ex-pats and earthly dreamers. They drag me from my room. The protesters have found a way through the border; now they're shuffling me outside into the field of snow. The trees are heavy with ice blossoms. The feather in my fingers, the tracks of dancers under my shoes, and the withering vision of Boogie Cops marching over the slush. The dancing people all arrested in cop-meshes. A strange crop of fruit dangling from some lonesome Tumtum tree. Original bodies, dead to the dream. Moonkeeper's corpse, just one more bruised apple, swinging. Lynch mob rhythm, pendulum style. Jodie and the Krunch, Ace and the wild 9, swinging dead from that same tree. All the love that I've ever lost, lost forever. The Jubjub birds have fluttered away into silence. The chances missed. Shadowgirl and Dogman, shadow-gone and dog-gone. My hands are tied behind my back. The feather floats away from my life. I remember a scream of livid despair rising from my throat, and then strangled by the noose that was placed around my neck, and tightened. A rope swung over a Tumtum branch. The rhythmless crowd of Boogies and Splicers and Refugees, all of them tugging on the rope . . .

At the last moment of my former life, one of the Boogies snatches the feather from the air. I vaguely recall the face of the highway she-cop, laughing in my face – "Choke on this, music-freak!" – as she rammed the feather into my mouth. I'm gagging on the noose and the feather, and lifted up into white heat.

Okay, like Move On Up, man; you know what I'm saying? Mayfield Demon virus to the rescue. I was let loose from the moment, totally Ian Curtis. My Dub-juicy soul floating away the dream . . .

I'm gagging on Moonkeeper feather. I'm flying to a new world. The dream of a dream. I'm playing edit-suite to the dead. Moon on the drums, Mingus on the bass, Hendrix on the guitar, Ian Curtis Mayfield (joined at the hip) on the vocals; myself on the controls and the all togetherness. I've been found at last.

Beat Heaven is where I'm telling this story from. I've been living here for more years than there are notes in one of Jimi's solos. The band is called The Remix Shadows. I chose that name myself, because I'm the Dub producer, and because this whole song is for Jodie and all the lost lovers of everywhere. The band is tight and the lyrics are written. I deem ourselves ready for a debut gig.

So we're coming back down to Earth. People get ready. Leave some space for the bass in your lives, and let this new disease find a home. And this time to infect only the rampant, the lustful, the nymphomatic. No more denial: I'm gonna spread my dancing juice throughout the land . . .

THE BIG SPACE FUCK

Kurt Vonnegut, Jr

Kurt Vonnegut is one of the handful of authors whose reputation has transcended the SF genre to make him one of the key names of postwar American fiction. His early SF novels, especially The Sirens of Titan *(1959) and* Cat's Cradle *(1963) are still avidly read, while later works such as* Slaughterhouse-Five *(1969),* Breakfast of Champions *(1973) and* Galapágos *(1985) extended and consolidated his reputation. His short fiction, collected in* Welcome to the Monkey House, *is equally impressive. "The Big Space Fuck", an uncollected and somewhat notorious story (believed to be the first commercially published story with the word "fuck" in the title), takes us into the Space Age from the perspective of 1972, when sueing one's parents could still seem like a joke, albeit a rather sick one . . .*

In 1977 it became possible in the United States of America for a young person to sue his parents for the way he had been raised. He could take them to court and make them pay money and even serve jail terms for serious mistakes they made when he was just a helpless little kid. This was not only an effort to achieve justice but to discourage reproduction, since there wasn't anything much to eat any more. Abortions were free. In fact, any woman who volunteered for one got her choice of a bathroom scale or a table lamp.

In 1979, America staged the Big Space Fuck, which was a serious effort to make sure that human life would continue to exist somewhere in the Universe, since it certainly couldn't continue much longer on Earth. Everything had turned to shit and beer cans and old automobiles and Clorox bottles. An interesting thing happened in the Hawaiian Islands, where they had been throwing trash down extinct volcanoes for years: a couple of the volcanoes all of a sudden spit it all back up. And so on.

This was a period of great permissiveness in matters of language, so even the President was saying shit and fuck and so on, without anybody's feeling threatened or taking offense. It was perfectly OK. He called the Space Fuck a Space Fuck and so did everybody else. It was a rocket ship with eight-hundred pounds of freeze-dried jizzum in its nose. It was going to be fired at the Andromeda Galaxy, two-million light years away. The ship was named the *Arthur C. Clarke*, in honor of a famous space pioneer.

It was to be fired at midnight on the Fourth of July. At ten o'clock that night, Dwayne Hoobler and his wife Grace were watching the countdown on television in the living room of their modest home in Elk Harbor, Ohio, on the shore of what used to be Lake Erie. Lake Erie was almost solid sewage now. There were man-eating lampreys in there thirty-eight feet long. Dwayne was a guard in the Ohio Adult Correctional Institution, which was two miles away. His hobby was making birdhouses out of Clorox bottles. He went on making them and hanging them around his yard, even though there weren't any birds any more.

Dwayne and Grace marveled at a film demonstration of how jizzum had been freeze-dried for the trip. A small beaker of the stuff, which had been contributed by the head of the Mathematics Department at the University of Chicago, was flash-frozen. Then it was placed under a bell jar, and the air was exhausted from the jar. The air evanesced, leaving a fine white powder. The powder certainly didn't look like much, and Dwayne Hoobler said so – but there were several hundred million sperm cells in there, in suspended animation. The original contribution, an average contribution, had been two cubic centimeters. There was enough powder, Dwayne estimated out loud, to clog the eye of a needle. And eight-hundred pounds of the stuff would soon be on its way to Andromeda.

"Fuck you, Andromeda," said Dwayne, and he wasn't being coarse. He was echoing billboards and stickers all over town. Other signs said, "Andromeda, We Love You," and "Earth has the Hots for Andromeda," and so on.

There was a knock on the door, and an old friend of the family, the County Sheriff, simultaneously let himself in. "How are you, you old motherfucker?" said Dwayne.

"Can't complain, shitface," said the sheriff, and they joshed back and forth like that for a while. Grace chuckled, enjoying their wit. She wouldn't have chuckled so richly, however, if she had been a little more observant. She might have noticed that the sheriff's jocularity was very much on the surface. Underneath, he had something troubling on his mind. She might have noticed, too, that he had legal papers in his hand.

"Sit down, you silly old fart," said Dwayne, "and watch Andromeda get the surprise of her life."

"The way I understand it," the sheriff replied, "I'd have to sit there for more than two-million years. My old lady might wonder what's become of me." He was a lot smarter than Dwayne. He had jizzum on the *Arthur C. Clarke*, and Dwayne didn't. You had to have an I.Q. of over 115 to have your jizzum accepted. There were certain exceptions to this: if you were a good athlete or could play a musical instrument or paint pictures, but Dwayne didn't qualify in any of those ways, either. He had hoped that birdhouse-makers might be entitled to special consideration, but this turned out not to be the case. The Director of the New York Philharmonic, on the other hand, was entitled to contribute a whole quart, if he wanted to. He was sixty-eight years old. Dwayne was forty-two.

There was an old astronaut on the television now. He was saying that he sure wished he could go where his jizzum was going. But he would sit at home instead, with his memories and a glass of *Tang*. *Tang* used to be the official drink of the astronauts. It was a freeze-dried orangeade.

"Maybe you haven't got two million years," said Dwayne, "but you've got at least five minutes. Sit thee doon."

"What I'm here for—" said the sheriff, and he let his unhappiness show, "is something I customarily do standing up."

Dwayne and Grace were sincerely puzzled. They didn't have the least idea what was coming next. Here is what it was: the sheriff handed each one of them a subpoena, and he said, "It's my sad duty to inform you that your daughter, Wanda June, has accused you of ruining her when she was a child."

Dwayne and Grace were thunderstruck. They knew that Wanda

June was twenty-one now, and entitled to sue, but they certainly hadn't expected her to do so. She was in New York City, and when they congratulated her about her birthday on the telephone, in fact, one of the things Grace said was, "Well, you can sue us now, honeybunch, if you want to." Grace was so sure she and Dwayne had been good parents that she could laugh when she went on, "If you want to, you can send your rotten old parents off to jail."

Wanda June was an only child, incidentally. She had come close to having some siblings, but Grace had had them aborted. Grace had taken three table lamps and a bathroom scale instead.

"What does she say we did wrong?" Grace asked the sheriff.

"There's a separate list of charges inside each of your subpoenas," he said. And he couldn't look his wretched old friends in the eye, so he looked at the television instead. A scientist there was explaining why Andromeda had been selected as a target. There were at least eighty-seven chronosynclastic infundibulae, time warps, between Earth and the Andromeda Galaxy. If the *Arthur C. Clarke* passed through any one of them, the ship and its load would be multiplied a trillion times, and would appear everywhere throughout space and time.

"If there's any fecundity anywhere in the Universe," the scientist promised, "our seed will find it and bloom."

One of the most depressing things about the space program so far, of course, was that it had demonstrated that fecundity was one hell of a long way off, if anywhere. Dumb people like Dwayne and Grace, and even fairly smart people like the sheriff, had been encouraged to believe that there was hospitality out there, and that Earth was just a piece of shit to use as a launching platform.

Now Earth really was a piece of shit, and it was beginning to dawn on even dumb people that it might be the only inhabitable planet human beings would ever find.

Grace was in tears over being sued by her daughter, and the list of charges she was reading was broken into multiple images by the tears. "Oh God, of God, of God—" she said, "she's talking about things I forgot all about, but she never forgot a thing. She's talking about something that happened when she was only four years old."

Dwayne was reading charges against himself, so he didn't ask Grace what awful thing she was supposed to have done when Wanda June was only four, but here it was: Poor little Wanda June drew pretty pictures with a crayon all over the new living-room wallpaper to make her mother happy. Her mother blew up and spanked her instead. Since that day, Wanda June claimed, she had not been able to look at any sort of art materials without trembling like a leaf and breaking out into cold sweats. "Thus was I deprived," Wanda June's lawyer had her say, "of a brilliant and lucrative career in the arts."

Dwayne meanwhile was learning that he had ruined his daughter's opportunities for what her lawyer called an "advantageous marriage and the comfort and love therefrom." Dwayne had done this, supposedly, by being half in the bag whenever a suitor came to call. Also, he was often stripped to the waist when he answered the door, but still had on his cartridge belt and his revolver. She was even able to name a lover her father had lost for her: John L. Newcomb, who had finally married somebody else. He had a very good job now. He was in command of the security force at an arsenal out in South Dakota, where they stockpiled cholera and bubonic plague.

The sheriff had still more bad news to deliver, and he knew he would have an opportunity to deliver it soon enough. Poor Dwayne and Grace were bound to ask him, "What made her *do* this to us?" The answer to that question would be more bad news, which was that Wanda June was in jail, charged with being the head of a shoplifting ring. The only way she could avoid prison was to prove that everything she was and did was her parents' fault.

Meanwhile, Senator Flem Snopes of Mississippi, Chairman of the Senate Space Committee, had appeared on the television screen. He was very happy about the Big Space Fuck, and he said it had been what the American space program had been aiming toward all along. He was proud, he said, that the United States had seen fit to locate the biggest jizzum-freezing plant in his "l'il ol' home town," which was Mayhew.

The word "jizzum" had an interesting history, by the way. It was as old as "fuck" and "shit" and so on, but it continued to be excluded from dictionaries, long after the others were let in. This was because so many people wanted it to remain a truly magic word – the only one left.

And when the United States announced that it was going to do a truly magical thing, was going to fire sperm at the Andromeda

Galaxy, the populace corrected its government. Their collective unconscious announced that it was time for the last magic word to come into the open. They insisted that *sperm* was nothing to fire at another galaxy. Only *jizzum* would do. So the Government began using that word, and it did something that had never been done before, either: it had standardized the way the word was spelled.

The man who was interviewing Senator Snopes asked him to stand up so everybody could get a good look at his codpiece, which the Senator did. Codpieces were very much in fashion, and many men were wearing codpieces in the shape of rocket ships, in honor of the Big Space Fuck. These customarily had the letters "U.S.A." embroidered on the shaft. Senator Snopes' shaft, however, bore the Stars and Bars of the Confederacy.

This led the conversation into the area of heraldry in general, and the interviewer reminded the Senator of his campaign to eliminate the bald eagle as the national bird. The Senator explained that he didn't like to have his country represented by a creature that obviously hadn't been able to cut the mustard in modern times.

Asked to name a creature that *had* been able to cut the mustard, the Senator did better than that: he named two – the lamprey and the bloodworm. And, unbeknownst to him or to anybody, lampreys were finding the Great Lakes too vile and noxious even for *them*. While all the human beings were in their houses, watching the Big Space Fuck, lampreys were squirming out of the ooze and onto land. Some of them were nearly as long and thick as the *Arthur C. Clarke*.

And Grace Hoobler tore her wet eyes from what she had been reading, and she asked the sheriff the question he had been dreading to hear: "What made her *do* this to us?"

The sheriff told her, and then he cried out against cruel Fate, too. "This is the most horrible duty I ever had to carry out—" he said brokenly, "to deliver news this heartbreaking to friends as close as you two are – on a night that's supposed to be the most joyful night in the history of mankind."

He left sobbing, and stumbled right into the mouth of a lamprey. The lamprey ate him immediately, but not before he screamed. Dwayne and Grace Hoobler rushed outside to see what the screaming was about, and the lamprey ate them, too.

It was ironical that their television set continued to report the countdown, even though they weren't around any more to see or hear or care.

"Nine!" said a voice. And then, "Eight!" And then, "Seven!" And so on.

POINTS OF VIEW

Kathe Koja

One of the rising US stars in both the horror and science fiction fields, Kathe Koja is a frequent contributor to magazines in each genre, and novels such as The Cipher *(1991),* Bad Brains *(1992) and* Skin *(1993) have brought high critical praise. "Points of View" is a sharp, disturbing story of sexual jealousy in the technological future. Some things* won't *change.*

Black slat blinds; the flavor of blood.

Afternoon, Robin stretched beside her, black T-shirt and bare ass, fast asleep or faking. Sophy rubbed a finger in the pain, found a smear, Rorschach of blood on the black-and-gold quilt: a queen on a chessboard, a donkey, a fly, more spoor of last night's rough fuck? Let the viewer decide. Like Robin's video drawings. She rolled to rise from the fat-pillowed futon and Robin stirred, angel's face annoyed, then burrowed deeper into dream. Of whom? Not me, Sophy thought. Hard splash of Stoly into half-full chrome water glass, alcohol and flat tapwater taste; and the iron of new blood. Into the bathroom, and she took the glass with her.

Under heartless fluorescents, a catalog of small bad surprises: ripped lip, yeah, and bruise like a flower, dark iris on the flesh beneath. On the investigating hand two nails broken, one torn almost free. Funny it didn't hurt more. Mouthful of vodka, insert sore finger and suck: purify, if not anesthetize. How had she come to be hurt, these ways? Drunk? Not so, or at least she didn't think so.

Back on the futon, nudging his weight, feeling with a feeling too much like gratitude the warmth of his long legs, their careless stretch like a dancer's, the smell of him all over the quilt, the pillows, on her fingers as she slowly stroked the seam of his bony jaw. Why was there no odor of *her* there? Was she simply too close to it, like the pulse of her blood and as unnoticed, or did the superior vitality of Robin's scent override her own? Superior vitality – that was Robin, his complaints of her tiredness, she was always tired lately. "Ask Hans Peter for something," he'd suggested, and Sophy had shaken her head, positively no, picturing Hans Peter and his constant, more than slightly maniacal grinning: a jack o'lantern burning silent nuclear light.

Hans Peter was a drug designer, but more importantly he was a patron, *the* patron, of Robin's art. Video drawing was not new – Brody pencil self-animated sketches mated to holocam footage – but Robin was: with the twisted innovation of genius he had, according to Hans Peter at least, stood the medium on its ear with his first exhibited drawing, "Doctors Feed the Hungry Dead Breakfast." It was slowly becoming a cult favorite, and its cold cerebral humor had instantly attracted Hans Peter's attention. Sophy felt she had never really understood it; where others saw powerful satire, a mocking convolution of conventional morals, she saw only sorrow and waste; she had never told Robin but he knew, and mocked her, too. "Tightassed Sophy," with that twist, that warmthless smile that was nonetheless so beautiful that when he called her, after the showing, she came, sad little leather bag of belongings, last week's haircut. He pulled her into bed by her breasts. She had been there, more or less, ever since.

Looking at him now, fallen angel, still she must smile, kept the smile as his eyes opened, unfathomed blue. He yawned, scratched his chest, asked her the time and when she gave it closed his eyes again; she might have been an appliance. But then eyes still shut he reached for her, commanding arm crooked round her neck, and with his other hand turned her face so he might kiss her, full and hard, on her aching mouth. She winced; she smiled. They slept again.

Another party, and Sophy careful to limit her drinks, as carefully watching her words, her smiles, the way she held herself, the way she talked or didn't. It was not so much a party as a business meeting, according to Robin, and she must get to know these people, know and remember them: their styles, their sponsors, their drug preferences and sexual fads. She tried, oh God she tried, but there were so many, and while different they were all, somehow, so terribly the same; she called someone named Allen Alice and half the room laughed, the other half sighed, and Robin stared at her like a stranger. She found at last a corner, sat, half a smile pinned to her face, silent until two people – "Kim" and "Tilman," sex obscure – approached her, made curious conversation, mostly with each other but the odd remark to her, and finally Tilman squealed, "I knew I knew you, you're the raincoat girl!" and Kim laughed, turned Sophy's unresisting chin like a parody of an oldtime director, wotta profile. Sophy smiled, bewildered, and Tilman started asking questions, how *about* that thing, the dancing, when he hit you didn't it *hurt*? "Looks like it did," touching her face, the bruise she had tried to conceal.

Then Robin, full lips compressed and grim, tight smile to Kim and Tilman as he dragged Sophy off and away, throwing her faux leather windbreaker at her, hustling her out the door with tiny pushes. "What were they talking about, I don't know what they were talking about," and Robin refusing to even look at her: "Don't talk to me, I have nothing whatever to say to you. Nothing." And he didn't. For two days.

She woke, a morning, to Robin laughing in the other room, the immaculate drawl of Hans Peter in reply, and then laughter again, from both. Hiss and click of the outer door locking, and Robin stood smiling at her from the bedroom doorway.

"A commission," too happy not to share it. "Hans Peter's putting up all the credit. A full-length drawing!" radiant as only Robin could be radiant, reaching to take her in a victory embrace. Kisses, her healed mouth hot under his, the pillows of the futon warm as a womb.

Afterwards he was all business, no time to discuss it with her now, he had calls to make, work to do, he needed absolute peace. She left him at his console, sun through the black blinds a deep dazzle on his hair, on the long matte slab: built-in keyboard, holo projector with unmarked keys and function board, so black market-new it still bore the gummy traces of peeled factory stickers. A discreet pile of printout was half-covered by a spill of magazines, faxes, newsprint, pages torn from all three, and as she carefully closed the door, his hand was sorting, eyelessly hunting the mess while the other sketched in the air, long steel glitter of the platinum Brody pencil. He was working, and she was happy.

On the kitchen counter, white and bare as any surgery, she found a blot of bubblepack, slim green triangles, green like the forest at night, like stained glass in a convent: a taste from Hans Peter. With a narrow frown she pushed them aside, into the counter's corner, then scrubbed her hands together as if they had been stained.

Bad headache.

The worst, raw shiver of pain and an ache twinned between her thighs, Robin's voice fussy and faraway: "Take this, Sophy," closing her hand around a cup, paper cup, her grip slow and defenseless. What is it? she wanted to say or maybe did, for Robins's answer: "I don't have *time* for this, I'm working. Just take it." Mouthing up a pill, its taste incongruous and sweet, as if it were sugarcoated. She swallowed the water, the merest motion of her body bringing new bright throbbing and she closed her eyes, lying absolutely still, and after a while heard or seemed to hear the sound of rain, no, a shower, water hitting the shower curtain, a loud staticky buzz, a sound familiar, but no time to sort impressions because now it was dark and she was glad.

"Can I see it?"

"Not yet," expansive, "not while it's in progress." Very carefully she asked if Hans Peter – and Robin laughed, reached over to tousle her hair. "Man's got a right to see what he's paying for. But don't worry, you'll be there for the premiere."

Shower-rain, water on plastic; the feel of fugue, subtle shift of bones resettling, the dance of muscles, eyesight gone low-resolution, consciousness eroded line by inexorable line, and Robin's face above her, pinking with delight; lips moving ("Bye-bye"), the noise of the water as loud in her ears as the roar of a tunneled train.

"Wake up."

Sophy stirred, legs in slow canter beneath the quilt, breasts bare and cold. "What?" as she tried to sit up, opened her eyes to Hans Peter in black wraparound shades and a luminous grin. Sophy jerked the quilt high; she saw her figure's motion, elongated by distortion, in the insect lenses of his eyes.

"Sorry if I scared you. Robin asked me to look in on you."

There was a pain in the back of her neck, like exercising too hard, the muscles sore and taut and hot. "Well, you looked. Now you can go."

"*Hey.*" Robin's face, staring in the doorway, flushed, eyes too bright. "You don't talk that way to a man like Hans Peter, *Sophy*. Hans Peter is my *friend*, *Sophy*." He curled an arm around Hans Peter's bony shoulders, squeezed. Hans Peter giggled, a soft sound like trickling water. "If it wasn't for him, I wouldn't *have* a career. Or Pauline."

A thing in her chest, like a punch: Pauline Pauline, lightspeed search backward through memory, names, faces at parties. "Who's Pauline?"

Incredibly, they both laughed, tandem sound. They might have been twins. Or actors.

"You want to know who Pauline is? I'll *show* you who Pauline is," and Robin reached for her, hands very hot, a bubble of sweat on his upper lip. His pupils were enormous. He dragged her off the futon, into the other room, her hands crossed futilely over her breasts and his breathing uneven and hard; smiling, a sweet smile, Hans Peter handed her a T-shirt, watched as she put it on. Turned to Robin, the faintest of frowns disturbing his luminescence: "Is this wise?" Robin, one-finger programming, fiddling with the playback, did not answer, and Hans Peter shrugged, took a seat at the opposite end of the room, Robin's favorite Myrtle chair; he winked at Sophy, who turned instantly away.

"Watch this," and Robin beside her, glittering, stern, a jailer.

Her own face, projected to three times its size.

"*What –*"

"Shut up, *Sophy*. Just watch."

The postures. The movements. Her. And nothing like her, *nothing*. A feeling in her throat like something crawling, the muscles in slow convulsion – not me, *not me*. Not up there, her smile, long and considering, a predator's elegant grin – no way hers but it *was*: no wizardly effect, no double, no clone even could be that eerily perfect; there, and *there*, the way she sometimes wiped the corner of one eye, an almost perfunctory habit, like nailbiting. ... The woman vaulted now through an elaborate freestyle combat dance, utterly conscious of her body and its energies in a way Sophy, the clumsy, never was. Robin beside her, laughing silently;

sweat ran down her sides, her armpits were soaked and sour.

The dance gone battle, and now before her an assailant in bull's mask and horns, brandishing some stick or stave, and the woman waited, feinted, there! a kick and another, fierce fluidity, ballet streetfighter, kicked again and bubbles burst and rose, blood bubbles then cartoon heat-bubbles as the woman grinned again, fullface, unSophy, swaggering through the shimmer to the camera's eye to confront it with her own, a rushing closeup that devoured all but that cryptic commando stare deep into the viewer's own; fade to gone.

Robin snapped the remote, tossed it into the air like a gleeful child.

"That's Pauline," he said.

"I said I was sorry!"

Sophy, head thick from hours of tears, rubbed a finger at her eye (then abruptly stopped). Leaden: "*Sorry*. You didn't tell me, you didn't even ask what I –" A long shiver poured down her skin, goosebumps sharp as scrapes though she was bundled to the throat in the futon quilt, mummied in a robe beneath. Robin half-lay, half-sat beside her, one pillow crosswise on his lap, fretfully kneading the tasseled ends.

"I knew you would never – I knew you would say no. You *know* you would have," and she nodded furiously, of *course* she would have said no, she would never have consented to something so monstrous. "It's just a mild dose, Soph, it brings on flip state but it doesn't hurt you. Hans Peter says –"

"Hans Peter! He's getting a free guinea pig, he'll say anything!"

"All I meant," with calm but pained dignity, "was that he *designed* the fucking thing, he *knows* what it can do."

"He knows. Right." She blew her nose, tissue wet and shredding; too many words to speak, too dreadful the terms. Flip state, *shit*, it was multiple personality, not a drug reaction but a whole new person, even Robin had admitted it, almost. She could not say the words aloud. Madness. A door opened that should never have been discovered, the unexpected stranger waiting, waiting for some pillpushing bastard like Hans Peter to slip off the lock. And Robin, don't forget Robin, propped in his director's chair, shiny pencil swift in the air like some trained bird of prey. The remarks at the party, Kim and Tilman and "the raincoat girl," how often had this happened, how many times? Who had seen her when she was *not*? Funny, it must be, to watch –

Sophy began to cry, again, slowly, monotonously. Robin flung down the pillow, sat up hingebacked and burst without preamble into loud baby tears.

"It's *not* bad," weeping, body swayed ever so slightly her way, "it's just flip state, that's *all*." I only gave you cancer. "Do you think I would let him hurt you? Do you think I would let *anybody* hurt you?" His whole chest trembled, avalanche of feeling, he was certainly a better actor than anyone in his drawings. With one notable exception. "Oh, Sophy," peering from between palms slick with mucus and tears, "I *love* you."

Her own tears cooling on her cheeks, she felt her hands rise, brainless puppets, to stroke his hair, caress the sweet wet planes of his skin, and as she did, watched her fingers, their movements, thinking, Flip state. And: Pauline.

Hans Peter's apartment, half a block of it at a block thousands of dollars better than the one she shared with Robin, and Sophy at the gate, a bored-sounding doorbot announcing her presence. Faint chiming sounds, Hans Peter's suppressed monitor smile, and Sophy's forehead hot as she stepped through gun-colored doors and into silence, the pink wash of lasers, fired light checking her one last time before the sanctum sanctorum. And Hans Peter, sipping the Polish brandy he affected, greeting her at the last door.

"Pardon the precautions," he said as she stepped silently past, "but in this life it pays to be cautious."

"Oh yeah? Is that why you let Robin fuck me up?"

Harsh, and angry bravado she did not really feel; what she felt was sick, and tired. Sick mostly. But there was no getting truth from Robin, and she had to have it, so she had to have it here.

" 'Fucked up'?" raising his eyebrows to make the quotes. "It's flip state, Sophy, and please, don't be bitter: it's a quality, an *ability*, that many people would like to share. Access to another part of your personality – your id, perhaps, or that tantalizing superego, or even just a construct of your own secret devising – make no mistake, Sophy, this is no pharmaceutical trick, this is *you*. A different Sophy, but Sophy all the same."

"That wasn't me up there."

"Oh, but it *was*." Enjoying himself, Sophy thought. "It's a part of you that goes, say, unaccessed in your daily life. The drug is a doorway, but the one who walks through – Sophy, Sophy, Sophy. Though *he* calls her Pauline." He sat on a sofa pink as a mouth, raised his glass, to her? Above his head a Japanese print, black and blue and shockingly ugly, a deliberate fart of bad taste in the suffocating couth of the room. "Enjoy it. It's making a kind of star of you, did you know that? Of brighter magnitude, maybe, than Robin, in that incestuous little garret colony scene he's trying so hard to crack. Though most of them have all the discriminating taste of a dog in a garbage can. So relax, have some fun with it. You've got nothing to worry about; my results are almost wholly positive. There *is* an addictive factor, but then the best things in life usually are."

It took a minute, even, to swallow. "What do you mean, addictive? What –"

A shrug, coathanger shoulders, not quite half a smile. "Entirely unavoidable. Well, not *entirely*, but it won't bother you a bit, you can eat it by the gramweight, nothing more than perhaps a headache the next morning. If you stop outright, though, *then* you may have a bit of –"

The door didn't try to stop her, nor Hans Peter, though the doorbot gave a glitched whinny as Sophy kicked past it, long scissor-stride and a clenched feeling in her throat, in the back of her neck, like fear but blacker, like rage but shot with yellow, long streaks like painful veins. No cab would pick her up so she walked the whole wild-eyed way, waiting, just waiting, just to get home.

Robin was gone: relief, disappointment. She poured mash whiskey, hands shaking, drinking from the bathroom water glass, its lip scummed with old toothpaste, the taste a warring mixture in her mouth. She stripped, turned on the shower, but the static-sound of the spray on the curtain repulsed her, drove her back into the other room to sit, more mash whiskey, temples humming, hunched into Robin's heavy midnight blue robe; even in her fury his scent calmed her, numbed the sharpest edges of her fear. The dead air of the room, the flat face of the monitor, gray as a brain and more gray and with one fist she pounded the remote to ON, whatever was in the box just *play* it.

Pauline.

This time, a different show.

Pauline naked, arched saunter, hair in elaborate braids shot through with long strands of neon thread, the same thread circling ankle, wrist, waist. Darkness, soft blur of neon movement through a space, familiar – God my God that's *here* – and climbing onto the futon to the body rising to greet her, as beautifully naked, full lips in welcoming pout: Robin. All the breath left Sophy's lungs.

In silence Robin knelt, with sparkling teeth undid the thread at her wrist, lips gleaming gaudy electric blue then purest white as he did the next, the one at her waist, pausing to lick the skin there with a tenderness so alien it hit Sophy like a slap. Pauline, hair blinking, on-off code of some bizarre devising, raised one long leg to bring the ankle to his lips so he might bite free the pink burn of light. She slipped down like water to lie beneath him, arms-propped and motionless above her, on his face a dreamy radiant gravity Sophy had never seen. He began to move, exquisitely, avid for her pleasure, slow thrusts like he never did, *never*, each calling forth from her a whisper, a wild hiss, a long sussuration as he slowed and stopped and bent his perfect head to blow a cool stream of air over her body, back and forth across her skin, her sweaty flesh

and Sophy's mouth clenched

and Pauline's eyes half-open

and Robin's rhythm rising, gaining, his hands grabbing hard at the futon

and Sophy leaning forward

and Pauline's cry, half-groan into his open mouth, "Oh *God*" as he pressed himself at last down upon her

and Sophy's shriek, her glass blowing through the air, the brown liquor floating in an eerie arc through the bodies now panting softly in rest, the smash of glass incongruous in the silence of the simulated world.

Fading to faraway charcoal, pinkish-black, and Robin's eyes, of course, the last to close, one final smug blink for the camera and then marching across the drifting holo-smoke the double-bars symbol for encryption engaged, Master Use Only, the worst of all somehow because it meant that this was made not to sell, not for money, just for Robin.

True darkness, twilight in the real world, and the sudden glow of the tape beginning again, he had set it for infinite repeat, making sure she must see it, oh the *bastard*, and she hammered at the remote, blackness again, ripped off his robe like it leeched at her flesh, dressed, first clothes she found, left. Mash whiskey in hand.

It took a while to find him, but he had only so many exits and she was in a determined mood, oh my, he wouldn't recognize her. And in fact he didn't, at first, not connecting this weaving steamed twisty walk, hair skewed, breath sour, with Sophy, and when he did – she saw it, the recognition flowing across his face like water, like blood – he flushed, too affronted to be truly angry, no, that would come later, it usually did. Unless he had her doppelganger, her double, penciled in his bed for tonight. *My* bed, too. Fucking me in my bed. In my *body*. Was she saying these things out loud? People were certainly staring.

It was a silent dance party, everyone in earbuds to one central tune or several, somebody's mix on the box tonight, eerie, the twitchings and flexings spastic, surreal, more autism than art. More and more were stopping, unplugging one curious ear or two, she was the better show. Performance art, they call this.

"– *home*," Robin was saying, "or the hospital, whichever you like. I'd take you there myself but I don't want to be seen with you."

"Oh, right," crowing to him, the air, the people watching, fuck them. "Maybe you'd rather I turn into Pauline. But I can't, can I? Unless you've got a taste on you, do you, Robin? Do you?" She slapped at the pockets of his velvet-look camo jacket, and he said something about she was embarrassing herself more than him and if she thought this was any and she screamed, literally, a scream as if she were being beaten with an iron bar, loud enough to pierce even the sludgey awareness of the last of the dancers, all of whom now frankly stared, giggled, shook their heads. One laughed outright and Sophy laughed, too, laughed herself all the way out the door where she found a cab without even trying, oh surely the fates were with her tonight, rode off, "Just drive," long strands of neon flowing by the window, strands like the neon in Pauline's hair.

I hate her I hate her, backseat litany with her nails eating away at her palms, I hate her I hate her I HATE HER and She's *me*, and the thought horrified her so she sat up, tried to, but the whiskey hugged her down and the cab kept going and she opened her eyes, one of her friends was dragging her into an elevator, her armpits ached from the pressure, she tried to talk but coughed into the taste of vomit instead.

"Boy, are you messed up," said the friend. "God must've

remembered my address for you," smiling, "but *I* had to pay the cab," and this time she did throw up, amazing postmodern slurry of color and the friend steered her around it, through a door, onto a sofa. "Be right back," but before he was it was morning, she was gagging dryly into a pillow that smelled, strong and pleasant, of dog. But it was only gagging, it passed, and the friend was there as all at once she remembered his name, Richard.

"Oh Richard, God, I'm sorry –" and on the heels of that a retching sob.

Richard's eyebrows were shaven free, and one of his eyes was tremendously bloodshot, red as his toenails. Sophy, squashed against his skinny bare chest, a St. Sebastian medal bobbing back and forth as her tears shook him and abruptly there were no more, and she laughed; and he laughed, too.

"Richard –"

"Save it. The only thing you haven't done yet is shit your pants and I don't think I could stand that. Now. You want tea? I'll get some of those oyster crackers, too, cures the crotch-rot, good for everything." Sophy laughed, a looser sound this time, drank the tea when it came, ate the crackers, small salty circles in her mouth.

"Now." Richard cinched his robe, austere white gi, always the sign he meant business. "You wanna talk, or should we just pretend that it was one hell of a party and let it go at that?"

It was hard to get started, and the words when they came went in slow confusing stumbles; in the end she told not the truth, enough only to put a narrow line in his forehead, his face at once years older, colder. "What you're saying," cinching the gi again, garotte, "is that he's got you on some kind of drug, right, and he's using you in his drawings. Right?"

She had not spoken of Pauline; it was too much to confess, even to him. "Right."

"And this drug is addictive?"

Small shamed nod, as if it were entirely her fault that this was so.

Long breath of air expelled through thinned lips. "Are you moved out or what? Because you can stay here, long as you want. You know that, if you don't know anything else, and I swear Sophy sometimes you don't."

"I guess."

Silence. He rubbed at his face, pulling his skin into a hound dog scowl. "I gotta shower, I gotta dance tonight, Cherry Novae, you ever been there?" distanced chatter, yelling from the shower, the noise of it raising goosebumps on her skin, a private frown, had Robin ruined her for showers, too? Baths, she would just take baths. When Richard left she watched a 2D movie, the scrawl of flatscreen pictures cheering her, soothing her so she slept, wrapped in a ratty plaid comforter on the dog-smelling sofa.

A rowboat, she sat in a rowboat drifting, empty oarlocks, her hands cool and motionless in her lap as the boat moved across a dead-calm lake, nosing its aimless way through a parting sheaf of algae. Farther off she saw blue, not water but a manmade color, and saw it to be a shirt, a man's shirt, a man floating facedown in the water. My God, oh my God as he floated closer, he and the boat on an intersecting line, she reached into the scummy water to turn him over; it was hard, he was heavy, but she did it, sweat in her eyes as she hauled him up and saw, with a choking cry, that it was Robin, unmarked, unmarred, but dead, dead as a sarcophagus, and weeping she kissed him, kissed his soft dead lips and his eyes boiled open, wide, a crazyman's wink and his green grin as with effortless power he ripped her out of the boat and down, into the waiting water, green as a forest at night, green as stained glass in a convent.

Sick shivering, waves of it, like a beaten animal trembling itself to death; it was worse than the cramping nausea, worse even than the feeling of being constantly dirty, filthy, her skin coated with slime, no matter how often she washed it was the same. Splashing her face, Richard standing beside her in his tiny cramped bathroom, rag in hand for wiping up her thin vomit.

"You can kick it, Sophy, come on."

Her pores felt big as shiny manholes. The water hurt her skin.

"Damn it, anybody can kick anything! I know! You check yourself in, you get some help, that's how it's *done*, you know it? You know it, Soph?" He touched her shoulder, his face wearing that line again, and others, painful lines of vast concern and she felt like weeping for pushing off his hand but she could *not*, could not *stand* the touch of a person's hand, any person, any kind of touch. It was all she could bear to touch herself.

"I'll call you," how unnatural, that voice of hers, the towel like raw paper crackling against her skin, oh God she was filthy again already. "I just, I just need to –"

"You just need a taste. *Right*," and the bitterness so intense, his turning-away magnified by her sickness, by the feeling of something live in her belly, some botched abortion roiling at last to vengeful life, and it made her scream, "It's not me it's not me IT'S NOT ME" over and over till the cab came.

He paid for that one, too.

Robin crouched atop the futon, braided hair half-undone, white curve of chunky china barely touching that richer, wetter curve, full underlip twisted between smile and scorn. The hair on his bare belly was gold, gold like a fairytale, honey-dark in the thatch beneath. He was naked except for his artistically ripped T-shirt: giddy shrunken head above the legend STICKLER FOR PUNISHMENT. Standing, legs ready to buckle, keys in hurting hand, Sophy believed it. Of herself.

"Got some coffee, there," little mocking nod towards the kitchen. "Or would you like something stronger?"

Her bones felt hollow. Her clothes were agony. Sidewalk salt, smeared on her boots, now smeared the indigo carpet; she imagined it, spoor, an eaten spot like a scar to mark her passing.

Robin drank, good to the last drop, set the cup into the clutter of the bedside table. Without looking his fingers scanned the mess, cigarettes, tissues, an empty glass, and extracted a bubblepack, slim green triangles. With as perfect a practiced motion he thumbed out two.

Her feet in her boots were burning. The kitchen, coffee sweet without sugar, her cold hands around the cup never warming. There was a scorched spot on her tongue, the coffee seared it so tears filled her eyes. Deliberately she drank more, held it in her mouth an awful second before swallowing, delaying the moment of ineffable surrender. Robin balanced the triangles on his thumbnails, his hands in little motions, as if he might begin juggling. Not smiling, "Go on. Sophy."

Tears, then, and she did not mark them, did not care or try, pity or rage or simple relief as she took the pills into her mouth, dry-swallowed, lay painfully back against the futon, still in coat and boots, to await the coming of the water. Her lids sagged, her hands fell palms-open, and the last thing she saw was

Robin, preening, showing himself as he stripped off his T-shirt.
   Welcome home, Pauline.

"Pig for it, aren't you." Obviously delighted. What was she a pig
for? Who cares. "Do you know you even smell different when –
don't shake your head at me, how would *you* know. You taste
different, too." Smiling, luxurious the memory. "All over."
   "How." Was that slur her?
   Smiling harder, "Better."

Hans Peter: "I think I'll have to cut you a quantity discount."
Robin laughed, distracted, pencil in hand. Sophy rubbed at her
temples, a headache groaning to life behind her dry eyes. She felt
like she had been fucking all night. Busy woman, that Pauline.
   Niagara, in her ears; Hans Peter settled himself in the Myrtle
chair. With any luck she was at least getting paid scale. Ha, ha, ha.
   Richard, on the phone: "– again. Can't you? *Please*, Sophy, *try*."
   Sophy, eyes closed, long distance: "I tried that. Twice. It really
doesn't work." She hung up, forgot she had.
   Fugue.
   Muscles, in rhythmic motion. A pain in her back, the back of her
neck, itchy feeling like writhing ants. Boy was it hot in here.
   Waking, when? later, Sophy remembered the heat, her skin felt
as if it glowed from bad sunburn. Robin, half-sleeping, rubbed a
caress down her arm, smiled sweet, *sweet*. Stopped both when he
saw who it was.
   "Why can't you be her all the time?" he said plaintively, and fell
back to sleep.

He ran the drawings over and over, he said to edit, but half the time
he wasn't even there when she was Sophy and so she sat, drinking
milk or sometimes water, watching Pauline. The absolute strangeness never wore off, but sometimes that in itself was a kind of
comfort: if not too strange to be happening, it was surely too
strange to believe.
   Sometimes people called for Pauline: Robin took the calls; it all
seemed to delight him. Once she called him Frankenstein, and he
laughed.
   "She's no monster," he said. "She's what *you* would be, if you
were worth a shit."

Slowly Sophy sat up, stared at him, dull-eyed. "I could kill myself, you know. I can still do that."

Fear then, anger, it was all rather gratifying: his career and his lover, down the drain in one fell swoop. She would have done it, too, in a minute. But she didn't like drains.

Blurry sound, the stretch of skin, sight lines clear and the lucidity terrifying, and Robin crouched before her, eyes narrow: "You glitching, babe?" a voice much too kind to be his, not talking to *her*; surely she was dreaming, Pauline's dreams.

Coming to? Yes, or something, smashing sound, the faux crystal water glasses one jagged wet glitter in the kitchen sink, smashing the very last one when Robin, Hans Peter behind, let himself in. He gaped, a singularly stupid look, Hans Peter prim in his disapproval.

Sophy smiled at them, a working, sagging grin, reached long to pinch Hans Peter's gray leather sleeve in a grotesque parody of playfulness. "Gotta dose for me, coach?"

His fingers were colder even than hers as he passed her the bubblepack. "Temperamental," he said, nodding toward the sink. "Like any actor, I suppose. But remember," including Robin in his gaze, remote, "the dosage increase – I don't recommend this and I don't condone it. And I won't be answerable for it."

Robin, leaping to the self-defense, amazing his reflexes: "I *told* her, I said –"

Sophy, numb hands, tucking the bubblepack into the pocket of her robe, smiling sideways through a falling curtain of unbraided hair, "I have to have some fun," and in a motion curiously balletic reached into the sink and flung a handful of broken glass at them, at their staring eyes, and they jumped, separate directions, as she laughed out loud, slapped a bleeding palm to the austere white counter, where it left a stain like the mark of the dead. It was, she thought, a Pauline thing to do.

Less and less hours as Sophy, Robin demanding in his worry, threatening to hide the drugs if she didn't stop it, slow down at least, and she laughed, literally in his face, pushing hers close to do it: "Go ahead," and laughed again through the grind in her skull; dreams, a state of constant subliminal bleedthrough, recalling things that never happened, charmed by the sense of shapes and

the taste of black licorice on her tongue, she had never been able
to bear licorice but now it was a thing to savor, that and the sound
of drums and water and someone's music, a feeling like chasing
memory, the Red Queen's endless race. Yes.

But what if *two* people are running?

Harsh boil of confusion, heat and her eyes, bounding open,
flapping, it seemed, like cartoon windowshades and her own
shock nothing as to Robin's: so vast as to be almost comical, seeing
Sophy staring out of Pauline's eyes, staring right at him. They were
in bed, he was just going in, and with convulsive grace she rolled,
throwing his weight and riding the momentum to rise astraddle,
his whole body limp beneath her and with all her strength she
punched him in the face, feeling something mash behind her
fingers as blood burst from his nose like a time-lapse flower,
pushed him half off the futon as his hands struggled to his face and
he stared, stared, the widest blue eyes in the world.

Cold bathroom floor, she took a shower, burning water, came
out to find Robin mute in the doorway. Under his nose the blood
was gelling. She slapped the bubblepack from his hands.

"You can forget that shit," she said.

Pushing past him, it was like pushing paper. Quickly, efficiently,
she dressed, brushed her hair into a long wet chignon. Robin
looked as if he might be sick, or cry. He made no move to wipe
away the blood. "Who are you?" he said.

"Nobody you know."

Sip of iced tea, ice cube rattled against her tooth. It hurt, a little.
The sugar in the tea was gritty as sand, the whole coffee shop
smelled like grease. Figured he would pick such a cheap place to
meet. Sophy said, "Have you ever read Bennett Braun? You
should."

Unshaven this morning, a curiously aged look to mouth and
eyes. Had she ever really loved that face, really? Honest answer:
yes. Honest question: why? He said, "Who's Bennett Braun?" in
a voice that did not know whether to be hard or soft, contemptuous or respectful.

"Pioneer in the field. Multiples. Oh come on," annoyed at his
ignorance, "multiple *personality*, you know, the stuff you turned
me on to. Flip state, remember?" He did not speak. "Did you know

there's such a thing as spontaneous integration? Most people need therapy to get them there, or get them ready. I didn't."

Miserable, he stirred his three-dollar coffee, sideways glance at her; he would never, now, look at her without wariness. It almost made her want to smile. Almost.

"In some people," lecturer's nod, "the original personality fracture is a reaction to a prolonged state of abuse or violence – a personality, or two, or several, are created to 'take the pain.' You see I've been busy. It's amazing what you can accomplish when you don't waste your time with fucking video drawings."

"You don't understand," rubbing at his lower lip, nervous continuous circle of finger on flesh, "you're the, I *need* you, I need you in my drawings. I need *Pauline*," a soft wail, he wanted to say more but she cut him off, neatly, like a surgeon.

"Hans Peter," she said, "was my midwife. Oh, do I owe him." She drank off the last of the tea. "You still don't get it, do you? *Pauline*," dragging out the word, "is not addicted. To anything. Never was. But now we're *both* clean as a whistle," pursed lips, little mocking noodle of sound. He did not move as she did, did not watch her leave. The chair he had chosen provided a full ray of gorgeous light, full on his averted, suffering face. She had to laugh, then.

At the apartment, leather bag filled and neat on the futon like a patient pet, and she took up the masters, all the tapes, all the hours she had watched, milk glass in hand. How many copies had he made, sold? Did it matter?

The phone went off, small startled buzz; she half-expected Robin but it was Richard, are you all right, you never called, how *are* you?

"Fine," she said, loading the first tape, thumb firm and cool on ERASE. "I'm fine." Images, flickering, dwindling down to gray, double-bars and no bars, the whole collection gone to slippery darkness, existence only in memory.

And memory is such a personal thing.

IT'S VERY CLEAN

Gene Wolfe

The Book of the New Sun (4 vols, 1980–83) brought Gene Wolfe to the very front rank of contemporary American SF writers, though he was a prolific producer of short stories long before that, much of his best work in that vein appearing in Damon Knight's Orbit *anthologies. His stories – some of the finest of the 1970s – have been collected in* The Island of Doctor Death and Other Stories and Other Stories *(1980) and* Gene Wolfe's Book of Days *(1981). "My heroes", he once wrote, "are often boys or young men trying to find a place in the world." Like this one:*

"It's very clean," the fat woman said. "You'll like it." She smiled, showing a gold tooth.

Miles nodded, too embarrassed to speak. He had told her he was twenty-one.

"You ready to go up now?" The woman held out her hand for money.

He needed time to quiet his stomach and steady his nerves. He managed to ask, "I wonder if you could show me how they work first."

"Sure. Matter of fact, we got a unit busted right now, and the man's up there workin' on it. You can see that." She motioned him to follow as she started toward the back of the building. "Usually I make customers use the stairs in front, but when I got to go up myself, I take the freight elevator."

They went through a door and left the Gilded Age behind. No more colored glass "Tiffany" lamps, fraudulent Oriental rugs, red velvet, or bead curtains. The floor and walls were concrete here. "You're real, aren't you?" Miles asked suddenly.

"Me?" The woman plucked at the front of her dress and peeked down her own bodice, her powdered chins pushed together like marshmallows in a box. "I think so. I haven't looked lately." She laughed again and pressed a button to start the elevator.

'I just meant . . ." The floor was lifting them.

"I know; it could be done, I suppose, but it's better to have somebody here to look after things, and that's me. Pull that handle there, will you?"

He did as she asked, sliding back the door, and they stepped into the gaslight era again.

"Mezzanine," the woman said gaily, "lingerie and sheets." She took his arm. "You'll have a swell time. You really will. Here's the one he's fixing."

She led him into what appeared to be a small bedroom decorated in the same opulent style as the corridor and the waiting room downstairs. A strikingly beautiful brunette in a pink negligee sat on the bed, apparently watching a man in overalls who had removed a portion of the paneling from a wall and was tinkering with the maze of wiring thus revealed.

The woman with the gold tooth asked him, "How is she? Ready to go again yet?"

He shook his head, removing a card covered with printed circuitry and slipping another into its place. "We'll try this." Looking at the girl on the bed, he asked, "How is it now, sweetheart?"

The girl tossed her head. "Dull. When are you going to stop fiddling with that and pay some attention to me?"

"Right now," the technician said. "Come over here and give me a kiss."

The girl got up, but seemed unable to straighten her left leg fully; she took a grotesque, hopping step, then fell forward, catching herself on her hands.

Wearily the technician strode over to her, picked her up, and replaced her on the bed. The girl looked at him angrily. "I'd be fine if you'd stop trying to make me walk. I can work." He ignored her and went back to the wiring panel in the wall.

The woman with the gold tooth said, "That's very commendable, Gloria, but we have to make you well first."

Miles asked, "The circuits in the wall control her?"

The technician nodded. "They're her brains, and what we call the motor functions are in there too. The things that decide how much each of the little electric servos in her ought to turn to make her move. Output to the body is UHF, but we keep the power low so the various units don't interfere with each other." He grinned and jerked his head. "Now, you take the layout right next door – the Lincoln exhibit. How would the tourists like it if they took their kids to see him and he started talking and acting like her? So, we keep the range down to fifteen feet. You try to take them farther than that, they lose their signal."

The woman with the gold tooth nudged Miles and said, "You ready to go now?" Miles nodded, and she led him out into the hall again.

He looked at the rows of doors; there seemed to be at least twenty on each side. "Do I get my choice?" he asked. It sounded more confident than he felt.

"Oh, no. I got customers in most of those. You come with me, though; I've got one that'll be perfect for you." Almost at the end of the hall she stopped in front of a door which stood open about two inches. "You'll like Jill," she said. "You want to use a script?"

"A script?"

"They used to have to use them before we got the programming so good. It still makes some customers feel more comfortable to have one. Mostly, you know, the older men."

"No," Miles said. "I don't think I want one."

"It's up to you. When you go inside, swinging the door back activates the girl. When it shuts, besides ensuring your privacy, it starts a timer, and you get a half-hour with her before she turns off. If you want more after that, you'll have to come downstairs and pay me for it. For the first time, you pay me now."

He knew but asked "How much?" anyway, for a moment hoping that the price had changed, that it would be more than he had, that he could leave without feeling he had backed down.

"Ten," the woman said. "Ten, Mondays through Thursdays; fifteen, Friday, Saturday, and Sunday; after one in the morning is by appointment only, and come into the park by the side entrance."

He handed her the money, and she tore a yellow ticket from a roll in her pocket and gave it to him. He stared at it, reflecting on what it might have been instead: a new jacket, or the uniform paperback edition of Günter Grass. He had saved the money coin by coin.

The woman was watching him. She said, "You just go inside now. That's all there is to it."

"Aren't you going to leave now? To tell the truth, I think I'd rather you did."

"I'll go as soon as you shut the door. Sometimes my customers, especially young guys like you, try to cheat by leaving it open. You go in now and just pretend like I'm not here."

He went in quickly, closing the door firmly behind him. This room was furnished just as the first had been, but was somewhat less brightly lit. The girl on the bed was red-haired and plump in a way he found attractive. There was a moment – only a fraction of a second, but he was sure he had seen it – before something like life animated her and she moved her head to look at him, brushing a stray lock of hair from her eyes. He smiled to himself.

"Hi," the girl said. "My name's Jill; come on in."

"Hello, Jill." He walked over to her, stood staring for a moment, then sat down beside her. She seemed perfect except for a smoothness of complexion that was almost too flawless, a doll-like roundness and conventional cuteness about her pert face.

"What do I call you, handsome?"

"Miles."

With small, white teeth like little bathroom tiles she nipped him lightly on the ear. "Okay, Miles, what do you want to do? I mean first?"

He stroked her hair, but she caught his hand and drew it through some opening in the gauzy robe she wore. "You're warm," he said.

"Of course I am. You wouldn't like it if I weren't, would you?"

"No. But don't do that." Her free hand had slipped into his lap, and when he pushed it aside, she began unfastening the buttons of his shirt. "Don't do that," he said again. "I thought you'd just, you know, lie there. Maybe kiss me."

She kissed him with lips as warm as blood and as smooth as rayon, and when she had finished, opened a drawer of her bedside table and offered him a script. "This one's called 'Passive'," she said. "It's very good."

It was dogeared and stained, and he knocked it away and said, "Let's get it over with."

"Listen, it's fun. Just relax and enjoy it." She lay down, her round face smiling mechanically up at him from the big, plump pillow. He wanted to turn off the lights or to close her eyes, but caught himself. They were doll's eyes, blue as the blue-glass chicken in which his grandmother had kept pins, and they were looking at the ceiling, not at him. He undressed slowly, hanging his clothes on a chair and reminding himself that he must keep track of the time.

"At my neck," she said when he sat down on the bed and he found a ribbon there and pulled it, so that her robe fell away.

When it was over, he rested, chest heaving.

His watch, when he looked at it, showed he had eight minutes left; and somehow he did not want to be in the room when the time ran out. He sat up. "Towels in the closet there," the girl said.

He dried himself and dropped the towel to the floor. "Listen," he said, "I don't suppose it matters to you, but you were just great." He tried to think of something further to say. "Really good. I feel like the pressure's off me – you know? I mean, I'm going to tell my friends."

The girl said, "Of course it matters to me. It's my work; I care."

"It was my first time. I mean, not my *first* time, you know, but my first with any kind of girl or someone like you. I wanted you to know."

"Your first time?" She sat up, the sheet drawn over her legs, and he saw the small, very white teeth scraping the top of her full lower lip. She said, "Miles, don't ever come back here."

He stared at her.

"It's not good for you. Not good for what you'll be like when you're older; I see them all the time. Do you understand?"

Near the door was a knob that controlled the lights. He turned them up until the room was as bright as a stage. "You're real," he said. "A real girl."

She said, "No, I'm not," but he had seen the look of fear.

"You're a real girl. They'd never program you to say something like that." He slapped her sharply, and her full cheek flushed red.

"Don't tell," she gasped, and he realized suddenly that he was not alone, naked in the brightly lit room. He covered himself with one hand, groping on the floor for the soiled towel with the other. The girl's eyes were filling with tears, and she choked on words. "I . . . I . . ."

"You what?"

"I . . . I only fill in. Just fill in. Only when some of the others are broken. I get half the money, but if you tell her, she won't ever let me work any more. Please don't tell."

He was shaking with anger. "You bet your sweet life I'm going to tell," he said. She turned off the lights so that he could dress, and when he stalked out, she followed almost to the top of the stairs, pleading while the others mocked her from their doorways; but he never looked back.

LOVE STORY IN THREE ACTS

David Gerrold

"David Gerrold" is the pseudonym of US author Jerrold David Friedmann, much of whose work has been in television; he has written a number of Star Trek *scripts and tie-ins. He is perhaps best known for his 1972 novel* When Harlie Was One, *which describes the evolution of intelligence in a computer, and for his time-travel novel,* The Man Who Folded Himself (1973). *Gerrold was one of the earliest writers to explore the sexual/technological future – as in this story from 1970.*

Act One

After a while John grunted and rolled off Marsha. He lay there for a bit, listening to the dawn whispering through the apartment, the sound of the air processor whirring somewhere, and the occasional rasp of his own breath and that of Marsha's too. Every so often, there was a short sharp inhalation, as if to say, "Yeah, well . . ."

"Yeah, well . . ." John muttered and began tugging at the metal reaction-monitor bands on his wrists. He sat on the edge of the bed, still pulling at the clasps, the fastenings coming loose with a soft popping sound. He reached down and unfastened similar bands from his ankles and let those fall carelessly to the floor.

Then he stood and *pad-padded* barefoot across the floor to the typewriter-sized console on the dresser. Behind him he heard the creak of the bed as Marsha levered herself up on one elbow. "What does it say?" she demanded.

"Just a minute, will you," John snapped. "Give me a chance." He ripped the readout from the computer and went through the motions of studying it. This was the deluxe model which recorded the actual moment-to-moment physical reactions of the band-wearers. The jagged spiky lines sprawled carelessly across the neat ruled graphs meant little to him – they were there for the technicians, not the laymen – but at the top of the sheet was the computer's printed analysis. Even before he looked at it, John knew it would be bad.

"Well . . . ?" Marsha demanded acidly, "did we enjoy ourselves?"

"Yeah . . ." he muttered. "About thirty-four percent . . ."

"Hell!" she said, and threw herself back on the bed. She lay there staring at the ceiling, "Hell . . ."

"I wish you wouldn't swear so much," he muttered, still looking at the readout.

"Hell," she said again, just to see him flinch. She reached over to the night stand and thumbed a cigarette out of the pack.

"And I wish you wouldn't smoke so much either. Kissing you is like kissing another man."

She looked back at him, "I've always wondered what your previous experience was. Your technique with women is terrible." She inhaled deeply as the cigarette caught flame.

"Aaaa," said John and padded into the bathroom. As he stood there, he gazed dourly at his hands. He could still see the imprint of the monitor bands on his wrists.

Every time they did it, she had to know, so they used the damned bands; and every time the score was lower than before – and so they both knew. Who needed a machine to tell him when he was enjoying himself in bed? You knew when it was good and you knew when it was bad. So who needed the machine?

He finished and flushed the toilet, then splashed his hands briefly under the faucet – more from a sense of duty than from any of cleanliness. He shook off the excess water, and padded out of the bathroom, not even bothering to turn off the light.

Marsha was sitting up in bed, still puffing on her cigarette. She took it out of her mouth and blew smoke at him, "Thirty-four percent. We've never gone that low before. When are you going to listen to some sense, John, and opt for the other unit?"

"I'm not a puppet – and I'm not going to let anyone make me one either! ... Be damned if I'm going to let some damn fool sweaty-handed technician plug wires into me ..." He started casting around for his slippers.

"At least talk to them, John – it won't kill you. Find out about it, before you say it's no good. Rose Schwartz and her husband got one and she says it's the greatest. She wouldn't be without it now." Marsha paused, brushed a straggling hair back over her forehead – and accidentally dropped cigarette ash on the sheets. He turned away in disgust while she brushed at it ineffectually, leaving a dim gray smudge.

John found one of his slippers and began pulling it on angrily. "At least go and find out about it ... ?" she asked. No answer. "John ... ?"

He kept tugging at his slipper, "Leave me alone, will you – I don't need any more goddamn machines!"

She threw herself back against the pillow. "The hell you don't."

He straightened up momentarily – stopped looking for his other slipper and glared at her, "I don't need a machine to tell me how to screw!"

She returned his stare, "Then why the hell does our score keep dropping? We've never gone *this low* before."

"Maybe, if you'd brush your teeth –"

"Maybe, if you'd admit that –"

"Aaaa," he said, cutting her off, and bent down to look under the bed.

She softened her tone, leaned toward him, "John ... ? Will you talk to the man at least? Will you?" he didn't answer; she went shrill again, "I'm talking to you! Are you going to talk to the man?"

John found his other slipper and straightened up, "No, dammit! I'm not going to talk to the man – and I'm not going to talk to you either, unless you start talking about something else. Besides, we can't afford it. Now, are you going to fix me my breakfast?"

She heaved herself out of the bed, pausing only to stub out her cigarette. "I'll get you your breakfast – but we can *too* afford it." She snatched her robe from where it hung on the door and stamped from the room.

John glared after her, too angry to think of an answer. "Aaaa," he said, and began looking for his undershorts.

Act Two

When we got back from lunch, there was a man waiting in his reception room, a neat-looking man with a moustache and slicked-back hair. He rose, "Mr Russell . . . ?"

John paused, "Yes . . . ?"

"I believe you wished to see me . . . ?"

"Do I? Who're you?"

With a significant look at the receptionist, "Ah, may I come in?"

John half-shrugged, stepped aside to let the man enter. He could always ask him to leave. Once inside, he said, "Now then, Mr uh . . . ?"

"Wolfe," said the man, as he sat down. He produced a gold-foil business card, "Lawrence Wolfe, of Inter-Bem."

"Uh –" said John, still standing, "I'm afraid there's been some misunderstanding?" He started to hand the card back, "I never –"

Wolfe smiled genially at him, "You must have, or I wouldn't be here." He rummaged through his briefcase, found a form, "Oh, here it is. Your wife was the one who called us." He looked up, "You knew about it, of course?"

"No, I –"

"Well, no matter. I have all the information already. All I need is your signature."

"Now look, Mr Wolfe. You're the one who's made a mistake. I don't need –"

"Mr Russell," he said calmly. "If you didn't need our services, your wife would not have called our office. Now, please sit down – you're making me nervous."

John stepped around behind his desk, but did not sit.

Wolfe looked at him patiently, "You'll be more comfortable."

John sat.

Wolfe said gently, "I understand your reluctance to accept the possibility that you might need a monitor-guidance system. It's not a very pleasant thing to realize that your capabilities are down – but by the same token, you can't begin to correct a fault until you admit that it exists. It is precisely that type of person,

person, Mr Russell – your type of person – who needs our services the most."

"Now, look," said John. "I haven't got time for a sales pitch. If you've got any literature, leave it and I'll look at it later. Right now –"

Wolfe cut him off, "Are you enjoying your sex life?"

"What?" the suddenness of the question startled him.

"I said, are you enjoying your sex life? And don't tell me you are, because I've got the figures right here in front of me. The only time thirty-four percent is something to brag about is when your median is thirty."

John glowered, but he didn't say anything.

Wolfe continued, "All right, I'll concede that you might be enjoying yourself. It's not unusual for a man to have a lower threshold than normal – but I can tell you that your wife is not enjoying her sex life – else she wouldn't have called us. People only call us when they're unhappy." Wolfe paused, then asked suddenly, "You're not cheating on her, are you?"

"Hell, no."

"Have you recently become a homosexual?"

John sneered, "Of course not."

"Do you use the fornixator?"

"You mean the mechanical masturbator?"

Wolfe was impassive, "It's been called that."

"No, I don't use it."

"I see," said Wolfe.

"You see what?"

"I see that if you were cheating on her, or using the fornixator, you'd have found your own particular choice of sexual outlet. If you were, I'd get up and walk out of here right now. It'd be obvious why she isn't enjoying sex with you – you're not enjoying it with her. You'd be getting your satisfaction elsewhere, and there'd be nothing that I – or anyone – could do about it. But, if you still love her – and if she's still your only sexual outlet . . . well, there is something I can do about that. You do love her, don't you?"

John hesitated. After a bit, "Well . . . yes, of course –"

"You want her to have the best, don't you?"

"Sure, but –"

"Then why don't you want her to be sexually satisfied?"

"I do, but –"

"Mr Russell," Wolfe said slowly, patiently as if explaining it to a child, "this is not the Victorian era. Women enjoy sex too." He leaned forward, became very serious, "Look, man, if you're sick, you go to a doctor and he makes you well again, doesn't he?"

"Yeah, I guess so."

"Sure, he does. Well, that's why I'm here. If you've got a sick sex life, you want to make it better again, don't you?"

John nodded.

Wolfe smiled, pleased at this concession, "You've got a monitor-reaction system now, don't you? Well, that's just for the diagnosis. But diagnosis isn't enough – now you need the treatment." Wolfe paused, noted the negative reaction on John's face. He changed his tone, became more serious, "Look, man, your score is way down – down to thirty-four. Doesn't that say to you that something's wrong? You *need* one of our guidance units."

"I can't afford it," John mumbled.

"You can't afford not to! This is to save your marriage, man! If you didn't need it, I wouldn't be sitting here right now. We don't lease our units to people who don't need them. Do you actually *want* a divorce, Mr Russell? That's where you're heading –"

John shook his head.

"Then what's your objection to the unit?"

John looked at the other man, "I'm not a puppet."

Wolfe leaned back in his chair, "Oh, so that's it." He started to close his case, then hesitated, "I really should get up and leave, you know. I really should. You've just shown me how absolutely little you know about the unit. But I'll stay – if only to clear up your misconceptions. I can't stand to see a man misinformed – especially about *my* company. I've got to clear this thing up. The guidance unit *is not* a puppeteer. It is a *guidance* unit – that's why it's called a guidance unit. If it were a control unit, we'd have *called* it a control unit."

"Oh," said John.

Wolfe rummaged around in his case, brought out a neat four-color photo, "Now, look. This is the unit – isn't it a beaut?"

John took the picture and looked at it. It showed a device resembling the one he already had at home sitting on his dresser, but slightly larger and with an additional set of controls.

"The unit monitors the sensitive areas of both you and your partner," said Wolfe. "It has a positive feedback reaction hooked into the guidance modules – all of which means that if your wife's responses indicate that she will react well to certain types of stimulation, then the guidance system will trigger the impulse within you to provide that stimulation. You can resist these impulses if you want to, but why bother? The machine is your friend – it wants you to enjoy yourself."

John looked up at him, "It works both ways . . . ?"

"Oh, yes, of course. She'll be responding to your needs just as you'll be responding to hers. Not only that, but the machine is programmed to guide you both to a simultaneous climax. That alone makes it all worthwhile."

"Yes, well, I don't know . . ."

"I *do* know, Mr Russell," Wolfe said persuasively. "The machine lets you be more sensitive. Your score is thirty-four today. How would you like it to be sixty tomorrow? And it'll get better as you become more experienced."

John shrugged, "You make it sound awfully good . . ."

"It is, Mr Russell. It is. I use one of these units myself – that is my wife and I do."

John looked at him. "You?"

"I know it may seem hard to believe, but it's true. Of course, I will admit that my wife and I never allowed our situation to reach the point that you and your wife have, but I can tell you that we have never regretted it."

"Never . . . ?" asked John.

"Never," said Wolfe, and he smiled proudly.

Act Three

After the installation men had left, John looked at his wife as if to say, "Now what?"

Marsha avoided his gaze. It was almost as if she were having second thoughts herself. "I'll get dinner," she said, and left the room.

Dinner was a silent meal, and they picked at it without relish. John had an irritating feeling of impatience, yet at the same time he dreaded the moment that was rushing down on both of them. Neither of them referred to the new machine waiting in the bedroom.

Finally, he pushed his plate away and left the table. He tried to interest himself in the television, but it was all reruns except for the movie, and he had seen that at the local theater last year – with Marsha, he remembered abruptly. He switched off the set disgustedly and picked up a magazine instead, but it was one that he had already read. He would have put it down, but Marsha came into the room, so he feigned interest in an article he had already been bored with once.

Marsha didn't speak; instead she pulled out her mending and began sewing at a torn sock. From time to time she gave a little exhalation of breath that was not quite a sigh.

It was his place to say something, John knew, but at the same time he didn't want to – it would be too much effort. He didn't feel like working at being nice tonight. He could feel the silence lying between them like a fence – and on either side of it the tethered dogs of their tempers waited for the unwary comment.

John dropped the magazine to the floor and stared at the opposite wall, the blank eye of the TV. He glanced over at Marsha, saw that she was already looking at him. He glanced away quickly, began rummaging through the rack for another magazine.

"You know," she said, "pretending that I'm not here won't make me go away. If you don't want to do it, just say so."

He dropped the magazine he was looking at, hesitated, then continued to rummage. "What's your hurry?" he said.

"You're just as curious as I am," she answered.

"No, I'm not. I really don't think that it's going to make that much difference. I only bought it for your sake." Then, having sunk his psychic barb, he returned his attention to the magazines.

She bent to her mending again, biting her lips silently, thinking of all the things she wanted to say, but knew she shouldn't. It wouldn't take much to make him storm out of the house and not come back until after the bars closed.

After a while, she bit off the end of the thread and said, "There's nothing to be afraid of," and immediately regretted having said it.

But he did not take offense. He just said, "I'm not afraid," and continued paging through an old copy of *Life*.

She put her mending down. "Remember when we were first married . . . ? How we used to stall all evening long – both pretending that *that* wasn't the only thing on our minds . . . ?"

He grunted. She couldn't tell whether it was a yes-grunt or a no-grunt.

"Don't you feel something like that now . . . ?" she asked. "I mean, doesn't it feel the same to you?"

"No, it doesn't," he said, and there was a hardness in his voice that made her back off.

She sighed and put her mending basket aside. She went into the kitchen and made coffee instead. Once she started to cry and had to blink back the tears. She thought that John hadn't heard, but suddenly he was standing at the kitchen door. "Now what's the matter?" he asked tiredly.

"Nothing," she snapped and took the cream out of the refrigerator and put it on the counter. "I burned myself, making you coffee."

"I don't want any," he said, then as an afterthought, "Thanks."

She put the cream back in the refrigerator and followed him into the living room, "Then what *do* you want? Do you want to go to bed?"

John looked at her. Who was this woman who had suddenly become a part of his life? Where had she come from? Why was he so reluctant even to touch her? He shoved the thought out of his mind. "I'm tired," he said.

"No, you're not," she snapped. "You don't want to. You always say you're tired when you don't want to." She pointed toward the bedroom, "Well, that thing's in there now, John – and it's not going away either. Sooner or later, you're going to have to see how it works. Why not tonight?"

He looked at her for a long moment, as if trying to remember the girl she had once been. Finally, "All right. I'll turn out the lights . . ."

She waited and they went into the bedroom together, without words. She started to help him out of his clothes, but he pushed her hands away and shrugged out of his shirt without letting her touch him. He unloosened his belt and let his pants drop to the floor.

And then, suddenly, she was standing in front of him – he hadn't even noticed when she'd shrugged out of her dress, but here she was, wearing only bra and panties. In the dim light she was only a silhouette and he had to rely on his memory to tell him what she looked like.

She slid into his arms and they stood there for a moment, without effort, without moving.

After a bit, she broke away and began looking for the wires and bands. "The pause that depresses . . ." she smiled at him, but he did not smile back. Instead, he sat down on the edge of the bed to wait.

She handed him the ankle and wrist bands and showed him how to attach the wires. "Mr Wolfe showed me how, but it's also in the instruction book. Bend down, so I can do your head." He did and she did.

"My turn now," she said. "Come on . . . "

He stood there, looking at her, conscious of the wires trailing from his wrists and ankles and from the top of his head. But she did not laugh. "Aren't you going to help me?" she demanded instead.

He glanced around and found that she had stacked her bands neatly on the night stand. With a minimum of effort, he clipped them to her forearms. He did not resist when she kissed him affectionately on the ear, but neither did he react. Marsha caught at his hand and held it, "It'll be good, John. I know." For the first time in a year, she looked into his eyes, "Trust me."

He looked back at her, this strange woman who was his wife, and his first impulse was to snap, "I'm doing it, aren't I?" But something in her glance held him back, and he just nodded instead.

Being careful of the wires, they climbed into bed.

For a while they lay side by side, she looking at him, he looking into the darkness. They listened to the sound of each other's breathing, like two titans in the dark. Finally, impatiently, she moved into his arms.

"They say you should relax," she whispered. "Let the machine do the guiding. But you do have to start it, John. You have to give the feedback and reaction systems something to start with . . ."

She lifted her face up, wanting to be kissed. He kissed it. He let his hands move incuriously over her body, feeling how her once-trim form had begun to pile up layers, had begun to turn to fat; the once-smooth skin was beginning to go rough and there were wrinkles. But he let his hands roam across her anyway, without direction, not noticing how they had already begun to quest and probe.

Marsha's hands too were moving across his body, through the sparse hair on his chest, up and along his never well-muscled arms, across the uneven pimple-stained skin of his back. Yet, he noticed, her hands seemed to be more gentle than they had seemed in the past, more sensitive, more knowing and more active. She was beginning to caress parts of his chest and legs, places that seemed to be more alive than he remembered them.

His hands too had taken on a life of their own – and yet, they were still his hands. He stroked, he fondled, he caressed with a technique and a skill he had never noticed in himself. And Marsha was reacting, responding, giving with an enthusiasm he had never before seen in this woman who was his wife.

Now he was moving and thrusting with a wholeness of being that had to be shared – it was too big for any one person – and he moved and thrust at her all the more wilfully, trying to push his sharing all the deeper into her. Marsha too seemed to be arching, thrusting, giving – as if she too had something overwhelming to give.

It was as if they were both doing the right thing at the right time and at the right place – and for one brief bright flash it reminded him of what it had been like when they had been young, and when nothing else had existed but each other and the bright surging world.

They forgot the wires, the bands, the guidance module on the dresser. Their external beings had disappeared and they immersed themselves in their lovemaking. It was a surging climbing wave, a bright crashing thing that built ever higher. Even higher.

And it was very good.

He smiled at her. She smiled back, and they kissed. It wasn't until the next morning they discovered the guidance module had not been connected.

KISS BOOTIES
NIGHT-NIGHT
Storm Constantine

Storm Constantine's novels, says The Encyclopedia of Science
Fiction, *"are all fundamentally concerned with sex and gender
(especially androgyny) ... Vigorous, erotic, highly visual, aes-
thetically informed by a late punk/Goth sensibility..." Her work
is proving immensely popular in the 1990s, from her* Wraethu
trilogy to more recent novels like Hermetech. *"Kiss Booties Night-
Night", an intriguing glimpse into a fetishistic future, was written
especially for this book.*

The sun, a fevered blister, hung low in a pagan sky of ceremonial
colours: purple, red, deepest orange. She stood among the rattling
sticks of petrified reeds, on the edge of the slow-moving slick they
called the river. Behind her, the manse was dark, but for the
winking violet lights of the security systems at eaves and porch.
The garden was so beautiful. She never grew tired of it: the rank
weeds; the blackened ivy over the walls of the ice-house; last year's
lilies not cleared away, fainting at the feet of this year's forced
growth that had been brought in from the hothouses of the city
centre, soon to die out here in the air.

  She put a tarless cigarette between her ink-lacquered lips and
drew in a stream of chemical fume. Her boots caught the light of
a security beam far across the river. Otherwise she was non-
reflecting, her skin pale and flat like bleached ashes, her dark
clothes a void against the descending night.

Maradissa Ferone, heiress. She played at having a career –
buying and selling the more intriguing artefacts from the past that
had escaped destruction into the present. She loved the past.
Sometimes, she designed parties, which she sold to the sons and
daughters of her dead parents' friends; Creatures of the Contemporary – as they styled themselves – who lived further up-river,
where the ugly old factories had been turned into apartments and
the river strained and treated to become something sterile, which
it was safe to touch, if not to drink.

Maradissa lived alone, although she was not reclusive. She was
often sighted in the more expensive night-haunts of the Industrial
Park, west of the river. Several times a year, she would throw a
themed party at the manse. Many people thought the decay was
contrived, but it was not. Maradissa took pleasure in watching the
slow dissolution of all that her mother had worked to achieve; the
manse, a rotting heritage. This was not a rebellion against her
mother, or her mother's success, but simply a statement that
everything was running *her* way, now. Unlike her peers, Maradissa
shunned cosmetic surgery, but for the decorative scarring on her
breasts and stomach. She was always the same sex.

Tonight, a hurrying air, a sense of imminence, volted through
her as she stood beside the river. Her skin prickled as she watched
the roiling surface of the water. When this feeling came, she
savoured it. It was fear. It was excitement. Life still held promise
in the throes of apprehension. She was dressed, ready to drive to
the Park, in period Gothic of the late twentieth century: tight, matt
black, and spikes. Her hair was a frothing black halo, teased and
stiff and lightless. Smoking the cigarette, she stoked her excitement. Sometimes she had to make it come like this; take in the
chemicals, watch the poisonous sunset, psych herself up.

She threw the remains of her cigarette into the river, smoothed
her taut black thighs, enjoying the feel of herself. There was power
in the fume she had taken, power in the lowering night, the colours
on the oily surface of the water. There were no seasons here and
the smells of the land were confections. She turned away from the
river.

Feeling watched.

She paused, knowing how the smoke could warp her senses,
kindle a feeling of agitation, of being an actress for an invisible
audience, bring with it a fleeting understanding of gods.

For a few sanctified moments, the silence of the garden was absolute, then the lilies rustled their thorns. Maradissa walked purposefully towards them. She was not afraid, and still young enough to believe in her own immortality. As she approached, something scrambled away from her; the foliage of life and death rattled loudly. Maradissa did not challenge, made no sound, although it was clear to her that whatever hid among the lilies was too large to be animal. Instead, she plucked an ivy cane from the ice-house wall and struck the place where the rustling had started.

Silence. Something crouched, something feared.

For a moment, Maradissa considered entering into the gripping shadows of the hanging plants. She even put one pointed boot upon the soil, then retreated. She would speak to her butler about it; the sniffers could inspect the grounds. She had no time to deal with intruders, certainly not those that ran from her.

He did not think she was beautiful, for to him she was beyond beauty, a goddess. She was remote and perfect, apparently unaware that her grounds were full of unseen gardening graduates, working to maintain the graveyard disarray that she loved. Michael had worked in her gardens now for nearly a month, and only during the last week had realized, or become aware of, the strong feelings she kindled within him. At first, he had seen her only briefly, whenever she left the house to climb into her car. He'd been fascinated by her appearance, the bizarre clothes. Other gardeners joked cruelly about her eccentricity. They were scornful, resentful, jealous of her wealth and luxuries. They liked to make lascivious comments, speculate about how well she'd perform in bed. Most were scathing. Their bitter envy made them want to debase her. Michael did not feel like that. His fantasies of her did not involve sex. He wanted to speak to her, worship at her feet. Those feet, clad in shiny black, forced into the pointed shape. It must hurt her.

Every evening before sundown, a bus came to pick up the gardeners and take them back to their apartments in the Colonies, but for the last two days, Michael had lingered behind when his colleagues went off-duty. He'd worked out that as the mistress of the house never entered the gardens during the day, she must do so after dark. And he was right. Hidden among the ragged foliage, he could watch her undisturbed for a glorious half-hour or so, before the security systems were activated. She was regal, mistress of her domain as she stalked around its boundaries.

His trespassing had terrified him at first, for he knew the very least penalty for discovery would be dismissal, but he could not resist this private pleasure. If he was careful, she need never know. But then, he wanted her to know. One day, he might even dare to make his presence known to her, an abject slave to her power. In part, he wanted to invoke her outrage. He had never felt this way before.

Now, he knew that she had sensed him in his hiding place. He'd watched her lean body become tense: so much shiny gloss in the ragged crêpe of the dried leaves around her. He'd scuttled backwards into the comfortless arms of an ancient rhododendron, and here, he had crouched down, peering through the thick leaves. She had walked towards him. He had smelled her perfume, the scent of her cigarette and the reek of the lacquer with which she styled her hair. He had never been able to study her so closely: a black and white ghost in the twilight. Her mouth, he realized, was small, its lack of generosity further emphasized by the severe black lipstick. This slight fault only made her more alluring. She'd stood, poised, a lithe cat ready to pounce, and he'd been frozen before her; terrified and longing for her predator eyes to fix upon him. Then, relaxing her muscles, she appeared to dismiss whatever sound had alerted her and wandered back towards the house.

Michael fell to his knees upon the damp earth. His heart pounded madly. She had known he was there, but she had not chased him off. Neither had she shown fear, but he'd not expected that, in any case. She had become a conspirator in his fantasy.

In the hallway of the house, Maradissa drew on her long black gloves and spoke to her magic mirror. In it, no reflection, but an image of her butler Leony, who lived some distance away in an apartment that Maradissa owned.

"Something in the gardens tonight," Maradissa said, admiring her long fingers in their velvet. "Not invited. Check it for me?"

Already Leony was reaching for the pads that would activate the sniffers. Late. They should have come on before sundown, but Maradissa's loitering by the river had probably deferred them.

"Nothing unsanctified," Leony said, looking at the display Maradissa could not see. "Staff working late?"

Maradissa pulled a face at the mirror. "They watched me."

Leony laughed. She was allowed certain privileges. "What do you expect?"

Maradissa smiled back, thinly. "No one stays here after sundown unless I request it. See to it, Lee." She made a pass across the mirror with her gloved hands.

"Your word, oh mistress, is my command," said Leony, a diminishing genie in the mirror as it clouded and darkened and veiled its magic.

Before the sniffers were released to patrol the grounds, Michael had slipped like a shadow over the wall. It took a long time to walk back to his apartment, and once there he felt too unnerved to eat his evening meal. As it lay cooling in its delivery slot, he lay on his bed, his stomach churning, and prayed to his goddess. She must hear him. He was her soul's servant.

Maradissa met her friends Crickforth and Evalie in the bar called The Bat Cavern on Eldritch Boulevard, at the edge of the park. It was a haunt favoured by all those who espoused Maradissa's chosen fashion period; a lot of black was seen around. Crickforth and Evalie were drinking bright green cocktails from triangular glasses.

"Babba, you just have to see!" Evalie announced as Maradissa slid onto the fishnet-covered seat beside her.

"See what?" Maradissa peeled off one of her gloves and put it beside her drink, lifted her glass with the ungloved hand.

"The most divine freaks!"

Maradissa looked at Crickforth. He had suffered a mild stroke recently, which had frozen the left side of his face. His parents had cut his allowance, owing to the fact that a new fashion drug had been responsible for the stroke, and were punishing him further by making him wait for corrective surgery. Crickforth, always an optimist, was using his deformity as a fashion accessory at present. He limped a bit and wore one black leather glove, a patch over his drooping eyelid. "She means the fetzers," he explained with half his mouth. "There's a Fetzer Nite on."

Maradissa sipped her drink. "Oh? So what?" She delivered an admonishing glance to Evalie.

Evalie poked Maradissa's arm. "Oh, where's your sense of

adventure? The fetzers represent *your* time, my bab, your time. Of course, you're interested."

Maradissa shook her head. "They most certainly *do not* represent my time, as you put it. What are you implying?"

Evalie would not be deterred. "But it was all the thing back then. Eighties' and Nineties' chic! Fetish nights, glamour-wear."

"A little more than that," Maradissa said, quietly.

Her remark was ignored. "Mara, we *must* go and see them."

"We wouldn't get in."

"With your contacts?" Evalie chided. "Don't be ridiculous."

Maradissa shrugged. For outrageous sights, they could visit any number of bars in the Park; there was always something to look at. The fetzers were something else. They thrived on debasement; or on debasing. Nowadays, there were therapies to see to that. Sexual and social neuroses could be worked out in group VR; safely. Maradissa had studied thoroughly the periods that interested her, but she was selective in what she adopted, or adapted, from the past. It was only a matter of time before the fetzers were persuaded to abandon their obsessions. Already, complaints had appeared on the bulletin boards. Whatever the fetzers had chosen to drag into the present, they had embellished and exaggerated it. Maradissa was aware of the rumours. It was unhealthy, and no protest about how it was all a kind of harmless fancy dress could convince those that saw it as a crack in the social seam. "I don't think we should risk corrupting Crickforth," Maradissa said, with a smile.

Crickforth grimaced. "It wasn't my idea!"

"Mara, don't be tiresome," Evalie said. "Have you no curiosity? It's bizarre the fetzers got a licence for tonight's meeting. Strings were tweaked, obviously!"

"Not really," Crickforth argued, wiping spittle from the dead corner of his mouth. "It's best to keep these things regulated."

"Well, whatever," Evalie said with a careless wave of her hand. "We could at least watch them going into the club."

Maradissa considered this suggestion. The mere thought of the fetzers made her feel annoyed – or angry – she wasn't sure which. Her father had once said to her, "You risk becoming what you resist"; to have a strong aversion to a thing somehow gave it power. "Where's it being held?"

"Key-mart's multi-storey," Evalie answered lightly, sensing compliance.

The night club had once been a car park, in the days when there had been a plague of cars. Below it, the converted aisles of the supermarket housed counsellors' booths, the tables and machines of sex yogis, and the darkened cells of light-therapists. Sometimes Maradissa and her friends took enlightenment drugs there or discussed non-existent dilemmas with earnest thin people. Naturally, the therapists and counsellors and self-appointed gurus had taken exception to the fetzer meeting taking place above their shrines, and had staged a non-violent protest outside, which everyone was ignoring.

The sidewalk was packed with neo-goths, zippers, body art flappers and haute couture junkies of every stripe. Chemical spliffs were passed freely among the cheerful throng that watched the fetzers walk up the ramp to the doors of the club. Most of the fetzers were in normal dress, clutching carryalls with a change of costume inside. They hurried past the onlookers with set expressions. Others, mainly middle-aged male transvestites, who were into it for laughs rather than illicit pleasure, paraded and minced and made lewd gestures at the crowd, which was catcalled appreciatively.

Maradissa despised them all. To her it was an embarrassing display.

"We *must* go in," said Evalie.

Maradissa glanced at Crickforth, who shrugged. "Could be fun."

Maradissa shook her head, exhaled a tolerant sigh and then pushed through the crowd. With her Ferone Corporation credit cards, she sailed past the door-keepers, Crickforth and Evalie in tow. People in the crowd, who knew them, shrieked out amused and gentle obscenities, at which Evalie, bringing up the rear, made dismissive signals.

Inside, it was cold, with localized areas of intense heat. Maradissa shivered. The air was red. "Changing room?" asked a uniformed receptionist.

Maradissa afforded him a scornful glance. "Bar."

In the event, Maradissa found it hard to be disgusted. The fetzers were playing at it. The occasion was no worse than a Gothic Renaissance night at the Pit Vault, only the costumes were sillier, and the music rather more vapid. Two men crawled past her on all-fours, leashed to a tall woman in badly-applied make-up, who was possibly a man. One sniffed Maradissa's feet. "Now puppies!" said the leash-woman, and tapped her charges affectionately with a whip that appeared to be made of embroidery silk. The puppies looked at one another and giggled; such a fun game. Maradissa eyed them condescendingly, while Evalie hooted in pleasurable distaste. After a while, the plethora of exposed genitals, naked breasts framed in straps and metal, bare tattooed buttocks and costumes of extreme brevity lost their shock value. Maradissa sat at the bar and gossiped with Evalie about people they knew. Crickforth was discussing the benefits of a new amenities centre in the Tech Park up-river, with a man who was encased in black leather from crown to toe, but for an open zip which exposed his mouth, and a hole at groin from which a flaccid penis hung.

"We could be anywhere, in any bar," Maradissa said, interrupting Evalie mid-sentence. "This is just another theme club. Only the clothes, or lack of them, make it different."

Evalie nodded. "Still, I wanted to come. I wanted to see."

Maradissa slid off her stool. "Can't help wondering what I'll find in the wash-room, though!"

"Want me to come with you?"

Maradissa rolled her eyes. "Ev, *please*!" She pushed her way into the crowd.

The fetzers were more friendly than members of other cult-groups Maradissa had met. Her own neo-Gothic culture tended towards cliquishness and aloofness. Here, everyone she passed smiled and greeted her as if she had known them for years. It seemed foolish to maintain a frosty attitude.

In the ladies' wash-room, both men and women clustered around the mirrors, squealing with laughter as they refreshed their face paint. A thin middle-aged man, clad only in leather straps and rather heavy make-up, grinned in Maradissa's face. "Great night, isn't it!"

Maradissa adopted a quizzical expression. "Mmm."

"Voyeuse!" The response was good-natured, rather than critical.

"No," Maradissa responded, and then restrained herself from

explaining why she was there. "It's interesting here, but rather tamer than I thought."

The man gave her a sly look. "There are levels of experience," he said. "You just have too look for them. Visit the Chamber, and then say tame."

"There is more?"

The man laughed. "There is always more. For those that want it."

But I don't want it, she thought. Still, there was no point in visiting this place without examining every option on the menu. She might discover something worth reporting to Evalie and Crickforth.

It took her some time to find the Chamber, because no one seemed willing to give explicit instructions concerning its location, but eventually, deep in the centre of the club, she found the entrance to the shrine of forbidden pleasures. There were curtains of shiny PVC across the doorway. As she lifted them and passed through, she noticed with amusement the health scanner that monitored her heart, before a mechanized voice breathed out an approving welcome.

Beyond, the light was redder, the air steamy. Figures were just moving shadows within the crimson fog. Maradissa heard the sounds; retching, laughter, groans, the slap of something yielding on flesh, something brittle shattering. Tribal music throbbed beneath this symphony of indulgence. On the floor, there was blood.

She felt both revolted and dazed. The light drew her in: through the sounds, through the steam peopled with indistinct forms. Occasionally, a seeking hand might reach out to stroke her, but she avoided their anonymous touch.

Crossing a slick-floored chamber, Maradissa entered a corridor of flesh – dampened latex fabric looped across the walls and ceiling, hanging down in writhing tatters. Here, there were sighs in the air and soft squeals of pleasure. Purple-pink light pulsed at the corridor's end, and Maradissa advanced towards it – cautiously, slightly in fear, slightly in anticipation. The flesh tunnel opened out into a vast chamber, where ribbons of incense curled around the cupreous scent of blood and the sharper, chemical reek of leisure anaesthetics.

Fascination and horror surged through Maradissa where she

stood at the threshold. The smoky air purled in upon itself like a veil drawing aside. *Come, sweet flesh. Enter in . . .*

The pleasure of machines. They were part biological, like alien robots, towering, spreading and curious. Metal black. Mannikins of subjection were mere bound scraps between the elegant pincers, the intestine coils of slinking alloy, the investigating probes, the scalpel-clawed prehensile digits. Their movement was hypnotic. Maradissa saw a swatch of hair hanging down from within an iron helmet. An arm shuddered pale within a tangle of dark cables. Above her, screens the size of hoardings advertised the forbidden sensuality. She understood that within the minds of these willing victims, the slow excoriation of flesh was twisted into dream-like virtual imagery that bloomed with mythic fantasy. Their pain was regulated to peaks they found acceptable. All was silent but for the slither of metal coils, the occasional mechanical hum. Every human mouth was plugged with rubber.

An undulating limb lifted up like the neck of a serpent from the tangled mass of flesh and machine. It turned an unwinking, glowing eye upon Maradissa, then snaked towards her slowly. A non-human voice breathed, "Welcome . . .", and in its echoless cadence, Maradissa heard the secret message of pleasures exquisite and undreamed of.

For one brief moment, she almost fell, mesmerized and willing, into the embrace of the fleshless arm. Then her stomach roiled involuntarily, and she had to turn away quickly, a hand to her mouth.

A woman had come into the Chamber behind her, blocking an easy exit. She was tall and fairly attractive, naked to the waist, clad in rubber leggings. Her torso was laced with bloody scars, and she held a thin blade in one hand. "Don't run, my pretty." The woman held out her hands to Maradissa. "You want to be here. I am the Priestess of Perversity. Come, I will lead you to a nest." She gestured at the machines.

Maradissa shook her head and tried to push past the woman, but the priestess grabbed hold of her arm. "Don't be afraid. It's your first time, isn't it?" Her voice was soft with reassurance.

"Let me past," Maradissa said, roughly pulling her arm from the priestess's hold. "I'm not meant to be here."

The priestess's expression changed slightly, hardened. She pulled back her lips into a sneering laugh and pressed the blade she held to her stomach. "Open up!" The scalpel-thin knife sliced into her flesh.

"You're sick!" Maradissa hissed, and made to push past her. She averted her head, not wanting to look at the fresh wound, afraid there would be no blood.

The woman blocked her way again and laughed. "Sick, huh? What are you doing here, little girl?"

Maradissa glanced up at her reflexively, could not help noticing the thin wet stream on the woman's upper belly. "I just . . . got lost."

The priestess shook her head. "Oh, really? I don't think so. You came here to see, didn't you? You're curious. Want to see how the big girls and boys play. That's OK. If you want to look, I can show you around."

Maradissa was momentarily paralysed by fear, unsure of whether the woman was right in her assumptions. Then, firmly, she shook her head. "No. Thank you."

"It's all right." The priestess smiled warmly. "Everyone has a first time."

Maradissa swallowed, tasted bile. "I'm not like you. Let me pass."

The priestess gestured at her. "Oh, no? Look at you in your pretty, kinky gear, your little painted face! You're not that different from us."

Maradissa recovered her composure, raised her hands like a barrier. "You've got it wrong," she said. "Excuse me, please. Or is assault part of your repertoire?"

The woman narrowed her eyes. "Only if you want it."

Maradissa uttered a short, dry laugh, rolled her eyes. "No, thank you. I'm not into pain."

The woman put her head on one side. "Aren't you?" She reached out and slid her hand down Maradissa's side. "I think everyone is, if they're honest. We're honest. This is reality. We are more healthy because of it. Come on, loosen up. Enjoy yourself. Don't waste your visit. You wouldn't be here if you didn't really want to be."

Maradissa backed away, affected her most haughty tone. "I'm not interested, actually. Please, excuse me. I have friends waiting and they'll come looking for me soon."

The woman folded her arms, the knife blade pointing into the air. She gave Maradissa's clothes and jewellery an assessing glance. "Oh, I see. It's a little rich kid come to gawp at the freaks, is it?"

"Yes, I'm rich," Maradissa agreed, unable to resist admitting it. "So what? You're no healthier than I am. You must hate yourself to cut your body like that. I happen to like my body, and I respect other people's."

The woman sneered. "Oh yeah? And that perfect nose is your own, is it? That faultless figure? You're into knives, girly, everyone's into knives!" She uttered a chilling screech of laughter, then pushed Maradissa back into the flesh tunnel, with the retort, "Go home to Mummy and Daddy. Your kind aren't wanted here."

Maradissa was burning with nausea and humiliated anger by the time she found Evalie at the bar. The injustice of being judged a surgery-junkie was almost as bad as what the Chamber had concealed in its bloody mists. She was not like them. It wasn't true. They were freaks. She was not. "I'm going," she snapped at Evalie. Crickforth had disappeared. "Stay if you want!"

"You've been ages," Evalie said, getting off her stool. "What happened? Are you OK?"

"No," Maradissa said. "I want to go home." For the first time in two years, she felt conscious of her age, and realized she was missing her mother.

On the way home, Evalie sympathized with Maradissa's revulsion, but was too eager for details, seemingly unaware that by describing what had happened, Maradissa felt she was somehow legitimizing it. The words should not be spoken. She dropped Evalie off at her parent's estate. "Stay here tonight," Evalie offered. "Don't go home alone."

Maradissa shook her head. "No. I'll be fine."

"Then, I'll come and stay with you, if you like."

"Ev, I'll be fine. Honestly. I was just taken by surprise back there, that's all. It'll soon be forgotten." Maradissa didn't want anyone to know how upset she was. She smiled and waved and drove away.

At home, Maradissa sat in her salon and drank some brandy, which she rarely touched. She was aware of feeling soiled. The house seemed cold and empty. She played some music disks, but the lyrics seemed too pertinent. Images filled her mind; the laughing, painted faces, the exposed bodies, then the hidden pleasures of the inner chamber and the Priestess of Perversity's grin as she opened up her flesh with a blade. Disgusting! How could people be like that? What was there in human nature that made it manifest? Something primitive. And yet, when Maradissa dreamed that night, she was held in the embrace of a metal lover without a face, who invaded her hungering body with devices too large for her to accommodate. She felt her flesh tear, but the pain was translated into a different sensation, like smelling the most exquisite perfume, tonguing the most exotic liqueur. Then she was screaming against the invasion, gathering an occult strength. She transformed herself into the metal lover and what shivered pale beneath her precise force filled her with an aching tenderness of feeling. She awoke disorientated, her body tensing to the receding pulse of erotic thrill.

Once she had dressed, Maradissa called Leony. "I'm not feeling too good," she said, keeping the mirror shadowed. "Make sure I'm not bothered, will you?"

"Do you need anything?"

"No. Just privacy for a while. I'm tired."

"Overdoing it, huh?" Leony laughed. Sometimes Maradissa went into retreat after lengthy, non-stop parties. "Listen, that intruder you spoke about last night. I've looked into it. A new staff member. Didn't understand the sundown regulation. It's all fixed now. I briefed his supervisor."

"Fine, fine. I just don't want to be pestered."

"Feed and medicate yourself properly."

"I will."

Michael had been horrified when his supervisor had confronted him about why he'd stayed behind at the manse the previous evening. Red-faced, he'd blurted an excuse about wanting to get a particular job finished. "We have set work schedules," the supervisor said, her eyes hard. "You don't get paid for overtime."

If she'd guessed Michael's true reason for lingering in the garden, she did not press the matter. Michael felt bereft, cheated. The supervisor didn't understand that Ms Ferone wanted him in her garden, and because their potential relationship had to be secret, the mistress could not reveal the truth.

All day, he worked near the house, peering through the windows at every opportunity. He saw his idol drifting from room to room, a glass in her hand. She seemed distracted – obviously agonizing over her decision to report his presence to the supervisor. She had made a mistake and would have to rectify it herself. Michael was powerless, her pawn. Sometimes, it seemed as if she was aware of his eyes, hidden in foliage beyond the windows, for she would start as if at a sudden sound, and glance through the panes. He longed to stand up, show himself, but knew that was not part of the ritual. He knew he would have to engineer a way to remain in the gardens after sundown again, but not yet. There would be a sign when it was time.

That evening, Michael had to go home with all his colleagues. He found he was glad to get back to his apartment, because he could lie on his bed and think about Maradissa. He imagined the click of spike heels upon the hard floor beyond his door, the tap that might come upon the laminated wood from sharp, lacquered nails. He imagined her coming in across the threshold, standing over him, saying, "You are mine."

For three days later Maradissa refused to go to the Park with any of her friends. She needed solitude, and spent a lot of time meditating, trying to face up to the demons spawned from the episode at the fetzer nite. She dressed herself in a loose purple robe, kept her hair clean and straight down her back, wore no make-up. She found she wanted to bathe frequently, as if there was something to wash away. It was as if she'd witnessed a terrible atrocity, and had to exorcise the trauma of it. Her mind was drawn to reinvent images of what the Chamber had contained, her thoughts colouring in more detail. Her meditations of calming scenes would mutate without her noticing it into hideous fantasies that left her feeling soiled and ashamed. Self-disgust prevented her from seeking outside therapy. The experiences exhausted her, numbed her with an unfamiliar weakness. She was used to feeling strong and in control.

Hiding in her manse, Maradissa ignored the calls piling up behind her mirror's surface. Let Leony deal with them, offer excuses for Maradissa's silence. She had more important things to attend to. She fought with her demons alone. The fetzers haunted her dreams, the secret fetzers of the inner Chamber. She dreamed that the Priestess of Perversity came looking for her. She scratched the windows of Maradissa's manse with sharp, metal claws, murmuring, "You want me to come. You want what I can give, what I can teach you." There were dreams, too, of tying faceless bodies down upon weird contraptions of wood and leather, anticipating with dread and desire an unknown torture that soon she would possess the knowledge to inflict. And the priestess was there to tell her, "You see. You *do* belong with us. You just didn't realize in what capacity."

During the day, she battled constantly with a feeling of being watched, sure there was an invisible presence beyond her windows staring in at her, compelling her to become aware of it. She chided herself for thinking it might be the Priestess, or some psychic emanation of the woman. Fleetingly, she remembered the incident in the garden before the fetzer experience. That must be it. A gardener looking in at her. Perhaps she should call Leony, but she felt too lethargic to bother. There was no sense of threat from the scrutiny, only an air of intense interest. Then, the night would come again, and Maradissa could not convince herself that it wasn't the fetzers who were watching her, bodilessly observing some weird kind of transformation taking place within her mind. The Priestess had cast a spell over her in the Chamber and now waited for her magic to take full effect. In the dark, contorted fetzer spirits surrounded the house.

One morning, Maradissa woke up angry. She would not be driven mad by what she'd witnessed in the Chamber. All the nightmares since were no more than phantoms of the mind. She leapt up from her bed and threw out her arms at the wan morning light beyond the windows. Enough! With this inner shout, it felt as if something inside her shattered and came out of her in a wave of emotion. She felt light-headed, as if there was more space around her. There were parts of other people's realities that were ugly, but they were not part of hers. She had fought the spell of the Chamber and won, defeated the demons of dark desire.

She called Evalie on the magic mirror.

"How are you?" Evalie asked. "I've tried to call for days, all I got was the butler. Everyone's been worried about you."

"A virus. I've beaten it!" Maradissa said cheerfully. "Now, I need some entertainment. Out tonight?"

"Yes! Yes! Pick me up?"
"OK. Usual time."

Michael knew that tonight had to be the night. It was impossible for him to linger behind after work, so at lunchtime, he'd pretend to be ill and took the rest of the day off. His goddess had seemed so miserable for days. His heart had ached to see her pale, forlorn face peering from the windows of the house. But, that morning, he'd caught a glimpse of her and had seen that her spirits had lifted. She'd been smiling again, that cool, aloof smile, and had no doubt made a decision.

As the gardeners' bus rolled off towards the Colonies, Michael was hiding near the gates to the Ferone manse. He waited until the bus was out of sight round a corner and then slipped between the metal portals as they ground ponderously shut. He knew that security systems would soon be in operation, but trusted that Maradissa would be aware of his presence and delay their activation. As her devotee, he was ready. He'd been alert for signs and now would act.

In the garden, Maradissa was dressed for the night. Spike-heeled boots, a catsuit of glistening black. She smoked beside the river. In her heart, a new feeling. The familiar kindling of excitement, the potential of the future, but tempered by serenity, a sense of separateness. Nothing could touch her now. She'd been reborn, stronger and more aware.

Then, the feeling of being watched sneaked up on her senses. She froze for a moment, a brief image of the Priestess of Perversity padding across her mind. Ridiculous. It was the gardener again. Immediately, she realized that the first time she had sensed him had not been because he'd been unaware of the regulations. It was so clear. He had been watching her, and watched her still. Slowly, she turned around, and saw him, this time, hiding in the lilies. A pale face through the dead and living leaves. She felt irritated, a little flattered perhaps, but resented the intrusion into her private time. The fume had empowered her. She was not afraid, and could defend herself against anything.

"Come out here!"

The man did not move. She could see the round holes of his eyes; he looked transfixed. An unfamiliar sensation shivered through her. When she walked towards him, she saw he was young. She had expected an older man.

"What are you doing here?"

He cowered down among the dead lilies, his hands steepled, trembling, before his face, as if in some kind of religious obeisance.

Maradissa laughed. "Why are you frightened. Don't be absurd. Explain yourself!"

He seemed to find his courage then, and made to scrabble backwards through the leafage. Maradissa grabbed his arm, and it was as if his flesh turned to fluid in her hold. He did not resist her, but hung there limply, leaning against her legs. Maradissa pushed him away. "Get off my premises. You'll lose your job for this!" She expected him to give her an appealing glance, say something. Instead, he lay there in the crackling foliage, beautiful and vulnerable. She saw, in his eyes, his feelings. How long had he watched here before he'd gathered the courage to stay after hours? He'd been reprimanded, but now risked dismissal, if not prosecution. What was he waiting for? What did he want from her?

Maradissa paused. It seemed that time condensed into a single moment, of which she was queen. She was conscious of her long limbs clad in shiny fabric, the slavering, fanged maw of her sex.

She straddled his fallen body, the heels of her boots digging into the soft soil. He lay still, waiting, his hair spread out over the crackling leaves. She imagined tearing the thin fabric of his shirt away, exposing his breast, like an empty canvas awaiting the marks of her nails.

Maradissa laughed uneasily, took a step to the side, stood over him. She felt dizzy. Time to go. She must dismiss him, go back to the house, call Leony, report the trespass. Evalie was expecting her and life must go on – it must!

The boy curled onto his side, still looking up at her with strange beseechment. He made no sound.

Maradissa extended one foot, placed it upon his face, so that her heel pressed against his trembling mouth. He reached up with grimed fingers, and the scent of leaf-mould was released, primal, almost anaesthetic.

He took hold of her foot, licked the leather. "Kiss booties night night," he said. And her heel drove into the soft flesh of his mouth.

CATMAN

Harlan Ellison

*The large number of awards (7 Hugos, 3 Nebulas, plus many more
from outside the SF/fantasy field) testify to Harlan Ellison's key
position as one of the greatest – if also one of the most controversial – short-story writers of our time. The tales which made him
famous are in his collections of the mid- to late-1960s:* Paingod
and Other Delusions *(1965),* I Have No Mouth and I Must Scream
(1967), Love Ain't Nothing But Sex Misspelled *(1968) and others.
His later work – less prolific but no less hard-hitting – is in* Strange
Wine *(1978),* Shatterday *(1980) and* Angry Candy *(1988).*
*"Catman", a novella from 1974, was his response to an invitation
to write "the* ultimate *future sex story", and it does not disappoint.
It involves a computer.*

The thief materialized in the shadow of a conversing waterfall. The
air sparked like a dust circuit for a moment, and then he was there;
back flat to the wall, a deeper black against the shadow, a stretch
fabric suit and hood covering every inch of his body from feet to
fingertips. Only his eyes were naked to the night. He stood there,
motionless, as the waterfall talked to itself. It had been programmed to deter suicides, and it was reciting reassurances.

"You don't really think you'll find peace in killing yourself, do
you?" the waterfall bubbled. "Who knows what lies on the other
side? Perhaps it'll be just the same, and you'll be aware of yourself
as an entity, but you'll be dead, and helpless to save yourself, and
you'll spend who-knows-how-long – perhaps an eternity – suffering the same anguish you knew when you were alive. But you'll be
trapped in death, and unable to get out. Wouldn't that be awful?

Instead, why don't we talk about what's troubling you—"

The thief dematerialized; the waterfall splashed on to itself.

He reappeared on the fiftieth level, in a frozen park. Standing beside a juniper encased in luminescent blue ice, he came into existence, checked the bag of electronic alarm-confounders, satisfied himself it was tied on securely, and started to wink-out again. He paused, half dematerialized, and stared across the park at the diorama of the Neanderthalers driving a herd of ibex off a cliff. The ice block was enormous, holding the cliff, the chasm, thirty of the graceful horned beasts, and half a hundred cavemen. It had been quarried from a site in Krapina, Yugoslavia by a timelock team that had frozen the moment 110,000 years before. It was an excellent display, art-directed by someone prestigious, perhaps Boltillon under a grant from Therox.

For a moment longer he considered the great scene, thinking how trapped they were, thinking how free he was, not even walls of ice to contain him. Then he vanished.

He came back to existence, brute matter, on the three-quarter-inch ledge outside a dreamcell apartment on the ninetieth level. He was flattened against the force screen that served as its outer wall. It was opaque, and he lay against it like a smear of rainbow oil. He could not be seen from inside, where the wealthy ones he intended to rob lay quietly, dreaming. But he could be seen by the scanning tower at the top of the Westminster Cathedral complex. Invisible beams blanketed London from the tower, watching. Registering intrusive action. He smiled and withdrew one of the confounders from the bag. It was a ladybug deranger; he palmed it onto the force screen wall and it tapped into the power source, and he felt the tension ease. Then he diffused himself, and reappeared inside the dreamcell.

The family lay in their pods, the gel rippling ever so slightly at every muscle spasm. The inner walls were a dripping golden lustrousness, molten metal running endlessly down into bottomless depths where the floor should have been. He had no idea what they were dreaming, but the women were laying moistly locked together in *soixante-neuf* and the men were wearing reflective metal headache bands over their eyes. The men were humming in soprano tones.

He vanished and reappeared in the lock room. The force screens were up, protecting the valuables, and the thief went down on his haunches, the bag of confounders dangling between his thighs. He whistled softly to himself, considering the proper tool, and finally withdrew a starfish passby. It scuttled across the floor and touched a screen with its dorsal cirri. The screens sputtered, changing hue, then winked out. The thief dematerialized and reappeared inside the vault.

He ignored the jewelry and the credit cards and selected the three pressure-capped tubes of Antarean soul-radiant, worth, on the black market, all the jewels in the lock room.

He disassembled himself and winked back into existence outside the force screen perimeter, retrieved the starfish, and vanished again, to appear on the ledge. The ladybug went into the bag, and he was gone once more.

When he materialized on the fifty-first level, in the Fuller Geodex, the Catman was waiting, and before the thief could vanish again, the policeman had thrown up a series of barriers that would have required everything in the bag to counteract, plus a few the thief had not considered necessary on this job.

The Catman had a panther, a peregrine falcon and two cheetahs with him. They were inside the barrier ring, and they were ready. The falcon sat on the Catman's forearm, and the cats began padding smoothly toward the thief.

"Don't make me work them," the Catman said.

The thief smiled, though the policeman could not see it. The hood covered the thief's face. Only the eyes were naked. He stared at the Catman in his skin cape and sunburst eagle's helmet. They were old acquaintances.

The cheetahs circled, narrowing in toward him. He teleported himself to the other side of the enclosed space. The Catman hissed at the falcon and it soared aloft, dove at the thief, and flew through empty space. The thief stood beside the Catman.

"Earn your pay," the thief said. His voice was muffled. It would make a voice-print, but not an accurate one; it would be insufficient in a court of law.

The Catman made no move to touch the thief. There was no point to it. "You can't avoid me much longer."

"Perhaps not." He vanished as the panther slid toward him on its belly, bunching itself to strike.

"But then, perhaps I don't want to," he said.

The Catman hissed again, and the falcon flew to his armored

wrist. "Then why not come quietly. Let's be civilized."

The thief chuckled deep in his throat, but without humor. "That seems to be the problem right there." The cheetahs passed through space he no longer occupied.

"You're simply all too bloody marvelous civilized; I crave a little crudeness."

"We've had this conversation before," said the Catman, and there was an odd note of weariness in his voice . . . for an officer of the law at last in a favorable position with an old adversary. "Please surrender quietly; the cats are nervous tonight; there was a glasscab accident on the thirty-sixth and they wafted a strong blood scent. It's difficult holding them in check."

As he spoke, the pavane of strike and vanish, hold and go, pounce and invisibility continued, around and around the perimeter ring. Overhead, the Fuller Geodex absorbed energy from the satellite power stars DayDusk&DawnCo, Ltd. had thrown into the sky, converted the energy to the city's use, providing from its silver mesh latticework the juice to keep London alive. It was the Geodex dome that held sufficient backup force to keep the perimeter ring strong enough to thwart the thief. He dodged in and out of reach of the cats; the falcon tracked him, waiting.

"It's taking you longer to do it each time," said the Catman.

The thief dematerialized five times rather quickly as the two cheetahs worked an inwardly spiraling pattern, pressing him toward a center where the panther waited patiently. "Worry about yourself," he said, breathing hard.

The falcon dove from the Catman's shoulder in a shallow arc, its wingspread slicing a fourth of the ring at head-height. The thief materialized, laying on his back, at the inner edge of the ring behind the Catman.

The panther bunched and sprang, and the thief rolled away, the stretch suit suddenly open down one side as the great cat's claws ripped the air. Then the thief was gone . . .

. . . to reappear behind the panther.

The thief held the ladybug deranger in his palm. Even as the panther sensed the presence behind him, the thief slapped the deranger down across the side of the massive head. Then the thief blinked out again.

The panther bolted, rose up on its hind legs and, without a sound, exploded.

Gears and cogs and printed circuits and LSI chips splattered against the inside of the perimeter ring . . . bits of pseudoflesh and infrared eyeballs and smears of lubricant sprayed across the invisible bubble.

The empty husk of what had been the panther lay smoking in the center of the arena. The thief appeared beside the Catman. He said nothing.

The Catman looked away. He could not stare at the refuse that had been black swiftness moments before. The thief said, "I'm sorry I had to do that."

There was a piping, sweet note in the air, and the cheetahs and the falcon froze. The falcon on the Catman's shoulder, the cheetahs sniffing at the pile of death with its stench of ozone. The tone came again. The Catman heaved a sigh, as though he had been released from some great oppression. A third time, the tone, followed by a woman's voice: "Shift end, Officer. Your jurisdiction ends now. Thank you for your evening's service. Goodspeed to you, and we'll see you nextshift, tomorrow at eleven-thirty P.M." The tone sounded once more – it was pink – and the perimeter ring dissolved.

The thief stood beside the Catman for a few more moments. "Will you be all right?"

The Catman nodded slowly, still looking away.

The thief watched him for a moment longer, then vanished. He reappeared at the far side of the Geodex and looked back at the tiny figure of the Catman, standing unmoving. He continued to watch till the police officer walked to the heap of matted and empty blackness, bent and began gathering up the remnants of the panther. The thief watched silently, the weight of the Antarean soul-radiant somehow oppressively heavy in the bag of confounders.

The Catman took a very long time to gather up his dead stalker. The thief could not see it from where he stood, so far away, but he knew the Catman was crying.

The air sparked around him . . . as though he had not quite decided to teleport himself . . . and in fact he had not been able to make the decision . . . and the air twinkled with infinitesimal scintillas . . . holes made in the fabric of normal space through which the displaced air was drawn, permitting the thief to teleport . . . the sparkling points of light actually the deaths of muons as they were sucked through into that not-space . . . and still he could not decide.

Then he vanished and reappeared beside the Catman.

"Can I help you?"

The Catman looked away quickly. But the thief saw the tears that had run down the Catman's black cheeks. "No, thank you, I'll be all right. I'm almost finished here." He held a paw.

The thief drew a deep breath. "Will you be home for dinner tonight?"

The Catman nodded. "Tell your mother I'll be along in a little while."

The thief went away from there, in twenty level leaps, quickly, trying not to see a black hand holding an even blacker paw.

They sit silently at the dinner table. Neil Leipzig cannot look at his father. He sits cross-legged on the thin pneumatic cushion, the low teak table before him; the *Estouffade de boeuf* on his plate vanishes and reappears. It is wallaby, smothered in wine sauce and "cellar vegetables" from sub-level sixteen-North. It continues to appear and disappear.

"Stop playing with your food," Neil Leipzig's mother says, sharply.

"Leave me alone; I'm not hungry," he says.

They sit silently. His father addresses his food, and eats quickly but neatly.

"How was your shiftday?" Neil Leipzig's mother says.

Neither of the men looks up. She repeats the question, adding, "Lew." His father looks up, nods abstractedly, does not answer, returns to his plate.

"Why is it impossible to get a civil word out of you in the evening," she says. There is an emerging tone in her voice, a tone of whitewater rapids just beyond the bend. "I ask: why is it impossible for you to speak to your family?"

Keep eating, don't let her do it to you again, Neil Leipzig thinks. He moves the cubes of soybean curd around in the *sauce madère* until they are all on the right side of the plate. *Keep silent, tough up*, he thinks.

"Lewis!"

His father looks up. "I think I'll go downstairs and take a nap, after dinner." His eyes seem very strange; there is a film over them; something gelatinous; as though he is looking out from behind a thick, semi-opaque membrane; neither Neil nor his mother can read the father's thoughts from those eyes.

She shakes her head and snorts softly, as though she is infinitely weary of dealing with those who persist in their arrogance and stupidity; there was none of that in what the father had said. *Let him alone, can't you?* Neil Leipzig thinks.

"We're out of deeps," the mother says.

"I won't need them," the father says.

"You know you can't sleep without a deep, don't try and tell me you can. We're out, someone will have to order more."

Neil Leipzig stands up. "I'll order them; finish your dinner."

He goes into the main room and punches out the order on the board. He codes it to his mother's personal account. Let *her* pay, he thinks. The confirmation tones sound, and he returns to the table. From the delivery chute comes the sound of the spansules arriving. He stands there staring down at his parents, at the top of his father's head, black and hairless, faintly mottled; at his mother's face, pale and pink, heavily freckled from the treatment machine she persists in using though the phymech advises her it is having a deleterious effect on her skin: she wants a tan for her own reasons but is too fair and redheaded for it to take, and she merely freckles. She has had plasticwork done on her eyes, they slant in a cartoon imitation of the lovely Oriental curve.

He is brown.

"I have to go out for a while."

His father looks up. Their eyes meet.

"No. Nothing like that," he lies. His father looks away.

His mother catches the exchange. "Is there something new between you two?"

Neil turns away. She follows him with her eyes as he starts for the tunnel to his own apartments. "Neil! What *is* all this? Your father acts like a burnout, you won't eat, I've had just about enough of this! Why do you two continue to torment me, haven't I had enough heartache from the both of you? Now you come back here, right here, right now, I want us to have this out." He stops.

He turns around. His expression is a disguise.

"Mother, do us both a favor," he says, quite clearly, "kindly shut your mouth and leave me alone." He goes into the tunnel, is reduced to a beam of light, is fired through the tunnel to his apartments seven miles away across the arcology called London, is retranslated, vanishes.

His mother turns to her husband. Alone now, freed of even the minor restraints imposed on her by the presence of her son, she assumes a familiar emotional configuration. "Lewis."

He wants to go lie down. He wants that very much.

"I want to know!"

He shakes his head gently. He merely wants to be left alone. There is very little of the Catman now; there is almost too much of Lewis Leipzig. "Please, Karin . . . it was a miserable shiftday."

She slips her blouse down off one perfect breast. The fine powder-white lines of the plasticwork radiate out from the meaty nipple, sweep down and around and disappear under the lunar curve. He watches, the film over his eyes growing darker, more opaque. "Don't," he says.

She touches a blue-enameled fingernail to the nipple, indenting it slightly. "There'll be bed tonight, Lewis."

He starts to rise.

"There'll be bed, and sex, and other things if you don't tell me, Lewis."

He slumps back into his round-shouldered dining position. He can hear the whine of generators far back in his memory. And the odor of dead years. And oil slicks across stainless steel. And the rough sensuality of burlap.

"He was out tonight. Robbery on the ninetieth level. He got away with three tubes of the Antarean soul-radiant."

She covers her breast, having won her battle with nasty weaponry, rotted memories. "And you couldn't stop him."

"No. I couldn't stop him."

"And what else?"

"I lost the panther."

Her expression is a combination of amazement and disgust. "He destroyed it?" Her husband nods; he cannot look at her. "And it'll be charged against your account." He does not nod; she knows the answer.

"That's it for the promotion, and that's it for the permutations. Oh, God, you're such a burnout . . . I can't stand you!"

"I'm going to lie down."

"You just sit there. Now listen to me, damn you, Lewis Leipzig. *Listen!* I will *not* go another year without being rejuvenated. You'll *get* that promotion and you'll get it bringing him in. Or I'll make you wish I'd never filed for you." He looks at her sharply.

She knows what he's thinking, knows the reply; but he doesn't say it; he never does.

He gets up and walks toward the dropshaft in the main room. Her voice stops him. "You'll make up your mind, Lewis."

He turns on her. The film is gone from his eyes. "It's our son, Karin. Our son!"

"He's a thief," she says. The edge in her voice is a special viciousness. "A thief in a time when theft is unnecessary. We have everything. Almost everything. You know what he does with what he steals. You know what he's become. That's no son of mine. Yours, if you want that kind of filth around you, but no son of mine. God knows I have little enough to live for, and I'm not going to allow your spinelessness to take *that* from me. I want my permutation. You'll do it, Lewis, or so help me God—"

He turns away again. Hiding his face from her, he says, "I'm only permitted to stalk him during regulation hours, you know that."

"Break the regs."

He won't turn around. "I'm a Catman. I can't do that. I'm bound."

"If you don't, I'll see that someone else does."

"I'm beginning not to care."

"Have it your way."

"Your way."

"My way then. But my way *whichever* way."

He vanishes into the main room and a moment later she hears the dropshaft hiss. She sits at the table staring into the mid-distance, remembering. Her face softens and flows and lines of weariness superimpose themselves over her one-hundred-and-sixty-five-year-old youthful face. She drops her face into her hand, runs the fingers up through her thick coppery hair, the metal fingernails making tiny clicking noises against the fibers and follicles. She makes a sound deep in her throat. Then she stiffens her back and rises. She stands there for several moments, listening to the past; she shrugs the robe from her slim, pale body and follows her husband's path to the dropshaft.

The dining salon is empty. From the main room comes the hiss of the dropshaft. Menials purr from the walls and clean up the dining area. Below, punishment and coercion reduce philosophies to diamond dust and suet.

Seven miles away, the thief reappears in his cool apartments. The sights and sounds of what he has overheard and seen between his parents, hidden in the main room till his father left his mother, tremble in his mind. He finds himself rubbing the palm of his left hand up the wall, rubbing over and over without control; his hand hurts from the friction but he doesn't stop. He rubs and rubs till his palm is bloody. Then he vanishes, illegally.

Sub-level one:eleven-Central was converted to ocean. Skipboats sliced across from Oakwood on the eastern shore to Caliban on the western cliffs. In the coves and underwater caves sportsmen hunted loknesses, bringing home trophies that covered large walls. Music was bubblecast across the water. Plankton beaneries bobbed like buoys near the tourist shores. Full Fathom Five had gotten four stars in *The Epicure* and dropshafts carried diners to the bottom to dine in elegance while watching the electro stims put on their regularly scheduled shows among the kelp beds. Neil Leipzig emerged into the pulsing ocher throat of the reception area, and was greeted by the maître d'.

"Good evening, Max. Would Lady Effim and her party be here yet?"

The maître d' smiled and his neck-slits opened and closed to reveal a pink moistness. "Not yet, Mr Leipzig. Would you care to wait at the bar? Or one of the rooms?"

"I'll be at the bar. Would you let them know I'm here when they arrive?"

The thief let the undulant carry him into the bar and he slid into a seat beside the great curved pressure window. The kelp beds were alive with light and motion.

"Sir?"

The thief turned from watching the light-play. A domo hovered at the edge of the starburst-shaped table. "Oh. A chin-chin, please, a little heavier on the Cinzano." The domo hummed a thankyou and swirled away. Neil Leipzig turned back to the phantasmagoria beyond the pressure window. A bubble of music struck the window and burst just beyond the thief's nose. He knew the tune.

"Neil."

The thief saw her reflection, dimly, in the window. He did not turn around for a moment, gathering his feelings. "Joice," he said, finally. "Nice to see you again."

"Then why don't you turn around so you *can*."

He let the seat turn him toward her.

She was still remarkable. He wanted to see dust marks on her loveliness, product of treachery and floating ethics, but he knew she had not really been treacherous, and if there had been an ethical failure, it had been his.

"May I sit?"

"I'm going to be joining a party in a few minutes, but please . . ." He waved her to the seat beside him. She settled into it, crossing her legs. The chiton opened and revealed smooth thigh vanishing up into ivory fabric. "How have you been?"

"I've been excellent, Neil. Breve sends his best."

"That was unnecessary."

"I'm trying to be reasonable, Neil. It's been a long time and I'm uncomfortable with it this way between us."

"Be comfortable. I've got it all straight."

"I'm trying to be friendly."

"Just be reasonable, that'll be enough."

The domo came bobbing through the room and hovered beside the table. It set the chin-chin down. The thief sipped and nodded acceptance. "Lady?" the domo hummed.

"Nothing for me, thanks."

The domo shot straight up and went away just below ceiling height.

"Are you still doing dust?" she asked.

He stiffened and his eyes came to her face with anger as he stopped watching the domo. "Your manners haven't improved any with time."

She started to say I'm sorry. But his anger continued to sheet: "If we run out on *that* topic, we can always discuss Breve's throat!"

"Oh, God, Neil, that's unfair . . . unfair and *lousy*!"

"I understand from one of the twinkle boys that Breve's using some new steroid vexing agent and a stim-sensitive synthetic that lets him vibrate it like mad. Must be terrific for you . . . when he's not with twinkles."

Joice pressed a fingertip against the room-call plate set into the surface of the starburst-shaped table. Near the reception area Max heard the tone on his console, noted it was Neil Leipzig's table, punched up an empty, and made a mental note to let Lady Effim know the thief was in a room, when she and her party arrived. At the starburst-shaped table, the number 22 pulsed in the translucent face of the room-call plate.

"All right. Neil. Enough already. Overkill doesn't become you."

She stood up.

"And mealy-mouth attempts at *bonhomie* don't become you."

He stood up.

"It's simply I see no reason why we have to be on the outs. There are still some good memories."

Side by side, they walked across the enormous dining room of the Full Fathom Five, toward the curving wall of glass-fronted private rooms.

"Look, Joice: I don't want to talk about it. You stopped to talk to *me*, remember? I didn't force myself on *you*."

"Just now, or three years ago?"

He couldn't help laughing. "Point for you," he said, opening the door to the private room. The magnifying glass of the room's front wall curved the diners beyond into a mere smear of moving color. From outside, the tableau in the room was cast large for anyone to watch.

"I'm sorry I said that about the dust," Joice said, slipping the soft fabric of the chiton off her shoulders. It floated to the floor like fog.

"I'm not sorry about my comments where Breve is concerned," Neil replied. Naked, he moved his shoulder blades in a loosening movement, realizing the scene with his parents had made him unbelievably tense. He slid into the free-fall cumulus fizz and lay on his back.

"Gardyloo!" she said, and dove into the mist beside him. Her long auburn hair floated wildly around her head.

"What the hell's all this in aid of, Joice?" the thief said. She rolled him under her, sitting astride his thighs, positioning herself above his erect penis.

"Peaceful coexistence," she said, and settled down slowly till he was deep up inside her.

"Has he filed for you?"

"No."

"Does he intend to?"

"I have no idea."

"You've gotten more *laissez-faire* since we were a pair. I can't recall a week when you weren't badgering me to file."

"I loved you."

"And you don't love Breve."

She moved her hips in a circular pattern. He contracted and expanded his penis in a steady pulse. She leaned back and rested her hands on his upper thighs, sliding up and down smoothly.

"I didn't say I don't love Breve. He just hasn't filed and it isn't a problem at the moment."

"Why don't *you* file for *him*?"

"Don't be cruel; you *know* Breve isn't in the Pool."

"So what *is* the problem? Twinkles?"

"Don't be ridiculous."

He freed one hand and, pressing her lower lips, very gently sought out and stroked the mercury heaviness of her clitoris. She shuddered and opened her eyes, then they slid closed once more.

"Then what is?"

"There's nothing wrong between us. He's doing very well, his work is going well, and I'm fulfilled. It's a good merging."

She spasmed, from deep in her stomach muscles, and he felt her contracting around him. When she climaxed it was with a succession of small ignitions. He continued touching her, maintaining a rhythm, and she spiraled upward through a chain of multiple orgasms till she dropped her upper body onto him, reached under to grasp his buttocks, and thrust herself up and down rapidly. He thought of metal surfaces.

She forced air through her clenched teeth and groaned from low in her throat, and he felt her rising for the final ascent. When it came, Neil held his breath and could feel the sudden cessation of her heartbeat. They rolled and turned in the free-fall mist, and Joice spasmed for half a minute.

They lay locked together for a time, and then she raised her head and looked down at him. "Nothing happened."

"For me. You're fine."

"Too much dust, Neil?"

"Too little interest."

"I don't believe that."

"Life is filled with little disappointments."

"You make me feel sad."

"Life is filled with little disappointments."

She pulled off him and reached for a moist and scented serviette in a dispenser on the wall. She dried herself between her legs and swam out of the fizz. Neil Leipzig lay on his back, at a forty-five degree angle to the floor, hanging artfully in mid-air, and watched her. "I don't regret losing you, Joice. I have more to work with, now that your appetites are satisfied at other groaning boards."

"Spare me the metaphors, Neil. Are you aware that in most circles you're considered ridiculous?"

"I seldom travel in those circles. It must get you dizzy."

"Hurting each other won't make the past more liveable."

"I don't live in the past."

"That's right, I forgot. You live in tin cans."

He felt his face getting hot. Too close, she'd come too close with that one. "Goodbye, Joice. Don't slam the door."

She draped the chiton over her arm, opened the door and stepped partially into the dining room proper. "Don't get metal splinters in your cock." She smiled a smile of victory and closed the door behind her. Softly.

He watched her striding across the Full Fathom Five to join a group of Twinkles, Dutchgirls, a Duenna . . . and Breve. As she moved, she was comically distorted by the magnifying window. It was like watching her stride through rainbows. She sat down with them and Breve helped her into the chiton. Neil smiled and with a shrug reached for a serviette.

The door opened, and the maître d' stuck his head in. "Mr Leipzig, Lady Effim and her party have arrived. The coral room. Would you like your drink sent over?"

"Thank you, Max. No, a fresh one, please. Chin-chin, a little heavier on the Cinzano. And tell Lady Effim I'll be there in a moment."

He lay in the fizz for a few minutes, thinking of metal surfaces, his eyes closed, fists clenched.

The thief had no real, concrete data on what Lady Effim's side-boys did to earn their keep, but he was gut certain it was at least partially sexual in nature; and Neil Leipzig did not dismiss the possibility that another part of their services dealt with various deaths; and that another substantial expenditure of their time in her behalf was legitimately connected with the continent she owned and exploited; and that other time was spent in *il*legitimate pursuits; and darker times spent in places, and doing things, the thief did not wish to dwell on.

The side-boys numbered three this time. Sometimes Lady Effim had six, sometimes eight, sometimes a squad. Never less than three. This time there were three.

One was obviously a twinkle: fishtailed hair parted in the middle, tinted blue-black like the barrel of a weapon, giving off the warm odor of musk and jasmine. Very slim; hands delicate and skin of the hands so pale Neil could see the calligraphy of blue veins clearly outlined; large nostrils that scooped air so the twinkle's chest rose and fell noticeably; skintight weskit suit with metal conchos and leather thongs down both sides; heavy on the jewelry.

"Neil, I'd like you to meet Cuusadou . . ."

The second was some kind of professional student: his like were to be found in the patiently seated waiting lines of the career bureaus, always ready to file for some obscure and pointless occupation – numismatist, dressage instructor, Neurospora geneticist, epitaphologist, worm rancher. His face was long and horsy; his tongue was long and he could bend its tip back on itself; he wore the current fashion, velvet jodhpurs, boots, rhodium manacles with jeweled locks, dark wrap-around glasses. He had bad skin and his fingernails were long, but the quicks were bitten and bloody down around the moons.

". . . and Fill . . ."

The third was a killer. He made no movement. His eyes stared straight ahead and Neil perceived the psychotic glaze. He did not look at the third man for more than a second. It was painful.

". . . and Mr Robert Mossman."

She invited him to join them, and Neil took the empty formfit where the domo had set his chin-chin. He settled into the chair and crossed his legs. "How've you been?"

Lady Effim smiled a long, thin smile of memories and expectations. "Warm. And you?"

"All right, I suppose."

"How is your father?"

"Excellent. He sends his best."

"That was unnecessary."

Neil laughed. "Less than an hour ago I said the same thing to someone. Excuse me; I'm a little cranky tonight."

She waved away his apology with a friendly, imperious gesture. "Has the city changed much?"

"Since when?"

"Last time." That had been six years earlier.

"Some. They turned the entire fourteenth level into crystal cultures. Beautiful. Peculiar. Waste of space. Helluva controversy, lot of people making speeches, the screens were full of it. I went off to the Hebrides."

She laughed. The crepe texture of her facial skin made it an exercise in origami. Neil gave it a moment's thought: having sex with this creature, this power, this force of nature. It was more than wealth that kept three such as these with this woman. Neil began to understand the attraction. The cheekbones, the timbre of her voice, ice.

"Still vanishing, Neil?" She said it with amusement.

"You're playing with me."

"Only a little. I have a great affection for you, darling. You know that. You amuse me."

"How are things in Australia?"

Lady Effim turned to Fill. For the answer.

"Cattle production is up two hundred percent, trawling acreage is yielding half a million barrels of lettuce a month, tithes are up point three three over last year at this time, and Standard & Poor's Index closed up eight points today."

Neil smiled. "What about all the standard poor bastards who were wiped out when the tsunami hit two weeks ago?"

Everyone stopped smiling. Lady Effim sat straighter and her left hand – which had been dangling a gold-link chain and baited fishhook in her jeroboam snifter of brandy in an attempt to snag the Antarean piranha before it bellied-up – the hand made a convulsive clenching movement. The killer's eyes came off dead center and snapped onto the thief with an almost audible click: the sound of armaments locked into firing position. Neil held his breath.

"Mr Mossman," Lady Effim said, slowly, "*no.*"

The air began to scintillate around Neil.

"Neil," said Lady Effim.

He stopped. The air settled. Mr Robert Mossman went back to rigidity.

Lady Effim smiled. It reminded the thief of an open wound. "You've grown suicidal in six years, Neil darling. Something unpleasant is happening to you; you're not the sweet, dashing lad I used to know. Death-wish?"

Neil smiled back, it seemed the thing to do. "Getting reckless in my declining years. I'm going to have to come visit your continent one of these days, m'Lady."

She turned to the twinkle. "Cuusadou, what are we doing for the company peasants who were affected by the disaster?"

The twinkle leaned forward and, with relish, said, "An absolutely splendid advertising campaign, Lady Effim: squawk, solids, car-cards, wandering evangelists, rumors, and in three days a major holo extravaganza. Our people have been on it since almost before the tide went out. Morale is very high. We've established competition between the cities: The one that mounts the most memorable mass burial ceremony gets a new sports arena. Morale is *very* high." He looked pleased.

"Thank you, darling," she said. She turned back to Neil. "I am a kind and benevolent ruler."

Neil smiled and spread his hands. "Your pardon."

It went that way for the better part of an hour.

Finally, Lady Effim said to Fill, "Darling, would you secure the area, please." The professional student fiddled with the jeweled lock on the right-wrist manacle, and a sliding panel in the manacle opened to reveal a row of tiny dials under a fingernail-sized meter read-out window. He turned the dials and a needle in the meter window moved steadily from one side to the other. When it had snugged up against the far side, he nodded obsequiously to Lady Effim.

"Good. We're alone. I gather you've been up to some nasty tricks, Neil darling. You haven't been teleporting illegally when you were offshift, have you?" She wore a nasty smile that should have been on display in a museum.

"I have something you want," Neil said, ignoring the chop. She knew he was breaking the regs at this very moment:

"I have to go out for a while."

His father looks up. Their eyes meet.

"No. Nothing like that," he lies. His father looks away.

He rubs and rubs till his palm is bloody. Then he vanishes, illegally.

"I'm sure you do, Neil *mon cher*. You always do. But what could *I* possibly have that would interest *you*? If you want something you go to the cornucopia and you punch it up and those cunning little atoms are rearranged cunningly and there you have it. Isn't that the way it's done?"

"There are things one can't get . . ."

"But those are illegal, darling. *So* illegal. And it seems foolish to want one of the few things you *can't* have in a world that permits virtually *every*thing."

"There are still taboos."

"I can't conceive of such a thing, Neil dear."

"Force yourself."

"I'm a woman of very simple tastes."

"The radiant."

It was only the most imperceptible of movements, but Neil Leipzig knew the blood had stopped pumping in Lady Effim's body. Beneath her chalky powder she went white. He saw the thinnest line of the biting edges of her teeth.

"So you did it."

Now the smile was Neil Leipzig's.

"A thief in a time of plenty. So you did it. You clever lad." Her eyes closed and she was thinking of the illegal Antarean drug. Here was a thrill she had never had. Farewell to ennui. She would, of course, have it, at any cost. Even a continent. It was a seller's market.

"What do you want?"

She would have it at any cost. Human lives: these three, his own. His father's.

His mother's.

"What do you want, Neil?"

His thoughts were a million miles away. A lie. They were only arcology levels above and across London.

"*You!* What do you want?"

So he told her.

He would have preferred the other three not be there. The look of revulsion on their faces – even the zombie Mr Robert Mossman's – made him defensive.

Lady Effim sneered. It did not become her. "You shall have it, Neil. As often as you care to go, God help you." She paused, looked at him in a new way. "Six years ago . . . when I knew you . . . were you . . ."

"No, not then."

"I never would have thought – of all the people I know, and you may be assured, dear boy, I know oddnesses beyond description – of all I know, I would have thought you were the last to . . ."

"I don't want to hear this."

"Of course not, how gauche of me. Of course, you shall have what you need. When I have. What. I. Need."

"I'll take you to it."

She seemed amused. "Take *me* there? Don't be silly, dear boy. I'm a very famous, very powerful, very influential person. I have no truck with stolen merchandise, not even any as exotic and lovely as soul-radiant." She turned to the killer. "Mr Mossman. You will go with Neil and obtain three tubes from where he has them secreted. No, don't look suspicious. Neil will deliver precisely what he has said he would deliver. He understands we are both dealing in good faith."

The twinkle said, "But he's . . ."

"It is not our place to make value-judgments, darling. Neil is a sweet boy, and what he needs he shall have." To Mr Robert Mossman: "When you have the three tubes, call me here." To the thief: "When I receive Mr Mossman's call, Fill will make the arrangements and you'll receive very explicit instructions where to go, and when. Is that satisfactory?"

Neil nodded, his stomach tight, his head beginning to hurt. He did not like their knowing.

"Now," Lady Effim said, "goodbye, Neil.

"I don't think I would care to see you again. Ever. You understand this contains no value-judgment, merely a preference on my part."

She did not offer her hand to be kissed as he and Mr Robert Mossman rose to leave the table.

The thief materialized on the empty plain far beyond the arcology of London. He was facing the gigantic structure and stared at it for minutes without really seeing it: eyes turned inward. It was near sunset and all light seemed to be gathered to the ivory pyramid that dominated the horizon. "Cradle of the sun," he said softly, and winked out of existence again. Behind him, the city of London rose into the clouds and was lost to sight. The apartments of the Prince of Wales were, at that moment, passing into darkness.

The next materialization was in the midst of a herd of zebra, grazing at tall stands of deep blue grass. They bolted at his appearance, shying sidewise and boiling away from him in a mass of flashing lines of black and white. He smiled, and started walking. The air vibrated with the smell of animal fur and clover. Walking would be a pleasure. And mint.

His first warning that he was not alone came with the sound of a flitterpak overhead. It was a defective: he should not have been able to hear its power-source. He looked up and a woman in torn leathers was tracking his passage across the veldt. She had a norden strapped to her front and he had no doubt the sights were trained on him. He waved to her, and she made no sign of recognition. He kept walking, into the darkness, attempting to ignore her; but his neck itched.

He vanished; to hell with her; he couldn't be bothered.

When he reappeared, he was in the trough of a dry wash that ran for several miles and came to an end, when he had vanished and reappeared again, at the mouth of a cave that angled downward sharply into the ground. He looked back along the channel of the arroyo. He was in the foothills. The mountains bulked purple and distant in the last fading colors of dusk. The horizon was close. The air was very clear, the wind was rising; there were no sounds but those of insects foretelling the future.

He approached the cave mouth and stopped. He sat down on the ground and leaned back on his elbows. He closed his eyes. They would come soon enough, he was certain.

He waited, thinking of nothing but metal surfaces.

In the night, they came for him.

He was half-asleep. Lying up against the incline of the arroyo, his thoughts fading in and out of focus like a radio signal from a transmitter beyond the hills. Oh, bad dreams. Not even subtle, not even artful metaphors. The spider was clearly his mother, the head pink and heavily freckled, redheaded, and slanting Oriental cartoon eyes. The Mameluke chained between the pillars was bald and old, and the face held an infinite weariness in its expression. The Praetorian with the flamethrower was himself, the searing wash of jellied death appearing and vanishing, being and being gone. He understood. Only a fool would not understand; he was weary, as his father was weary, but he was no fool. He burned the webbing. Again and again. Only to have it spring into existence each time. He came fully awake before the cone-muzzle of the weapon touched his shoulder.

Came awake with the web untouched, covering the world from

horizon to horizon, the spider crawling down the sky toward the weary black man hanging between the pillars.

"You were told I'd be coming," he said. It was only darkness in front of him, but darkness *within* a darkness, and he knew someone stood there, very close to him, the weapon pointed at his head.

He knew it. Only a fool would not have known. Now he was awake, and he was no fool.

The voice that answered from the deeper darkness was neither male nor female, neither young nor old, neither deep nor high. It sounded like a voice coming from a tin cup. Neil knew he had been honorably directed; this was the place, without doubt. He saluted Lady Effim's word of honor with a smile. The voice from the tin cup said, "You're supposed to giving me a word, isn't it?"

"The word you want is *Twinkle*."

"Yeah, that was to being the word. I'm to your being took downstairs now. C'mon."

The thief rose and brushed himself off.

He saw movement from the corner of his eye. But when he turned to look, there was nothing.

He followed the shadow as it moved toward the cave mouth. There was no Moon, and the faraway ice-chips of the stars gave no heat, gave no light. It was merely a shadow he followed: a shadow with its weapon carried at port arms.

They passed into the mouth of the cave, and the dirt passage under their feet began to slope down sharply almost at once. There were two more shadows inside the mouth of the cave, hunkered down, looking like piles of rags, features indistinct, weapon barrels protruding from the shapeless masses like night-blooming flowers of death.

One of them made a metallic sound when it brushed against the wall. It. Neither he nor she. It.

Neil Leipzig followed the shadow down the steep slope, holding on to the rock wall for support as his feet sought purchase. Ahead of him, his guide seemed to be talking to himself very, very softly. It sounded like a mechanical whirring. The guide was not a domo.

"Here you'll stop it," the guide said, when they had descended so deep into the cave passage that the temperature was cool and pleasant. He moved in the darkness, and the thief saw a heat-sensitive plate in the rock wall suddenly come to life with light as the guide touched it. Then a door irised open in the rock wall, and light flooded out, blinding him for a moment. He covered his eyes. The guide gave him a shove through the iris. It was neither polite help nor surly indignity. He merely shoved Neil through to get him inside. It was an old-style elevator, not a dropshaft and not a light-ray tunnel. He had no idea how long it had been here, but probably before the arcology of London.

He looked at his guide in the full light.

He felt, for the first time since . . . he felt for the first time that he wanted to go home, to stop, to go back, to return to himself before . . . to return to the past . . .

The guide was a gnome of spare human parts and rusting machinery. He was barely four feet tall, the legs bowed with the enormous weight of a metal chest like the belly of an old-time wood-burning stove. The head was hairless and the left half was a metal plate devoid of eyes, or nose, or mouth, or skin, or sweat, or pore. It was pocked and flaking metal, riveted through in uneven lines to the bone of the half of the head that was still flesh-covered. His left arm was fastened at the shoulder by a pot-metal socket covered with brazing marks. Depending from the socket were long, curved, presumably hollow levers containing sole-noids; another ball socket for elbow, another matched pair of hollow levers, ball socket wrist, solenoid fingers. His right arm was human. It held the cone-muzzled weapon: an archaic but nonetheless effective disruptor. Input sockets – some of them the ancient and corroded models housewives had found in the walls of their homes, into which they had plugged vacuum cleaners and toasters – studded both thighs, inside and out. His penis was banded with expansible mesh copper. He was barefoot; the big toe was gone on the right foot; it had been replaced with a metal stud.

Neil Leipzig felt sick. Was this—?

He stopped the thought. It had never been like this before, no reason to think it would be like this here. It couldn't be. But he felt sick. And filthy.

He was certain he had seen movement out of the corner of his eye, up there in the arroyo.

The elevator grounded, and the door irised open. He stepped out ahead of the gnome. They were in an underground tunnel, higher and wider than the one above, well lit by eterna lamps set into the tunnel's arched roof. The guide set off at a slow lope, and the thief followed him; illegal, yes . . . but how did they *live* down here, like troglodytes; was this the look of his future . . . he erased the thought . . . and could not stop thinking it.

They rounded a bend and kept going. The tunnel seemed to stretch on indefinitely. Behind him, around the bend, he thought he heard the elevator door close and the cage going back up. But he could not be certain.

They kept on in a straight line for what seemed an eighth of a mile, and when it became clear to Neil that they were going to keep going for many miles in this endless rabbit run, the guide took a sudden right turn into a niche in the right-hand wall the thief had not even suspected was there.

The niche opened into a gigantic cavern. Hewn from solid rock for a purpose long forgotten, decades before, it stretched across for several miles and arched above them in shadows the thief's eyes could not penetrate. Like the pueblo Amerinds of old, whoever lived here had carved dwellings from the rock faces and ledges. From the floor of the cavern below them, all the way up into the shadows, Neil could see men and women moving along the ledges, busy at tasks he could not name. Nor would he have bothered:

All he could see, all he could believe, was the machine that dominated the cavern floor, the computer that rose up and up past the ledge on which they stood, two hundred feet high and a quarter mile in diameter.

"*Mekcoucher*," the half-human gnome said, his voice filled with—

Neil looked down at him. The expression was beatific. Love. Awe, love, desire, respect, allegiance, love. The blasted little face twisted in what was supposed to be a sigh of adoration. Love. Mek-coo-*shay*. The French had invented the word, but the dregs of the Barcelona arcology had conceived the deed. *Mekcoucher*.

The thief touched the gnome's head. The guide looked up without surliness or animosity. His eye was wet. His nose, what there was of his nose, was running. He sobbed, and it came from deep in his stove chest, and he said again, a litany, "*Mekcoucher*. This am all I be here about, dearest shine bright. Fursday, this Fursday, I me I get turn." Neil felt a terrible kinship and pity and recycling of terror. This little thing, here beside him on this ledge, this remnant of what had once been a man, before it had begun dreaming of metal surfaces, of electric currents, of shining thighs, this thing had been no better than Neil Leipzig. Was *this* the future?

Neil could understand the gnome's orison to the machine. It was an installation to inspire homage, to lift up the heart; it was so large and so complex, it inspired deification, idolatry; it was a machine to engender devotion.

It was a sex-partner to consume one such as Neil Leipzig with trembling lust.

They started down the ledge toward the floor of the cavern, the thief with his arm around the gnome's shoulders, both of them moist-eyed and finding it difficult to breathe. At one point, Neil asked the gnome if they could stop, if they could sit down with their backs to the rock wall and just look at the incredible bulk and shapes and shining metal surfaces of the machine in the center of their world.

And they sat, and they watched.

"This is where my place I been stay long time," said the gnome, staring across at the machine. They were now only a hundred feet above the floor of the cavern, and the computer rose up before them, filling their eyes.

Neil asked the gnome his name. "Fursday," he said. "This Fursday, I me I get turn to joy."

A life centralized around his love-partner. No name other than the name that told everyone he would go to Heaven on Thursday. Neil shuddered, but it was a trembling of expectation and desire. And it was there, sitting and remembering the first time, three years earlier ... remembering the times since ... inadequate, searching, fulfilling but not fulfilling the way *this* installation, *this* carnal machine could fulfill ... he knew it ... he felt it ... his bones vibrated like tuning forks, his heart was pudding.

And it was there, sitting beside the gnome, that Mr Robert Mossman found him.

He came down the ledge behind them, walking lightly, never dislodging a shard of limestone, hardly breathing, the pounder in his right hand. The pounder hit the brain with a laser beam that had the impact of a cannonball dropped from a great height. It could turn the inside of the victim's skull to gruel without marring the outside surface. It made for neat corpses. It was final. It was utterly illegal.

The thief knew there had been noise behind them in the tunnel; there had been movement in the arroyo.

He cursed Lady Effim's word of honor.

He said nothing as the killer came down on them. Mr Robert Mossman stopped and aimed the weapon at Neil Leipzig's left eye.

"Hey!" Fursday said, seeing the silent killer for the first time. "You aren't being to come down here! I'm me I told to bring him, this one down. Stop!"

Mr Robert Mossman tracked the pen-point muzzle of the pounder through mere seconds of arc and squeezed the butt of the weapon. Light slashed across the space between them and hit the gnome with the impact of a slammed door. The recoil shuddered the killer; the little metal man was lifted and slung along the ledge. He fell flat onto his back, his human arm hanging over the edge. Neil froze for only a moment, then made a movement toward the gnome's weapon. He knew he would never make it. He could feel the pressure of Mr Robert Mossman's palm squeezing the pounder. He anticipated the slam of nova heat in his brain, and his eyes filled with light.

But it didn't come. He could not turn around. He knew the killer was savoring the moment. And *in* that moment Neil Leipzig heard the rush of displaced air, the most terrible scream in the world, and the sounds of a struggle.

He turned in time to see the falcon tear away half the killer's face and, pinions beating a blurred breaststroke against the air, the falcon bore Mr Robert Mossman over backward.

The killer fell screaming to the rocks below. The falcon skimmed above him, observing, making note of finality, and when it was satisfied that its prey was dead, it dove, ripped loose a piece of meat, and arced back up into the air, banking and turning on a wingtip, and flew to rest on the Catman's shoulder.

The smouldering ember eyes of the two cheetahs stared back at the thief.

The Catman came down the sloping ledge and helped his son to his feet. "Come home now," he said.

Neil Leipzig looked at his father, the lines of tension and sadness and weariness imprinted like circuits across the face. He moved a step closer and then he had his arms around the black man. They stood that way for seconds, and then the Catman's arms came up and circled the thief's back. They stood silently, holding each other.

When they separated, Neil was able to speak. "You didn't stay home, you followed me; all the way from the Five?"

The Catman nodded.

"But how?"

"You to the meeting, then him after you. Come home."

"Dad, it isn't your onshift, you can get yourself in a bad way. Go now, before anyone sees you." The single dead eye of the gnome stared up at the hidden roof of the cavern. Neil thought of metal surfaces. His palms were wet. The air sparkled with scintillance; he stopped it.

"You won't come back with me?"

"I can't. Please, Dad."

"You've seen what this is like. You're my son. I can't let you do it."

"Dad, go *away*. Please! I know what I'm doing."

"Neil."

"*Please*, Dad! I'm begging you. Go away."

"And nothing up there matters more than this?"

"You're not turned away? It doesn't make you sick? Not even here, not even seeing this, not even here will you make a stand? My God, Dad, can't you see you're more destroyed than I'll *ever* be, no matter *what* I do?"

"Make a stand? I'm here, aren't I?"

"Go away!" Then, trying to hurt him because he did not want him hurt, he said, "Your wife is waiting for you."

"Stop it, Neil. She was your mother once."

"The once and never mother to the pervert thief. And you, her consort. Lovely. You want me to come back to that? I won't let my eyes see it again. Not ever."

"How long have you been—"

"How long have I been like this?" He waved an arm at the great machine. "Three years."

"But there was Joice, we thought, your mother and I thought."

"It didn't work. It wasn't enough."

"Neil, *please*, it's not for you. It's—"

"It's what, Dad, it's what? Perverted? Nauseating? Destructive? Pointless? I could apply them all to the way you live with her."

"Will they come up here after us?" He nodded toward the ledges of cave dwellings and the people moving about them.

"I don't think so, I don't know, but I don't think so. Everything was arranged. I don't know why that one—" and he indicated the body of Mr Robert Mossman below, "—I don't know why he came after me. But that doesn't matter. Go back. Get out of here. Your promotion, your job, it's almost time for the permutations, God knows that bitch won't give you a moment's peace if she doesn't get rejuvenated. *You're offshift, Dad!* You've never even *bent* a reg before . . . please get the hell out of here and leave me alone."

"You don't understand her."

"I don't *want* to understand her. I've lived with her for twenty-eight years."

"You won't come back with me?"

"No."

"Then let me stay."

The cheetahs closed their eyes and dropped their heads onto their paws. The falcon shrugged and ruffled itself.

"You're out of your mind. Do you know what I'm here for . . . of course you know . . . go *home*!"

So they walked down past the still body of the little metal and flesh gnome, down the ledge, down to the floor of the great cavern, the thief, the policeman and the animals padding along behind. They paused at the body of Mr Robert Mossman, and Neil Leipzig, to make certain he knew what he was walking into, took the killer's communication phone from his ring finger, called Lady Effim, and told her what had happened. She said, "I apologize, Neil. My companions are, how can I put it meaningfully, *devoted* to me. Mr Mossman was very much on his own. I regret his death, but I regret even more that this has caused you to doubt my word. You have my assurance everything was ordered correctly for your arrival. You won't be troubled again. And again, I ask your pardon." He turned her off and he went with his father to the village of the computer.

"For the last time: will you leave now? I don't want you to see this."

"I'll stay. I'll be right over here. Perhaps later . . ."

"No. Even if I go back, I'll only come here again. I know what I need."

"I'll have to keep tracking you."

"That's your job."

The thief held a tiny inhalation tube filled with soft, feathery yellow dust. He had received it from the hand of the cyborg woman who ran the computer's village. It was called The Dust, and spoken of reverently. It was much finer and looked more potent than any Dust Neil Leipzig had ever used. He knew what was going to happen, and could only guess at the intensity of the experience.

The world aboveground was free, totally and utterly free. There were no boundaries, no taboos beyond causing other's harm. And even in such a world, *this* was forbidden. The last, the final, the ultimate sexual experience.

"I'll wait."

He didn't answer. He removed his clothes, walked to the towering bulk of the computer and touched it.

The crackle-finish surface of its north flank was smooth and cool to his touch. He felt sensuality pulsing in the machine. They had exposed the leads for him, and he paused for a moment to consider what obligations they must owe Lady Effim for them to give him The Dust, to permit him *Mekcoucher* time with their love-partner. The dwellers in this subterranean hideaway. They were *all* like Fursday. Advanced stages of love commitment to this machine. Part metal, part human, totally the computer's property. Helpless to deny their passion. He grabbed the leads.

The blue lead went into the surgically implanted socket on the inside of his right thigh, the red input lead went into the socket on the inside of his left thigh. The "stim" electrodes found their proper areas through his hair and scalp. He merely placed the medusa cap on his head and they wriggled to their proper clips, sank their fangs, wire snakes. One lead hooked him into the plethysmograph and the Lissajous oscilloscope and the GSR galvanometer. The velcro band containing a million black-dot photocells was ready and he wrapped it around his penis. Then he snorted The Dust, the yellow wonder from Barcelona.

He lay up against the metal body of the machine, arms out cruciform, legs spread, cheek flat to the waiting surface. He could feel the expectancy in the computer, hungry lover.

He thought of the first time he had made love to Joice, the feel of her flesh. It was not enough.

Then he contracted the muscles in his thighs and closed the circuits.

Instantly, the metal of the machine began to flow. He felt himself sinking into the north flank of the computer. His fingers penetrated the metal as easily as if it had been modeling clay. He began to get proprioceptive feedback from muscle activity . . . he could feel the whorls on his fingertips as sucking whirlpools, dark swirling waters that drew his blood and bones through the flesh and out into the machine, spinning the essence of his physical being away from its skin container . . . his chest began to harden, to vibrate with sound like a thunder sheet of aluminum . . . the soles of his feet melted and his arches flattened and his lower legs oozed into puddles of mercury . . . he sank into the machine, was enclosed, its arms around him, welcoming him . . .

The Dust blew in hurricane clouds through his body and puffed out through the great smooth apertures in his head and back and buttocks. The Dust mingled with lubricant and it was altered, even as he was altered.

He perceived with purest immediacy the sense of his positioning of arms and legs and ferrite cores and LSI circuits and bowels and conductors and limbs and body and plates and fissures and counterweights and glands and wiring in the immediate environment that he was the machine had begun to be him.

Then the auditory and visual feedback began, delayed responses, an instant later than they should have been. He spoke: *Oh, good* and it repeated from another mouth a moment later, *ood.* Echolalia.

He felt his penis engorging with blood and felt the density of light increasing in the capillaries as the plethysmograph measured his arousal in a new language the machine he was the machine interpreted . . . the density of light decreased . . . increased . . . decreased . . . increased . . .

He spiraled upward into the machine – Lissajous pattern oscilloscope sine and cosine waves from the x and y axes actually came together, pulsated in three dimensions and he teased himself the machine he the man with vernier knob stimulation – it came out green and the machine trembled, began to secrete testosterone, estrogen, progesterone . . .

She, the machine, he, the machine, she, the man, he, the machine . . . the man, he becoming she becoming machine . . .

His heart was pudding.

The Lissajous pulsations became hallucinations in the sex

organs of the computer . . . galvanic skin response on the galvanometer . . . aching in his spine . . .

Sinking slowly into a sea of oil. Great skyscraper bulk of metalflesh slowly warmly moistly sinking into a sea of blue-black oil. Pumping. Pumping. Wet closing over his head, running in waves over his naked body. Invisible mat of hair covering every plate and surface, a fine golden down, soaking up oil, engorging, coming to climax.

Her breasts were warm, the rivets sensitive to each feather caress of electric stim. Her vagina filled with soft, melting things that went up and up and roughened the oil-slick inner surfaces, sliding to touch and knead the vulva. *So good. Ood.*

His memory, he could see everything in his memory, stored in the banks, every moment of his life from the first dripping emergence from the vats, the running, the extruding, the rolling, the flattening, the cutting, the shaping, the forming, the welding. Every moment of his life: the instant he was first engaged, the circuits closing, the surge of power, the first inputs, the primary runs, every boring clearing procedure, every exercise, every erroneous output.

His mother, his father, great cats and the wet scent of their breath, like coolant on overheated coils, the soft taste of Joice in his mouth, her body moving beneath him, sinking into her, tiniest folding of her labia around his penis, the rising to orgasm, the overloading, the heat, the peace of darkness.

Then he altered his stroke and felt the change to precognitive anticipatory feedback, telling himself how it would feel, fulfilling his own prophecies, the smell of flesh on metal, metal on flesh, the colors of whirling information, increments of semen and fused capacitors.

He was the teleport, additional human faculties, soft sponge pineal gland, polluted adrenaline, strange eyes, this was the best for me the very best I've ever hungry metal lover. They began to converge . . . everything began to converge. He, the machine called Neil Leipzig, was the x axis; he, the machine called love-partner, was the y axis; they began to converge; identical sine waves, out of phase.

His pattern was a growing. The machine's was a throbbing. He passed the machine at a higher level every pulse. The machine grew frantic and drank more power. He tried to catch up, chasing the nymphomaniacal peaks as the machine beckoned him, teased him, taunted him, drew him on, then flashed away. He extended on metal limbs, the machine's soft flesh grew sunburned and dark and leather tough.

Then he peaked out, it, she, peaked out, unable to draw more power from her source. They exchanged modes, as the point of destructive interference denied quantum mechanics and was reached: a millisecond of total sound and utter silence. Orgasm: metal became flesh, human became machine.

The interference pattern was a grating whine that became more and more pure as they came into phase. The machine, in its human throat, began to vibrate in sympathy. She, who had been Neil Leipzig at the start, captured the exponential pattern that had been his, the machine, captured it as it fell away.

They circled, and the image on the Lissajous screen became a circle as she captured the machine and held her in phase again. Prolate and oblate: two dimensional images slowing, softening, dimming, the message of release and surcease .986, 1.0014, .9999986, 1.00000000014 . . .

The first thing he heard was the sound of the two cheetahs attacking something, agony and fury. The first thing he saw was the dying point of green light on the oscilloscope screen. The first thing he felt was the rough metal of his chest against the sweat-soaked north flank of his love-partner.

He was dry. As though he had given the machine a transfusion, as if it had sucked all the juices from him. He understood why Joice and all the others, as free as they had been, had been unable to arouse him in times past, how the first *Mekcoucher* with its promises of *this*, had led him farther and farther into the inevitability of what he had just experienced.

Now, for the first time in his life, he knew what passion could lead through, what it led to inexorably. And he knew he could never go back. He would stay here, in this terrible place, with these others who shared his lover, and this was all he wanted.

He fell away from the machine and lay on the rock floor of the cavern. His breath had to be drawn in stages. His head reeled. His hand lay on his metal chest.

He wanted to sleep, but the sounds of conflict were louder now, insistent, crowding through the pain and satiation his body felt at one and the same time. He rolled over on his stomach, his chest clanking against the rock floor. *It was the best for you, too,* he thought. *The best you ever had, love-partner. You will never forget me. If I die today, you'll remember always, in every last memory cell.*

At the base of the nearest ledge, the Catman's cheetahs were struggling with one of the love-partner's people. He was down and they were savaging him, but clearly trying to avoid killing him. The thief had seen the technique before. It was called putting, as in *stay put*. The rest of the colony had no part in the melee, and were, in fact, watching with some pleasure – if pleasure could be discerned on faces that were partially metal masks.

A tall, limping, old woman with copper legs came across from the crowd. She hobbled to Neil as the Catman commanded, "Heel!" and the cheetahs left their chewed and semi-conscious prey. The Catman joined the copper-legged old woman.

The falcon looked sleepy. It was an illusion.

"Will you can stay be here with love-partner?" the old woman said. There was a tone of pleading in her voice. "Tewsday," she said, indicating the pile of worked-over flesh and metal the cheetahs had put, "he was for crazy of you with the love-partner. But I'm the saying one for your give machine love never before that fire hot. If you'll be stay this place us can make you what my is being, first lover."

The Catman moved a step closer. "Neil!"

There was raw horror on his face. He had seen his son's body vanish into the machine, had seen the machine turn soft and swallow the thief, had seen the machine sweat and go mad with lust, had seen his son emerge with his parts altered. Neil Leipzig looked at his father, and at the old woman. "I'll stay. Now go and take Tewsday for repair."

The old woman hobbled away, and the crowd went back into their rock-wall dwellings. Neil Leipzig stood facing the Catman.

"You can't. My God, Neil, *look* at you, and this is only the first time. That thing *eats* what it loves. Do you want to end up like—"

He waved a hand at the retreating mob of half-humans.

"This is where I belong. I haven't belonged up there for a long time."

"Neil, please, I'll do anything you want; resign my commission, we can go away to another city . . ."

"Dad," he said, "I have always loved you. More than I've ever been able to tell you. I always wanted you to fight back. That's all I ever wanted."

"You don't understand your mother. She's had bad times, too."

"It's all in aid of nothing. Look at you. You haven't got a dream left in the world. We're killing you a little at a time. It's time I stopped contributing to it and did something final."

"But not this, not down here, son . . ."

But the thief was gone. The air twittered with bright scintillas of fading light.

The first jump brought him back to the world embedded in the earth a quarter of a mile beneath the arroyo. Had he made such a teleportational error earlier, he would have died. But mating with the machine had altered him. The love-partner had never known a teleport, and in the exchange of modes he had been made less than machine but more than mortal. He expanded his personal space and vanished again. The second jump took him to the surface, and he winked it, out in an instant – seen by no living thing, for even the guards were dead, having been pounded by Mr Robert Mossman.

The night welcomed him, accepted his mote-outlined shadow, and took no further notice as he vanished again, reappeared, vanished, and in seconds materialized in his mother's bedroom high in London.

He leaned over and grasped her by the wrist, and wrenched her from the doze cocoon where she lay, supple and naked, the powder-white marks of the plasticwork making longitudinal lines on her breasts that glowed faintly in the night light. Her eyes snapped open as he dragged her free.

"Come along, Mom. We have to go now."

Then, clutching her naked body to his naked body, he vanished.

Before merging with the machine, he could not have carried someone with him. But everything was changed now. Vastly changed.

The Catman was high on the ledge leading to the elevator when the thief reappeared with his mother. The cheetahs padded alongside and the falcon was on the wing. The climb was a difficult one for a man that age, even with unnumbered rejuvenations. The Catman was too far away to do anything to stop him.

"Neil!"

"You're free, Dad. You're free now. Don't waste it!"

The Catman was frozen for only a moment. And in that moment Neil Leipzig carried the semiconscious body of his mother to the love-partner. The Catman screamed, a high and desolate scream because he knew what was happening. He began running down the ledge, screaming to his falcon to intercept, screaming to his cheetahs to get there before him, screaming because he could never make it in time.

The thief plugged himself in, his mother pressed flat between his naked metalflesh body and the fleshmetal north flank of his love-partner.

He flexed his thigh muscles, closed the contacts . . .

. . . and offered himself and the suddenly howling woman as the ultimate troilism.

The machine flowed, the oscilloscope formed a design no living creature had ever seen in more than three dimensions, and then, in an instant, it was over. The machine absorbed what it could not refuse, and there was only the single point of green light on the screen, and endless silence once more beneath the earth.

The Catman reached the machine, saw the beads of sweat mixed with blood that dotted the north flank, and heard fading moans of brutality that repeated soundlessly.

The Catman sits alone in a room, remembering.

The child never knew. It was not the mother. The mother always loved, but had no way of showing it. The father had never loved, and had every way of reinforcing it, day after day.

The Catman sits and mourns. Not for the child, gone and without sorrow. For the woman.

For the bond of circumstances that held them together through days and nights of a special kind of love forged in a cauldron of hate.

He will never forgive the child for having destroyed that love out of hate.

He will sit alone now. He has nothing left to live for. He hopes the child burns in a terrible Hell, even as he burns in his own. And after a while, there is always the conversing waterfall.

LOVE AND SEX AMONG THE INVERTEBRATES

Pat Murphy

*Pat Murphy's polished and inventive stories have been appearing
regularly since the early 1980s, "Rachel in Love" winning a
Nebula award in 1988 – as did her second novel,* The Falling
Woman. *Some of her fiction reflects her work at the Exploratorium,
a San Francisco museum promoting interaction between its visitors and the arts and sciences. "Love and Sex Among the Invertebrates", selected as one of the best stories of 1990, posits a
post-disaster world where sex reappears in a very strange form
indeed.*

This is not science. This has nothing to do with science. Yesterday,
when the bombs fell and the world ended, I gave up scientific
thinking. At this distance from the blast site of the bomb that took
out San Jose, I figure I received a medium-sized dose of radiation.
Not enough for instant death, but too much for survival. I have
only a few days left, and I've decided to spend this time constructing the future. Someone must do it.

It's what I was trained for, really. My undergraduate studies
were in biology – structural anatomy, the construction of body
and bone. My graduate studies were in engineering. For the past
five years, I have been designing and constructing robots for use
in industrial processing. The need for such industrial creations is
over now. But it seems a pity to waste the equipment and materials
that remain in the lab that my colleagues have abandoned.

I will put robots together and make them work. But I will not try to understand them. I will not take them apart and consider their inner workings and poke and pry and analyze. The time for science is over.

The pseudoscorpion, Lasiochernes pilosus, is a secretive scorpionlike insect that makes its home in the nests of moles. Before pseudoscorpions mate, they dance – a private underground minuet – observed only by moles and voyeuristic entomologists. When a male finds a receptive female, he grasps her claws in his and pulls her toward him. If she resists, he circles, clinging to her claws and pulling her after him, refusing to take no for an answer. He tries again, stepping forward and pulling the female toward him with trembling claws. If she continues to resist, he steps back and continues the dance: circling, pausing to tug on his reluctant partner, then circling again.

After an hour or more of dancing, the female inevitably succumbs, convinced by the dance steps that her companion's species matches her own. The male deposits a packet of sperm on the ground that has been cleared of debris by their dancing feet. His claws quiver as he draws her forward, positioning her over the package of sperm. Willing at last, she presses her genital pore to the ground and takes the sperm into her body.

Biology texts note that the male scorpion's claws tremble as he dances, but they do not say why. They do not speculate on his emotions, his motives, his desires. That would not be scientific.

I theorize that the male pseudoscorpion is eager. Among the everyday aromas of mole shit and rotting vegetation, he smells the female, and the perfume of her fills him with lust. But he is fearful and confused: a solitary insect, unaccustomed to socializing, he is disturbed by the presence of another of his kind. He is caught by conflicting emotions: his all-encompassing need, his fear, and the strangeness of the social situation.

I have given up the pretense of science. I speculate about the motives of the pseudoscorpion, the conflict and desire embodied in his dance.

I put the penis on my first robot as a kind of joke, a private joke, a joke about evolution. I suppose I don't really need to say it was a private joke – all my jokes are private now. I am the last one left, near as I can tell. My colleagues fled – to find their families, to seek refuge in the hills, to spend their last days running around, here and there. I don't expect to see anyone else around anytime soon. And if I do, they probably won't be interested in my jokes. I'm sure that most people think the time for joking is past. They don't see that the bomb and the war are the biggest jokes of all. Death is the biggest joke. Evolution is the biggest joke.

I remember learning about Darwin's theory of evolution in high school biology. Even back then, I thought it was kind of strange, the way people talked about it. The teacher presented evolution as a *fait accompli*, over and done with. She muddled her way through the complex speculations regarding human evolution, talking about *Ramapithecus*, *Australopithecus*, *Homo erectus*, *Homo sapiens*, and *Homo sapiens neanderthalensis*. At *Homo sapiens* she stopped, and that was it. The way the teacher looked at the situation, we were the last word, the top of the heap, the end of the line.

I'm sure the dinosaurs thought the same, if they thought at all. How could anything get better than armor plating and a spiked tail. Who could ask for more?

Thinking about the dinosaurs, I build my first creation on a reptilian model, a lizardlike creature constructed from bits and pieces that I scavenge from the industrial prototypes that fill the lab and the storeroom. I give my creature a stocky body, as long as I am tall; four legs, extending to the side of the body then bending at the knee to reach the ground; a tail as long as the body, spiked with decorative metal studs; a crocodilian mouth with great curving teeth.

The mouth is only for decoration and protection; this creature will not eat. I equip him with an array of solar panels, fixed to a sail-like crest on his back. The warmth of sunlight will cause the creature to extend his sail and gather electrical energy to recharge his batteries. In the cool of the night, he will fold his sail close to his back, becoming sleek and streamlined.

I decorate my creature with stuff from around the lab. From the trash beside the soda machine, I salvage aluminum cans. I cut them into a colorful fringe that I attach beneath the creature's chin, like the dewlap of an iguana. When I am done, the words on the soda cans have been sliced to nonsense: Coke, Fanta, Sprite, and Dr Pepper mingle in a collision of bright colors. At the very end, when the rest of the creature is complete and functional, I make a cock of copper tubing and pipe fittings. It dangles beneath his belly, copper bright and obscene looking. Around the bright copper, I weave a rat's nest of my own hair, which is falling out by the handful. I like the look of that: bright copper peeking from a clump of wiry black curls.

Sometimes, the sickness overwhelms me. I spend part of one day in the ladies' room off the lab, lying on the cool tile floor and rousing myself only to vomit into the toilet. The sickness is nothing that I didn't expect. I'm dying, after all. I lie on the floor and think about the peculiarities of biology.

For the male spider, mating is a dangerous process. This is especially true in the spider species that weave intricate orb-shaped webs, the kind that catch the morning dew and sparkle so nicely for nature photographers. In these species, the female is larger than the male. She is, I must confess, rather a bitch; she'll attack anything that touches her web.

At mating time, the male proceeds cautiously. He lingers at the edge of the web, gently tugging on a thread of spider silk to get her attention. He plucks in a very specific rhythm, signaling to his would-be lover, whispering softly with his tugs: "I love you. I love you."

After a time, he believes that she has received his message. He feels confident that he has been understood. Still proceeding with caution, he attaches a mating line to the female's web. He plucks the mating line to encourage the female to move onto it. "Only you, baby," he signals. "You are the only one."

She climbs onto the mating line – fierce and passionate, but temporarily soothed by his promises. In that moment, he rushes to her, delivers his sperm, then quickly, before she can change her mind, takes a hike. A dangerous business, making love.

Before the world went away, I was a cautious person. I took great care in my choice of friends. I fled at the first sign of a misunderstanding. At the time, it seemed the right course.

I was a smart woman, a dangerous mate. (Odd – I find myself writing and thinking of myself in the past tense. So close to death that I consider myself already dead.) Men would approach with caution, delicately signaling from a distance: "I'm interested. Are you?" I didn't respond. I didn't really know how.

An only child, I was always wary of others. My mother and I lived together. When I was just a child, my father had left to pick up a pack of cigarettes and never returned. My mother, protective and cautious by nature, warned me that men could not be trusted. People could not be trusted. She could trust me and I could trust her, and that was all.

When I was in college, my mother died of cancer. She had known of the tumor for more than a year; she had endured surgery and chemotherapy, while writing me cheery letters about her gardening. Her minister told me that my mother was a saint – she hadn't told me because she hadn't wanted to disturb my studies. I realized then that she had been wrong. I couldn't really trust her after all.

I think perhaps I missed some narrow window of opportunity. If, at some point along the way, I had had a friend or a lover who had made the effort to coax me from hiding, I could have been a different person. But it never happened. In high school, I sought the safety of my books. In college, I studied alone on Friday nights. By the time I reached graduate school, I was, like the pseudoscorpion, accustomed to a solitary life.

I work alone in the laboratory, building the female. She is larger than the male. Her teeth are longer and more numerous. I am welding the hip joints into place when my mother comes to visit me in the laboratory.

"Katie," she says, "why didn't you ever fall in love? Why didn't you ever have children?"

I keep on welding, despite the trembling of my hands. I know she isn't there. Delirium is one symptom of radiation poisoning. But she keeps watching me as I work.

"You're not really here," I tell her, and realize immediately that talking to her is a mistake. I have acknowledged her presence and given her more power.

"Answer my questions, Katie," she says. "Why didn't you?"

I do not answer. I am busy and it will take too long to tell her about betrayal, to explain the confusion of a solitary insect confronted with a social situation, to describe the balance between fear and love. I ignore her just as I ignore the trembling of my hands and the pain in my belly, and I keep on working. Eventually, she goes away.

I use the rest of the soda cans to give the female brightly colored scales: Coca-Cola red, Sprite green, Fanta orange. From soda cans, I make an oviduct, lined with metal. It is just large enough to accommodate the male's cock.

The male bowerbird attracts a mate by constructing a sort of art piece. From sticks and grasses, he builds two close-set parallel walls that join together to make an arch. He decorates this structure and the area around it with gaudy trinkets: bits of bone, green leaves, flowers, bright stones, and feathers cast off by gaudier birds. In areas where people have left their trash, he uses bottle caps and coins and fragments of broken glass.

He sits in his bower and sings, proclaiming his love for any and all females in the vicinity. At last, a female admires his bower, accepts his invitation, and they mate.

The bowerbird uses discrimination in decorating his bower. He chooses his trinkets with care – selecting a bit of glass for its glitter, a shiny leaf for its natural elegance, a cobalt-blue feather for a touch of color. What does he think about as he builds and decorates? What passes through his mind as he sits and sings, advertising his availability to the world?

I have released the male and I am working on the female when I hear rattling and crashing outside the building. Something is happening in the alley between the laboratory and the nearby office building. I go down to investigate. From the mouth of the alley, I peer inside, and the male creature runs at me, startling me so that I step back. He shakes his head and rattles his teeth threateningly.

I retreat to the far side of the street and watch him from there. He ventures from the alley, scuttling along the street, then pauses by a BMW that is parked at the curb. I hear his claws rattling against metal. A hubcap clangs as it hits the pavement. The creature carries the shiny piece of metal to the mouth of the alley and then returns for the other three, removing them one by one. When I move, he rushes toward the alley, blocking any attempt to invade his territory. When I stand still, he returns to his work, collecting the hubcaps, carrying them to the alley, and arranging them so that they catch the light of the sun.

As I watch, he scavenges in the gutter and collects things he finds appealing: a beer bottle, some colorful plastic wrappers from candy bars, a length of bright yellow plastic rope. He takes each find and disappears into the alley with it.

I wait, watching. When he has exhausted the gutter near the mouth of the alley, he ventures around the corner and I make my move, running to the alley entrance and looking inside. The alley floor is covered with colored bits of paper and plastic; I can see wrappers from candy bars and paper bags from Burger King and McDonald's. The yellow plastic rope is tied to a pipe running up one wall and a protruding hook on the other. Dangling from it, like clean clothes on the clothesline, are colorful pieces of fabric: a burgundy-colored bath towel, a paisley print bedspread, a blue satin bedsheet.

I see all this in a glance. Before I can examine the bower further, I hear the rattle of claws on the pavement. The creature is running at me, furious at my intrusion. I turn and flee into the laboratory, slamming the door behind me. But once I am away from the alley, the creature does not pursue me.

From the second-story window, I watch him return to the alley and I suspect that he is checking to see if I have tampered with anything. After a time, he reappears in the alley mouth and crouches there, the sunlight glittering on his metal carapace.

In the laboratory, I build the future. Oh, maybe not, but there's no one here to contradict me, so I will say that it is so. I complete the female and release her.

The sickness takes over then. While I still have the strength, I drag a cot from a back room and position it by the window, where I can look out and watch my creations.

What is it that I want from them? I don't know exactly.

I want to know that I have left something behind. I want to be sure that the world does not end with me. I want the feeling, the understanding, the certainty that the world will go on.

I wonder if the dying dinosaurs were glad to see the mammals, tiny ratlike creatures that rustled secretively in the underbrush.

When I was in seventh grade, all the girls had to watch a special presentation during gym class one spring afternoon. We dressed in our gym clothes, then sat in the auditorium and watched a film called *Becoming a Woman*. The film talked about puberty and menstruation. The accompanying pictures showed the outline of a young girl. As the film progressed, she changed into a woman, developing breasts. The animation showed her uterus as it grew a lining, then shed it, then grew another. I remember watching with awe as the pictures showed the ovaries releasing an egg that united with a sperm, and then lodged in the uterus and grew into a baby.

The film must have delicately skirted any discussion of the source of the sperm, because I remember asking my mother where the sperm came from and how it got inside the woman. The question made her very uncomfortable. She muttered something about a man and woman being in love – as if love were somehow all that was needed for the sperm to find its way into the woman's body.

After the discussion, it seems to me that I was always a little confused about love and sex – even after I learned about the mechanics of sex and what goes where. The penis slips neatly into the vagina – but where does the love come in? Where does biology leave off and the higher emotions begin?

Does the female pseudoscorpion love the male when their dance is done? Does the male spider love his mate as he scurries away, running for his life? Is there love among the bowerbirds as they copulate in their bower? The textbooks fail to say. I speculate, but I have no way to get the answers.

My creatures engage in a long, slow courtship. I am getting sicker. Sometimes, my mother comes to ask me questions that I will not answer. Sometimes, men sit by my bed – but they are less real than my mother. These are men I cared about – men I thought I might love, though I never got beyond the thought. Through their translucent bodies, I can see the laboratory walls. They never were real, I think now.

Sometimes, in my delirium, I remember things. A dance back at college; I was slow-dancing, with someone's body pressed close to mine. The room was hot and stuffy and we went outside for some air. I remember he kissed me, while one hand stroked my breast and the other fumbled with the buttons of my blouse. I kept wondering if this was love – this fumbling in the shadows.

In my delirium, things change. I remember dancing in a circle with someone's hands clasping mine. My feet ache, and I try to stop, but my partner pulls me along, refusing to release me. My feet move instinctively in time with my partner's, though there is no music to help us keep the beat. The air smells of dampness and mold; I have lived my life underground and I am accustomed to these smells.

Is this love?

I spend my days lying by the window, watching through the dirty glass. From the mouth of the alley, he calls to her. I did not give him a voice, but he calls in his own way, rubbing his two front legs together so that metal rasps against metal, creaking like a cricket the size of a Buick.

She strolls past the alley mouth, ignoring him as he charges toward her, rattling his teeth. He backs away, as if inviting her to follow. She walks by. But then, a moment later, she strolls past again and the scene repeats itself. I understand that she is not really oblivious to his attention. She is simply taking her time, considering her situation. The male intensifies his efforts, tossing his head as he backs away, doing his best to call attention to the fine home he has created.

I listen to them at night. I cannot see them – the electricity failed two days ago and the streetlights are out. So I listen in the darkness, imagining. Metal legs rub together to make a high creaking noise. The sail on the male's back rattles as he unfolds it, then folds it, then unfolds it again, in what must be a sexual display. I hear a spiked tail rasping over a spiny back in a kind of caress. Teeth chatter against metal – love bites, perhaps. (The lion bites the lioness on the neck when they mate, an act of aggression that she accepts as affection.) Claws scrape against metal hide, clatter over metal scales. This, I think, is love. My creatures understand love.

I imagine a cock made of copper tubing and pipe fittings sliding into a canal lined with sheet metal from a soda can. I hear metal sliding over metal. And then my imagination fails. My construction made no provision for the stuff of reproduction: the sperm, the egg. Science failed me there. That part is up to the creatures themselves.

My body is giving out on me. I do not sleep at night; pain keeps me awake. I hurt everywhere, in my belly, in my breasts, in my bones. I have given up food. When I eat, the pains increase for a while, and then I vomit. I cannot keep anything down, and so I have stopped trying.

When the morning light comes, it is gray, filtering through the haze that covers the sky. I stare out the window, but I can't see the male. He has abandoned his post at the mouth of the alley. I watch for an hour or so, but the female does not stroll by. Have they finished with each other?

I watch from my bed for a few hours, the blanket wrapped around my shoulders. Sometimes, fever comes and I soak the blanket with my sweat. Sometimes, chills come, and I shiver under the blankets. Still, there is no movement in the alley.

It takes me more than an hour to make my way down the stairs. I can't trust my legs to support me, so I crawl on my knees, making my way across the room like a baby too young to stand upright. I carry the blanket with me, wrapped around my shoulders like a cape. At the top of the stairs, I rest, then I go down slowly, one step at a time.

The alley is deserted. The array of hubcaps glitters in the dim sunlight. The litter of bright papers looks forlorn and abandoned. I step cautiously into the entrance. If the male were to rush me now, I would not be able to run away. I have used all my reserves to travel this far.

The alley is quiet. I manage to get to my feet and shuffle forward through the papers. My eyes are clouded, and I can just make out the dangling bedspread halfway down the alley. I make my way to it. I don't know why I've come here. I suppose I want to see. I want to know what has happened. That's all.

I duck beneath the dangling bedspread. In the dim light, I can see a doorway in the brick wall. Something is hanging from the lintel of the door.

I approach cautiously. The object is gray, like the door behind it. It has a peculiar, spiraling shape. When I touch it, I can feel a faint vibration inside, like the humming of distant equipment. I lay my cheek against it and I can hear a low-pitched song, steady and even.

When I was a child, my family visited the beach and I spent hours exploring the tidepools. Among the clumps of blue-black mussels and the black turban snails, I found the egg casing of a horn shark in a tidepool. It was spiral-shaped, like this egg, and when I held it to the light, I could see a tiny embryo inside. As I watched, the embryo twitched, moving even though it was not yet truly alive.

I crouch at the back of the alley with my blanket wrapped around me. I see no reason to move – I can die here as well as I can die anywhere. I am watching over the egg, keeping it safe.

Sometimes, I dream of my past life. Perhaps I should have handled it differently. Perhaps I should have been less cautious, hurried out on the mating line, answered the song when a male called from his bower. But it doesn't matter now. All that is gone, behind us now.

My time is over. The dinosaurs and the humans – our time is over. New times are coming. New types of love. I dream of the future, and my dreams are filled with the rattle of metal claws.

A CONEY ISLAND
OF THE MIND

Maureen F. McHugh

*One of the brightest new SF names of the 1990s, Maureen F.
McHugh lived for some years in China before returning to her
native Ohio: an experience reflected in her acclaimed first novel,
China Mountain Zhang, which won the prestigious Tiptree Memorial Award. Her second novel, Half the Day is Night was
recently published, and her short stories appear regularly in the
leading SF magazines. "A Coney Island of the Mind" explores
some of the possibilities of Virtual Reality in one of the seedier
corners of cyberspace.*

Reality Parlor.

He pays his money and goes back to the cubicle with the
treadmill and pulls on the waldos, puts on the heavy eyeless, earless
helmet. He grabs for the handlebars suspended before him, blind
in the helmet that smells intimately of someone else's hair.

Now he can see. Not the handlebars hung from the ceiling on a
tapewrapped cable, not the treadmill. He is the cat with future feet.
He sees a schematic of a room; all the lines of the room are in pink
neon on velvet black, and in his ears instead of the seasound of the
helmet he hears the sound of open space. A room sounds different
than a helmet even where there's nothing to hear.

A keyboard appears, or rather a line drawing of a keyboard with
all the letters on the keys in glowing neon blue. Over it in neon blue
letters is the message, "Please type in your user ID."

"Cobalt," he types, letting go of the handlebars. The waldos give him the sensation of hitting keys, give him feedback. His password is nagasaki.

A neon pink door draws itself in the velvet wall in front of him. The keyboard disappears and the handlebars appear in pink neon schematic until he grabs them. Then they disappear from sight, but he can still feel them, safe in his gloved hands. He starts forward [the treadmill lurches a bit under his blind feet but it always does that at first so he is accustomed to it, doesn't really think about it, just kind of expects it and forgets about it] through the door which opens up ahead of him, pulling apart like elevator doors into the party.

The party isn't a schematic, the party looks real. The party is a big space full of people dressed all ways – boys with big hair and girls with latex skulls and NPC in evening gowns and tuxes – and as he comes out of the elevator he looks to the right, to the mirrors, and sees himself, sees Cobalt, sees a Tom Sawyer in the twenty-first century, a flagboy in a bluesilk jacket and thigh high boots with a knotwork of burgundy cords at the hips. All angles in the face, smooth face like a razor, a face he had custom configured in hours of bought-time at the reality parlor, not playing the reality streets, not even looking, just working on his own look. Cobalt eyes like lasers, and blue-steel braids for hair.

Edgelook, whatta-look, hot damn.

Not what he looks like at all in the mundane world of Cincinnati, Ohio, but he isn't in Cincinnati, ho, flagboy, he's not in Kansas anymore, he is at *the party*. Here he is, a serious dog, a democratic dog, but he doesn't think he'll spend a lot of time at the party today, looking around he doesn't see anyone he knows. Not that that means they aren't there, because anybody can look like anything, but if they don't have a handle he recognizes and they don't go calling out to Cobalt then they don't want to be the people he knows, right? And anyway, this afternoon the partyroom is full of off-the-racks, look-like-your-favorite-movie-star or take-a-basic-template-what-color-are-your-eyes-your-hair-look-like-a-manne-quin which he can't abide because he's looking for people with style so he angles over toward the far wall [his real feet, his mundane feet in their grass-stained sneakers that he wears when he mows the lawn just keep heading straight ahead on the treadmill, if he angles he'll step off the treadmill, but he turns the handlebars to the left and he's done it so long that he doesn't get confused by his feet saying one direction and the handlebars telling him another] to the far wall, full of blank doorways, and he stops to read the menu.

It's better now that he's turned eighteen, more choices. Games and Adventures, Simulations, Tanks and Airplanes and Spaceships – but he's not really interested in a lot of that because he's on a treadmill, not sitting down, so back to games and Adventures, Places to Go and Things to Do, where he is likely to find some people he knows, someone to hang out with; Quixote and Bushman and Taipei.

"Any messages?" he asks out loud.

Soft chime that can be heard over the whole room of the party (except that no one else does). No messages. Nobody in the swim? Then he'll look for a place where maybe he'll meet serious dogs. He almost selects Chinatown but changes his mind and [left hand lets go of the handlebars and reaches out] pushes the button for Coney Island.

[Feedback through the waldo, it feels like pushing something.]

A line of electricity forms at the top of the door, a forcefield, an edge of static that rolls down like a window shade only draws down an opening on a place.

Black night on the boardwalk with the ferris wheel and the parachute drop all decked out in colored lights off in the distance. Cobalt steps through the door and his feet thump the hollow wood of the boardwalk. The booths spill bright white and yellow light onto the boards. He can hear the ocean. A guy selling hotdogs. Coney fucking Island.

So he walks down the boardwalk, checking out the crowd, checking out how much is just program – the sailor and his girl at the Toss The Ring who are always at the Toss The Ring every time he comes – and how much is real people. It's a quiet night on the boardwalk.

Maybe he should go back to the party, check out Chinatown. Hey, he's here, maybe he'll just dogtrot on down the boardwalk, out toward the rides, see if there's someone. Then he'll go back to Chinatown.

Moving along the boardwalk, past the cotton candy, past the tattoo parlor, past the place where the counter is a two-tone Cadillac, dog gone, dog going, into a dog eat dog world.

And the queens (who are mostly black and tall and female and camp, that being the current fashion in queens) are calling "Hey sweetcakes," "Hey, be my blueboy," "Are you hotwired, babyface?" "Are you wired for sound?" Which he's not because he rents time in a fucking public reality parlor (no pun intended) where they aren't going to supply equipment to wire your crotch.

But it's all just noise, white noise, background hiss, the sound of Coney Island and not what he's looking for anyway although who's to say what he'd be looking for if he had the option? But he doesn't, so he isn't, he's looking for his mates, his team, his dogpack. He's checking under the boardwalk behind the Chinese food place, and watching the Mustangs crawl up the street because Quixote likes simulations, likes to drive fast cars in crazy places. Watching for spies because Taipei likes adventure games where he fights off attackers, watches for gang members because they all like to play Warriors and Coney Island is where it starts, where they catch the subway to the cemetery in the Bronx.

But the streets are all full of programming, of nonplayer characters, and kids without style, which is to say that this night Coney Island is empty.

So he's thinking that he'll check one more place, maybe take in a movie, or call up the airlock and go on to Chinatown, and he stops where he can see the ocean and looks for a moment, the stone dark ocean rolling and making that sound, hypnotizing him and he likes it because there isn't much ocean in Cincinnati, hell, there isn't even much sin in Cincinnati.

She leans next to him with a star hanging off her ear, one lone star in the smoke nebula of her hair, no off-the-rack handle but a costume full of style, like himself, like the dogpack, this woman has taken some time. "Hey blueboy," she says.

"Hey yourself," he says and imagines she smells like perfume, smells like ash. She has full breasts and brown skin in the yellow light. She has yellow snake eyes, not like dice, like rattlesnakes, and hair that doesn't act like real hair at all but fills some indefinite space, swallows light, absorbs light, no reflections. Soft looking. Nice touch, that. She's a chimera, she's not content to take a strictly human template, she's diddled the programming.

He's a lucky dog.

They make noise in the night, what's your name, Cobalt what's yours? (Rattlesnake, he wonders, or cobra, coral snake, black racer, asp, gila monster, his mind all in a rush before she answers –)

Lamia.

Which isn't what he expects at all and doesn't mean a thing except it sounds liquid. He wishes he had more access, he wishes he had programmed something, an ashen rose maybe, to pull out of the air and give to her, but all he has are things that are useful in adventure games; a smoke bomb, a rope, a bottle that can be broken and used like a knife.

"That's pretty," he says.

She reaches out and takes his hand. And sighs happily.

The ocean rolls in.

"Squeeze," she says in a throaty whisper.

For a moment he doesn't understand but then he squeezes her hand and she half-closes her eyes. "Flagboy," she says, "I think I like you."

"Want to walk on the beach?" he asks.

She shrugs and kneads his fingers, he can feel her hand, all the bones of it and her long fingers, and she can feel his because of the waldos. He pulls her toward the steps and she gives a throaty, gaspy laugh.

She's wearing high heels, spikes with toes like cloven hooves – except that her feet don't look human. Her smoky hair has horns, then it's a halo, a madonna veil, all smoke. She follows him in a clatter across the hollow boards and down the steps into the sand. Their footsteps become silent [it never feels any different, because his feet are still on the treadmill, and his right hand is still on the handlebars, but his left holds the air and the waldos mimic the pressure of her hand].

"Not so tight," she says and he loosens his grip on her hand.

Eyes and hands, eyes and ears and hands. How real is real?

The light from the star in her hair falls on her bare shoulders, on her collarbones. Her clothing has no reason to stay covering her breasts but it does. She wouldn't feel it if he touched her breasts, not unless she's wearing a hotsuit. Could she be wearing a hotsuit, have her whole body wired for touch? Does she have a place at home, a treadmill, the whole bit? Spoiled Fifth Avenue girl? LA girl? Maybe she's forty years old, he doesn't know. Maybe she's ugly.

Interesting thought, that. He looks at her smoky hair and her skin and the hollow leading into her heart shaped top and squeezes her hand and she sighs. Huuuhhh.

And he sighs, too. Maybe she's ugly, or fat, or old. Maybe she is blind, or deformed. Maybe she is married. Wild thought that this beautiful girl can be anything.

His heart is pounding. She stops and they are facing each other, holding hands. If they kissed, there would be nothing but air. Strange to feel her through his palm and fingers, the waldos giving him all the feelings of her hand, of the weight of her body behind the hand, and knowing that he could pass his arm through her. She is nothing but light. If he thinks about it he can feel the weight of the helmet on his head.

And her hand. All the bones and tendons and ligaments, the elastic play of her muscle. He finds her fingers, presses them one-by-one. She is watching him with slit pupiled snake eyes gone from amber to green, although he can't remember when that happened. The ocean roars behind them.

He laces his fingers through hers. "Where are you?" he asks, although it's rude to ask people that.

"On the boardwalk," she says, her voice coming out in a breath. She is watching him, lazily intent, and he is playing with her hand. She closes her eyes and catches her lip in her teeth. Her face is so strange.

"Don't stop," she whispers and he doesn't know what she is talking about and then he realizes it is her hand, her hand in his blue gloved one. Her face is almost empty of expression, but small things seem to be happening in it independent of anything that is in his face.

"Squeeze," she says again.

Confused, he does, and feels her squeezing rhythmically back, pulsing little squeezes, and he realizes in horror just –

[She's hotwired her hand.]

– as she comes. Eyes shut, her smoky hair rising in horns, she gasps a little. He jerks his hand away, but she is standing there oblivious, and it's too late anyway.

[You take a hotsuit and re-wire the crotch so the system thinks it's a hand, then anytime someone touches your hand . . .]

He is embarrassed, angry, shocked. He doesn't know if he should just go or not.

[His fingers squeezing her and he didn't know.]

"Blueboy," she says, and sits down on the sand. "Oh Christ, blueboy."

He will go and he does [turning the handlebars; feet, as always, straight on the treadmill] and starts back for the steps.

"Come on," she says, "what's so awful about it?"

"You didn't tell me," he says, all indignation.

"Prissy little virgin," she says, and laughs behind him.

"Airlock," he says, which is a system command, a gateway back to the party. The line of static starts at the height of a door, and the forcefield rolls down like a window shade.

"Huff on out of here," she says. "Righteous little bitch. Are you a girl?"

"What!?" he says.

Which makes her laugh. "Well, I guess not, sweetcakes, but for a moment I sure thought you were."

Sweetcakes. [Somewhere in Cincinnati his cheeks are burning.]

"I'm glad," she says, "because I'm not into girls. I just like wearing girl bodies because I like you righteous boys, you sweet straight boys."

He starts to step into the party and stops. "What?" he says.

"Draws you all like moths to a flame," she said. Or he said, or it said.

His first swift thought is that he'll have to change his look, never look like this again, abandon Cobalt, be something else.

She laughs that ashen laugh. "Go on home, blueboy."

And he does, steps back into the party, leaves Coney Island behind. The party, neutral ground, where he shakes his head, dog shaking water off his coat. He blinks in the lights of the party. Thinks of going home, going back to Cincinnati, to thinking about Ohio State in the fall.

Trying not to think about feet like hooves, high heels.

What a frigging nut case!

Bad luck, Quixote is waving across the space. Cobalt doesn't know, just wants to go home.

"Where you been," Quixote says, "you're looking democratic."

Shrugs. What's he going to say, I met this girl – I met this girl and her hand . . . he starts to smile, what a dog story. Quixote is going to be green.

"You won't believe what happened to me in Coney Island," Cobalt says.

He doesn't have to tell everything.

"No way!" Quixote says.

It's a dog eat dog world, sometimes.

THE GIRL WHO WAS PLUGGED IN

James Tiptree, Jr

The extraordinary stories which appeared in quick succession between 1970 and 1977 under the name "James Tiptree, Jr" were widely assumed to be the work of a man – they were praised by some critics for the muscularity of their prose – and the news that their author was really Alice Sheldon (1915–87) came as a revelation to many. She had worked for the US government, including a spell in the Pentagon, then retrained as an experimental psychologist, and her stories were concerned with sex, identity, occasionally ecology and almost invariably death. They are collected in Ten Thousand Light Years From Home *(1973),* Warm Worlds and Otherwise *(1975),* Star Songs of an Old Primate *(1978) and* Out of the Everywhere . . . *(1981). The following novella won the author her first Hugo award, and has since been hailed as an important precursor of the Cyberpunk movement of the 1980s.*

Listen, zombie. Believe me. What I could tell you – you with your silly hands leaking sweat on your growth-stocks portfolio. One-ten lousy hacks of AT&T on twenty-percent margin and you think you're Evel Knievel. AT&T? You doubleknit dummy, how I'd love to show you something.

Look, dead daddy. I'd say. See for instance that rotten girl?

In the crowd over there, that one gaping at her gods. One rotten girl in the city of the future. (That's what I said.) Watch.

She's jammed among bodies, craning and peering with her soul yearning out of her eyeballs. Love! Oo-ooh, love them! Her gods are coming out of a store called Body East. Three youngbloods, larking along loverly. Dressed like simple street-people but ... smashing. See their great eyes swivel above their nosefilters, their hands lift shyly, their inhumanly tender lips melt? The crowd moans. Love! This whole boiling megacity, this whole fun future world loves its gods.

You don't believe gods, dad? Wait. Whatever turns you on, there's a god in the future for you, custom-made. Listen to this mob. "I touched his foot! Ow-oow, I TOUCHED Him!"

Even the people in the GTX tower up there love the gods – in their own way and for their own reasons.

The funky girl on the street, she just loves. Grooving on their beautiful lives, their mysterioso problems. No one ever told her about mortals who love a god and end up as a tree or a sighing sound. In a million years it'd never occur to her that her gods might love her back.

She's squashed against the wall now as the godlings come by. They move in a clear space. A holocam bobs above but its shadow never falls on them. The store display screens are magically clear of bodies as the gods glance in and a beggar underfoot is suddenly alone. They give him a token. "Aaaaah!" goes the crowd.

Now one of them flashes some wild new kind of timer and they all trot to catch a shuttle, just like people. The shuttle stops for them – more magic. The crowd sighs, closing back. The gods are gone.

(In a room far from – but not unconnected to – the GTX tower a molecular flipflop closes too, and three account tapes spin.)

Our girl is still stuck by the wall while guards and holocam equipment pull away. The adoration's fading from her face. That's good, because now you can see she's the ugly of the world. A tall monument to pituitary dystrophy. No surgeon would touch her. When she smiles, her jaw – it's half purple – almost bites her left eye out. She's also quite young, but who could care?

The crowd is pushing her along now, treating you to glimpses of her jumbled torso, her mismatched legs. At the corner she strains to send one last fond spasm after the godlings' shuttle. Then her face reverts to its usual expression of dim pain and she lurches onto the moving walkway, stumbling into people. The walkway junctions with another. She crosses, trips and collides with the

casualty rail. Finally she comes out into a little place called a park.
The sportshow is working, a basketball game in 3-di is going on
right overhead. But all she does is squeeze onto a bench and huddle
there while a ghostly free-throw goes by her ear.

After that nothing at all happens except a few furtive hand-
mouth gestures which don't even interest her bench-mates.

But you're curious about the city? So ordinary after all, in the
FUTURE?

Ah, there's plenty to swing with here – and it's not all that *far*
in the future, dad. But pass up the sci-fi stuff for now, like for
instance the holovision technology that's put TV and radio in
museums. Or the worldwide carrier field bouncing down from
satellites, controlling communication and transport systems all
over the globe. That was a spin-off from asteroid mining, pass it
by. We're watching that girl.

I'll give you just one goodie. Maybe you noticed on the sportshow
or the streets? No commercials. No ads.

That's right. NO ADS. An eyeballer for you.

Look around. Not a billboard, sign, slogan, jingle, sky-write,
blurb, sublimflash, in this whole fun world. Brand names? Only in
those ticky little peep-screens on the stores and you could hardly
call that advertising. How does that finger you?

Think about it. That girl is still sitting there.

She's parked right under the base of the GTX tower as a matter
of fact. Look way up and you can see the sparkles from the bubble
on top, up there among the domes of godland. Inside that bubble
is a boardroom. Neat bronze shield on the door: Global Transmissions Corporation – not that that means anything.

I happen to know there are six people in that room. Five of them
technically male, and the sixth isn't easily thought of as a mother.
They are absolutely unremarkable. Those faces were seen once at
their nuptials and will show again in their obituaries and impress
nobody either time. If you're looking for the secret Big Blue
Meanies of the world, forget it. I know. Zen, do I know! Flesh?
Power? Glory? You'd horrify them.

What they do like up there is to have things orderly, especially
their communications. You could say they've dedicated their lives
to that, to freeing the world from garble. Their nightmares are
about hemorrhages of information; channels screwed up, plans
misimplemented, garble creeping in. Their gigantic wealth only

worries them, it keeps opening new vistas of disorder. Luxury? They wear what their tailors put on them, eat what their cooks serve them. See that old boy there – his name is Isham – he's sipping water and frowning as he listens to a databall. The water was prescribed by his medistaff. It tastes awful. The databall also contains a disquieting message about his son, Paul.

But it's time to go back down, far below to our girl. Look! She's toppled over sprawling on the ground.

A tepid commotion ensues among the bystanders. The consensus is she's dead, which she disproves by bubbling a little. And presently she's taken away by one of the superb ambulances of the future, which are a real improvement over ours when one happens to be around.

At the local bellevue the usual things are done by the usual team of clowns aided by a saintly mop-pusher. Our girl revives enough to answer the questionnaire without which you can't die, even in the future. Finally she's cast up, a pumped-out hulk on a cot in the long, dim ward.

Again nothing happens for a while except that her eyes leak a little from the understandable disappointment of finding herself still alive.

But somewhere one GTX computer has been tickling another, and toward midnight something does happen. First comes an attendant who pulls screens around her. Then a man in a business doublet comes daintily down the ward. He motions the attendant to strip off the sheet and go.

The groggy girl-brute heaves up, big hands clutching at bodyparts you'd pay not to see.

"Burke? P. Burke, is that your name?"

"Y-yes." Croak. "Are you . . . policeman?"

"No. They'll be along shortly, I expect. Public suicide's a felony."

". . . I'm sorry."

He has a 'corder in his hand. "No family, right?"

"No."

"You're seventeen. One year city college. What did you study?"

"La – languages."

"H'm. Say something."

Unintelligible rasp.

He studies her. Seen close, he's not so elegant. Errand-boy type.

"Why did you try to kill yourself?"

She stares at him with dead-rat dignity, hauling up the gray sheet. Give him a point, he doesn't ask twice.

"Tell me, did you see Breath this afternoon?"

Dead as she nearly is, that ghastly love-look wells up. Breath is the three young gods, a loser's cult. Give the man another point, he interprets her expression.

"How would you like to meet them?"

The girl's eyes bug out grotesquely.

"I have a job for someone like you. It's hard work. If you did well you'd be meeting Breath and stars like that all the time."

Is he insane? She's deciding she really did die.

"But it means you never see anybody you know again. Never, *ever*. You will be legally dead. Even the police won't know. Do you want to try?"

It all has to be repeated while her great jaw slowly sets. *Show me the fire I walk through.* Finally P. Burke's prints are in his 'corder, the man holding up the big rancid girl-body without a sign of distaste. It makes you wonder what else he does.

And then – THE MAGIC. Sudden silent trot of litterbearers tucking P. Burke into something quite different from a bellevue stretcher, the oiled slide into the daddy of all luxury ambulances – real flowers in that holder! – and the long jarless rush to nowhere. Nowhere is warm and gleaming and kind with nurses. (Where did you hear that money can't buy genuine kindness?) And clean clouds folding P. Burke into bewildered sleep.

. . . Sleep which merges into feedings and washings and more sleeps, into drowsy moments of afternoon where midnight should be, and gentle businesslike voices and friendly (but very few) faces, and endless painless hyposprays and peculiar numbnesses. And later comes the steadying rhythm of days and nights, and a quickening which P. Burke doesn't identify as health, but only knows that the fungus place in her armpit is gone. And then she's up and following those few new faces with growing trust, first tottering, then walking strongly, all better now, clumping down the short hall to the tests, tests, tests, and the other things.

And here is our girl, looking—

If possible, worse than before. (You thought this was Cinderella transistorized?)

The disimprovement in her looks comes from the electrode jacks peeping out of her sparse hair, and there are other meldings of flesh and metal. On the other hand, that collar and spinal plate are really an asset; you won't miss seeing that neck.

P. Burke is ready for training in her new job.

The training takes place in her suite and is exactly what you'd call a charm course. How to walk, sit, eat, speak, blow her nose, how to stumble, to urinate, to hiccup – DELICIOUSLY. How to make each noseblow or shrug delightfully, subtly different from any ever spooled before. As the man said, it's hard work.

But P. Burke proves apt. Somewhere in that horrible body is a gazelle, a houri who would have been buried forever without this crazy chance. See the ugly duckling go!

Only it isn't precisely P. Burke who's stepping, laughing, shaking out her shining hair. How could it be? P. Burke is doing it all right, but she's doing it through something. The something is to all appearances a live girl. (You were warned, this is the FUTURE.)

When they first open the big cryocase and show her her new body she says just one word. Staring, gulping, "How?"

Simple, really. Watch P. Burke in her sack and scuffs stump down the hall beside Joe, the man who supervises the technical part of her training. Joe doesn't mind P. Burke's looks, he hasn't noticed them. To Joe, system matrices are beautiful.

They go into a dim room containing a huge cabinet like a one-man sauna and a console for Joe. The room has a glass wall that's all dark now. And just for your information, the whole shebang is five hundred feet underground near what used to be Carbondale, Pa.

Joe opens the sauna-cabinet like a big clamshell standing on end with a lot of funny business inside. Our girl shucks her shift and walks into it bare, totally unembarrassed. *Eager.* She settles in face-forward, butting jacks into sockets. Joe closes it carefully onto her humpback. Clunk. She can't see in there or hear or move. She hates this minute. But how she loves what comes next!

Joe's at his console and the lights on the other side of the glass wall come up. A room is on the other side, all fluff and kicky bits, a girly bedroom. In the bed is a small mound of silk with a rope of yellow hair hanging out.

The sheet stirs and gets whammed back flat.

Sitting up in the bed is the darlingest girl child you've EVER seen. She quivers – porno for angels. She sticks both her little arms straight up, flips her hair, looks around full of sleepy pazazz. Then she can't resist rubbing her hands down over her minibreasts and belly. Because, you see, it's the godawful P. Burke who is sitting there hugging her perfect girl-body, looking at you out of delighted eyes.

Then the kitten hops out of bed and crashes flat on the floor.

From the sauna in the dim room comes a strangled noise. P. Burke, trying to rub her wired-up elbow, is suddenly smothered in *two* bodies, electrodes jerking in her flesh. Joe juggles inputs, crooning into his mike. The flurry passes; it's all right.

In the lighted room the elf gets up, casts a cute glare at the glass wall and goes into a transparent cubicle. A bathroom, what else? She's a live girl, and live girls have to go to the bathroom after a night's sleep even if their brains are in a sauna cabinet in the next room. And P. Burke isn't in that cabinet, she's in the bathroom. Perfectly simple, if you have the glue for that closed training circuit that's letting her run her neural system by remote control.

Now let's get one thing clear. P. Burke does not *feel* her brain is in the sauna room, she feels she's in that sweet little body. When you wash your hands, do you feel the water is running on your brain? Of course not. You feel the water on your hand, although the "feeling" is actually a potential-pattern flickering over the electrochemical jelly between your ears. And it's delivered there via the long circuits from your hands. Just so, P. Burke's brain in the cabinet feels the water on her hands in the bathroom. The fact that the signals have jumped across space on the way in makes no difference at all. If you want the jargon, it's known as eccentric projection or sensory reference and you've done it all your life. Clear?

Time to leave the honey-pot to her toilet training – she's made a booboo with the toothbrush, because P. Burke can't get used to what she sees in the mirror—

But wait, you say. Where did that girl-body come from?

P. Burke asks that too, dragging out the words.

"They grow 'em," Joe tells her. He couldn't care less about the flesh department. "PDs. Placental decanters. Modified embryos, see? Fit the control implants in later. Without a Remote Operator it's just a vegetable. Look at the feet – no callus at all." (He knows because they told him.)

"Oh . . . oh, she's incredible . . ."

"Yeah, a neat job. Want to try walking-talking mode today? You're coming on fast."

And she is. Joe's reports and the reports from the nurse and the doctor and style man go to a bushy man upstairs who is some kind of medical cybertech but mostly a project administrator. His reports in turn go – to the GTX boardroom? Certainly not, did you think this is a *big* thing? His reports just go up. The point is, they're green, very green. P. Burke promises well.

So the bushy man – Doctor Tesla – has procedures to initiate. The little kitten's dossier in the Central Data Bank, for instance. Purely routine. And the phase-in schedule which will put her on the scene. This is simple: a small exposure in an off-network holoshow.

Next he has to line out the event which will fund and target her. That takes budget meetings, clearances, coordinations. The Burke project begins to recruit and grow. And there's the messy business of the name, which always gives Doctor Tesla an acute pain in the bush.

The name comes out weird, when it's suddenly discovered that Burke's "P." stands for "Philadelphia". Philadelphia? The astrologer grooves on it. Joe thinks it would help identification. The semantics girl references *brotherly love, Liberty-Bell, main-line, low teratogenesis,* blah-blah. Nicknames Philly? Pala? Pooty? Delphi? Is it good, bad? Finally "Delphi" is gingerly declared goodo. ("Burke" is replaced by something nobody remembers.)

Coming along now. We're at the official checkout down in the underground suite, which is as far as the training circuits reach. The bushy Doctor Tesla is there, braced by two budgetary types and a quiet fatherly man whom he handles like hot plasma.

Joe swings the door wide and she steps shyly in.

Their little Delphi, fifteen and flawless.

Tesla introduces her around. She's child-solemn, a beautiful baby to whom something so wonderful has happened you can feel the tingles. She doesn't smile, she . . . brims. That brimming joy is all that shows of P. Burke, the forgotten hulk in the sauna next door. But P. Burke doesn't know she's alive – it's Delphi who lives, every warm inch of her.

One of the budget types lets go a libidinous snuffle and freezes. The fatherly man, whose name is Mr Cantle, clears his throat.

"Well, young lady, are you ready to go to work?"

"Yes, sir," gravely from the elf.

"We'll see. Has anybody told you what you're going to do for us?"

"No, sir." Joe and Tesla exhale quietly.

"Good." He eyes her, probing for the blind drain in the room next door.

"Do you know what *advertising* is?"

He's talking dirty, hitting to shock. Delphi's eyes widen and her little chin goes up. Joe is in ecstasy at the complex expressions P. Burke is getting through. Mr Cantle waits.

"It's, well, it's when they used to tell people to buy things." She swallows. "It's not allowed."

"That's right." Mr Cantle leans back, grave. "Advertising as it used to be is against the law. *A display other than the legitimate use of the product, intended to promote its sale.* In former times every manufacturer was free to tout his wares any way, place or time he could afford. All the media and most of the landscape was taken up with extravagant competing displays. The thing became uneconomic. The public rebelled. Since the so-called Huckster Act sellers have been restrained to, I quote, displays in or on the product itself, visible during its legitimate use or in on-premises sales." Mr Cantle leans forward. "Now tell me, Delphi, why do people buy one product rather than another?"

"Well . . ." Enchanting puzzlement from Delphi. "They, um, they see them and like them, or they hear about them from somebody?" (Touch of P. Burke there; she didn't say, from a friend.)

"Partly. Why did *you* buy your particular body-lift?"

"I never had a body-lift, sir."

Mr Cantle frowns; what gutters do they drag for these Remotes?

"Well, what brand of water do you drink?"

"Just what was in the faucet, sir," says Delphi humbly. "I – I did try to boil it—"

"Good God." He scowls; Tesla stiffens. "Well, what did you boil it in? A cooker?"

The shining yellow head nods.

"What *brand* of cooker did you buy?"

"I didn't buy it, sir," says frightened P. Burke through Delphi's lips. "But – I know the best kind! Ananga has a Burnbabi. I saw the name when she—"

"Exactly!" Cantle's fatherly beam comes back strong; the Burnbabi account is a strong one, too. "You saw Ananga using one so you thought it must be good, eh? And it is good or a great human being like Ananga wouldn't be using it. Absolutely right. And now, Delphi, you know what you're going to be doing for us. You're going to show some products. Doesn't sound very hard, does it?"

"Oh, no, sir . . ." Baffled child's stare; Joe gloats.

"And you must never, *never* tell anyone what you're doing." Cantle's eyes bore for the brain behind this seductive child.

"You're wondering why we ask you to do this, naturally. There's a very serious reason. All those products people use, foods and healthaids and cookers and cleaners and clothes and cars – they're all made by *people*. Somebody put in years of hard work designing and making them. A man comes up with a fine new idea for a better product. He has to get a factory and machinery, and hire workmen. Now. What happens if people have no way of hearing about his product? Word-of-mouth is far too slow and unreliable. Nobody might ever stumble onto his new product or find out how good it was, right? And then he and all the people who worked for him – they'd go bankrupt, right? So, Delphi, there has to be *some way* that large numbers of people can get a look at a good new product, right? How? By letting people see you using it. You're giving that man a chance."

Delphi's little head is nodding in happy relief.

"Yes, sir, I do see now – but sir, it seems so sensible, why don't they let you—"

Cantle smiles sadly.

"It's an overreaction, my dear. History goes by swings. People overreact and pass harsh unrealistic laws which attempt to stamp out an essential social process. When this happens, the people who understand have to carry on as best they can until the pendulum swings back." He sighs. "The Huckster Laws are bad, inhuman laws, Delphi, despite their good intent. If they were strictly observed they would wreak havoc. Our economy, our society would be cruelly destroyed. We'd be back in caves!" His inner fire is showing; if the Huckster Laws were strictly enforced he'd be back punching a databank.

"It's our duty, Delphi. Our solemn social duty. We are not breaking the law. You will be using the product. But people wouldn't understand, if they knew. They would become upset just as you did. So you must be very, very careful not to mention any of this to anybody."

(And somebody will be very, very carefully monitoring Delphi's speech circuits.)

"Now we're all straight, aren't we? Little Delphi here" – He is speaking to the invisible creature next door – "Little Delphi is going to live a wonderful, exciting life. She's going to be a girl people watch. And she's going to be using fine products people will be glad to know about and helping the good people who make them. Yours will be a genuine social contribution." He keys up his pitch; the creature in there must be older.

Delphi digests this with ravishing gravity.

"But sir, how do I—?"

"Don't worry about a thing. You'll have people behind you whose job it is to select the most worthy products for you to use. Your job is just to do as they say. They'll show you what outfits to wear to parties, what suncars and viewers to buy and so on. That's all you have to do."

Parties – clothes – suncars! Delphi's pink mouth opens. In P. Burke's starved seventeen-year-old head the ethics of product sponsorship float far away.

"Now tell me in your own words what your job is, Delphi."

"Yes sir. I – I'm to go to parties and buy things and use them as they tell me, to help the people who work in factories."

"And what did I say was so important?"

"Oh – I shouldn't let anybody know, about the things."

"Right." Mr Cantle has another paragraph he uses when the subject shows, well, immaturity. But he can sense only eagerness here. Good. He doesn't really enjoy the other speech.

"It's a lucky girl who can have all the fun she wants while doing good for others, isn't it?" He beams around. There's a prompt shuffling of chairs. Clearly this one is go.

Joe leads her rout, grinning. The poor fool thinks they're admiring her coordination.

It's out into the world for Delphi now, and at this point the up-channels get used. On the administrative side account schedules are opened, subprojects activated. On the technical side the reserved bandwidth is cleared. (That carrier field, remember?) A new name is waiting for Delphi, a name she'll never hear. It's a long string of binaries which have been quietly cycling in a GTX tank ever since a certain Beautiful Person didn't wake up.

The name winks out of cycle, dances from pulses into modulations of modulations, whizzes through phasing, and shoots into a giga-band beam racing up to a synchronous satellite poised over Guatemala. From there the beam pours twenty thousand miles back to earth again, forming an all-pervasive field of structured energies supplying tuned demand-points all over the Can-Am quadrant.

With that field, if you have the right credit rating you can sit at a GTX console and operate a tuned ore-extractor in Brazil. Or – if you have some simple credentials like being able to walk on water – you could shoot a spool into the network holocam shows running day and night in every home and dorm and rec. site. *Or* you could create a continentwide traffic jam. Is it any wonder GTX guards those inputs like a sacred trust?

Delphi's "name" appears as a tiny analyzable nonredundancy in the flux, and she'd be very proud if she knew about it. It would strike P. Burke as magic; P. Burke never even understood robotcars. But Delphi is in no sense a robot. Call her a waldo if you must. The fact is she's just a girl, a real-live girl with her brain in an unusual place. A simple real-time on-line system with plenty of bit-rate – even as you and you.

The point of all this hardware, which isn't very much hardware in this society, is so Delphi can walk out of that underground suite, a mobile demand-point draining an omnipresent fieldform. And she does – eighty-nine pounds of tender girl flesh and blood with a few metallic components, stepping out into the sunlight to be taken to her new life. A girl with everything going for her including a meditech escort. Walking lovely, stopping to widen her eyes at the big antennae system overhead.

The mere fact that something called P. Burke is left behind down underground has no bearing at all. P. Burke is totally unselfaware and happy as a clam in its shell. (Her bed has been moved into the waldo cabinet room now.) And P. Burke isn't in the cabinet; P. Burke is climbing out of an air-van in a fabulous Colorado beef preserve and her name is Delphi. Delphi is looking at live Charolais steers and live cottonwoods and aspens gold against the blue smog and stepping over live grass to be welcomed by the reserve super's wife.

The super's wife is looking forward to a visit from Delphi and her friends and by a happy coincidence there's a holocam outfit here doing a piece for the nature nuts.

You could write the script yourself now, while Delphi learns a few rules about structural interferences and how to handle the tiny time lag which results from the new forty-thousand-mile parenthesis in her nervous system. That's right – the people with the leased holocam rig naturally find the gold aspen shadows look a lot better on Delphi's flank than they do on a steer. And Delphi's face improves the mountains too, when you can see them. But the nature freaks aren't quite as joyful as you'd expect.

"See you in Barcelona, kitten," the head man says sourly as they pack up.

"Barcelona?" echoes Delphi with that charming little subliminal lag. She sees where his hand is and steps back.

"Cool, it's not her fault," another man says wearily. He knocks back his grizzled hair. "Maybe they'll leave in some of the gut."

Delphi watches them go off to load the spools on the GTX transport for processing. Her hand roves over the breast the man had touched. Back under Carbondale, P. Burke has discovered something new about her Delphi-body.

About the difference between Delphi and her own grim carcass.

She's always known Delphi has almost no sense of taste or smell. They explained about that: Only so much bandwidth. You don't have to taste a suncar, do you? And the slight overall dimness of Delphi's sense of touch – she's familiar with that, too. Fabrics that would prickle P. Burke's own hide feel like a cool plastic film to Delphi.

But the blank spots. It took her a while to notice them. Delphi doesn't have much privacy; investments of her size don't. So she's slow about discovering there's certain definite places where her beastly P. Burke body *feels* things that Delphi's dainty flesh does not. H'mm! Channel space again, she thinks – and forgets it in the pure bliss of being Delphi.

You ask how a girl could forget a thing like that? Look. P. Burke is about as far as you can get from the concept *girl*. She's a female, yes – but for her, sex is a four-letter word spelled P-A-I-N. She isn't quite a virgin. You don't want the details; she'd been about twelve and the freak-lovers were bombed blind. When they came down they threw her out with a small hole in her anatomy and a mortal one elsewhere. She dragged off to buy her first and last shot and she can still hear the clerk's incredulous guffaws.

Do you see why Delphi grins, stretching her delicious little numb body in the sun she faintly feels? Beams, saying, "Please, I'm ready now."

Ready for what? For Barcelona like the sour man said, where his nature-thing is now making it strong in the amateur section of the Festival. A winner! Like he also said, a lot of strip-mines and dead fish have been scrubbed but who cares with Delphi's darling face so visible?

So it's time for Delphi's face and her other delectabilities to show on Barcelona's Playa Neuva. Which means switching her channel to the EurAf synchsat.

They ship her at night so the nanosecond transfer isn't even noticed by that insignificant part of Delphi that lives five hundred feet under Carbondale, so excited the nurse has to make sure she eats. The circuit switches while Delphi "sleeps," that is, while P. Burke is out of the waldo cabinet. The next time she plugs in to open Delphi's eyes it's no different – do you notice which relay boards your phone calls go through?

And now for the event that turns the sugarcube from Colorado into the PRINCESS.

Literally true, he's a prince, or rather an Infante of an old Spanish line that got shined up in the Neomonarchy. He's also eighty-one, with a passion for birds – the kind you see in zoos. Now it suddenly turns out that he isn't poor at all. Quite the reverse; his old sister laughs in their tax lawyer's face and starts restoring the family hacienda while the Infante totters out to court Delphi. And little Delphi begins to live the life of the gods.

What do gods do? Well, everything beautiful. But (remember Mr Cantle?) the main point is Things. Ever see a god empty-handed? You can't be a god without at least a magic girdle or an eight-legged horse. But in the old days some stone tablets or winged sandals or a chariot drawn by virgins would do a god for life. No more! Gods make it on novelty now. By Delphi's time the hunt for new god-gear is turning the earth and seas inside-out and sending frantic fingers to the stars. And what gods have, mortals desire.

So Delphi starts on a Euromarket shopping spree squired by her old Infante, thereby doing her bit to stave off social collapse.

Social what? Didn't you get it, when Mr Cantle talked about a world where advertising is banned and fifteen billion consumers are glued to their holocam shows? One capricious self-powered god can wreck you.

Take the nose-filter massacre. Years, the industry sweated years to achieve an almost invisible enzymatic filter. So one day a couple of pop-gods show up wearing nose-filters like *big purple bats*. By the end of the week the world market is screaming for purple bats. Then it switched to bird-heads and skulls, but by the time the industry retooled the crazies had dropped bird-heads and gone to injection globes. Blood!

Multiply that by a million consumer industries and you can see why it's economic to have a few controllable gods. Especially with the beautiful hunk of space R&D the Peace Department laid out for and which the taxpayers are only too glad to have taken off their hands by an outfit like GTX which everybody knows is almost a public trust.

And so you – or rather, GTX – find a creature like P. Burke and give her Delphi. And Delphi helps keep things *orderly*, she does what you tell her to. Why? That's right, Mr Cantle never finished his speech.

But here come the tests of Delphi's button-nose twinkling in the torrent of news and entertainment. And she's noticed. The feedback shows a flock of viewers turning up the amps when this country baby gets tangled in her new colloidal body-jewels. She registers at a couple of major scenes, too, and when the Infante gives her a suncar, little Delphi trying out suncars is a tiger. There's a solid response in high-credit country. Mr Cantle is humming his happy tune as he cancels a Benelux subnet option to guest her on a nude cook-show called Wok Venus.

And now for the superposh old-world wedding! The hacienda has Moorish baths and six-foot silver candelabras and real black horses and the Spanish Vatican blesses them. The final event is a grand gaucho ball with the old prince and his little Infanta on a bowered balcony. She's a spectacular doll of silver lace, wildly launching toy doves at her new friends whirling by below.

The Infante beams, twitches his old nose to the scent of her sweet excitement. His doctor has been very helpful. Surely now, after he has been so patient with the suncars and all the nonsense—

The child looks up at him, saying something incomprehensible about "breath". He makes out that she's complaining about the three singers she had begged for.

"They've changed!" she marvels. "Haven't they changed? They're so dreary. I'm so happy now!"

And Delphi falls fainting against a gothic vargueno.

Her American duenna rushes up, calls help. Delphi's eyes are open, but Delphi isn't there. The duenna pokes among Delphi's hair, slaps her. The old prince grimaces. He has no idea what she is beyond an excellent solution to his tax problems, but he had been a falconer in his youth. There comes to his mind the small pinioned birds which were flung up to stimulate the hawks. He pockets the veined claw to which he had promised certain indulgences and departs to design his new aviary.

And Delphi also departs with her retinue to the Infante's newly discovered yacht. The trouble isn't serious. It's only that five thousand miles away and five hundred feet down P. Burke has been doing it too well.

They've always known she has terrific aptitude. Joe says he never saw a Remote take over so fast. No disorientations, no rejections. The psychomed talks about self-alienation. She's going into Delphi like a salmon to the sea.

She isn't eating or sleeping, they can't keep her out of the body-cabinet to get her blood moving, there are necroses under her grisly sit-down. Crisis!

So Delphi gets a long "sleep" on the yacht and P. Burke gets it pounded through her perforated head that she's endangering Delphi. (Nurse Fleming thinks of that, thus alienating the psychomed.)

They rig a pool down there (Nurse Fleming again) and chase P. Burke back and forth. And she loves it. So naturally when they let her plug in again Delphi loves it too. Every noon beside the yacht's hydrofoils darling Delphi clips along in the blue sea they've warned her not to drink. And every night around the shoulder of the world an ill-shaped thing in a dark burrow beats its way across a sterile pool.

So presently the yacht stands up on its foils and carries Delphi to the program Mr Cantle has waiting. It's long-range; she's scheduled for at least two decades' product life. Phase One calls for her to connect with a flock of young ultra-riches who are romping loose between Brioni and Djakarta where a competitor named PEV could pick them off.

A routine luxgear op, see; no politics, no policy angles, and the main budget items are the title and the yacht which was idle anyway. The storyline is that Delphi goes to accept some rare birds for her prince – who cares? The *point* is that the Haiti area is no longer radioactive and look! – the gods are there. And so are several new Carib West Happy Isles which can afford GTX rates, in fact two of them are GTX subsids.

But you don't want to get the idea that all these newsworthy people are wired-up robbies, for pity's sake. You don't need many if they're placed right. Delphi asks Joe about that when he comes down to Baranquilla to check her over. (P. Burke's own mouth hasn't said much for a while.)

"Are there many like me?"

"Nobody's like you, buttons. Look, are you still getting Van Allen warble?"

"I mean, like Davy. Is he a Remote?"

(Davy is the lad who is helping her collect the birds. A sincere redhead who needs a little more exposure.)

"Davy? He's one of Matt's boys, some psychojob. They haven't any channel."

"What about the real ones? Djuma van O, or Ali, or Jim Ten?"

"Djuma was born with a pile of GTX basic where her brain should be, she's nothing but a pain. Jimsy does what his astrologer tells him. Look, peanut, where do you get the idea you aren't real? You're the realest. Aren't you having joy?"

"Oh, Joe!" Flinging her little arms around him and his analyzer grids. "Oh, *me gusto mucho, muchissimo!*"

"Hey, hey." He pets her yellow head, folding the analyzer.

Three thousand miles north and five hundred feet down a forgotten hulk in a body-waldo glows.

And is she having joy. To waken out of the nightmare of being P. Burke and find herself a peri, a stargirl? On a yacht in paradise with no more to do than adorn herself and play with toys and attend revels and greet her friends – her, P. Burke, having friends! – and turn the right way for the holocams? Joy!

And it shows. One look at Delphi and the viewers know: DREAMS CAN COME TRUE.

Look at her riding pillion on Davy's sea-bike, carrying an apoplectic macaw in a silver hoop. Oh, *Morton, let's go there this winter!* Or learning the Japanese chinchona from that Kobe group, in a dress that looks like a blowtorch rising from one knee, and which should sell big in Texas. *Morton, is that real fire?* Happy, happy little girl!

And Davy. He's her pet and her baby and she loves to help him fix his red-gold hair. (P. Burke marveling, running Delphi's fingers through the curls.) Of course Davy is one of Matt's boys – not impotent exactly, but very *very* low drive. (Nobody knows exactly what Matt does with his bitty budget but the boys are useful and one or two have made names.) He's perfect for Delphi; in fact the psychomed lets her take him to bed, two kittens in a basket. Davy doesn't mind the fact that Delphi "sleeps" like the dead. That's when P. Burke is out of the body-waldo up at Carbondale, attending to her own depressing needs.

A funny thing about that. Most of her sleepy-time Delphi's just a gently ticking lush little vegetable waiting for P. Burke to get back on the controls. But now and again Delphi all by herself smiles a bit or stirs in her "sleep". Once she breathed a sound: "Yes."

Under Carbondale P. Burke knows nothing. She's asleep too, dreaming of Delphi, what else? But if the bushy Dr Tesla had heard that single syllable his bush would have turned snow-white. Because Delphi is TURNED OFF.

He doesn't. Davy is too dim to notice and Delphi's staff boss, Hopkins, wasn't monitoring.

And they've all got something else to think about now, because the cold-fire dress sells half a million copies, and not only in Texas. The GTX computers already know it. When they correlate a minor demand for macaws in Alaska the problem comes to human attention: Delphi is something special.

It's a problem, see, because Delphi is targeted on a limited consumer bracket. Now it turns out she has mass-pop potential – those macaws in *Fairbanks*, man! – it's like trying to shoot mice with an ABM. A whole new ball game. Dr Tesla and the fatherly Mr Cantle start going around in headquarters circles and buddy-lunching together when they can get away from a seventh-level weasel boy who scares them both.

In the end it's decided to ship Delphi down to the GTX holocam enclave in Chile to try a spot on one of the mainstream shows. (Never mind why an Infanta takes up acting.) The holocam complex occupies a couple of mountains where an observatory once used the clear air. Holocam total-environment shells are very expensive and electronically superstable. Inside them actors can move freely without going off-register and the whole scene or any selected part will show up in the viewer's home in complete 3-di, so real you can look up their noses and much denser than you get from mobile rigs. You can blow a tit ten feet tall when there's no molecular skiffle around.

The enclave looks – well, take everything you know about Hollywood-Burbank and throw it away. What Delphi sees coming down is a neat giant mushroom-farm, domes of all sizes up to monsters for the big games and stuff. It's orderly. The idea that art thrives on creative flamboyance has long been torpedoed by proof that what art needs is computers. Because this showbiz has something TV and Hollywood never had – *automated inbuilt viewer feedback*. Samples, ratings, critics, polls? Forget it. With that carrier field you can get real-time response-sensor readouts from every receiver in the world, served up at your console. That started as a thingie to give the public more influence on content.

Yes.

Try it, man. You're at the console. Slice to the sex-age-educ-econ-ethno-cetera audience of your choice and start. You can't miss. Where the feedback warms up, give 'em more of that. Warm – warmer – *hot!* You've hit it – the secret itch under those hides, the dream in those hearts. You don't need to know its name. With your hand controlling all the input and your eye reading all the response you can make them a god . . . and somebody'll do the same for you.

But Delphi just sees rainbows, when she gets through the degaussing ports and the field relay and takes her first look at the insides of those shells. The next thing she sees is a team of shapers and technicians descending on her, and millisecond timers everywhere. The tropical leisure is finished. She's in gigabuck mainstream now, at the funnel maw of the unceasing hose that's pumping the sight and sound and flesh and blood and sobs and laughs and dreams of *reality* into the world's happy head. Little Delphi is going plonk into a zillion homes in prime time and nothing is left to chance. Work!

And again Delphi proves apt. Of course it's really P. Burke down under Carbondale who's doing it, but who remembers that carcass? Certainly not P. Burke, she hasn't spoken through her own mouth for months. Delphi doesn't even recall dreaming of her when she wakes up.

As for the show itself, don't bother. It's gone on so long no living soul could unscramble the plotline. Delphi's trial spot has something to do with a widow and her dead husband's brother's amnesia.

The flap comes after Delphi's spots begin to flash out along the world-hose and the feedback appears. You've guessed it, of course. Sensational! As you'd say, they IDENTIFY.

The report actually says something like InskinEmp with a string of percentages meaning that Delphi not only has it for anybody with a Y-chromosome, but also for women and every thing in between. It's the sweet supernatural jackpot, the million-to-one.

Remember your Harlow? A sexpot, sure. But why did bitter hausfraus in Gary and Memphis know that the vanilla-ice-cream goddess with the white hair and crazy eyebrows was *their baby girl*? And write loving letters to Jean warning her that their husbands weren't good enough for her? Why? The GTX analysis don't know either, but they know what to do with it when it happens.

(Back in his bird sanctuary the old Infante spots it without benefit of computers and gazes thoughtfully at his bride in widow's weeds. It might, he feels, be well to accelerate the completion of his studies.)

The excitement reaches down to the burrow under Carbondale where P. Burke gets two medical exams in a week and a chronically inflamed electrode is replaced. Nurse Fleming also gets an assistant who doesn't do much nursing but is very interested in access doors and identity tabs.

And in Chile, little Delphi is promoted to a new home up among the stars' residential spreads and a private jitney to carry her to work. For Hopkins there's a new computer terminal and a full-time schedule man. What is the schedule crowded with?

Things.

And here begins the trouble. You probably saw that coming too.

"What does she think she is, a goddam *consumer rep*?" Mr Cantle's fatherly face in Carbondale contorts.

"The girl's upset," Miss Fleming says stubbornly. "She *believes* that, what you told her about helping people and good new products."

"They are good products," Mr Cantle snaps automatically, but his anger is under control. He hasn't got where he is by irrelevant reactions.

"She says the plastic gave her a rash and the glo-pills made her dizzy."

"Good god, she shouldn't swallow them," Doctor Tesla puts in agitatedly.

"You told her she'd use them," persists Miss Fleming.

Mr Cantle is busy figuring how to ease this problem to the weasel-faced young man. What, was it a goose that lays golden eggs?

Whatever he says to level Seven, down in Chile the offending products vanish. And a symbol goes into Delphi's tank matrix, one that means roughly *Balance unit resistance against PR index*. This means that Delphi's complaints will be endured as long as her Pop Response stays above a certain level. (What happens when it sinks need not concern us.) And to compensate, the price of her exposure-time rises again. She's a regular on the show now and response is still climbing.

See her under the sizzling lasers, in a holocam shell set up as a walkway accident. (The show is guesting an acupuncture school shill.)

"I don't think this new body-lift is safe," Delphi's saying. "It's made a funny blue spot on me – look, Mr Vere."

She wiggles to show where the mini-grav pak that imparts a delicious sense of weightlessness is attached.

"So don't leave it *on*, Dee. With your meat – watch that deck-spot, it's startling to synch."

"But it I don't wear it it isn't honest. They should insulate it more or something, don't you see?"

The show's beloved old father, who is the casualty, gives a senile snigger.

"I'll tell them," Mr Vere mutters. "Look now, as you step back bend like this so it just shows, see? And hold two beats."

Obediently Delphi turns, and through the dazzle her eyes connect with a pair of strange dark ones. She squints. A quite young man is lounging alone by the port, apparently waiting to use the chamber.

Delphi's used by now to young men looking at her with many peculiar expressions, but she isn't used to what she gets here. A jolt of something somber and knowing. *Secrets.*

"Eyes! Eyes, Dee!"

She moves through the routine, stealing peeks at the stranger. He stares back. He knows something.

When they let her go she comes shyly to him.

"Living wild, kitten." Cool voice, hot underneath.

"What do you mean?"

"Dumping on the product. You trying to get dead?"

"But it isn't right," she tells him. "They don't know, but I do, I've been wearing it."

His cool is jolted.

"You're out of your head."

"Oh, they'll see I'm right when they check it," she explains. "They're just so busy. When I tell them—"

He is staring down at little flower-face. His mouth opens, closes. "What are you doing in this sewer anyway? Who are you?"

Bewilderedly she says, "I'm Delphi."

"Holy Zen."

"What's wrong? Who are you, please?"

Her people are moving her out now, nodding at him.

"Sorry we ran over, Mister Uhunh," the script girl says.

He mutters something but it's lost as her convoy bustles her toward the flower-decked jitney.

(Hear the click of an invisible ignition-train being armed?)

"Who was he?" Delphi asks her hairman.

The hairman is bending up and down from his knees as he works.

"Paul. Isham. Three," he says and puts a comb in his mouth.

"Who's that? I can't see."

He mumbles around the comb, meaning "Are you jiving?" Because she has to be, in the middle of the GTX enclave.

Next day there's a darkly smoldering face under a turban-towel when Delphi and the show's paraplegic go to use the carbonated pool.

She looks.

He looks.

And the next day, too.

(Hear the automatic sequencer cutting in? The system couples, the fuels begin to travel.)

Poor old Isham senior. You have to feel sorry for a man who values order: when he begets young, genetic information is still transmitted in the old ape way. One minute it's a happy midget with a rubber duck – look around and here's this huge healthy stranger, opaquely emotional, running with God knows who. Questions are hear where there's nothing to question, and eruptions claiming to be moral outrage. When this is called to Papa's attention – it may take time, in that boardroom – Papa does what he can, but without immortality-juice the problem is worrisome.

And young Paul Isham is a bear. He's bright and articulate and tender-souled and incessantly active and he and his friends are choking with appallment at the world their fathers made. And it hasn't taken Paul long to discover that *his* father's house has many mansions and even the GTX computers can't relate everything to everything else. He noses out a decaying project which adds up to something like, Sponsoring Marginal Creativity (the free-lance team that "discovered" Delphi was one such grantee). And from there it turns out that an agile lad named Isham can get his hands on a viable packet of GTX holocam facilities.

So here he is with his little band, way down the mushroom-farm mountain, busily spooling a show which has no relation to Delphi's. It's built on bizarre techniques and unsettling distortions pregnant with social protest. An *underground* expression to you.

All this isn't unknown to his father, of course, but so far it has done nothing more than deepen Isham senior's apprehensive frown.

Until Paul connects with Delphi.

And by the time Papa learns this, those invisible hypergolics have exploded, the energy-shells are rushing out. For Paul, you see, is the genuine article. He's serious. He dreams. He even reads – for example, *Green Mansions* – and he wept fiercely when those fiends burned Rima alive.

When he hears that some new GTX pussy is making it big he sneers and forgets it. He's busy. He never connects the name with this little girl making her idiotic, doomed protest in the holocam chamber. This strangely simple little girl.

And she comes and looks up at him and he sees Rima, lost Rima the enchanted bird girl, and his unwired human heart goes twang.

And Rima turns out to be Delphi.

Do you need a map? The angry puzzlement. The rejection of the dissonance Rima-hustling-for-GTX-My-Father. Garbage, cannot be. The loitering around the pool to confirm the swindle . . . dark eyes hitting on blue wonder, jerky words exchanged in a peculiar stillness . . . the dreadful reorganization of the image into Rima-Delphi *in my Father's tentacles*—

You don't need a map.

Nor for Delphi either, the girl who loved her gods. She's seen their divine flesh close now, heard their unamplified voices call her name. She's played their god-games, worn their garlands. She's even become a goddess herself, though she doesn't believe it. She's not disenchanted, don't think that. She's still full of love. It's just that some crazy kind of *hope* hasn't—

Really you can skip all this, when the loving little girl on the yellow-brick road meets a Man. A real human male burning with angry compassion and grandly concerned with human justice, who reaches for her with real male arms and – boom! She loves him back with all her heart.

A happy trip, see?

Except.

Except that it's really P. Burke five thousand miles away who loves Paul. P. Burke the monster, down in a dungeon, smelling of electrode-paste. A caricature of a woman burning, melting, obsessed with true love. Trying over twenty-double-thousand miles of hard vacuum to reach her beloved through girl-flesh numbed by an invisible film. Feeling his arms around the body he thinks is hers, fighting through shadows to give herself to him. Trying to taste and smell him through beautiful dead nostrils, to love him back with a body that goes dead in the heart of the fire.

Perhaps you get P. Burke's state of mind?

She has phases. The trying, first. And the shame. The SHAME. *I am not what thou lovest.* And the fiercer trying. And the realization that there is no, no way, none. Never. *Never* . . . A bit delayed, isn't it, her understanding that the bargain she made was forever? P. Burke should have noticed those stories about mortals who end up as grasshoppers.

You see the outcome – the funnelling of all this agony into one dumb protoplasmic drive to fuse with Delphi. To leave, to close out the beast she is chained to. *To become Delphi.*

Of course it's impossible.

However her torments have an effect on Paul. Delphi-as-Rima is a potent enough love object, and liberating Delphi's mind requires hours of deeply satisfying instruction in the rottenness of it all. Add in Delphi's body worshipping his flesh, burning in the fire of P. Burke's savage heart – do you wonder Paul is involved?

That's not all.

By now they're spending every spare moment together and some that aren't so spare.

"Mister Isham, would you mind staying out of this sports sequence? The script calls for Davy here."

(Davy's still around, the exposure did him good.)

"What the difference?" Paul yawns. "It's just an ad. I'm not blocking that thing."

Shocked silence at his two-letter word. The script girl swallows bravely.

"I'm sorry, sir, our directive is to do the *social sequence* exactly as scripted. We're having to respool the segments we did last week, Mister Hopkins is very angry with me."

"Who the hell is Hopkins? Where is he?"

"Oh, please, Paul. *Please*."

Paul unwraps himself, saunters back. The holocam crew nervously check their angles. The GTX boardroom has a foible about having things *pointed* at them and theirs. Cold shivers, when the image of an Isham nearly went onto the world beam beside that Dialadinner.

Worse yet, Paul has no respect for the sacred schedules which are now a full-time job for ferret boy up at headquarters. Paul keeps forgetting to bring her back on time and poor Hopkins can't cope.

So pretty soon the boardroom data-ball has an urgent personal action-tab for Mr Isham senior. They do it the gentle way, at first.

"I can't today, Paul."

"Why not?"

"They say I have to, it's *very* important."

He strokes the faint gold down on her narrow back. Under Carbondale, Pa., a blind mole-woman shivers.

"Important. Their importance. Making more gold. Can't you see? To them you're just a thing to get scratch with. A *huckster*. Are you going to let them screw you, Dee? Are you?"

"Oh, Paul—"

He doesn't know it but he's seeing a weirdie; Remotes aren't hooked up to flow tears.

"Just say no, Dee. No. Integrity. You have to."

"But they say, it's my job—"

"You won't believe I can take care of you, Dee, baby, baby, you're letting them rip us. You have to choose. Tell them, no."

"Paul . . . I w-will . . ."

And she does. Brave little Delphi (insane P. Burke). Saying "No, please, I promised, Paul."

They try some more, still gently.

"Paul, Mr Hopkins told me the reason they don't want us to be together so much. It's because of who you are, your father."

She thinks his father is like Mr Cantle, maybe.

"Oh great. Hopkins. I'll fix him. Listen, I can't think about Hopkins now. Ken came back today, he found out something."

They are lying on the high Andes meadow watching his friends dive their singing kites.

"Would you believe, on the coast the police have *electrodes in their heads*?"

She stiffens in his arms.

"Yeah, weird. I thought they only used PP on criminals and the army. Don't you see, Dee – something has to be going on. Some movement. Maybe somebody's organizing. How can we find out." He pounds the ground behind her: "We should make *contact*! If we could only find out."

"The, the news?" she asks distractedly.

"The news." He laughs. "There's nothing in the news except what they want people to know. Half the country could burn up and nobody would know it if they didn't want. Dee, can't you take what I'm explaining to you? They've got the whole world programmed! Total control of communication. They've got everybody's minds wired in to think what they show them and want what they give them and they give them what they're programmed to want – you can't break in or out of it, you can't get *hold* of it anywhere. I don't think they even have a plan except to keep things going round and round – and God knows what's happening to the people or the earth or the other planets, maybe. One great big vortex of lies and garbage pouring round and round getting bigger and bigger and nothing can ever change. If people don't wake up soon we're through!"

He pounds her stomach softly.

"You have to break out. Dee."

"I'll try, Paul, I will—"

"You're mine. They can't have you."

And he goes to see Hopkins, who is indeed cowed.

But that night up under Carbondale the fatherly Mr Cantle goes to see P. Burke.

P. Burke? On a cot in a utility robe like a dead camel in a tent, she cannot at first comprehend that he is telling *her* to break it off with Paul. P. Burke has never seen Paul. *Delphi* sees Paul. The fact is, P. Burke can no longer clearly recall that she exists apart from Delphi.

Mr Cantle can scarcely believe it either but he tries.

He points out the futility, the potential embarrassment for Paul. That gets a dim stare from the bulk on the bed. Then he goes into her duty to GTX, her job, isn't she grateful for the opportunity, etcetera. He's very persuasive.

The cobwebby mouth of P. Burke opens and croaks.

"No."

Nothing more seems to be forthcoming.

Mr Cantle isn't dense, he knows an immovable obstacle when he bumps one. He also knows an irresistible force: GTX. The simple solution is to lock the waldo-cabinet until Paul gets tired of waiting for Delphi to wake up. But the cost, the schedules! And there's something odd here . . . he eyes the corporate asset hulking on the bed and his hunch-sense prickles.

You see, Remotes don't love. They don't have real sex, the circuits designed that out from the start. So it's been assumed that it's *Paul* who is diverting himself or something with the pretty little body in Chile. P. Burke can only be doing what comes natural to any ambitious gutter-meat. It hasn't occurred to anyone that they're dealing with the real hairy thing whose shadow is blasting out of every holoshow on earth.

Love?

Mr Cantle frowns. The idea is grotesque. But his instinct for the fuzzy line is strong; he will recommend flexibility.

And so, in Chile:

"Darling, I don't have to work tonight! And Friday too – isn't that right, Mr Hopkins?"

"Oh, great. When does she come up for parole?"

"Mr Isham, please be reasonable. Our schedule – surely your own production people must be needing you?"

This happens to be true. Paul goes away. Hopkins stares after him wondering distastefully why an Isham wants to ball a waldo. (How sound are those boardroom belly-fears – garble creeps, creeps in!) It never occurs to Hopkins that an Isham might not know what Delphi is.

Especially with Davy crying because Paul has kicked him out of Delphi's bed.

Delphi's bed is under a real window.

"Stars," Paul sleepily. He rolls over, pulling Delphi on top. "Are you aware that this is one of the last places on earth where people can see the stars? Tibet, too, maybe."

"Paul . . ."

"Go to sleep. I want to see you sleep."

"Paul, I . . . I sleep so *hard*, I mean, it's a joke how hard I am to wake up. Do you mind?"

"Yes."

But finally, fearfully, she must let go. So that five thousand miles north a crazy spent creature can crawl out to gulp concentrates and fall on her cot. But not for long. It's pink dawn when Delphi's eyes open to find Paul's arms around her, his voice saying rude, tender things. He's been kept awake. The nerveless little statue that was her Delphi-body nuzzled him in the night.

Insane hope rises, is fed a couple of nights later when he tells her she called his name in her sleep.

And that day Paul's arms keep her from work and Hopkin's wails go up to headquarters where the sharp-faced lad is working his sharp tailbone off packing Delphi's program. Mr Cantle defuses that one. But next week it happens again, to a major client. And ferret-face has connections on the technical side.

Now you can see that when you have a field of complexly heterodyned energy modulations tuned to a demand-point like Delphi there are many problems of standwaves and lashback and skiffle of all sorts which are normally balanced out with ease by the technology of the future. By the same token they can be delicately unbalanced too, in ways that feed back into the waldo operator with striking results.

"Darling – what the hell! What's wrong? DELPHI!"

Helpless shrieks, writhings. Then the Rima-bird is lying wet and limp in his arms, her eyes enormous.

"I . . . I wasn't supposed to . . ." she gasps faintly, "They told me not to . . ."

"Oh my god – *Delphi*."

And his hard fingers are digging in her thick yellow hair. Electronically knowledgeable fingers. They freeze.

"You're a *doll*! You're one of those PP implants. They control you. I should have known. Oh God, I should have known."

"No, Paul," she's sobbing. "No, no, no—"

"Damn them. Damn them, what they've done – you're not *you*—"

He's shaking her, crouching over her in the bed and jerking her back and forth, glaring at the pitiful beauty.

"No!" She pleads (it's not true, that dark bad dream back there). "I'm Delphi!"

"My father. Filth, pigs – damn them, damn them, damn them."

"No, no," she babbles. "They were good to me—" P. Burke underground mouthing, "They were good to me – Aah-aaaah!"

Another agony skewers her. Up north the sharp young man wants to make sure this so-tiny interference works. Paul can scarcely hang onto her, he's crying too. "I'll kill them."

His Delphi, a wired-up slave! Spikes in her brain, electronic shackles in his bird's heart. Remember when those savages burned Rima alive?

"I'll *kill* the man that's doing this to you."

He's still saying it afterward but she doesn't hear. She's sure he hates her now, all she wants is to die. When she finally understands that the fierceness is tenderness she thinks it's a miracle. *He knows – and he still loves!*

How can she guess that he's got it a little bit wrong?

You can't blame Paul. Give him credit that he's even heard about pleasure-pain implants and snoops, which by their nature aren't mentioned much by those who know them most intimately. That's what he thinks is being used on Delphi, something to *control* her. And to listen – he burns at the unknown ears in their bed.

Of waldo-bodies and objects like P. Burke he has heard nothing.

So it never crosses his mind as he looks down at his violated bird, sick with fury and love, that he isn't holding *all* of her. Do you need to be told the mad resolve jelling in him now?

To free Delphi.

How? Well, he is, after all, Paul Isham III. And he even has an idea where the GTX neurolab is. In Carbondale.

But first things have to be done for Delphi, and for his own stomach. So he gives her back to Hopkins and departs in a restrained and discreet way. And the Chile staff is grateful and do not understand that his teeth don't normally show so much.

And a week passes in which Delphi is a very good, docile little ghost. They let her have the load of wildflowers Paul sends and the bland loving notes. (He's playing it coony.) And up in headquarters weasel boy feels that *his* destiny has clicked a notch onward and floats the word up that he's handy with little problems.

And no one knows what P. Burke thinks in any way whatever, except that Miss Fleming catches her flushing her food down the

can and next night she faints in the pool. They haul her out and
stick her with IVs. Miss Fleming frets, she's seen expressions like
that before. But she wasn't around when crazies who called
themselves Followers of the Fish looked through flames to life
everlasting. P. Burke is seeing Heaven on the far side of death, too.
Heaven is spelled P-a-u-l, but the idea's the same. *I will die and be
born again in Delphi*.

Garbage, electronically speaking. No way.

Another week and Paul's madness has become a plan. (Remember, he does have friends.) He smolders, watching his love paraded
by her masters. He turns out a scorching sequence for his own
show. And finally, politely, he requests from Hopkins a morsel of
his bird's free time, which duly arrives.

"I thought you didn't *want* me any more," she's repeating as
they wing over mountain flanks in Paul's suncar. "Now you
know—"

"Look at me!"

His hand covers her mouth and he's showing her a lettered card.

DON'T TALK THEY CAN HEAR EVERYTHING WE SAY.

I'M TAKING YOU AWAY NOW.

She kisses his hand. He nods urgently, flipping the card.

DON'T BE AFRAID. I CAN STOP THE PAIN IF THEY TRY TO HURT YOU.

With his free hand he shakes out a silvery scrambler-mesh on a
power pack. She is dumbfounded.

THIS WILL CUT THE SIGNALS AND PROTECT YOU DARLING.

She's staring at him, her head going vaguely from side to side, No.
"Yes!" He grins triumphantly. "Yes!"

For a moment she wonders. That powered mesh will cut off the
field, all right. It will also cut off Delphi. But he is *Paul*. Paul is
kissing her, she can only seek him hungrily as he sweeps the suncar
through a pass.

Ahead is an old jet ramp with a shiny bullet waiting to go. (Paul
also has credits and a Name.) The little GTX patrol courier is built
for nothing but speed. Paul and Delphi wedge in behind the pilot's
extra fuel tank and there's no more talking when the torches start
to scream.

They're screaming high over Quito before Hopkins starts to
worry. He wastes another hour tracking the beeper on Paul's
suncar. The suncar is sailing a pattern out to sea. By the time
they're sure it's empty and Hopkins gets on the hot flue to

headquarters the fugitives are a sourceless howl above Carib West.

Up at headquarters weasel boy gets the squeal. His first impulse is to repeat his previous play but then his brain snaps to. This one is too hot. Because, see, although in the long run they can make P. Burke do anything at all except maybe *live*, instant emergencies can be tricky. And – Paul Isham III.

"Can't you order her back?"

They're all in the GTX tower monitor station, Mr Cantle and ferret-face and Joe and a very neat man who is Mr Isham senior's personal eyes and ears.

"No sir," Joe says doggedly. "We can read channels, particularly speech, but we can't interpolate organized pattern. It takes the waldo op to send one-to-one—"

"What are they saying?"

"Nothing at the moment, sir." The console jockey's eyes are closed. "I believe they are, ah, embracing."

"They're not answering," a traffic monitor says. "Still heading zero zero three zero – due north, sir."

"You're certain Kennedy is alerted not to fire on them?" the neat man asks anxiously.

"Yes, sir."

"Can't you just turn her off?" The sharp-faced lad is angry. "Pull that pig out of the controls!"

"If you cut the transmission cold you'll kill the Remote," Joe explains for the third time. "Withdrawal has to be phased right, you have to fade over to the Remote's own autonomics. Heart, breathing, cerebellum would go blooey. If you pull Burke out you'll probably finish her too. It's a fantastic cybersystem, you don't want to do that."

"The investment." Mr Cantle shudders.

Weasel boy puts his hand on the console jock's shoulder, it's the contact who arranged the No-no effect for him.

"We can at least give them a warning signal, sir." He licks his lips, gives the neat man his sweet ferret smile. "We know that does no damage."

Joe frowns, Mr Cantle sighs. The neat man is murmuring into his wrist. He looks up. "I am authorized," he says reverently, "I am authorized to, ah, direct a signal. If this is the only course. But minimal, minimal."

Sharp-face squeezes his man's shoulder.

In the silver bullet shrieking over Charleston Paul feels Delphi arch in his arms. He reaches for the mesh, hot for action. She thrashes, pushing at his hands, her eyes roll. She's afraid of that mesh despite the agony. (And she's right.) Frantically Paul fights her in the cramped space, gets it over her head. As he turns the power up she burrows free under his arm and the spasm fades.

"They're calling you again, Mister Isham!" the pilot yells.

"Don't answer. Darling, keep this over your head damn it how can I—"

An AX90 barrels over their nose, there's a flash.

"Mister Isham! Those are Air Force jets!"

"Forget it," Paul shouts back. "They won't fire. Darling, don't be afraid."

Another AX90 rocks them.

"Would you mind pointing your pistol at my head where they can see it, sir?" the pilot howls.

Paul does so. The AX90s take up escort formation around them. The pilot goes back to figuring how he can collect from GTX too, and after Goldsboro AB the escort peels away.

"Holding the same course," Traffic is reporting to the group around the monitor. "Apparently they've taken on enough fuel to bring them to towerport here."

"In that case it's just a question of waiting for them to dock." Mr Cantle's fatherly manner revives a bit.

"Why can't they cut off that damn freak's life-support," the sharp young man fumes. "It's ridiculous."

"They're working on it," Cantle assures him.

What they're doing, down under Carbondale, is arguing.

Miss Fleming's watchdog has summoned the bushy man to the waldo room.

"Miss Fleming, you will obey orders."

"You'll kill her if you try that, sir. I can't believe you meant it, that's why I didn't. We've already fed her enough sedative to affect heart action; if you cut any more oxygen she'll die in there."

The bushy man grimaces. "Get Doctor Quine here fast."

They wait, staring at the cabinet in which a drugged, ugly madwoman fights for consciousness, fights to hold Delphi's eyes open.

High over Richmond the silver pod starts a turn. Delphi is sagged into Paul's arm, her eyes swim up to him.

"Starting down now, baby. It'll be over soon, all you have to do is stay alive, Dee."

". . . Stay alive . . ."

The traffic monitor has caught them. "Sir! They've turned off for Carbondale – Control has contact—"

"Let's go."

But the headquarters posse is too late to intercept the courier wailing into Carbondale. And Paul's friends have come through again. The fugitives are out through the freight dock and into the neurolab admin port before the guard gets organized. At the elevator Paul's face plus his handgun get them in.

"I want Doctor – what's his name, Dee? Dee!"

". . . Tesla . . ." She's reeling on her feet.

"Doctor Tesla. Take me down to Tesla, fast."

Intercoms are squalling around them as they whoosh down, Paul's pistol in the guard's back. When the door slides open the bushy man is there.

"I'm Tesla."

"I'm Paul Isham. *Isham*. You're going to take your flaming implants out of this girl – now. Move!"

"What?"

"You heard me. Where's your operating room? Go!"

"But—"

"Move! Do I have to burn somebody?"

Paul waves the weapon at Dr Quine, who has just appeared.

"No, no," says Tesla hurriedly. "But I can't, you know. It's impossible, there'll be nothing left."

"You screaming well can, right now. You mess up and I'll kill you," says Paul murderously. "Where is it, there? And wipe the feke that's on her circuits now."

He's backing them down the hall, Delphi heavy on his arm.

"Is this the place, baby? Where they did it to you?"

"Yes," she whispers, blinking at a door. "Yes . . ."

Because it is, see. Behind that door is the very suite where she was born.

Paul herds them through it into a gleaming hall. An inner door opens and a nurse and a gray man rush out. And freeze.

Paul sees there's something special about that inner door. He crowds them past it and pushes it open and looks in.

Inside is a big mean-looking cabinet with its front door panels ajar.

And inside that cabinet is a poisoned carcass to whom something wonderful, unspeakable, is happening. Inside is P. Burke the real living woman who knows that HE is there, coming closer – Paul whom she had fought to reach through forty thousand miles of ice – PAUL is here! – is yanking at the waldo doors—

The doors tear open and a monster rises up.

"Paul darling!" croaks the voice of love and the arms of love reach for him.

And he responds.

Wouldn't you, if a gaunt she-golem flab-naked and spouting wires and blood came at you clawing with metal studded paws—

"Get away!" He knocks wires.

It doesn't much matter which wires, P. Burke has so to speak her nervous system hanging out. Imagine somebody jerking a handful of your medulla—

She crashes onto the floor at his feet, flopping and roaring "PAUL-PAUL-PAUL" in rictus.

It's doubtful he recognizes his name or sees her life coming out of her eyes at him. And at the last it doesn't go to him. The eyes find Delphi, fainting by the doorway, and die.

Now of course Delphi is dead, too.

There's a total silence as Paul steps away from the thing by his foot.

"You killed her," Tesla says. "That was her."

"Your control." Paul is furious, the thought of that monster fastened into little Delphi's brain nauseates him. He sees her crumpling and holds out his arms. Not knowing she is dead.

And Delphi comes to him.

One foot before the other, not moving very well – but moving. Her darling face turns up. Paul is distracted by the terrible quiet, and when he looks down he sees only her tender little neck.

"Now you get the implants out," he warns them. Nobody moves.

"But, but she's dead," Miss Fleming whispers wildly.

Paul feels Delphi's life under his hand, they're talking about their monster. He aims his pistol at the gray man.

"You. If we aren't in your surgery when I count three I'm burning off this man's leg."

"Mr Isham," Tesla says desperately, "you have just killed

the person who animated the body you call Delphi. Delphi herself is dead. If you release your arm you'll see what I say is true."

The tone gets through. Slowly Paul opens his arm, looks down. "Delphi?"

She totters, sways, stays upright. Her face comes slowly up.

"Paul . . ." Tiny voice.

"Your crotty tricks," Paul snarls at them. "Move!"

"Look at her eyes," Dr Quine croaks.

They look. One of Delphi's pupils fills the iris, her lips writhe weirdly.

"Shock." Paul grabs her to him. "*Fix* her!" He yells at them, aiming at Tesla.

"For God's sake . . . bring it in the lab." Tesla quavers.

"Goodbye-bye," says Delphi clearly. They lurch down the hall, Paul carrying her, and meet a wave of people.

Headquarters has arrived.

Joe takes one look and dives for the waldo room, running into Paul's gun.

"Oh no, you don't."

Everybody is yelling. The little thing in his arm stirs, says plaintively, "I'm Delphi."

And all through the ensuing jabber and ranting she hangs on, keeping it up, the ghost of P. Burke or whatever whispering crazily "Paul . . . Paul . . . Please, I'm Delphi . . . Paul?"

"I'm here, darling, I'm here." He's holding her in the nursing bed. Tesla talks, talks, talks unheard.

"Paul . . . don't sleep . . ." The ghost-voice whispers. Paul is in agony, he will not accept, WILL NOT believe.

Tesla runs down.

And then near midnight Delphi says roughly, "Ag-ag-ag—" and slips onto the floor, making a rough noise like a seal.

Paul screams. There's more of the *ag-ag* business and more gruesome convulsive disintegrations, until by two in the morning Delphi is nothing but a warm little bundle of vegetative functions hitched to some expensive hardware – the same that sustained her before her life began. Joe has finally persuaded Paul to let him at the waldo-cabinet. Paul stays by her long enough to see her face change in a dreadfully alien and coldly convincing way, and then he stumbles out bleakly through the group in Tesla's office.

Behind him Joe is working wet-faced, sweating to reintegrate the fantastic complex of circulation, respiration, endocrines, midbrain homeostases, the patterned flux that was a human being – it's like saving an orchestra abandoned in midair. Joe is also crying a little; he alone had truly loved P. Burke. P. Burke, now a dead pile on a table, was the greatest cybersystem he has ever known and he never forgets her.

The end, really.

You're curious?

Sure, Delphi lives again. Next year she's back on the yacht getting sympathy for her tragic breakdown. But there's a different chick in Chile, because while Delphi's new operator is competent, you don't get two P. Burke's in a row – for which GTX is duly grateful.

The real belly-bomb of course is Paul. He was *young*, see. Fighting abstract wrong. Now life has clawed into him and he goes through gut rage and grief and grows in human wisdom and resolve. So much so that you won't be surprised, some time later, to find him – where?

In the GTX boardroom, dummy. Using the advantage of his birth to radicalize the system. You'd call it "boring from within".

That's how he put it, and his friends couldn't agree more. It gives them a warm, confident feeling to know that Paul is up there. Sometimes one of them who's still around runs into him and gets a big hello.

And the sharp-faced lad?

Oh, he matures too. He learns fast, believe it. For instance, he's the first to learn that an obscure GTX research unit is actually getting something with their loopy temporal anomalizer project. True, he doesn't have a physics background, and he's bugged quite a few people. But he doesn't really learn about that until the day he stands where somebody points him during a test run—

—and wakes up lying on a newspaper headlined NIXON UNVEILS PHASE TWO.

Lucky he's a fast learner.

Believe it, zombie. When I say growth I mean *growth*. Capital appreciation. You can stop sweating. There's a great future there.

MEMORIES OF THE BODY
Lisa Tuttle

A US-born writer resident in the UK (currently Scotland) since 1980, Lisa Tuttle was an early graduate of the Clarion SF writers' workshop and quickly established herself as a masterful writer of short stories of fantasy, horror and science fiction. Some of her best have been collected in A Nest of Nightmares *(1986)*, A Spaceship Built of Stone and Other Stories *(1987) and* Memories of the Body *(1992), which takes its title from the following sharp-edged tale of sexual tension in a technological future . . .*

As she plunged the long-bladed butcher's knife into her husband's chest, Cerise realized she had wanted to kill him for years.

She had always kept her anger hidden, not only from others, but from herself as well. She deplored violence, and believed hers was a peaceful nature. She had tried to understand her husband's changing moods and needs, and when he left her she had wept, and gone on loving. Now, however, her long-denied anger was as real as the knife in her hand, and she hated him.

Murder was wonderful. Patrick let out a little moan when she stabbed him, and she echoed his sound as she sometimes did in bed, to encourage him.

She pulled the knife out and gazed at his thin, naked body, loved for so long. She wanted to cut it to pieces, to stab him in a hundred places. She bared her teeth and swung at him.

He tried to stop her, grabbing hold of the blade. He cried out. Blood stained his pale hands.

"Stupid!" she said. With a hard, impatient turn of her wrist she freed the knife from his grasp and severed two of his fingers.

"What'll I cut off next?" she asked. She was breathing hard and her body tingled, as aroused as she had ever been by love-making. "Why don't you try to get away? Turn around, I'll stab you in the back."

He stared down at his ruined hand and took one stumbling step backwards. She went after him, cutting him twice, opening his stomach.

"I bet you never thought I could do this. You thought you could get away with anything. You thought I was weak, I bet. Thought I'd kill myself sooner than hurt you. Stand still, damn you."

With the next stab, the knife sank deep into his abdomen, buried to the hilt, slipping in her grasp.

'Cerise . . ." Blood bubbled on his lips as he spoke. There was blood everywhere, and a terrible, sweet smell. In sudden silence, Patrick fell to his knees, then toppled forward, onto the knife, and lay still.

She felt a surge of disappointment. She wasn't ready for it to be over. She crouched down and tried to lift him, but the body was a dead weight. "Pat?" she said. Her smile lost its shape, and she began to pant, the smell of death so thick she could hardly breathe. She gagged, and then vomited, and then wept.

Later, she stared through a blur of tears at the little bald spot on the back of his head. She wished she could apologize to him. The hate was all gone now. She hadn't always hated him. "Oh, Pat," she said softly. "I loved you. I really, really did."

Cerise continued to crouch beside the body while the clock above the bed clicked away the seconds, still dazed with discovery, astonished by her own emotions.

The murder had been Hewitt's idea – she had agreed to it under pressure, only to please him. He would go on feeling threatened by her ex-husband forever, it seemed, unless she would agree to kill him. But even when she went down to that fancy kitchenware shop in the new mall and picked out the scariest-looking knife she could find she wasn't really planning on using it. She was sure that when it came right down to it she would chicken out. Self-defence would be hard enough, but to strike first, to kill in cold blood . . . And to kill someone she had loved! She wasn't an aggressive person. She didn't even like competitive sports, and she hated arguments. That was how she'd agreed to this, in fact. To stop the arguments she and Hewitt were having about love. She had told herself she was only doing it for Hewitt, but from the moment she had seen Patrick again, Hewitt had been nowhere in her thoughts.

Cerise rose on shaky legs and went into the bathroom to wash off the blood, glancing at the button beside the light-switch. If she pushed it, a member of the Timber Oaks staff would be with her within seconds. She decided she wanted to be clean, dressed and made-up, back in control before anyone saw her. She was sure that was how Hewitt would have done it when he murdered his wife.

Still naked, Cerise leaned through the doorway to look at the clock. Without her lenses, she had to squint to make out the time. It was almost four, much later in the afternoon than she had imagined. They had told her she could stay the night if she wanted, or even for a couple of days. But Hewitt was expecting her for dinner. He obviously didn't think murder should take very long. She wondered how Hewitt had killed his wife, and imagined that he had despatched her with great efficiency. He'd probably walked in, said her name, shot her with one of his guns, fired again to make sure, and then drove back to the office to finalize a couple of deals. Hewitt had offered to show her a videotape of the murder, but Cerise, disliking violence, had refused.

Cerise tried to estimate how long it would take her to drive back to town, and thought about rush-hour traffic. She would be late, but she really had to wash her hair. There might be blood in it, or something else. She wished she wasn't having dinner with Hewitt tonight. He was going to take one look at her and know that she'd had sex with Patrick before she killed him.

The sex hadn't been part of the deal. Not that anything had been said, but she knew Hewitt's attitude. The murder might have been for Hewitt, but there was no way she could pretend the sex had been.

She turned the shower on hard and stepped under it, wishing she could wash away her guilt as easily as the blood.

I shouldn't have had sex with him, she thought. Then said aloud, "It." It, not him. That wasn't Patrick's body lying on the bedroom floor; it never had been Patrick. She had to remind herself now of what she had willingly – wilfully – forgotten during the past few hours. It was only a machine she'd murdered, a sophisticated facsimile of Patrick; not a person, only a fax.

On her senior trip in high school Cerise had met a fax of the President. So far as she knew, that was the only one, until the Patrick-fax, but from Hewitt she knew that more and more of the rich and powerful were having facsimiles made to act as decoys, and to be held in reserve against the day when medical science made possible, and age or illness made desirable, a full-body transplant. Hewitt didn't have his own – yet. He said he was waiting until they'd been perfected. He said they were still only machines, not much better than animated dolls. He was particularly contemptuous of people who had sex with faxes. He claimed to find it an inexplicable perversion.

But it wasn't like that. It wasn't the make-believe that Cerise had imagined – neither the murder nor the sex. From the moment she saw him, when his eyes met hers and he smiled with delighted recognition, she could not believe it wasn't her own Patrick, brought to this place by some trick or miracle. And when he kissed her – oh, she could never resist him when he kissed her like that. So they had made love. For hours. And it was wonderful – more like her best fantasies than anything she'd ever had with her husband in reality. Everything was perfect. And then . . .

Then the inevitable, fatal quarrel. She couldn't remember how it had started, or even what it had been about. It had been everything they'd ever disagreed about, the worst fight they'd ever had. None of her attempts to placate him had worked. All the old weapons had come out, and all the old hurts, and then Cerise had stopped backing down. When tears choked her throat and the words would not come, instead of giving in and crying she went for the knife. She had shut him up forever. She had killed him.

Cerise turned off the shower and leaned against the wall, almost too weak to go on standing.

I really killed him, she thought. I really did it.

She just made it across the room to press the button before she slid down the wall and passed out on the wet tiles.

Cerise spent the night at Timber Oaks after all – the night, and the following day. Someone phoned Hewitt to postpone her dinner date. They took care of everything; that was part of the deal.

Not all of its services were strictly legal – nevertheless, Timber Oaks was a registered clinic, with trained psychiatrists on staff. They recognized the guilt and anguish Cerise was suffering, and they knew how to deal with it. Their main effort, at first, was to get her to accept that there had been no real murder. There was no victim. No one had been hurt. She had simply acted out her aggressions on a machine programmed for that very purpose.

Shown the body of the fax, shown the software, shown how it worked and was neither living nor dead, Cerise could not lose the feeling that she had done wrong, and that someone had been hurt. "Maybe it's true that nobody is dead, but I didn't know that – I really meant to kill him when I stabbed him; I really wanted him to die."

"That was the Patrick in your head," said the psychiatrist. "The real Patrick is still alive; it's only *your* Patrick who is dead. You killed the Patrick in your head; you programmed the fax from your memories, and then you killed what you had created. You murdered an illusion. Do you really think that's the same as killing a person? You know the faxes don't feel anything – they don't think – it's all programming, not life."

"I know," said Cerise. "Of course it's not the same as if I really killed Patrick – I know that. But I *could* have killed Patrick, I would have if he'd been there. That's what's so scary. I never thought I'd be able to kill. Not only am I able to, but I could glory in it – I'd never felt like that before! What's to stop me from doing it again?"

"The same things that have always stopped you. We all have unacceptable emotions inside us . . . we learn ways of dealing with them. Yours aren't out of control – they never were. Don't forget, you knew that wasn't really Patrick. Even as you thought you were killing him, a part of you knew perfectly well it was only a fax, and that you had permission to act out your aggressions on it. You're still in touch with reality; I very much doubt you would ever confuse what happened here at Timber Oaks with what happens outside."

Cerise listened, and argued, and gradually let herself be convinced. It was time to leave this place, go home, see Hewitt, and try to come to terms with what she had learned about herself. She tucked the videotape they gave her – hard proof of what she'd done – away in her bag, wondering if she would ever be able to watch it.

The next evening, as she gazed at Hewitt across a table in one of the city's most expensive restaurants, Cerise saw for the first time how much he was like Patrick, and was surprised that she had never noticed before.

Both were rather thin, pale-skinned men with fair, wispy hair. Hewitt didn't appear to be going bald, but Cerise remembered a patch of hair with a slightly different texture than the rest, and she suspected a transplant. Both men had charming smiles, disarmingly innocent faces, and self-righteous natures. If Hewitt was better-tempered than Patrick, Cerise now thought that was only because he had enough money to smooth his way, and Patrick, although not poor, was always struggling.

The waiter filled their glasses with champagne and went away.

"Well," said Hewitt, raising his glass in a toast to her. "Was it a success?"

"That depends on how you define success."

"How do you feel about your ex-husband now?"

She had woken that morning feeling a great weight gone. There was a burden she no longer had to bear. An old wound had finally healed. "I feel . . . relieved," she said. "Accepting. It's over. As if he died a long time ago. He doesn't matter anymore."

Hewitt smiled. "You still think the murder was only for my benefit?"

"Maybe I feel better about Patrick but worse about myself," Cerise said. "I'm not sure it was worth it if the only way I could get free of Patrick was to murder him."

"We all have violent impulses," said Hewitt. "Isn't it better to face up to them and get them out in the open instead of repressing them and pretending they aren't there?"

"Yes, yes, I talked to the shrink, too." Cerise looked away from Hewitt's eyes – the same colour as Patrick's – at the bubbles in her champagne. "It was so real," she said. "That's what makes it so hard. I really didn't know it was going to be like that."

"If it wasn't real, there wouldn't be much point," Hewitt said. "You have to believe in it, or it isn't any good. I didn't just want you to kill some doll . . . I wanted you to get rid of your husband, once and for all . . . the image that you were still carrying around inside you. That's what I was jealous of – not the real man."

"You don't have to be jealous any more," said Cerise wearily.

"I know. And I'm grateful. I know it couldn't have been easy for you. This isn't a thank-you present," he said, putting a small black velvet box on the table. "It's because I love you."

She knew what it was, and she wished she didn't. She didn't move to pick it up. She looked at him.

"I want you to marry me," he said.

"Oh, Hew," she said, shaking her head. "I wish you wouldn't. I – it's too soon."

"Am I being insensitive? Do you need time to mourn your husband?" His voice was still gentle, but there was a brittle edge to the words.

"Well, maybe I do," she said, although she'd already realized that her mourning for Patrick was, finally, over. "I just think I need some more time, to be sure."

"You've been divorced for more than a year, and you've known me for nearly six months. How long does it take? I know how I feel about you."

Just then the waiter arrived with their appetizers. Hewitt frowned down at his plate. "What is this? Frozen? Or fresh?"

"I'm sure it's fresh, sir."

"That's what the menu said, but I doubt it. Just a minute." Hewitt took a small taste and shook his head. "That's not fresh. Take it back."

"Of course. I'm sorry you didn't like it, sir."

"I don't like second best," said Hewitt. "Frozen is second best. I only eat the real thing."

Cerise looked down at her own plate, not seeing what was on it, knowing that she would be making the worst mistake of her life if she married Hewitt Price.

After the waiter had gone Hewitt looked at her and shrugged. "I'm not going to push," he said. "I'm willing to wait. If you need time, take your time. Keep the ring."

"No, I can't. It wouldn't be right."

"I'm not going to take it back to the store," he said. "And I'm not going to want to give it to anybody else."

She shook her head.

He gave her a look that said she was being unreasonable, but put the little box back in his pocket.

Gradually, somehow, the evening got back on keel. Marriage wasn't mentioned again. They talked about a planned skiing trip, and mutual friends, and a book Hewitt was reading. She felt that he had forgiven her, and although she had wanted to be alone, at the end of the evening, when he assumed she was coming home with him, she couldn't say no. She was a little tense when they made love, but she didn't think he noticed – he was drunk, and fell asleep quickly. Despite her dissatisfaction and misgivings, so did she.

It was late morning when she woke, the big house was quiet around her, and Hewitt was gone. He had left her a note, suggesting a place to meet for dinner, the key to one of the cars, and a Gold American Express card in her name "in case you want to do some shopping".

She closed her eyes, feeling a tug of purely material desire.

"I will not marry you for your money," she said aloud, but the conviction she had felt the previous evening was lacking. She went into the bathroom to take a shower, and tried to remember what it was like making love with Hewitt. Instead, she kept remembering how it had been with Patrick before she killed him. She was aroused, and thought of looking at her tape, to remember it better. How could she have been so happy one moment, so violently angry the next? Just as well as the sex, she remembered what it had been like to kill. If she married Hewitt, would she some day be wanting to murder him? It seemed all too likely. But she doubted whether Hewitt would be willing to buy her a Hewitt-fax. Far more likely that he would order his own Cerise-fax, and kill her. She wondered what he was like as a murderer.

Cerise emerged from the shower, dried off and then wrapped herself in a huge, soft towel, although she knew she was alone, and the house was warm. The video library was downstairs, but she didn't think he would keep such a personal tape with all the others.

She was right. She found it – the Timber Oaks logo on the back marked it out at once – among the small selection of pornography Hewitt kept on the shelf behind the bedroom video system.

She felt like a spy, fearful of being caught as she slid the cassette into the player. It didn't help at all to remind herself that Hewitt had once offered to show it to her. He wasn't with her now, and she had different reasons for wanting to see it. Wiping sweaty hands on the towel, blinking eyes that suddenly felt too dry, she sank onto the bed, staring at the screen.

She recognized the bland good taste of a Timber Oaks bedroom at once. A pretty young woman with red-gold hair, wearing a dark blue silk kimono, was standing beside the bed, looking apprehensive, when the door opened and Hewitt came in.

"You wanted to see me?" said Hewitt. He was wearing a salmon-coloured suit – the height of fashion three years ago – and holding a square black leather case in one hand.

"Oh, darlin', I've missed you so," said the woman, whom Cerise guessed to be a fax of Hewitt's ex-wife, Penny. Her voice was soft and slightly husky with a distinctive East Texas twang.

"Missed me, or missed my money?"

"Oh, Hewitt, how can you even ask? I've missed you. Let me show you how I've missed you." As she spoke, she opened her kimono and shrugged out of it. It dropped with a silken whisper on the floor.

Cerise tucked her towel more firmly closed. She wondered if Hewitt thought her breasts were too small.

Hewitt put his case down on a chair. Now, thought Cerise. Now the gun, or the knife, would come out, now he would kill her. But he left the case where it was, went to the naked woman, and began to kiss her breasts and neck while she sighed and seemed to melt against him. After about a minute he lifted her in his arms and carried her to the bed.

She put up a small show of resistance. "Let me . . . you get undressed, too," she said.

"No hurry," he said. "Plenty of time." He pushed her back, and knelt before her, between her legs.

Shocked, Cerise managed to lurch off the bed and across to the video, to punch the fast-forward button. So Hewitt had his dark secret, too – sex with a fax! She felt too embarrassed to watch. But even at top speed the sex seemed to go on and on: every time she stopped it, there was some new pornographic position to be flinched away from.

When she saw the gun, she returned the tape to normal speed.

The gun, a small, snub-nosed, silver pistol, was in Hewitt's right hand, carefully pointed away from the woman, who was watching him apprehensively. They were both naked, sitting on the bed.

"You said you'd do anything for me," said Hewitt. "How can I believe you?"

"I would – I would do anything for you. Almost. But you can't ask me to kill myself!"

"Can't I?"

"You wouldn't if you loved me. People don't. Oh, Hew, I'd die happily if it would save your life, but I'm not going to kill myself. Ask me something else to prove I love you."

"All right," he said. He gazed at her steadily. "It's a real sacrifice I'm going to ask you for, Penny."

She nodded eagerly.

"Would you give up other men for me?"

"Of course!"

"Would you give up your beauty?"

Something flickered in her yes. "You wouldn't love me if I was ugly."

"Is that what you think? You're wrong. Maybe I fell in love with the way you looked, but now I love you . . . I'll love you no matter what, as long as you're alive. That's my problem. That, and not being able to believe you really love me. I need proof, Penny."

Penny closed her eyes and said, "All right." Then she opened them. "What do you want me to do?"

"I want you to scar yourself. I want you to mark your face to prove you're mine." He leaned away from her, towards the bedside table. He came back with a razor-blade held delicately between thumb and forefinger of the hand without the gun. "Use this. Just one little cut. On your face." With the pistol, he traced a line on his own cheek. "Show me you mean it."

Penny straightened up, and took the blade from him with her right hand. Staring straight ahead at nothing, as if into a mirror, she raised her hand to her right cheekbone, placed the cutting edge of the razor there, and then drew it down in a curving sweep to the corner of her mouth. It was the delicate, assured gesture of a woman applying make-up. When she took her hand away red blossomed in tiny dots, which formed a crescent and then began to run. Within seconds half of her face was awash with blood, dripping onto her neck and shoulders.

"Again," said Hewitt. "The other side."

Obediently she lifted her hand, then stopped and hurled the blade away from her. "It hurts," she said plaintively. "It stings. Is there some spray or something in the bathroom to make it stop hurting?"

"Go and get the razor. You're not finished."

She frowned. "Oh, yes I am. That's enough."

"It's not enough," he said. "It'll never be enough."

"It'll have to be," she said. "I'm through."

"Oh, yes," he said. "You're through."

He raised his hand and squeezed the trigger. Penny's face exploded.

Cerise choked on a scream and backed away, her towel falling off and making her feel even more vulnerable. As she scrambled to find her clothes she heard two more gunshots from the television, and then the sound of Hewitt weeping.

Hypocrite, she thought. Murderer. Murderer!

Hewitt hadn't destroyed a fax; he had killed his wife. She recalled his stubborn determination to have only the best, never to settle for something which wasn't "real" and knew that Hewitt wouldn't have been content with a make-believe murder. He was rich enough to buy whatever he wanted – apparently even his wife's death.

Cerise wondered if Timber Oaks was behind it. Had they helped him replace the real woman with a fax? Or had he pulled a switch and fooled them, too? Although she had never met Hewitt's ex-wife, Cerise knew some of Hewitt's friends were still in touch with her. After her own experience at Timber Oaks, she did not doubt that a fax could deceive even Penny's most intimate friends.

She dressed as quickly as she could. The feeling of possessing dangerous knowledge made her too nervous to linger any longer in Hewitt's house than she absolutely must. She took one of Hewitt's cars because her own was on the other side of town, and drove to a nearby service station to use the telephone.

There was a listing for a Penny K. Price, and Cerise dialled the number without stopping to think what she would say.

"Could I speak to Penny, please?"

"This is she."

The back of her neck prickled at those familiar East Texas vowels. "I'm . . . uh, my name is Cerise Duval, and I wondered . . . I wondered if I could come visit you."

A brief silence, while Cerise cursed herself for rushing into this without some plausible lie, and then the voice said, "You're Hewitt's girlfriend."

"That's right."

"Is Hewitt with you?"

"No, I'm by myself. I wondered if I could just drive over now . . . if you're not too busy."

"I'm not busy. You want to see me?"

Cerise bit her lip. "Yes."

"Oh, well, why not. Come on over." She gave directions to her house.

At Timber Oaks, Cerise had been shown the easiest way to tell a fax from a human being. There was a slot in the back of the neck – covered by a flap of fax-flesh – for the insertion of software, and there were sockets (also covered by fax-flesh) at the base of the spine and just under the heart. Unless Penny wore a bikini to receive visitors, Cerise wouldn't have the opportunity to check for power points, but it shouldn't be too hard to find the software slot.

The Penny who opened the door to her looked exactly like the woman on the tape. It had been more than three years since her murder, but she hadn't aged a single day. "Cerise?"

"Yes. I hope you don't mind my coming over like this?"

Penny shook her head. "That's fine. I wasn't doing anything special . . . Would you like some coffee? Or a diet soda?"

"Coffee would be nice, if it isn't any trouble."

"No trouble at all. I was just about to put some on for myself." They both had fallen into the rituals of politeness, and Cerise wondered how they would ever get out. She followed the other woman into a large, light kitchen and hovered in the doorway, watching Penny take coffee pot and filters from a cupboard. She's not real, she told herself. Why wait? It was never going to be any less embarrassing, any more possible. Penny's back was to her. Now. Cerise moved swiftly across the floor, reaching for the back of Penny's neck.

Penny yelped, and dropped the box of paper filters, but she didn't pull away. Instead, after the first seconds of tensed surprise she relaxed and stood still, even inclining her head slightly to make it easier for Cerise.

There was nothing beneath her hair but warm, soft flesh, and no matter how Cerise prodded and pulled at it, that flesh did not give way, or part, or pull up. In a swelter of embarrassment, she withdrew.

"I'm sorry, I hope I didn't hurt you, I just . . ." There was no way she was going to be able to think of an acceptable explanation.

Not turning around, not looking at her, Penny said, "There isn't a software slot because there isn't any software. Just my brain."

"I'm sorry," Cerise said again, helplessly. "You must think I'm horrible. The thing is, I saw a tape . . ."

Penny turned around. She didn't look angry or surprised. "And you thought that Hewitt had murdered me and replaced me with a fax. The perfect crime."

"Look, I know about Timber Oaks," Cerise said. "I went there to murder my husband – a fax of him, I mean, of course. But I know Hewitt – and I just didn't believe he would have been satisfied with a make-believe murder."

Penny nodded. "You're right. You do know Hewitt. Do you still want that coffee?"

"Oh, yes, please." She watched Penny pick up the filters and, with a quick sideways glance, go to the sink to fill a kettle. "Don't worry, I'm not going to grab you and try to find your sockets."

"If you'll just wait till we've had our coffee I'll take my clothes off and show them to you."

"Look, I'm sorry, I really am. It was stupid of me."

"It wasn't stupid," Penny said, stopping and looking directly at her. "And I wasn't joking."

"What do you mean?"

"I've still got my brain, so I'm still me, right?" said Penny. "That's what Hewitt said. That's what I tell myself. But this . . ." She gave herself a thump, flat-handed, on the breastbone. "Hewitt bought this for me. It's not the body I was born with. It's a fax. But I'm not. Supposedly."

"Your whole body," said Cerise slowly. "Your whole body's a replacement?"

Penny nodded.

"I've heard about the others they did that to . . . there's one man they've kept alive for five or six years now, isn't there?"

" 'Kept alive'," Penny repeated with a particular emphasis.

"Well, that's how they say it, that's how they talk about it on the news, you know."

"Like they had him in a machine. Like this was an iron lung." Again, Penny patted her breastbone. "Still, he was dying. I wasn't. I was the first young, healthy subject, so far as I know. There are more than the ones you hear about on the news. Rich old men who don't want to die. But they have to be convinced they're dying, first – they don't want to make the switch too soon, in case it goes wrong, in case it doesn't work, or in case it's not really what they've been told. In case it isn't really like life."

"Is it like life?"

"Oh, yes, it's like life." Penny extended her arm. "Here. Feel. Can you tell any difference?"

A little reluctantly, Cerise did as she was asked. Warm, human flesh. But she knew that already, more intimately. She shook her head. "I mean for you. Is it the same for you? Is it really just like life?"

"It's like life," said Penny. "It's like life." She was shaking her head as she spoke. "Hewitt explained it to me. You don't feel things with your body, you know. The feeling is in your head. You touch my hand, but I don't feel it with my hand. The nerves in my hand send a message to my brain, and my brain decides what it feels like, and what I feel about it. It's all in the brain. If I was in a coma, the things that were done to my body wouldn't register. They wouldn't matter. I wouldn't feel them unless my brain knew about them. So this body works just like my old body. It all works perfectly well, and in some ways it's better. It's in better shape."

Cerise watched Penny pour boiling water, and the fragrance of fresh coffee rose gently between them.

"Why did you do it?" Cerise asked.

Penny sighed. "I did it for Hewitt." She looked down, then directly at Cerise. "And maybe for the money. Partly that, but mostly it was for him. Hewitt thinks he bought me. He thought I married him for his money . . . well, of course the money was part of it. If he'd been some broke college kid, the marriage probably wouldn't have happened. But everybody thought he was such a great catch, and I really wanted to get away from home, and get married, and I though it would be so great to be his wife, to be Mrs Hewitt Price. It was OK for a while and then . . . then it wasn't. I don't know what happened. It was like I couldn't believe in it anymore; I was just going through the motions. Everything looked OK on the surface; Hewitt thought everything was fine. But there wasn't anything underneath. Maybe I stopped loving him – or maybe I just grew up and realized I never had loved him, and a beautiful house full of expensive things couldn't make up for that. That was when I told Hewitt I wanted out." She poured the coffee into blue mugs and put them on the kitchen table. They both sat. Cerise put her hands around the mug, holding the warmth, and waited for Penny to go on.

"Hewitt just went crazy. He was sure there was somebody else. There wasn't. I guess it's a good thing there wasn't, because I think Hewitt would have killed him, really killed him. He always had this thing about other men – I don't know why, since I'm sure I never gave him any cause to be jealous.

"I felt horribly guilty, of course. After all, it wasn't Hewitt's fault I wasn't happy. He gave me everything. He didn't drink, he never hit me . . . but I wanted out. I couldn't go on like I was, just to make Hewitt happy. Hewitt seemed to think I should, and I guess I thought he was right – I had made a promise, after all, when we married; and he'd kept *his* promise. So I was in the wrong, and I owed Hewitt something. We both believed that. He'd fulfilled his part of the bargain, and I hadn't. I owed him something. So . . . I gave him what he wanted. I gave him my body."

Cerise blew on her coffee, thinking of Hewitt's jealousy. She remembered how he had questioned her about her marriage, and how he had wanted her to kill Patrick. She had been shocked at first, but he was persuasive, and he wanted it so much. It was something she was doing for him, not for herself, and so she had let him talk her into it. Cerise no longer believed in such altruism. People couldn't talk you into things you really didn't want to do. She said to Penny, "How much did he pay you?"

Penny smiled ruefully. "A lot. He made it worth my while. If I left him, he let me know I'd have nothing: no money, no job, nobody to take care of me. Just my freedom, whatever that meant. But if I let him kill me, he'd make sure I was comfortable. A nice place to live, a steady income, a car . . . and this perfect body. This body won't get sick or fat or old. At the time, that seemed really important. I'd always been terrified of getting old and falling apart physically, afraid of being ugly, and having nobody love me. And the money . . . I'd never had to support myself, you see. I never had a job; I didn't even finish college. He was offering me the perfect way out, I thought. I could buy my future with my body. That was the same thing I did when I got married. I guess I should have realized that. I guess I only got what I deserved."

"What's that?"

"This pretty surface. It's like my marriage. All the parts are there, but they don't add up. There's something missing. I don't know what, and I don't know how to change it. I could get out of my marriage. I don't know how to get out of *this*."

"Wait a minute – I thought you said it was just like life?"

"That's it," said Penny. "*Like* life. Not life itself. It looks perfect from the outside, but it's not."

"Didn't you just tell me—"

"Everything works," Penny said. "All the nerves and senses. But they're not mine. I'm the only one who knows that I'm not living anymore. That I can't live. I can only remember." She gestured at her coffee, still untouched on the table before her. "I know what coffee tastes like. I drink it, and I think I'm tasting that cup, but really I'm remembering coffee I've had in the past. If you dumped salt in it without me seeing, I wouldn't know it, I wouldn't taste any difference."

"That sounds like something wrong with your sense of taste," Cerise said.

"No, you don't understand; that's a bad example. It's hard to explain. But life is change . . . and I can't change anymore; I can't have new experiences. I don't have a future, just a past. It's all fake, memories of life, recycled to make me think I'm still living. I had a boyfriend for a while, but then I realized that I was responding to him, to everything he did or said, as being *like* Hewitt, or *like* Mark, or like Johnny or somebody else I used to know. I could never know *him*."

"But you've never met *me* before. How about that? Do I remind you of someone you already know? And what about this conversation?"

"Oh, I can see you," said Penny, sounding very tired. "You don't understand. I can hear you, touch you . . . the information still comes in. It's like watching television . . . but watching television isn't life. It can tell you about life, but it also gets in the way. Ever since the transplant, there's always something between me and life. This body. It works for me, but it isn't me. I thought I was trapped before. I didn't know what it meant to be trapped."

Cerise couldn't understand what Penny was talking about. She was reminded of Hewitt's claims to supersensitivity, the way he would take two things she thought were basically the same and call one superior and the other worthless.

"What do you do all day?" Cerise asked. "How do you live?"

"There's the money from Hewitt, so I – oh, you mean how do I spend my time? Well, two days a week I have my volunteer work at the hospital. I see people socially, go to parties . . . There's the bridge club. I go shopping. I like to read, and I watch a lot of television. Except that I'm living by myself, it's not that much different from how I spent my time when I was married to Hewitt."

"Maybe that's what's wrong. Maybe it wasn't Hewitt who trapped you, but a whole way of life. You left him, but you didn't change anything else. You need to change your life, do something totally different, to make you feel alive again. Move to another city, travel, find a new lover, get yourself a job . . ." She shrugged, impatient because it seemed so obvious.

But Penny was shaking her head, rejecting what Cerise said even before she finished. "You don't understand," she said again. "I can't change my life. It's too late for that. I can't make myself feel alive because I'm *not* alive."

"Then Hewitt might as well have killed you," Cerise said. "He might as well have done what I thought he did and killed you and put a fax here in your place . . . a fax would probably do a better job of it than you; a fax would probably think it was happy!"

"He might as well have killed me," Penny agreed, apparently deaf to the other woman's irritation. "He took my life away . . . he might as well have killed my brain, too. Sometimes I wonder if I *can* die now, or if I'll just go on living in this body forever . . . sometimes I think he took my death away from me as well as my life. I died, and I didn't even get to experience it! My own death . . . Hewitt sent me a tape – the same tape you saw – of him killing me. At first I thought it was horrible, I thought it was horribly cruel of him to show me what he'd done. But now I'm glad I can see it. I'm glad I know. It's the only evidence I have. I watch it a lot. I look at myself again and again . . . I watch myself die, and I try to imagine what it was like. I try to *feel* it." She gave Cerise a wistful smile. "It's the only death I have."

Cerise felt the hairs prickle on the back of her neck. My brain is telling my body to do that because of what Penny is telling me, she thought. She wondered if Penny was crazy. She sounded like a hypochondriac, inventing problems where there were none. And yet . . . what could it be like to lose your whole body, every part of it except the brain, and not die, to go on living in an altered, artificial form? It was impossible to imagine, so maybe it was impossible to explain. Whatever it was, whether it was Penny's madness or Hewitt's crime, Cerise realized she'd had enough of it.

"I'm sorry," she said. "I really am sorry you're not happy. But I have to go now. Thank you for the coffee."

"You're welcome," Penny said. "I'll show you out . . . it was very nice meeting you . . . I'm so glad you decided to call. Please do come again."

Her ordinary, unthinking politeness struck Cerise as surreal, but it took a positive effort to stop herself from joining in with the expected response.

Filling in the gap left by the other woman's silence Penny went on, "Any time . . . it would be so nice to see you again. And why don't you bring Hewitt next time?"

Cerise stopped by the door and turned to give Penny a hard look. "You don't mean that. Do you?"

"Why, of course."

"You actually want to see Hewitt again? After what he did to you? Why?"

"He won't see me," Penny said. "As far as he's concerned, I'm dead. He killed me, and he paid me for the privilege. I've tried to call him . . . His lawyer told me if I make any more attempts to contact him he'll stop my monthly payments. But I thought maybe if you said something to him . . . you could tell him that you phoned me; I didn't get in touch with you; he couldn't blame me."

"I just don't understand why you want to see him."

"I don't either. I probably shouldn't be saying this to you, of all people, but I'd go back to him if he'd have me. I think about him all the time. Sometimes he seems like the only thing in the world, the only real thing, the only one I care about. If we could get back together, I think maybe we could work things out, maybe it would be all right; he could make it all right."

Cerise felt sick. There was no doubting Penny's sincerity. "But he's the one who killed you – I mean, did this to you, made you like this."

Penny nodded. "That's why. He destroyed me, so he's the one who can save me. It makes sense, don't you see?"

"No. No it doesn't. You can't go back. You're not the same person who married Hewitt. You've got to stop living in the past. You're *not* dead, unless you decide to be. Stop remembering – do something new; *live*."

"If I stop remembering, I will die," Penny said. "Remembering is all I have. But I can't expect you to understand that. You've still got your life. You've got Hewitt."

"You didn't have to let him kill you," Cerise said.

They looked at each other as if across a great divide. Cerise felt she didn't breathe again until she was outside the house, alone on the quiet, suburban street. Then, the sense of freedom she felt was intoxicating.

She took the videotape they had given her at Timber Oaks out of her bag, threw it to the ground and stamped on it until the plastic broke, then pulled the tape free of its protective casing. No one would ever watch this tape; she would not be able to send it to Patrick now. She wished her own memories could be destroyed as easily, but at least she knew they belonged to the past, like Hewitt. She could cope with the past because she still had a future. She put the keys in the ignition, closed the car door, and walked away from it.

RANDY KARL TUCKER, or, THE EDUCATION OF A MOLDIE-LOVER

Rudy Rucker

Great-great-great grandson of the philosopher Hegel, Rudolf von Bitter Rucker is a former underground cartoonist, a professor of mathematics, the author of several works on mathematical philosophy – and one of SF's wild talents, whose novels and stories combine abstruse mathematical concepts with outrageous storytelling and sheer high spirits. White Light *(1980),* The Sex Sphere *(1983) and* The Secret of Life *(1985) form a sort of sequence of journeys through transreal spacetime, while* The 57th Franz Kafka *collects some of his most bizarre short stories. Rucker is currently engaged on a series of robot novels which began with* Software *(1982) and continued with* Wetware *(1988); the following story (published here for the first time) will be incorporated into the third of these,* Freeware, *coming soon.*

Randy Karl Tucker grew up near the Dixie Highway in tacky Shively, down in the southwest corner of Louisville. About a century earlier, Dixie Highway had been the main road into town from the Army base at Fort Knox, thirty miles south of Louisville, and Shively had been a place where soldiers would come to taste the calm pleasures of civilian life – or to gamble at Churchill downs and get drunk and sleep with floozies. Many of the soldiers ended up marrying Shively women; over the years it became a solid little community, with its full share of godless lowlifes, professional Christians, and dazed white trash.

Randy's mother Sue Tucker was bi, on the butch side, though cutely tomboyish to some male eyes. She was a master plumber with her own business that she ran out of her truck and her little house's garage. Mostly she did repairs, though now and then she'd do contract work for remodelling.

Sue didn't like to talk about Randy's father, but children hear everything, and over the years Randy had learned that his father had been a random guy who'd happened to make it with Sue in the course of a big sex party down at the La Mirage Health Club in downtown Louisville on Hallowe'en, 2031. According to Sue, the guy had been masked behind a flickercladding Happy Cloak, disguised as a woman in fact, and she'd never found out who he was.

There were men around when Randy was quite young, but at the time he entered adolescence, Sue Tucker was in lesbian mode. One of Sue's favourite girlfriends was a femme named Honey Weaver – a stocky, bleached-blonde waitress with large breasts and a weak chin. Soon after Randy's sixteenth birthday, Sue Tucker selected Honey to be the one to instruct Randy Karl about sex, the idea being that, as a lesbian, Honey would teach Randy a proper respect for women.

"Randy Karl," Sue said one September afternoon in 2048, after coming home to find Randy squirmingly watching porno on the uvvy once again. "Turn off that kilp. It's anti-woman."

"Oh, come on, Sue." He always called his mother by her first name. "It don't hurt none. At least let me do it till I need glasses." He was a mournful-looking lad with a long thin face. He hadn't gotten his growth yet and was only a little over five feet tall. He wore his hair in a flat-top. He was dressed in a white T-shirt and khakis; the khakis had a nasty bulge in them from Randy's watching the filth on the uvvy.

"Randy Karl, it's high time you learned what's what. I want you to go on over to Honey Weaver's right now."

"Huh? What for?"

"She's having a problem with her drain. You can fix that for her can't you?"

Randy had often helped his mother on jobs, but this was the first time she'd offered to let him go out on his own.

"Will I git paid union wage?"

"And then some."

Randy put together a tool-box and walked down the street to Honey's – she lived two and a half blocks away, in a house exactly like the Tucker's: a three-room bungalow with cheap ceramic siding and a concrete front stoop.

Honey came to the door in a loosely fastened pink wrapper.

"Oh hi there, Randy, Sue told me you were on your way. I just changed out of my waitress clothes. Come on in." As she opened the door, her wrapper slid a bit further open, and Randy could see her bare breasts and a flash of her pubic hair. "What you starin' at boy?" said Honey with a gentle laugh. "Ain't you never seen a live woman before?"

"I— " choked Randy, setting down his box of tools with a clatter. "Honey, I— "

"You're all excited," purred Honey. "You cute little thing." She stretched out her arms so that her wrapper fell wide open. "Come here, Randy. Hug me and kiss my tits."

Randy exulted in the smell and feel of Honey's pillowy breasts, breasts that smelled of sweat and perfume, breasts that rubbed Randy's face with stiff nipples. Honey snaked her hand down and undid Randy's pants. Before he knew what was happening, she'd gotten out his stiff little dick and he'd come off into her insistent, intimate fingers. He was so surprised and embarrassed that he burst into tears.

"There, there," said Honey, smiling down at him and rubbing his sperm onto her breasts. "That makes nice smooth skin. I like milking a little boy like you, Randy Karl. Would you like to see my vagina?"

"Yes, Honey, I surely would."

"Kneel down on the floor in front of me."

Randy knelt on the smooth plastic floor, and Honey stepped up close to Randy with her fragrant bushy crotch right at the level of his face. She adjusted her legs a bit, straddling them wider, and now Randy could see the details of her genitalia.

"Kiss my pussy, Randy Karl, lick on it all over."

Randy started in gingerly, but then Honey seized his head with both hands and pressed his face tight between her legs. Honey's fragrant soft tissues felt luxurious, extravagant, intoxicating. Randy kissed and licked and sucked and moaned. Honey began a rapid rhythmic bucking of her pelvis against Randy's mouth, a bucking that cascaded into chaotic shudders. And then she sank down to the floor beside Randy.

Randy crawled up onto Honey, hoping to sink his painfully stiff erection into her – but she balked.

"I don't want no man's dick in me never again, Randy Karl, not even yours." She sat up, looking a little dazed. Outside it was dusk; the door was slightly open, and through the screen-door Randy could see people down on the sidewalk passing by. But the kitchen lights were off and the people couldn't see in. "If you do one more favour for me Randy, I'll milk you off again."

"Sure, Honey. I'll do anything you say. This is the most fun I ever had." At this moment Honey looked sublimely beautiful to Randy, even with the roll of fat at her waist and with her stark lack of a chin.

"Wait right here."

Honey went into her bedroom and got something. A long, soft, plastic thing in the shape of a dick. It was dark blue with shifting highlights of gold.

"This here's my limpware dildo," said Honey. "Since I'm a dyke, I call it a she. Her name is Angelika. Angelika, this is Randy Karl Tucker. Randy, meet Angelika."

The dildo twitched and simpered in Honey's hand. It – she – actually had a little voice. Randy recognized that Angelika was made of imipolex with a DIM; she was like a moldie, only not so smart. Randy had hardly ever seen any moldies or even limpware in Shively before. There were enough militant Christian Heritagists around to keep that kind of thing out of sight.

"Stick Angelika in me, Randy Karl," said Honey, laying back on the floor. "It's what your Mommy always does for me. And get over on one side of me so's I can reach your dick."

Angelika was lively and vibrant in Randy's hand. She hummed as if in pleasurable anticipation. Noticing an odd smell, Randy held the dildo up to his nose and sniffed it. The limpware gave off a gamey, foetid odour quite unlike Honey's funky musk.

"That's the way moldies smell," Honey explained. "It seems right nasty at first, but later you get used to it. It's sexy! Spray out more smell, Angelika!"

The dildo chirped and hissed, and the sharp moldie stink got ten times stronger. Randy could feel his blood pounding in his temples. He'd never been so aroused in his entire life.

"Come on, Randy!" urged Honey. "We're still just gittin' started!"

Over and over for the next two years – the rest of his time in high school – Randy kept coming back for sex with Honey, and Honey kept thinking of new things for them to do. When she noticed how interested Randy was in seeing her to the bathroom, she bought a big moldie imipolex sheet that Randy would lie down on naked while Honey urinated all over him, especially on his face. The sheet's name was Sammie-Jo.

Randy's grades dropped as he wandered around in a haze, continually thinking of things like the scent of Honey's hot urine mingled with the rank odour of Sammie-Jo. He made some halfhearted attempts to date the girls he went to high school with, but nothing could come close to Honey Weaver, Angelika, and Sammie-Jo. Randy was becoming sexually addicted to imipolex.

One of Honey's motives for the whole affair was to focus Sue Tucker's attention on Honey's sexuality. Honey loved to tell Sue all the intimate details of what she did with Randy. At first, Sue was compulsively, unwholesomely fascinated; during those unpleasant months Randy would sometimes catch his mother watching him with a bright, quizzical expression. But finally Sue's motherly instincts won out and she banished all interest in her son's sex-life.

This turned out to be a net loss for Honey, because Sue's interest in Honey's sexuality got repressed right alongside the visions of Randy servicing Honey. Sue had several screaming arguments with Honey on the uvvy before she could get Honey to stop calling her up with the latest details. After a year or so, the irregular love-triangle became so galling to Sue that she stopped talking to Honey entirely.

In the spring of Randy Karl's senior year in high school, Sue flipped back to being het. She started a steady relationship with an unpleasant, foppish man named Lewis. Lewis had a moustache grown out so long that it was possible to twirl the ends, which was something Lewis frequently did. Lewis was a site-manager for the company building London Earl Estates, a cut-rate housing development in Okalona, Kentucky, twenty miles south of Shively. Sue was doing a lot of the plumbing contracting at London Earl, which is how she met Lewis, who spent his days there in a trailer-office. Lewis was a martinet and a weakling, but Sue seemed to enjoy him. She was quite a bit smarter than him, and she was generally able to get him to do whatever she wanted him to.

As soon as Lewis moved in with Sue, he started pressuring Randy to leave, but Sue stuck up for her son. She moved Randy's room out into the garage so Randy and Lewis wouldn't get in each other's way so much, and she began passing Randy all of her plumbing work other than the contracts out at London Earl Estates. Randy already had his Journeyman Plumber certification, and she wanted him to make Master Plumber before leaving home.

"Technology can come and go, Randy Karl," Sue liked to tell Randy. "But people are always going to use pipes. These days we got soft pipes and smart pipes, but they're still pipes. There's no other way to move water around, and nobody knows how to handle pipes except plumbers. Once you're a Master Plumber, you're fixed for life."

Randy was happier than he'd ever been that spring. His sex-thing with Honey was going hot and heavy. And he made great money after school and on the weekends. He was getting really good at the new plumbing technologies. His favourite was the pipe-gun that would grow a plastic pipe right under a house's crawl-space, a snaky crawling pipe that would zig and zag where you told it to. He liked living in the garage, and Sue was proud of how fast he was learning.

The end to this golden age came on 20 June 2050, the day after Randy graduated from high school.

Randy woke up late; it was nearly noon. Some of his class-mates had thrown a big party after the graduation and for once they'd let Randy come. He still felt giddy from the beer, pot, bourbon, and snap he'd had the night before. Randy wasn't used to drinking and doping. How had he gotten home? Oh yeah, he'd walked, stopping every few blocks to puke into people's yards. What a toot!

He rolled over on his side, taking a mental inventory of himself. He felt pretty good. He was all through with school. He sat up on the edge of his bed and looked around the garage – at his dresser and desk sitting among the drums of raw pipe-plastic and the cabinets of plumbing-machine parts. His clothes-hangers dangled from a wire slung up under the ceiling. Sue's truck and Lewis's hydrogen-cycle were gone. Randy was all through with school. He had a stubborn erection; the sensory amplification of his hangover/stoneover made him riggish. He decided to go on over to Honey's; today was her day off.

Randy put on a sleeveless T-shirt, baggy shorts and plastic sandals.

He ate some milk and bread out of his mother's fridge, and ambled down the street towards Honey's.

It was a hot Kentucky day, the air so thick with humidity that your skin got slick with sweat if you moved fast. The cracks in the old concrete streets and sidewalks were lush with weeds. Gnats whined everywhere. The weeds and the bushes and grasses exuded a steamy warmth. Each of the Shively houses was just like the one next to it, each the same ceramic-coated box, each with a slightly different trim pattern around the front door.

Honey was home all right, but when Randy walked in, she turned red-faced and tearful. "Don't come near me!" cried Honey. "No more! All them things you and me did was wrong, Randy Karl!"

"Now what are you talkin' about, Honey? Are you mad Sue wouldn't let me ask you to graduation?"

"Everything we done was wrong!" repeated Honey. "Especially the things with Angelika and – and with Sammie-Jo. Dr Dicky Pride at the Shively Heritage House told me so. Yes, when you and your Mamma didn't ask me to your graduation last night, I went to the service at the Heritage House. And now I've done been born again. I was up past midnight with Dr Pride a-prayin' over me."

At first Randy thought Honey was playing with him, and he began to beseech her and to abase himself like she'd taught him to do. "Forgive me, Mistress Honey. Your will is my will. Do anything you like to me," said Randy, grovelling at her feet and unzipping his fly. "But, um, please do something. I'm horny as hell from all that beer and snap I had last night."

"Only thing you and me might ever do together again, Randy Karl Tucker, is goin' to meetings over to the Shively Heritage House," said Honey, flouncing to the other side of the room and sitting down in a straight-backed chair with her arms crossed. "I'm through bein' the goddamn Whore of Babylon. I've cleansed my body's temple."

"Um – what about Angelika and Sammie-Jo? Can I have 'em?"

"Dr Pride said I should bring them into the Heritage House, but – yeah, you take 'em. I'd be ashamed to bring them in. What if Dr Pride asked me to hold them up and like go, 'This is my dildo that my boy-toy and his Mommy and me fucked each other with so many taahms, and this is the sheet I used to piss on him with and—'" Honey's voice broke into shrill brittle laughter, or was it tears. She was still sitting in the chair across the room. She stretched out her trembling arm to point at the closet where she kept her imipolex sex-toys. "Take 'em the hell out of here right now, Randy Karl! Take 'em and git!" She was crying hard again, and Randy tried to pet her, but there was no way.

He took Sammie-Jo and Angelika home and masturbated with them. It was OK, though nowhere near as hot as it had always been with Honey at the controls. Angelika and Sammie-Jo weren't smart enough to be really fun. For the first time Randy started wondering what it would be like to have sex with fully intelligent and autonomous moldies instead of with these imipolex DIM-equipped toys. After he'd come, he washed Angelika and Sammie-Jo, let them lay out in the sun for a while, and then put in the back of one of the cabinet drawers near his bed in the garage.

Randy kept on mooning around Honey's the rest of that summer – mowing her lawn, doing her dishes, anything at all – but to no avail. The only thing Honey liked to do anymore was to go to meetings at the Shively Heritage House. So in August Randy started going with her.

Randy was certainly no Mr Sophisticated, but he'd never seen such a bunch of losers, geeks, and feebs as he found at the Heritage House meetings – all the people raving about Jesus and the Heritage Of Man and about how much they hated the moldies. The Heritagists were highly exercised over the Moldie Citizenship Act that the California senator Stahn Mooney had managed to railroad through Congress back in 2038. Even though Mooney had been out of office for years now, Congress still hadn't mustered the will to repeal that hellacious moldie-lovin' Act. What an outrage! Another big area of interest was, of course, all the perverse permutations of sex made possible by moldies, uvvies, and imipolex.

Randy would try and catch Honey's eye sometimes when Dicky Pride would go off about moldies and imipolex – Randy fondly remembering the steamy sessions with Honey and her toys – but Honey would just look away. Her small mind had shifted gears and there was nothing to do about it.

Meanwhile Randy was doing more and more plumbing. The customers Sue had given him were passing his name onto their friends; he was known for doing fast, solid work for the best price around. He was a whiz with the pipe-gun. But it was getting really hard to live at home. Lewis was in his face all the time, acting as if he was Randy's father or something, what a joke. Lewis had picked up some king of drug habit, a cocaine analog called pepp. Like coke, pepp had the effect of making stupid people think they were smart. And the smarter Lewis felt, the more insufferable he became. It was time for Randy to move out, but now it turned out that Sue didn't want him to, and she was stalling on the Master Plumber's certificate to keep Randy at home.

At Christmas, Honey's mother in Indianapolis died of cancer, and Honey, the sole child, moved there with her new Heritagist girlfriend Nita to take over her mother's comfortable estate: a paid-up retrofitted tract home near the Speedway and a well-deployed range of cash credits on the $Web. Dr Dicky Pride alerted the Indianapolis branch of the Human Heritage Council, and they were prepared to welcome the grieving Honey and Honey's companion with open arms.

When Randy heard Honey was moving, he went over to her house and asked her if he could leave town with her and Nita. But Honey chose to be a real bitch about it.

"Face it Randy, you was nothing more than my boy-toy. A kid I liked to piss on. Get over it. It was only because of Sue that you was important to me. And by the way, you can tell Sue she's a cold-hearted xoxxin' bitch."

This was way too frank. Randy felt small and used; used and abused. His poor young heart broke clean through that day, and it would never really heal again.

What with his non-existent social life and the bad situation at home, Randy kept going to the Shively Heritage House meetings that winter. No matter what he thought about the Heritagists' beliefs, he had the ability to blend in with them real well. He'd seen an uvvy show once about some beetles that live in anthills because they can trick the ants into feeding them. The Heritage House was an anthill Randy could live in.

Dr Dicky Pride liked asking Randy to repair little things, and soon – it wasn't clear which of them proposed it – Randy had been asked to move into the Heritage House as a "seminarian". The Heritage House – really just an over-sized Shively home – had a big garage with a second floor, and Dr Pride turned the garage over to Randy rent-free.

Sue gave Randy some of her older plumbing equipment, and Randy used his savings to buy his own pipe-gun and his own whipped-to-shit panel truck. The day Randy moved out, Sue finally pulled the right strings to get Randy his Master Plumber's certificate.

Randy lived alone up in the room over the Heritage House garage, and for sex he still had Angelika and Sammie-Jo. Whenever Randy asked them to, which was just about every night, Angelika would turn into a vaginal sheath with an extra flap that would ruck up tight and caressing around Randy's balls, while at the same time Sammie-Jo would smother Randy's face with a divinely smelly moldie hood pursed into the folded shapes of clitoris and labia. When he was finished, Randy always made sure to open the window wide to air out the toy moldies' cheesy reek. And in the mornings he let the algae-veined limpware goodies "feed" by sitting out in the daylight while he dressed and had breakfast.

One rainy night in March, there were footsteps up the stairs to Randy's room just while Randy was in the midst of an onanistic sex party. A pass-key slid into his lock and the door swung open. A trapezoid of light came in from the stairwell to lie across Randy Karl's engorged nudity.

"Hi Randy." Dr Dicky Pride stepped into the room, closed the door behind him and turned on the light. "Don't be embarrassed, son, I expected to find you this way. I've been able to smell what you do up here nights. And of course Honey told me all about you." Dr Pride was carrying a pink imipolex dildo, slender and not so long as Angelika. He waggled it rakishly, then ran his nose along the length of the moldie imipolex penis – sniffing it full savourily. Though it was a cold night, Dr Pride's face was damp with perspiration.

"Isn't he a beauty, Randy Karl? I call him Dr Jerry Falwell."

"What do you want?" said Randy, pulling his bed-sheet up to his chin to cover him and Angelika and Sammie-Jo. "You shouldn't of barged in here, Dr Pride."

"Struggle though we might, we're both miserable cheeseballs, son. We've got to stick together. Do me like you did Honey. Or I can do you. You're a very attractive and virile young man."

"I ain't gonna do nothing with you, Dr Pride. You've been good to me, I know. But I just ain't interested in sex with people no more, and if I was a-goin' to do anything, it would be with a woman. I'll move out of here as soon as you like. But no way am I a-stickin' Dr Jerry Falwell up your butt for you. Now, please git on out of here and leave me alone."

Randy and Dr Pride didn't explicitly mention the incident to each other during the following days, but they both agreed that it was time for Randy to graduate from being a seminarian, and to leave the Shively Heritage House.

"You ought to go on a mission, Randy Karl," suggested Dr Pride. "The Human Heritage Council is very well-connected – and I'm talking worldwide. We've got Heritage Houses and missionaries everywhere. The Council can act as a very effective placement service. I've already sent in my very top recommendation for you, by the way. Uvvy in to the Council's central server and see what they can find for you. A spirited young man like you needs to get out and see the world!"

Dr Pride left Randy alone with the Heritage House uvvy, and Randy logged into the Council's central machine, a huge asimov slave computer located under a mountain in Salt Lake City, Utah, just like the Mormons' genealogy computer. The uvvy fed Randy an image showing an a-life clerk in a sterile virtual reality office. The clerk was meant to look like a wholesome young daughter of the Great Plains, but the illusion was unconvincing. The silicon computation was crude enough that Randy could see the facets of her body's polygonal meshes, and several of the facets were incorrectly coloured in. For a few moments the figure sat stiff and blank, but then some signal from Randy's uvvy animated her.

"Hello there," she said. Her voice was shrill and perky. "You're Randy Karl Tucker from the Shively, Kentucky, Heritage House, I believe? Yes? Terrif. You can call me Jenny. How can I help you?"

"Um, I'm a-thinkin' about gettin' out of town," said Randy. "Like a mission or a job somewheres else? I've got me a Master Plumber's certificate."

"Yes, we already have that information, Randy." Jenny woodenly pretended to look through some papers on her desk. "Master plumber is very good. And your minister Dr Pride speaks very highly of you. I wonder – could you tell me frankly what you think of him?"

"Well, he's a good preacher. He packs 'em in."

"We've heard some rumours that he's a . . . cheeseball?"

"I ain't never had sex with him, and I don't plan to. So don't ask me. Just help me get to heck outta here."

"What kind of sex do you like, Randy?" Jenny morphed her faces' polygons into a conspiratorial smile. A few of her cheeks' smaller triangles flickered to black, making it look as if Jenny had blackheads. Or stubble. "You can tell Jenny. Jenny knows lots of secrets. Do you like toy moldies?"

"Looky here, I thought this was supposed to be a job-search session. And what if I am interested in moldies. That's a good enough reason to be a Heritagist, ain't it? Just like it's all drunks that goes to AA."

Jenny emitted a laugh. "I won't pry any further, Randy. I just wanted to make sure you don't mind being around moldies and imipolex. Because the job I've found for you – have you ever heard of Bangalore, India? Look."

A world globe appeared in front of Jenny and rotated to bring India into view, hanging like a fat udder from the Asian landmass. A little red dot pulsed down in the centre of the teat's tip.

"It's on a plateau and has a pleasant climate," said Jenny. "It's quite modern and Western, very high-tech. It's one of the only cities in India that sells beer on tap. Hindustan Aeronautics is there, also Indian Telephone Industries, Bharat Electronics, and Emperor Staghorn Beetle Larvae Limited. The world's largest manufacturer of imipolex. Emperor Staghorn needs a pipe-fitter; a master plumber."

"The folks who make moldie plastic are gonna take the Heritagists' advice on who to hire?" said Randy. "That don't make sense."

"Oh, they'll take our advice," said Jenny. "Indirectly. Like I said, we've got a lot of contacts, and a lot of people owe us favours. We can get you hired, Randy, I guarantee it. And you'll be surprised how big the salary is. All we want is that you uvvy me every month or two and tell me about anything interesting you see. And remember, you'll be working around moldies and imipolex every day." Jenny smiled again and put on a Kentucky accent. "Hell, Randy Karl, you'll be happy as a pig in a potato-patch."

"Shitfire!" Randy finally allowed himself to get excited. "India? Do they speak English there?"

"You bet! Just say the word, Randy, and you've got the job. We'll even find you a place to live and buy your plane tickets."

"I'll do it!"

"Be at the Louisville airport tomorrow at 9 a.m. They'll be holding your passport and your tickets for you at the Humana Airlines counter."

Randy packed his few possessions into his panel truck, told Dr

Pride good-bye, and drove over to Sue's house to tell her. It was six o-clock of a dark Friday evening.

Lewis answered the door. "Sue's not here," he said shortly.

"I'll come in and wait," said Randy.

"She's not coming back till Sunday night," said Lewis, fingering his moustache. He was twitchy from pepp. "She's gone up to Indianapolis to visit that goddamn dyke whore Honey Weaver. Your old girlfriend. And as long as Sue's not home, you're not welcome." Lewis made as if to close the door, but Randy stuck his foot in it.

"Don't slam my own door on me, you poncey son of a bitch."

"You mess with me, son, and you're in for a world of hurt," snapped Lewis. "I've got a gun. What the hell are you doing here anyway?" He peered out at Randy's laden truck. "Don't tell me you want to move back in! Xoxx-ass loser."

"I'll be spending tonight in the garage like I used to," said Randy shortly. "And you'd best not disturb me."

He cruised out for some burgers, and brought a six-pack of grape soda back to the garage. The back of the garage was still set up more or less like Randy's room; he'd only taken a few of his things with him when he moved over to the Heritage House. Randy took out the suitcase he'd gotten for his high school graduation and carefully began going through his life's accumulation of stuff, trying to figure out which things he'd need in India. What the hell would it be like there?

Finally Randy's bag was ready, and he filled in another hour unpacking the plumbing supplies from his truck and storing them back in with Sue's stuff. He was fooling around with his beloved pipe-gun when Lewis appeared in the garage, pepped to the pits. He had an old-fashioned Wild-West gunpowder pistol in his right hand. What an asshole.

"I said you're not welcome here, Randy," said Lewis, pointing out the garage door like some kind of plantation overseer. "Out."

Randy felt himself looking down submissively. He always got scared when people yelled at him; he always gave in and looked away. But tonight he caught himself doing it, and he realized he didn't want to give in any more. He touched the pipe-gun's controls, which set a growing white snake of two-inch plastic pipe to creeping across the garage floor, hidden from Lewis's view by the truck.

"I mean it," said Lewis, stepping closer and waving his gun. "Get your trashy ass out of here, Randy Karl Tucker." He actually twirled his moustache after he said this.

Randy had the pipe form a right angle and flow out from under the truck just in time to tangle with Lewis's feet. Lewis stumbled, looked down, and suddenly the pipe grew a tee at its end and accelerated straight up, punching Lewis in the crotch. The man doubled in pain, dropping his pistol.

Randy's fingers danced across the pipe-gun controls, and in seconds, Lewis was imprisoned in a tight cage of pipes. When Lewis opened his mouth to yell, Randy grew a skilful circle of pipe tight around his head, gagging him so that he could do no more than grunt and moan.

"How would you like it I send a pipe right up your butt and out the top of your head?" asked Randy rhetorically. "But I don't need the hassle of the clean-up. After tomorrow I'm gone. Goin' to India, Lewis. Not Indiana, my man, but India. It'll be real different there, for true." Randy opened up the back of his emptied panel truck and threw in a couple of canvas tarps. "Stay nice and quiet, Lewis, if you don't want that there plastic pipe enema." Randy found a dolly and used it to lever the caged Lewis into the back of the truck, loosely wrapping the cage in the tarps in case Lewis did try to make noise. "You can breathe, can't you? Maybe I should trim off that moustache for you? To hell with it. You'll be OK. Tell Sue good-bye for me when you see her Sunday." Randy shut the truck door, took his suitcase, closed up the garage, and spent the night on the couch watching porno on the uvvy, just like old times, with tattered Angelika and Sammie-Jo for company.

It turned out that Randy liked India a lot. He liked the chaos and disorganization of the city streets – the sweepers, the priests, the bright-clothed women with alert eyes, the thin barefoot men in plastic shirts or no shirt at all, the older men in white jackets, the wildly bearded holymen, the nose-rings and pouchy eyes and orange cloth, the hundred castes and colours and languages. There was always a hubbub, but nobody really hurried. There was always time to talk. Everyone seemed to speak at least a bit of English – idiosyncratic British-and-Sanskrit-tinged English – and to be happy to practise it on Randy Karl. People were kind to Randy in India, and kindness had been something in short supply throughout his life so far.

The Emperor Staghorn Beetle Larvae Ltd fab was about ten miles east of Bangalore. Initially Randy commuted there by train every day. It was a huge, rectangular structure, windowless and tightly secured lest moldies break in to steal the precious imipolex. At any given time there were twenty to a hundred moldies flying or hopping around outside the Emperor Staghorn Beetle Larvae building, drawn to the source of imipolex like bees drawn to honey. Arriving at Emperor Staghorn for his first day's work, Randy was thrilled to see so many moldies. One of them approached him as he walked to the fab from the train.

"Hello there," said the moldie, a womanly figure clothed in what looked like bracelets, bangles, necklaces, belts and a golden crown. "I'm Parvati. Are you new here?" Parvati stood very close to Randy. Randy noticed that her many pieces of jewelry were in fact shiny bumps and ridges of her imipolex flesh.

"Yes ma'am," said Randy. "I'm a-startin' on as a pipe-fitter." Surreptitiously he sniffed the air, tasting of the moldie's odour and finding it good. "Do you work here, too?"

"I wish I did," said Parvati. "All that gorgeous imipolex. What is your name?"

"Randy Karl Tucker. I'm from Kentucky."

"How extremely interesting. Randy, you will learn that the Emperor Staghorn employees are allowed to buy imipolex at cost from the company store. Be sure always to purchase as much as you can afford, and I can trade it for whatever you want. Food, money, intoxicants, sexual intimacy, maid-service, sky-rides, jungle tours, diving in the Arabian Sea – there are a plethora of possibilities." Parvati's voice had an enchanting lilt to it.

"Emperor Staghorn employees can buy imipolex?" said Randy. "That's good. I like imipolex. Fact is" Randy looked around. The other commuters had already bustled past him and were queuing up at the Emperor Staghorn entrance. "Fact is, I think I may be a cheeseball."

"I already love you, Randy," said Parvati, planting a divinely smelly kiss on his cheek. "Run along and enjoy your new job, dear boy. Remember Parvati on payday! We will have a very heavy date!"

Waiting for Randy inside the Emperor Staghorn building was a plump, golden-skinned man wearing dirty white pants and a dirty white jacket with many pockets holding many things. He was shiny bald on top, with a wreath of iron-gray curls.

"Greetings, Mr Tucker," he said, extending his hand. "I am Neeraj Doriswamy, the Plumbing Supervisor and, by virtue of this office, your *de facto* boss. I am welcoming you to Emperor Staghorn Beetle Larvae Ltd."

"Thank you kindly," said Randy. "I'm right proud to be here."

Doriswamy stared out through the glass door at the figure of Parvati. She'd grown a few extra arms and was smoothly undulating in a sacred dance. "She was certainly chatting you up, Mr Tucker."

"Well, um, yeah," said Randy. "She asked me about having a date with her. I think she's kinda sexy. I hope it's – "

"Oh, it's perfectly all right to fraternize with moldies, Randy. Indeed, Emperor Staghorn is even employing a few moldies here and there. They provide most of our custom chipmoulds. But these highly skilled moldie employees are wealthy nabobs, of a much higher caste than the moldies who beg for imipolex outside our fab gates. Shall I call you Randy and you call me Neeraj?"

"Sure thing, Neeraj."

"Capital. Let's continue our conversation while we are walking this way." Neeraj led Randy off down a long hall that ran along one side of the fab building. The right wall was blank, and the left was punctuated with thick-glassed windows looking into the fab proper. The people inside were dressed in white coveralls, with white boots and face-masks. Meanwhile Neeraj kept talking, his voice a steady, musical flow.

"Yes, the street-moldies are very friendly to Emperor Staghorn employees because of course they are hoping you will be giving them imipolex. Some of us have moldie servants. When I was a younger man, I kept a moldie who was flying me to work like a great bird! Devilishly good fun. But finally it was becoming too great a financial outlay for a father of five. And too dodgy."

"Dodgy?" asked Randy. "You mean like risky? To keep a moldie?"

"I will be telling you in due time what precautions you must be taking in your dodgy relations with low-caste moldies," said Neeraj, starting to open a big door in the left wall. A breeze of pressurized air wafted out. "But that can wait a little bit. We are entering the pre-gowning area. We'll get suited up and go into the main part of the fab, which is a clean-room. Here we are allowing less than one dust particle per cubic metre of air."

"Imipolex is that xoxxin' sensitive?"

"Imipolex is a very highly structured quasicrystal," said Neeraj. "While we are manufacturing the layers, the accidental inclusion of a dust particle can spoil the long-range Penrose correlations. And of course we are also producing the hybridized chipmould cultures here, and contamination by a wild fungus spore or by a stray algal germ cell would be disastrous. Keep in mind Randy, that in the air, for instance, of the train you ride to work, there are perhaps a million particles per cubic metre, and very many of the particles are biologically active."

The door to the pre-gowning room closed behind them. The floor was covered with sticky adhesive to catch the dust from their feet. Following Neeraj's example, Randy sat down on a bench and pulled some disposable blue covers over his shoes.

"Ram-ram, Neeraj," said a leathery brown woman sitting behind a counter. "Is this our new Mr Tucker?"

"Indeed. Randy, this is Roopah, Roopah this is Randy."

"Here are your building suit, your shoes, and your ID badge," said Roopah, setting what looked like tight-cuffed blue pyjamas and white bowling shoes on the counter. "Press your thumb on this pad, Randy, so that your locker can recognize you. Your locker number is 239."

In the locker room, they stashed their street-clothes and put on the blue building suits and the white plastic shoes. They washed their hands and put on hair nets and safety glasses. Beyond the locker room lay a medium clean zone – with a mere ten thousand particles per cubic metre. Here the air already felt purer than any that Randy had ever breathed; the odourless air flowed effortlessly into his lungs.

They passed a break room where some of the fab workers were having non-dusty snacks like apple juice and yogurt. Then they went into a second locker room: the gowning room proper. They put on latex gloves. They wiped off their safety glasses and their ID badges – wiped everything three times with lint-free alcohol-soaked cloths. They put on white hoods and overalls. Randy had hoped the suits might be live imipolex, but they were just brainless plastic.

"We call these bunny suits," said Neeraj, cheerfully pulling his hands up under his chin and making a chewing face like a rabbit. "And the floppy white galoshes are fab booties."

They pulled the fab booties over their white bowling shoes. They pulled vinyl gloves over their latex gloves. Neeraj gave Randy a face-mask equipped with a small fan that drew in new air and pumped Randy's exhalations through a filter. This was starting to feel a teensy bit . . . obsessive. But Randy liked being obsessive.

Now Neeraj led Randy through a tile corridor lined with nozzles blasting out air. "This is the air-shower," said Neeraj. "You are turning around three times as you are walking through. Notice that the floor in here and in the fab is a grating. The floors have suction pumps and the ceilings are filled with fans. The entire air of the fab is completely changed ten times in a minute."

Slowly moving through the air-shower, with his filthy invisible human particles being sucked out through the floor grate, Randy thought of a Bible phrase: I was glad when they said unto me, let us go into the house of the Lord.

Beyond the air-shower lay the temple of moldie creation. The lights were bright and yellow; they gave the fab a strange, under-world feeling. The rushing air streamed down past Randy from ceiling to floor. White-garbed figures moved about; all of them were dressed exactly the same. Everyone's labours revolved around glowing cylindrical slugs of imipolex, the slugs ranging in size from breakfast sausages on up to giant bolognas four feet long.

The fab was perhaps the size of a football field, and it had high fifteen-foot ceilings to accommodate an overhead monorail system that carried the partially processed slugs of imipolex from station to station.

The crude imipolex itself was manufactured in a series of vats, vacuum chambers and distillation columns fed by slurries of chemicals piped up from somewhere below the floor.

Four or five different types of imipolex were used to make a completed slug, and the slugs were built up in successive layers like onions. At one end of the fab was a bay where the successive layers of imipolex were added.

Some of the imipolexes could be relaxed into a dissolved phase, so these new layers could be added to a slug simply by dipping it into a vat. Others of the imipolexes were too highly polymerized and gel-like for dipping. These were smeared on using roller-devices, or were laminated on in sheets.

After each new layer was deposited, the slugs were cycled through three more stages: holographic nanoetching, rare-earth metal doping, and chipmould infection. Depending on its size, a completed slug of imipolex might include twenty to two hundred layers, with each layer being separately etched, doped and infected.

As Randy and his boss moved down the main corridor on their tour, people kept recognizing Neeraj and coming over to pat him on the back or on the arm or on the stomach – they were like worker-ants exchanging greetings while tending their larvae.

"We are touching each other very much here," said Neeraj. "Perhaps we are using so much body language because it is hard to see each other's faces. Or maybe it is because everyone is so clean."

The only human contamination Randy could sense was the meaty smell of his own breath bouncing around inside his face-mask. He wished he could tear off the mask and inhale the clean pure air of the fab. But then he would exhale, and the fab wouldn't like that – detectors would notice the increased number of parti-cles-per-cubic-metre, and lights would flash.

Later they went downstairs to the sub fab, the floor below the fab. Like the break area, the sub fab was only kept at ten thousand particles per cubic metre, and you didn't have to wear a face-mask.

The sub fab was a techno dream, the ultimate mad scientist's lab. It held all the devices needed to support the machines of the fab. The electrical generators were here, the plumbing, the tanks of acids, the filtering systems, the vacuum lines, the particle monitoring equipment – miles of wires and pipes and cables in an immaculately painted concrete room. This was where Randy was to begin work, maintaining and upgrading the sub fab's plumbing.

The apartment the Heritagists had found for Randy was in a sterile high-rise right next to the Bangalore airport. Most of the people living in it were non-Indian workers and scientists imported by the various high-tech industries of Bangalore. After a tense, alienated week there, Randy decided to move into town, into the real India, into a dim room in an ancient stone building on the side of a hill between the orchid-filled Lalbagh Gardens and the bustling Gandhi Bazaar.

The sheer diversity of India soothed Randy: in tense Louisville, everyone was good or bad, rich or poor, black or white – but in the streets of Bangalore there were hundreds of shadings on every scale, and life's daily workings were all the more richly woven.

The building with Randy's room was called Tipu Bharat; Tipu being the name of a former Indian prince, and Bharat being the Indian word for India. The walls of Tipu Bharat were worked with carved designs like necklaces and set with arched, pillared niches holding miniature bright imipolex statues of gods, animated icons that waved their tiny arms and seemed to watch the passers-by. There was an open terrace on the roof where the Tipu Bharat roomers could sit and stare out towards the Eastern or the Western Ghats, the distant mountain ranges that enclosed the high plateau of Bangalore.

Near the Gandhi Bazaar was a street of the naked holymen called sadhus; day and night the sadhus sat in streetside booths, each with a small incense burner, a blanket, a fly-whisk, and a tacked-up collection of shimmering religious art, much of it made of imipolex. Sometimes one of the sadhus would put on a show: hammer a sharpened stick into his head, build a fire in the street and walk on its coals, suck blood from the neck of a live chicken, or do something even more fantastic and disgusting. Randy often walked down to watch them in the evenings.

"The moldie you are always fabulating with outside the fab," said Neeraj on the morning of Randy's first monthly payday, a Saturday. "Is she calling herself Parvati?"

"Mm-hmm," said Randy. "Do you know her?"

"No, no, I only recognize the shape she is wearing – Parvati is the goddess who is the wife of the god Shiva. In the Hindu religion, Shiva's wife is extremely important; she has many different names and many different forms. One form is Parvati the beautiful, but another of her forms is the black Kali who rides a lion, brandishes a knife and wears a necklace of chopped-off human heads. The risk in becoming very intimate with a moldie Parvati is that she may unexpectedly become a Kali and take your head. Like all women, my wife is both Parvati and a Kali, not to mention an Uma and a Durga, but my wife is human and I do not need to worry so much about her really and truly taking my head. You are planning to buy Parvati a slug of imipolex from the company store today and to have a heavy date with her, are you not?"

Randy blushed. "Not that it's really any of your all's goddamn business, Neeraj."

"I do not disapprove, Randy, but I am saying this: Keep your head. Some moldies play the game of sticking a tendril up a man's nose and implanting a control unit in his brain. This is called a thinking cap. You have never heard of this practice?"

"Can't say as I have."

"If you are going to spend time with moldies, and perhaps to be sexually intimate with them, it is a good practice, first of all, to be wearing a protective barrier in the back of your nose. There is a temporary self-installing titaniplast device of this nature available in the company store. Come along, I'll walk over there with you and make sure that my rumbustious young horn-doggie is equipped with the proper protection."

One whole end of the employee's store was filled with bins of lusciously glowing imipolex sausages. The set-up reminded Randy of the fireworks stands in Indiana; rank upon rank of magical cylinders lying there, arranged by size and waiting for ignition. The colourful patterns on the imipolex were alive and constantly changing, albeit in calm and rhythmic ways. The slugs came in a range of standard sizes that ranged from a hundred grams up to two kilograms.

Randy picked out a five-hundred gram sausage, which was nearly at the limit of what he could comfortably afford. Neeraj showed him where the nose-blockers were, and also made sure that Randy bought one of the small imipolex patches that Neeraj called leech-DIMs.

"Leech-DIMs are making a moldie very confused," said Neeraj. "But we are not fully understanding why. Leech-DIMs were invented only last year by Sri Ramanujan, one of Emperor Staghorn's finest limpware engineers. As long as you have a leech-DIM handy, you can instantly bollox up a threatening moldie. You are very fortunate to be able to buy one; at this point in time they are available solely through the Emperor Staghorn Beetle Larvae company store."

The leech-DIMs were small ragged patches of plastic, no bigger than the joint of your thumb, no two of them looking quite similar. They were so diverse as to resemble organically grown objects – like some tropical tree's aerial seeds perhaps, or like by-the-wind-sailor jellyfish collected from some lonely, windward beach.

The leech-DIMs were shockingly expensive, with one leech-DIM costing nearly the equivalent of three months' pay: a quarter of a year's earnings! Randy tried hard to get out of buying one, but

Neeraj was adamant; he and Randy argued so loudly that soon a clerk came over to inform Randy that Emperor Staghorn Beetle Larvae employees were in fact required to use appropriate cautions with moldies, and that yes, he could buy on credit.

So Randy equipped himself and took Parvati to his room in the Tipu Bharat and presented her with his five-hundred gram slug of imipolex. The slug was two inches in diameter and nearly a foot long. It was circled by colourful stripes that smoothly undulated through a repeating standing-wave pattern that bounced from one end of the sausage to the other.

"Oh Randy," exclaimed Parvati, exhaling a heady cloud of spores. She took the gift sausage in both hands. "My darling! It's beautiful. Five hundred grams! I'll incorporate it right away."

She pressed the imipolex against her breasts, and the sausage's stripes began to twist and flow like cream in coffee. The sausage deformed itself into the shape of a nonlinear dumbbell, and concentric circles appeared in the two ends. The ends domed themselves up and merged with Parvati's flesh: now her enlarged breasts were covered with what looked like shiny gold and copper filigree, very arabesque and fractal. Parvati held her arms up high and twirled around. "Do you like it, Randy?"

"You're beautiful, Parvati. What do you say we have some fun now?" The nose-blocker deadened the sound of Randy's voice in his own ears. Parvati sashayed forward, undid Randy's pants, then drew him down onto his bed. Randy's youth and lust were such that he was able to reach three climaxes in twenty minutes – three deep, aching ejaculations.

And then he lay there, spent and happy, staring out at the darkening sky. A single bright evening star appeared in the top of the window: Venus. Parvati's soft form was all around him, partly under him and partly over him. She ran a caressing hand across his face, poked softly at his nose, and slipped a thin finger into his nostril.

"Now don't you be a-tryin' to give me no thinkin'-cap," cried Randy, jerking upright in sudden terror. He snatched his leech-DIM up from where he'd left it under the corner of the bed and held it out protectively. "I mean it, Parvati!"

She drew her puddled shape back into a more human form. "I was only teasing you, Randy. I know you're wearing a nose-blocker. I can tell by the sound of your voice. Is that a leech-DIM you're holding?

I've heard of them, but I've never seen one. Don't you trust me?"

"My boss, Neeraj, he told me you might try and put a controller on my brain."

"If I could count on you to bring me imipolex on every single payday, then why would I need to control you? You'd already be doing everything I want you to do. Can I count on you, Randy?"

"You can if you'll promise to come see me in between paydays, Parvati . I can't wait a whole 'nother month to grease my wrench. My old limpware sex-toys – they're whipped to shit."

"Show them to me."

Randy pulled Sammie-Jo and Angelika out of the bottom drawer of his dresser. They smelled rotten, and their colours had turned muddy grey.

"Whew!" said Parvati. "They'll be completely dead in a week to ten days. That is exactly how I do not want to end up."

"Do you want them?"

"I should say not. Most distasteful. Bury them. Or set them afire."

"What am I gonna do for sex?"

"I'll come and see you twice a week," said Parvati softly. "Every Saturday and perhaps every Tuesday. I'll be your steady girlfriend. How would you like that?"

"It'd be swell! Hey, if you're my girlfriend, why don't you come on and walk around the neighbourhood with me? You can help explain stuff to me, and maybe – maybe you can help me buy some new sex toys. Also I'd like to get something to eat."

They went to the Mavalli Tiffin Rooms, a vegetarian snack place near the Lalbagh Gardens park. Randy got them a table in front, near a window, in case Parvati's smell were a problem. But the moldie's presence didn't disturb anyone; indeed the other groups in the room seemed pleasantly amused by the singular pair made by Randy the hillbilly cheeseball and Parvati the moldie goddess – the couple were visible proof of Bangalore's modernity and advancing technological prowess!

After eating some pancakes stuffed with gnarly yellow roots, Randy took Parvati to see the sadhus. The sadhus were greatly excited at the sight of Parvati. Two of the sadhus heaped some thorny branches on the ground and rolled in them till they bled; another thrust a long staff through a hole in his penis and worked it up and down. Still another sadhu fed a well-worn imipolex snake down his throat and then – with much bucking of his stomach muscles – he pushed the snake out of his anus. Parvati acknowledged the sadhus' homage with graceful motions of her arms. Randy stood right behind her, with his hands tight around her waist. Parvati's smells and motions were nectar to him.

"I used to see guys like the sadhus at the Kentucky State Fair," said Randy. "We called 'em carnival geeks. There was a time I thought I might grow up to be one. Hey, do you wanna go help me pick out some imipolex sex-toys?"

"Don't fritter your money away on toys, Randy," said Parvati, pushing her bottom against Randy's crotch and growing some temporary butt-fingers to fondle him secretly. "All of your extra money should come to me. If you promise to bring me 750 grams of imipolex instead of 500 next payday, we can go back up to your room right now. And I'll come make love to you three times a week."

As they started to leave, the sadhus began holding out begging-bowls to Parvati and clamouring for "moksha". Parvati stretched out her left arm and lumps seemed to move out along the back of her hand. And then the tips of her fingers popped out four black nuggets like wrinkled marbles. The sadhus began fighting savagely over them.

"What's that?" asked Randy.

"Those are lumps of chipmould mycelium, technically known as sclerotia, but commonly called camote in the Americas and moksha in India. They are a powerful psychedelic, greatly prized by the sadhus."

By now the camote nuggets had been devoured by four lucky sadhus who lay prostrate in adoration at Parvati's feet. Randy and Parvati picked their way around them, and headed back towards the Tipu Bharat. It was getting late, and beggars were bedding down for the night on the sidewalks. When a man in a turban rode past on a unicycle, Parvati pulled Randy into a dark doorway.

"Look out for that one," she whispered. "He's a dacoit – a mugger from a gang."

They lingered in the shadows after the dacoit was gone, hugging and kissing and feeling each other, until suddenly a moldie came plummeting down out of the sky and landed in front of them. He was shaped like a lithe, nude Indian man, but with leathery wings, four arms, and a shiny crown like Parvati's. He had an enormous, uncircumcised penis. Parvati cupped her enlarged new breasts and ingratiatingly hefted them at the interloper. He glared at her with his mouth open, apparently talking to Parvati via direct moldie radio waves.

"It is none of your affair," shouted Parvati suddenly. "You should be grateful to me!"

The four-armed moldie gave Randy a rough shove that sent him sprawling, then leapt up in the air and flew away.

"Who in the world was that?" asked Randy, shakily getting to his feet. "Looked like one mean motherfucker!"

"That was my husband, Shiva the destroyer. Ridiculous as it may seem, he's jealous of you. As if sex with a human could possibly mean anything to me. Shiva thinks I should come back to our nest right away? I'll teach him a little lesson in etiquette. I'll spend the entire night with you."

Back in Randy's room they had sex again, and then Parvati started looking bored. "I'm bound and determined to stay here all night, Randy, but I'm not conditioned to sleep anywhere other than in the security of my home nest. What shall we do?"

"Maybe we should take like a drug-trip together," said nude Randy. "You give me a lump or two of that camote stuff, and I'll put the leech-DIM on you." He held the postage-stamp-sized leech-DIM out to her on the palm of his hand.

"What an odd idea," said Parvati. "For a moldie and a human to 'take like a drug-trip together'. You're quite the singular cheeseball, Randy Karl Tucker." She peered at his leech-DIM. "Let me try it just for a minute at first. Put it on me, and count a minute by your watch, and then remove it right away. I want to see if I like it."

Randy pressed the leech-DIM against Parvati's left shoulder – like a vaccination. The leech-DIM had been dry and papery to the touch, but as soon as the leech touched Parvati it softened, and then quickly twitched itself into a position of maximum contact.

Parvati's skin lit up like a Christmas tree, and her limbs shank back into her body-mass. She lay there on Randy's bed like a living mandala. Once the minute was up, it took a bit of effort to pry up an edge of the leech, but after that was done Randy could easily peel it off. Parvati's usual shape gradually returned, her limbs and head slowly growing out from the mandala.

"Goodness me," said Parvati. "That was really something." She gestured fluidly, and two chipmould sclerotia appeared in the palm of her hand: one black, and one a hard gem-like blue. "Eat these, Randy, and put the leech-DIM on me. We'll make a night-long debauch of it."

Randy ate the camote. It was crunchy but juicy, and bitter with alkaloids. He started feeling the effects almost immediately. With wooden fingers he put the now-soft leech-DIM back on Parvati and lay down on the bed with her, wrapping himself tight around the pulsing egg of her body.

The camote took Randy on an express-ride to a classic mystical vision: he saw God in the form of an all-pervading white light. The light recognized Randy and spoke to him. "I love you, Randy," it said. "I'll always love you. I'm always here." Filigreed multi-dimensional patterns of tubes surrounded Randy like pipes all around him, wonderfully growing and branching pipes leading from Randy out through the white light and, in the distance homing in on – someone else. Parvati. "Randy?" came her voice. "Is that you? Are we in this dream together?" "Yes oh yes we are," answered Randy. "Let's fly together," said Parvati, and her essence flowed through the pipes to mingle with Randy's, and then they were adrift together in a sky of lovely shapes, endlessly many shapes of infinite intricacy, all gladly singing to the pair of flying lovers.

When Randy woke up, he was lying on the floor with Parvati's tissues completely surrounding his head. He was breathing through a king of nozzle Parvati had pushed into his mouth. For a moment Randy feared she was attacking him, and then, peeling her off himself, he feared she was dead. But once he removed her leech-DIM, Parvati livened up and began pulling herself back together. The hot morning sun streamed in Randy's window, and the thousand noises of the street came drifting in – the chattering voices, the bicycle bells, the vendors' cries, the Indian radio music, the swish and shuffle of moving bodies – a moiré of sound vibrations filling the air like exquisite ripples in a three-dimensional pond.

"Wow,' said Parvati.

"Did you have a good time?"

"It was – wonderful."

ALL MY DARLING DAUGHTERS

Connie Willis

"I have written everything from screwball comedies to mysteries to fairy tales and found to my delight that science fiction welcomes them all." SF has welcomed Connie Willis too, awarding her several Hugos and Nebulas since her début in 1971 – two of each in a single year when her short story "Even the Queen" won both awards, as did her novel Doomsday Book: *a unique achievement. "All My Darling Daughters", a hard-hitting story about a troubled adolescent on an orbiting boarding-school of the future, first appeared as an original in Willis's collection* Fire Watch, *as it was deemed too strong for magazine publication. A second collection,* Impossible Things, *has recently appeared.*

> Barrett: I'll have her dog . . . Octavius.
> Octavius: Sir?
> Barrett: Her dog must be destroyed. At once.
> Octavius: I really d-don't see what the p-poor little beast has
>   d-done to . . .
>
> *The Barretts of Wimpole Street*

The first thing my new roommate did was tell me her life story. Then she tossed up all over my bunk. Welcome to Hell. I know, I know. It was my own fucked fault that I was stuck with the stupid little scut in the first place. Daddy's darling had let her grades slip till she was back in the freshman dorm and she would stay there until the admin reported she was being a good little girl again. But he didn't have to put me in the charity ward, with all the little scholarship freshmen from the front colonies – frightened virgies one and all. The richies had usually had their share of jig-jig in boarding school, even if they were mostly edge. And they were willing to learn.

Not this one. She wouldn't know a bone from a vaj, and wouldn't know what went into which either. Ugly, too. Her hair was chopped off in an old-fashioned bob I thought nobody, not even front kids, wore any more. Her name was Zibet and she was from some godspit colony called Marylebone Weep and her mother was dead and she had three sisters and her father hadn't wanted her to come. She told me all this in a rush of what she probably thought was friendliness before she tossed her supper all over me and my nice new slickspin sheets.

The sheets were the sum total of good things about the vacation Daddy Dear had sent me on over summer break. Being stranded in a forest of slimy slicksa trees and noble natives was supposed to build my character and teach me the hazards of bad grades. But the noble natives were good at more than weaving their precious product with its near frictionless surface. Jig-jig on slickspin is something entirely different, and I was close to being an expert on the subject. I'd bet even Brown didn't know about this one. I'd be more than glad to teach him.

"I'm so *sorry*," she kept saying in a kind of hiccup while her face turned red and then white and then red again like a fucked alert bell, and big tears seeped down her face and dripped on the mess. "I guess I got a little sick on the shuttle."

"I guess. Don't bawl, for jig's sake, it's no big deal. Don't they have laundries in Mary Boning It?"

"Marylebone Weep. It's a natural spring."

"So are you, kid. So are you." I scooped up the wad, with the muck inside. "No big deal. The dorm mother will take care of it."

She was in no shape to take the sheets down herself, and I figured Mumsy would take one look at those big fat tears and assign me a new roommate. This one was not exactly perfect. I could see right now I couldn't expect her to do her homework and not bawl giant tears while Brown and I jig-jigged on the new sheets. But she didn't have leprosy, she didn't weigh eight hundred pounds, and she hadn't gone for my vaj when I bent over to pick up the sheets. I could do a lot worse.

I could also be doing some better. Seeing Mumsy on my first day back was not my idea of a good start. But I trotted downstairs with the scutty wad and knocked on the dorm mother's door.

She is no dumb lady. You have to stand in a little box of an entryway waiting for her to answer your knock. The box works on the same principle as a rat cage, except that she's added her own little touch. Three big mirrors that probably cost her a year's salary to cart up from earth. Never mind – as a weapon, they were a real bargain. Because, Jesus Jiggin' Mary, you stand there and sweat and the mirrors tell you your skirt isn't straight and your hair looks scutty and that bead of sweat on your upper lip is going to give it away immediately that you are scared scutless. By the time she answers the door – five minutes if she's feeling kindly – you're either edge or you're not there. No dumb lady.

I was not on the defensive, and my skirts are never straight, so the mirrors didn't have any effect on me, but the five minutes took their toll. That box didn't have any ventilation and I was way too close to those sheets. But I had my speech all ready. No need to remind her who I was. The admin had probably filled her in but good. And I'd get nowhere telling her they were my sheets. Let her think they were the virgie's.

When she opened the door I gave her a brilliant smile and said, "My roommate's had a little problem. She's a new freshman, and I think she got a little excited coming up on the shuttle and—"

I expected her to launch into the "supplies are precious, everything must be recycled, cleanliness is next to godliness" speech you get for everything you do on this godspit campus. Instead she said, "What did you do to her?"

"What did I – look, she's the one who tossed up. What do you think I did, stuck my fingers down her throat?"

"Did you give her something? Samurai? Float? Alcohol?"

"Jiggin' Jesus, she just got here. She walked in, she said she was from Mary's Prick or something, she tossed up."

"And?"

"And what? I may look depraved, but I don't think freshmen vomit at the sight of me."

From her expression, I figured Mumsy might. I stuck the smelly wad of sheets at her. "Look," I said, "I don't care what you do. It's not my problem. The kid needs clean sheets."

Her expression for the mucky mess was kinder than the one she had for me. "Recycling is not until Wednesday. She will have to sleep on her mattress until then."

Mary Masting, she could knit a sheet by Wednesday, especially with all the cotton flying around this fucked campus. I grabbed the sheets back.

"Jig you, scut," I said.

I got two months' dorm restricks and a date with the admin.

I went down to the third level and did the sheets myself. It cost a fortune. They want you to have an *awareness* of the harm you are doing the delicate environment by failing to abide, etc. Total scut. The environment's about as delicate as a senior's vaj. When Old Man Moulton bought this thirdhand Hell-Five, he had some edge dream of turning it into the college he went to as a boy. Whatever possessed him to even buy the old castoff is something nobody's ever figured out. There must have been a Lagrangian point on the top of his head.

The realtor must have talked hard and fast to make him think Hell could ever look like Ames, Iowa. At least there'd been some technical advances since it was first built or we'd all be *floating* around the godspit place. But he couldn't stop at simply gravitizing the place, fixing the plumbing, and hiring a few good teachers. Oh, no, he had to build a sandstone campus, put in a football field, and plant *trees!* This all cost a fortune, of course, which put it out of the reach of everybody but richies and trust kids, except for Moulton's charity scholarship cases. But you couldn't jig-jig in a plastic bag to fulfill your fatherly instincts back then, so Moulton had to build himself a college. And here we sit, stuck out in space with a bunch of fucked cottonwood trees that are trying to take over.

Jesus Bonin' Mary, cottonwoods! I mean, so what if we're a hundred years out of date. I can take the freshman beanies and the pep rallies. Dorm curfews didn't stop anybody a hundred years ago either. And face it, pleated skirts and cardigans make for easy access. But those godspit trees!

At first they tried the nature-dupe stuff. Freeze your vaj in winter, suffocate in summer, just like good old Iowa. The trees were at least bearable then. Everybody choked in cotton for a month, they baled the stuff up like Mississippi slaves and shipped it down to earth and that was it. But finally something was too expensive even for Daddy Moulton and we went on even-clime like all the other Hell-Fives.

Nobody bothered to tell the trees, of course, so now they just spit and drop leaves whenever they feel like it, which is all the time. You can hardly make it to class without choking to death.

The trees do their dirty work down under, too, rooting happily away through the plumbing and the buried cables so that nothing works. Ever. I think the whole outer shell could blow away and nobody would ever know. The fucked root system would hold us together. And the admin wonders why we call it Hell. I'd like to upset their delicate balance once and for all.

I ran the sheets through on disinfect and put them in the spin. While I was sitting there, thinking evil thoughts about freshmen and figuring how to get off restricks, Arabel came wandering in.

"Tavvy, hi! When did you get back?" She is always too sweet for words. We played lezzies as freshmen, and sometimes I think she's sorry it's over. "There's a great party," she said.

"I'm on restricks," I said. Arabel's not the world's greatest authority on parties. I mean, herself and a plastic bone would be a great party. "Where is it?"

"My room. Brown's there," she said languidly. This was calculated to make me rush out of my pants and up the stairs, no doubt. I watched my sheets spin.

"So what are you doing down here?" I said.

"I came down for some float. Our machine's out. Why don't you come on over? Restricks never stopped you before."

"I've been to your parties, Arabel. Washing my sheets might be more exciting."

"You're right," she said, "it might." She fiddled with the machine. This was not like her at all.

"What's up?"

"Nothing's up." She sounded puzzled. "It's samurai-party time without the samurai. Not a bone in sight and no hope of any. That's why I came down here."

"Brown, too?" I asked. He was into a lot of edge stuff, but I couldn't quite imagine celibacy.

"Brown, too. They all just sit there."

"They're on something, then. Something new they brought back from vacation." I couldn't see what she was so upset about.

"No," she said. "They're not on anything. This is different. Come see. Please."

Well, maybe this was all a trick to get me to one of Arabel's scutty parties and maybe not. But I didn't want Mumsy to think she'd hurt my feelings by putting me on restricks. I threw the lock on the spin so nobody'd steal the sheets and went with her.

For once Arabel hadn't exaggerated. It was a godspit party, even by her low standards. You could tell that the minute you walked in. The girls looked unhappy, the boys looked uninterested. It couldn't be all bad, though. At least Brown was back. I walked over to where he was standing.

"Tavvy," he said, smiling, "how was your summer? Learn anything new from the natives?"

"More than my fucked father intended." I smiled back at him.

"I'm sure he had your best interests at heart," he said. I started to say something clever to that, then realized he wasn't kidding. Brown was just like I was. He had to be kidding. Only he wasn't. He wasn't smiling anymore either.

"He just wanted to protect you, for your own good."

Jiggin' Jesus, he had to be on something. "I don't need any protecting," I said. "As you well know."

"Yeah," he said, sounding disappointed. "Yeah." He moved away.

What in the scut was going on? Brown leaned against the wall, watching Sept and Arabel. She had her sweater off and was shimmying out of her skirt, which I have seen before, sometimes even helped with. What I had never seen before was the look of absolute desperation on her face. Something was very wrong. Sept stripped, and his bone was as big as Arabel could have wanted, but the look on her face didn't change. Sept shook his head almost disapprovingly at Brown and went down on Arabel.

"I haven't had any straight-up all summer," Brown said from behind me, his hand on my vaj. "Let's get out of here."

Gladly. "We can't go to my room," I said. "I've got a virgie for a roommate. How about you?"

"No!" he said, and then more quietly, "I've got the same problem. New guy. Just off the shuttle. I want to break him in gently."

You're lying, Brown, I thought. And you're about to back out of this, too. "I know a place," I said, and practically raced him to the laundry room so he wouldn't have time to change his mind.

I spread one of the dried slickspin sheets on the floor and went down as fast as I could get out of my clothes. Brown was in no hurry, and the frictionless sheet seemed to relax him. He smoothed his hands the full length of my body. "Tavvy," he said, brushing his lips along the line from my hips to my neck, "your skin's so soft. I'd almost forgotten." He was talking to himself.

Forgotten what, for fucked's sake, he couldn't have been without any jig-jig all summer or he'd be showing it now, and he acted like he had all the time in the world.

"Almost forgotten . . . nothing like . . ."

Like what? I thought furiously. Just what have you got in that room? And what has it got that I haven't? I spread my legs and forced him down between them. He raised his head a little, frowning, then he started that long, slow, torturing passage down my skin again. Jiggin' Jesus, how long did he think I could wait?

"Come on," I whispered, trying to maneuver him with my hips. "Put it in, Brown. I want to jig-jig. Please."

He stood up in a motion so abrupt that my head smacked against the laundry-room floor. He pulled on his clothes, looking . . . what? Guilty? Angry?

I sat up. "What in the holy scut do you think you're doing?"

"You wouldn't understand. I just keep thinking about your father."

"My *father*? What in the scut are you talking about?"

"Look, I can't explain it. I just can't . . ." And left. Like that. With me ready to go off any minute and what do I get? A cracked head.

"I don't have a father, you scutty godfucker!" I shouted after him.

I yanked my clothes on and started pulling the other sheet out of the spin with a viciousness I would have liked to have spent on Brown. Arabel was back, watching from the laundry-room door. Her face still had that strained look.

"Did you see that last charming scene?" I asked her, snagging the sheet on the spin handle and ripping a hole in one corner.

"I didn't have to. I can imagine it went pretty much the way mine did." She leaned unhappily against the door. "I think they've all gone bent over the summer."

"Maybe." I wadded the sheets together into a ball. I didn't think that was it, though. Brown wouldn't have lied about a new boy in his room in that case. And he wouldn't have kept talking about my father in that edge way. I walked passed Arabel. "Don't worry,

Arabel, if we have to go lezzy again, you know you're my first choice."

She didn't even look particularly happy about that.

My idiot roommate was awake, sitting bolt upright on the bunk where I'd left her. The poor brainless thing had probably been sitting there the whole time I'd been gone. I made up the bunk, stripped off my clothes for the second time tonight, and crawled in. "You can turn out the light any time," I said.

She hopped over to the wallplate, swathed in a nightgown that dated as far back as Old Man Moulton's college days, or farther. "Did you get in trouble?" she asked, her eyes wide.

"Of course not. I wasn't the one who tossed up. If anybody's in trouble, it's you," I added maliciously.

She seemed to sag against the flat wallplate as if she were clinging to it for support. "My father – will they tell my father?" Her face was flashing red and white again. And where would the vomit land this time? That would teach me to take out my frustrations on my roommate.

"Your father? Of course not. Nobody's in trouble. It was a couple of fucked sheets, that's all."

She didn't seem to hear me. "He said he'd come and get me if I got in trouble. He said he'd make me go home."

I sat up in the bunk. I'd never seen a freshman yet that wasn't dying to go home, at least not one like Zibet, with a whole loving family waiting for her instead of a trust and a couple of snotty lawyers. But Zibet here was scared scutless at the idea. Maybe the whole campus was going edge. "You didn't get in trouble," I repeated. "There's nothing to worry about."

She was still hanging onto that wallplate for dear life.

"Come on" – Mary Masting, she was probably having an attack of some kind, and I'd get blamed for that, too. "You're safe here. Your father doesn't even know about it."

She seemed to relax a little. "Thank you for not getting me in trouble," she said and crawled back into her own bunk. She didn't turn the light off.

Jiggin' Jesus, it wasn't worth it. I got out of bed and turned the fucked light off myself.

"You're a good person, you know that," she said softly into the darkness. Definitely edge. I settled down under the covers, planning to masty myself to sleep, since I couldn't get anything any other way, but very quietly. I didn't want any more hysterics.

A hearty voice suddenly exploded into the room. "To the young men of Moulton College, to all my strong sons, I say—"

"What's that?" Zibet whispered.

"First night in Hell," I said, and got out of bed for the thirtieth time.

"May all your noble endeavors be crowned with success," Old Man Moulton said.

I slapped my palm against the wallplate and then fumbled through my still-unpacked shuttle bag for a nail file. I stepped up on Zibet's bunk with it and started to unscrew the intercom.

"To the young women of Moulton College," he boomed again, "to all my darling daughters." He stopped. I tossed the screws and file back in the bag, smacked the plate, and flung myself back in bed.

"Who was that?" Zibet whispered.

"Our founding father," I said, and then remembering the effect the word "father" seemed to be having on everyone in this edge place, I added hastily, "That's the last time you'll have to hear him. I'll put some plast in the works tomorrow and put the screws back in so the dorm mother won't figure it out. We will live in blessed silence for the rest of the semester."

She didn't answer. She was already asleep, gently snoring. Which meant so far I had misguessed every single thing today. Great start to the semester.

The admin knew all about the party. "You *do* know the meaning of the word restricks, I presume?" he said.

He was an old scut, probably forty-five. Dear Daddy's age. He was fairly good-looking, probably exercising like edge to keep the old belly in for the freshman girls. He was liable to get a hernia. He probably jig-jigged into a plastic bag, too, just like Daddy, to carry on the family name. Jiggin' Jesus, there oughta be a law.

"You're a trust student, Octavia?"

"That's right." You think I'd be stuck with a fucked name like Octavia if I wasn't?

"Neither parent?"

"No. Paid mother-surr. Trust name till twenty-one." I watched his face to see what effect that had on him. I'd seen a lot of scared faces that way.

"There's no one to write to, then, except your lawyers. No way to expel you. And restricks don't seem to have any appreciable effect on you. I don't quite know what would."

I'll bet you don't. I kept watching him, and he kept watching me, maybe wondering if I was his darling daughter, if that expensive jism in the plastic bag had turned out to be what he was boning after right now.

"What exactly was it you called your dorm mother?"

"Scut," I said.

"I've longed to call her that myself a time or two."

The sympathetic buildup. I waited, pretty sure of what was coming.

"About this party. I've heard the boys have something new going. What is it?"

The question wasn't what I expected. "I don't know," I said and then realized I'd let my guard down. "Do you think I'd tell you if I knew?"

'No, of course not. I admire that. You're quite a young woman, you know. Outspoken, loyal, very pretty, too, if I may say so."

Um-hmm. And you just happen to have a job for me, don't you?

"My secretary's quit. She likes younger men, she says, although if what I hear is true, maybe she's better off with me. It's a good job. Lots of extras. Unless, of course, you're like my secretary and prefer boys to men."

Well, and here was the way out. No more virgie freshman, no more restricks. Very tempting. Only he was at least forty-five, and somehow I couldn't quite stomach the idea of jig-jig with my own father. Sorry, sir.

"If it's the trust problem that's bothering you, I assure you there are ways to check."

Liar. Nobody knows who their kids are. That's why we've got these storybook trust names, so we can't show up on Daddy's doorstep: Hi, I'm your darling daughter. The trust protects them against scenes like that. Only sometimes with a scut like the admin here, you wonder just who's being protected from whom.

"Do you remember what I told my dorm mother?" I said.

"Yes."

"Double to you."

Restricks for the rest of the year and a godspit alert band welded onto my wrist.

"I know what they've got," Arabel whispered to me in class. It was the only time I ever saw her. The godspit alert band went off if I even mastied without permission.

"What?" I asked, pretty much without caring.

"Tell you after."

I met her outside, in a blizzard of flying leaves and cotton. The circulation system had gone edge again. "Animals," she said.

"Animals?"

"Little repulsive things about as long as your arm. Tessels, they're called. Repulsive little brown animals."

"I don't believe it," I said. "It's got to be more than beasties. That's elementary school stuff. Are they bio-enhanced?"

"You mean pheromones or something?" She frowned. "I don't know. I sure didn't see anything attractive about them, but the boys – Brown brought his to a party, carrying it around on his arm, calling it Daughter Ann. They all swarmed around it, petting it, saying things like 'Come to Daddy.' It was really edge."

I shrugged. "Well, if you're right, we don't have anything to worry about. Even if they're bio-enhanced, how long can beasties hold their attention? It'll all be over by midterm."

"Can't you come over? I never see you." She sounded like she was ready to go lezzy.

I held up the banded wrist. "Can't. Listen, Arabel, I'll be late to my next class," I said, and hurried off through the flailing yellow and white. I didn't have a next class. I went back to the dorm and took some float.

When I came out of it, Zibet was there, sitting on her bunk with her knees hunched up, writing busily in a notebook. She looked much better than the first time I saw her. Her hair had grown out some and showed enough curl at the ends to pick up on her features. She didn't look strained. In fact she looked almost happy.

"What are you doing?" I hoped I said. The first couple of sentences out of float it's anybody's guess what's going to come out.

"Recopying my notes," she said. Jiggin', the things that make some people happy. I wondered if she'd found a boyfriend and that was what had given her that pretty pink color. If she had, she was doing better than Arabel. Or me.

"For who?"

"What?" She looked blank.

"What boy are you copying your notes for?"

"Boy?" Now there was an edge to her voice. She looked frightened.

I said carefully, "I figure you've got to have a boyfriend." And watched her go edge again. Mary doing Jesus, that must not have come out right at all. I wondered what I'd really said to send her off like that.

She backed up against her bunk wall like I was after her with something and held her notebook flat against her chest. "Why do you think that?"

Think what? Holy scut. I should have told her about float before I went off on it. I'd have to answer her now like it was still a real conversation instead of a caged rat being poked with a stick, and hope I could explain later. "I don't know why I think that. You just looked –"

"It's true, then," she said, and the strain was right back, blinking red and white.

"What is?" I said, still wondering what it was the float had garbled my innocent comment into.

"I had braids like you before I came here. You probably wondered about that." Holy scut, I'd said something mean about her choppy hair.

"My father ..." – she clutched the notebook like she had clutched the wallplate that night, hanging on for dear life. "My father cut them off." She was admitting some awful thing to me and I had no idea what.

"Why did he do that?"

"He said I tempted . . . men with it. He said I was a – that I made men think wicked thoughts about me. He said it was my fault that it happened. He cut off all my hair."

It was coming to me finally that I had asked her just what I thought I had: whether she had a boyfriend.

"Do you think I – do that?" she asked me pleadingly.

Are you kidding? She couldn't have tempted Brown in one of his bone-a-virgin moods. I couldn't say that to her, though, and on the other hand, I knew if I said yes it was going to be toss-up time in dormland again. I felt sorry for her, poor kid, her braids chopped off and her scut of a father scaring the hell out of her with a bunch of lies. No wonder she'd been so edge when she first got here.

"Do you?" she persisted.

"You want to know what I think," I said, standing up a little unsteadily. "I think fathers are a pile of scut." I thought of Arabel's story. Little brown animals as long as your arm and Brown saying, "Your father only wants to protect you." "Worse than a pile of scut," I said. "All of them."

She looked at me, backed up against the wall, as if she would like to believe me.

"You want to know what my father did to me?" I said. "He didn't cut my braids off. Oh, no, this is lots better. You know about trust kids?"

She shook her head.

"Okay. My father wants to carry on his precious name and his precious jig-juice, but he doesn't want any of the trouble. So he sets up a trust. He pays a lot of money, he goes jig-jig in a plastic bag, and presto, he's a father, and the lawyers are left with all the dirty work. Like taking care of me and sending me someplace for summer break and paying my tuition at this godspit school. Like putting one of these on me." I held up my wrist with the ugly alert band on it. "He never even saw me. He doesn't even know who I am. Trust me. I know about scutty fathers."

"I wish . . ." Zibet said. She opened her book and started copying her notes again. I eased down onto my bunk, starting to feel the post-float headache. When I looked at her again, she was dripping tears all over her precious notes. Jiggin' Jesus, everything I said was wrong. The most I could hope for in this edge place was that the boys would be done playing beasties by midterms and I could get my grades up.

By midterms the circulation system had broken down completely. The campus was knee-deep in leaves and cotton. You could hardly walk. I trudged through the leaves to class, head down. I didn't even see Brown until it was too late.

He had the animal on his arm. "This is Daughter Ann," Brown said. "Daughter Ann, meet Tavvy."

"Go jig yourself," I said, brushing by him.

He grabbed my wrist, holding on hard and pressing his fingers against the alert band until it hurt. "That's not polite, Tavvy. Daughter Ann wants to meet you. Don't you, sweetheart?" He held the animals out to me. Arabel had been right. Hideous little things. I had never gotten a close look at one before. It had a sharp little brown face, with dull eyes and a tiny pink mouth. Its fur was coarse and brown, and its body hung limply off Brown's arm. He had put a ribbon around its neck.

"Just your type," I said. "Ugly as mud and a hole big enough for even you to find."

His grip tightened. "You can't talk that way to my . . ."

"Hi." Zibet said behind me. I whirled around. This was all I needed.

"Hi," I said, and yanked my wrist free. "Brown, this is my roommate. My *freshman* roommate. Zibet, Brown."

"And this is Daughter Ann," he said, holding the animal up so that its tender pink mouth gaped stupidly at us. Its tail was up. I could see tender pink at the other end, too. And Arabel wonders what the attraction is?

"Nice to meet you, freshman roommate," Brown muttered and pulled the animal back close to him. "Come to Papa," he said, and stalked off through the leaves.

I rubbed my poor wrist. Please, please let her not ask me what a tessel's for? I have had about all I can take for one day. I'm not about to explain Brown's nasty habits to a virgie.

I had underestimated her. She shuddered a little and pulled her notebooks against her chest. "Poor little beast," she said.

"What do you know about sin?" she asked me suddenly that night. At least she had turned off the light. That was some improvement.

"A lot," I said. "How do you think I got this charming bracelet?"

"I mean really doing something wrong. To somebody else. To save yourself." She stopped. I didn't answer her, and she didn't say anything more for a long time. "I know about the admin," she said finally.

I couldn't have been more surprised if Old Scut Moulton had suddenly shouted, "Bless you, my daughter," over the intercom.

"You're a good person. I can tell that." There was a dreamy quality to her voice. If it had been anybody but her I'd have thought she was masting. "There are things you wouldn't do, not even to save yourself."

"And you're a hardened criminal, I suppose?"

"There are things you wouldn't do," she repeated sleepily, and then said quite clearly and irrelevantly, "My sister's coming for Christmas."

Jiggin', she was full of surprises tonight. "I thought you were going home for Christmas," I said.

"I'm never going home," she said.

"Tavvy!" Arabel shouted halfway across campus. "Hello!"

The boys are over it, I thought, and how in the scut am I going to get rid of this alert band? I felt so relieved I could have cried.

"Tavvy," she said again. "I haven't seen you in weeks!"

"What's going on?" I asked her, wondering why she didn't just blurt it out about the boys in her usual breakneck fashion.

"What do you mean?" she said, wide-eyed, and I knew it wasn't the boys. They still had the tessels, Brown and Sept and all the rest of them. They still had the tessels. It's only beasties, I told myself fiercely, it's only beasties and why are you so on edge about it? Your father has your best interests at heart. Come to Daddy.

"The admin's secretary quit," Arabel said. "I got put on restricks for a samurai party in my room." She shrugged. "It was the best offer I'd had all fall."

Oh, but you're trust, Arabel. You're trust. He could be your father. Come to Papa.

"You look terrible," Arabel said. "Are you doing too much float?"

I shook my head. "Do you know what it is the boys do with them?"

"Tavvy, sweetheart, if you can't figure out what that big pink hole is for—"

"My roommate's father cut her hair off," I said. "She's a virgie. She's never done anything. He cut off all her hair."

"Hey," Arabel said, "you are really edging it. Listen, how long have you been without jig-jig? I can set you up, younger guys than the admin, nothing to worry about. Guaranteed no trusters. I could set you up."

I shook my head. "I don't want any."

"Listen, I'm worried about you. I don't want you to go edge on me. Let me ask the admin about your alert band at least."

"No," I said clearly. "I'm all right, Arabel. I've got to get to class."

"Don't let this tessel thing get to you, Tavvy. It's only beasties."

"Yeah." I walked steadily away from her across the spitting, leaf-littered campus. As soon as I was out of her line of sight, I slumped against one of the giant cottonwoods and hung on to it like Zibet had clung to that wallplate. For dear life.

Zibet didn't say another thing about her sister until right before Christmas break. Her hair, which I had thought was growing out, looked choppier than ever. The old look of strain was back and getting worse every day. She looked like a radiation victim.

I wasn't looking that good myself. I couldn't sleep, and float gave me headaches that lasted a week. The alert band started a rash that had worked its way halfway up my arm. And Arabel was right. I was going edge. I couldn't get the tessels off my mind. If you'd asked me last summer what I thought of beasties, I'd have said it was great fun for everyone, especially the animals. Now the thought of Brown with that hideous little brown and pink thing on his arm was enough to make me toss up. I keep thinking about your father. If it's the trust thing you're worried about, I can find out for you. He has your best interests at heart. Come to Papa.

My lawyers hadn't succeeded in convincing the admin to let me go to Aspen for Christmas, or anywhere else. They'd managed to wangle full privileges as soon as everybody was gone, but not to get the alert band off. I figured if the dorm mother got a good look at what it was doing to my arm, though, she'd let me have it off for a few days and give it a chance to heal. The circulation system was working again, blowing winds of hurricane force all across Hell. Merry Christmas, everybody.

On the last day of class, I walked into our dark room, hit the wallplate, and froze. There sat Zibet in the dark. On my bed. With a tessel in her lap.

"Where did you get that?" I whispered.

"I stole it," she said.

I locked the door behind me and pushed one of the desk chairs against it. "How?"

"They were all at a party in somebody else's room."

"You went in the boys' dorm?"

She didn't answer.

"You're a freshman. They could send you home for that," I said, disbelieving. This was the girl who had gone quite literally up the wall over the sheets, who had said, "I'm never going home again."

"Nobody saw me," she said calmly. "They were all at a party."

"You're edge," I said. "Whose is it, do you know?"

"It's Daughter Ann."

I grabbed the top sheet of my bunk and started lining my shuttle bag with it. Holy scut, this would be the first place Brown would look. I rifled through my desk drawer for a pair of scissors to cut some air slits with. Zibet still sat petting the horrid thing.

"We've got to hide it," I said. "This time I'm not kidding. You really are in trouble."

She didn't hear me. "My sister Henra's pretty. She has long braids like you. She's good like you, too," and then in an almost pleading voice, "she's only fifteen."

Brown demanded and got a room check that started, you guessed it, with our room. The tessel wasn't there. I'd put it in the shuttle bag and hidden it in one of the spins down in the laundry room. I'd wadded the other slickspin sheet in front of it, which I felt was fitting irony for Brown, only he was too enraged to see it.

"I want another check," he said after the dorm mother had given him the grand tour. "I know it's here." He turned to me. "I know you've got it."

"The last shuttle's in ten minutes," the dorm mother said. "There isn't time for another check."

"She's got it. I can tell by the look on her face. She's hidden it somewhere. Somewhere in this dorm."

The dorm mother looked like she'd like to have him in her Skinner box for about an hour. She shook her head.

"You lose, Brown," I said. "You stay and you'll miss your shuttle and be stuck in Hell over Christmas. You leave and you lose your darling Daughter Ann. You lose either way, Brown."

He grabbed my wrist. The rash was almost unbearable under the band. My wrist had started to swell, puffing out purplish-red over the metal. I tried to free myself with my other hand, but his grip was as hard and vengeful as his face. "Octavia here was at a samurai party in the boys' dorm last week," he said to the dorm mother.

"That's not true," I said. I could hardly talk. The pain from his grip was making me so nauseated I felt faint.

"I find that difficult to believe," the dorm mother said, "since she is confined by an alert band."

"This?" Brown said, and yanked my arm up. I cried out. "This thing?" He twisted it around my wrist. "She can take it off any time she wants. Didn't you know that?" He dropped my wrist and looked at me contemptuously. "Tavvy's too smart to let a little thing like an alert band stop her, aren't you, Tavvy?"

I cradled my throbbing wrist against my body and tried not to black out. It isn't beasties, I thought frantically. He would never do this to me just for beasties. It's something worse. Worse. He must never, never get it back.

"There's the call for the shuttle," the dorm mother said. "Octavia, your break privileges are canceled."

Brown shot a triumphant glance at me and followed her out. It took every bit of strength I had to wait till the last shuttle was gone before I went to get the tessel. I carried it back to the room with my good hand. The restricks hardly mattered. There was no place to go anyway. And the tessel was safe. "Everything will be all right," I said to the tessel.

Only everything wasn't all right. Henra, the pretty sister, wasn't pretty. Her hair had been cut off, as short as scissors could make it. She was flushed bright red and crying. Zibet's face had gone stony white and stayed that way. I didn't think from the looks of her that she'd ever cry again. Isn't it wonderful what a semester of college can do for you?

Restricks or no, I had to get out of there. I took my books and camped down in the laundry room. I wrote two term papers, read three textbooks, and, like Zibet, recopied all my notes. He cut off my hair. He said I tempted men and that was why it happened. Your father was only trying to protect you. Come to Papa. I turned on all the spins at once so I couldn't hear myself think and typed the term papers.

I made it to the last day of break, gritting my teeth to keep from thinking about Brown, about tessels, about everything. Zibet and her sister came down to the laundry room to tell me Henra was going back on the first shuttle. I said goodbye. "I hope you can come back," I said, knowing I sounded stupid, knowing there was nothing in the world that could make me go back to Marylebone Weep if I were Henra.

"I am coming back. As soon as I graduate."

"It's only two years," Zibet said. Two years ago Zibet had the same sweet face as her sister. Two years from now, Henra too would look like death warmed over. What fun to grow up in Marylebone Weep, where you're a wreck at seventeen.

"Come back with me, Zibet," Henra said.

"I can't."

Toss-up time. I went back to the room, propped myself on my bunk with a stack of books, and started reading. The tessel had been asleep on the foot of the bunk, its gaping pink vaj sticking up. It crawled onto my lap and lay there. I picked it up. It didn't resist. Even with it living in the room, I'd never really looked at it closely. I saw now that it couldn't resist if it tried. It had tiny little paws with soft pink underpads and no claws. It had no teeth, either, just the soft little rosebud mouth, only a quarter of the size of the opening at the other end. If it had been enhanced with pheromones, I sure couldn't tell it. Maybe its attraction was simply that it had no defenses, that it couldn't fight even if it wanted to.

I laid it over my lap and stuck an exploratory finger a little way into the vaj. I'd done enough lezzing when I was a freshman to know what a good vaj should feel like. I eased the finger farther in.

It screamed.

I yanked the hand free, balled it into a fist, and crammed it against my mouth hard to keep from screaming myself. Horrible, awful, pitiful sound. Helpless. Hopeless. The sound a woman must make when she's being raped. No. Worse. The sound a child must make. I thought, I have never heard a sound like that in my whole life, and at the same instant, this is the sound I have been hearing all semester. Pheromones. Oh, no, a far greater attraction than some chemical. Or is fear a chemical, too?

I put the poor little beast onto the bed, went into the bathroom, and washed my hands for about an hour. I thought Zibet hadn't known what the tessels were for, that she hadn't had more than the vaguest idea what the boys were doing to them. But she had known. Known and tried to keep it from me. Known and gone into the boys' dorm all by herself to steal one. We should have stolen them all, all of them, gotten them away from those scutting god-fucking . . . I had thought of a lot of names for my father over the years. None of them was bad enough for this. Scutting Jesus-jiggers. Fucking piles of scut.

Zibet was standing in the door of the bathroom.

"Oh, Zibet," I said, and stopped.

"My sister's going home this afternoon," she said.

"No," I said, "Oh, no," and ran past her out of the room.

I guess I had kind of a little breakdown. Anyway, I can't account very well for the time. Which is edge, because the thing I remember most vividly is the feeling that I needed to hurry, that something awful would happen if I didn't hurry.

I know I broke restricks because I remember sitting out under the cottonwoods and thinking what a wonderful sense of humor Old Man Moulton had. He sent up Christmas lights for the bare cottonwoods, and the cotton and the brittle yellow leaves blew against them and caught fire. The smell of burning was everywhere. I remember thinking clearly, smokes and fires, how appropriate for Christmas in Hell.

But when I tried to think about the tessels, about what to do, the thoughts got all muddy and confused, like I'd taken too much float. Sometimes it was Zibet Brown wanted and not Daughter Ann at all, and I would say, "You cut off her hair. I'll never give her back to you. Never." And she would struggle and struggle against him. But she had no claws, no teeth. Sometimes it was the admin, and he would say, "If it's the trust thing you're worried about, I can find out for you," and I would say, "You only want the tessels for yourself." And sometimes Zibet's father said, "I am only trying to protect you. Come to Papa." And I would climb up on the bunk to unscrew the intercom but I couldn't shut him up. "I don't need protecting," I would say to him. Zibet would struggle and struggle.

A dangling bit of cotton had stuck to one of the Christmas lights. It caught fire and dropped into the brown broken leaves. The smell of smoke was everywhere. Somebody should report that. Hell could burn down, or was it burn up, with nobody here over Christmas break. I should tell somebody. That was it, I had to tell somebody. But there was nobody to tell. I wanted my father. And he wasn't there. He had never been there. He had paid his money, spilled his juice, and thrown me to the wolves. But at least he wasn't one of them. He wasn't one of them.

There was nobody to tell. "What did you do to it?" Arabel said. "Did you give it something? Samurai? Float? Alcohol?"

"I didn't . . ."

"Consider yourself on restricks."

"It isn't beasties," I said. "They call them Baby Dear and Daughter Ann. And they're the fathers. They're the fathers. But the tessels don't have any claws. They don't have any teeth. They don't even know what jig-jig is."

"He has her best interests at heart," Arabel said.

"What are you talking about? He cut off all her hair. You should have seen her, hanging onto the wallplate for dear life! She struggled and struggled, but it didn't do any good. She doesn't have any claws. She doesn't have any teeth. She's only fifteen. We have to hurry."

"It'll all be over by midterms," Arabel said. "I can fix you up. Guaranteed no trusters."

I was standing in the dorm mother's Skinner box, pounding on her door. I did not know how I had gotten there. My face looked back at me from the dorm mother's mirrors. Arabel's face: strained and desperate. Flashing red and white and red again like an alert band: my roommate's face. She would not believe me. She would put me on restricks. She would have me expelled. It didn't matter. When she answered the door, I could not run. I had to tell somebody before the whole place caught fire.

"Oh, my dear," she said, and put her arms around me.

I knew before I opened the door that Zibet was sitting on my bunk in the dark. I pressed the wallplate and kept my bandaged hand on it, as if I might need it for support. "Zibet," I said. "Everything's going to be all right. The dorm mother's going to confiscate the tessels. They're going to outlaw animals on campus. Everything will be all right."

She looked up at me. "I sent it home with her," she said.

"What?" I said blankly.

"He won't . . . leave us alone. He – I sent Daughter Ann home with her."

No. Oh, no.

"Henra's good like you. She won't save herself. She'll never last the two years." She looked steadily at me. "I have two other sisters. The youngest is only ten."

"You sent the tessel home?" I said. "To your *father*?"

"Yes."

"It can't protect itself," I said. "It doesn't have any claws. It can't protect itself."

"I told you you didn't know anything about sin," she said, and turned away.

I never asked the dorm mother what they did with the tessels they took away from the boys. I hope, for their own sakes, that somebody put them out of their misery.

PAIRPUPPETS
Manuel Van Loggem

One of Holland's leading novelists and playwrights, Manuel Van Loggem has occasionally written fantasy stories, some with science-fictional content. Het Liefdeleven der Priargen (1968, translated as "The Love Life of the Priargs") collects some of these. "Pairpuppets," translated by its author, is his best-known story, and shows how love might be in a rather more remote future.

1

"It's the end of our mutual service time," Eric said softly to himself, "and I'm not glad."

He was standing at the window and looking out over the polder far below him. The carefully calculated disorder of renovated mills and sham farms held less attraction for him than usual. He knew that he was on the brink of a new period in his life. Far away, on the lines of the horizon, he saw the contours of the gigantic machines that emitted a faint and incessant humming as the only evidence of their otherwise inscrutable activity; they glimmered faintly like a weak imitation of a reluctant sunset. "Like secret signals from outerspace invaders," Eric thought. He shook his head as if to drive out the waspish buzzing of continuous whining thoughts in his brain.

"Why do I think of aliens?"

He once had been on an instruction tour of the power stations. He knew that there was no living creature in the immense rooms where the computers drew their flashing runes on the glass screens.

Only the contented purring of tame nuclear forces could be heard, like a smile in sound. They brought into movement the innumerable pivots, axles, and junctions through which all the vital necessities of life were distributed through the country.

Eric became conscious of a vague sense of fear caused by the sight of the vast expanse filled with rows of factories cleverly integrated with the artificial landscape. He recovered, however, quickly.

It was almost time for his appointment with his girl friend Tina. Her imminent visit filled him with lust, slightly dulled by weak vibrations of an almost imperceptible boredom. The delights of her body were known to him to the last details, as if they were the results of a programmed pleasure pattern, punched on a tape and tuned to his carnal receptors. "Fixed habits are bad for passion," he thought. "It really seems to mark the end of our service time. I should be glad to get a new partner, but I'm not."

He had agreed with Tina to perform the mating from behind this evening, with hand-and-mouth foreplay for half an hour, as was explained in the third chapter of the *Handbook for Fornication*. Eric knew that in former times the drive for pairing had been discharged in unbridled frenzy without any training. Much misery had been the result. Now good mating manners were already taught to children at the end of their anal phase.

With a certain sadness Eric remembered his initial experience after the first signs of sexual maturity had manifested themselves. He'd had the luck to be assigned to a wise, motherly initiator. His delights then must have equaled the religious thrills of ancient saints as described in books of cultic lore. He remembered the fever of orgasm when his thoughts had melted away in the heat of passion. His body had been engulfed by a white hollowness, giving him the sensation of becoming one with everything that existed. He now remained painfully himself in his polite and skilled mating bouts with Tina.

She arrived at the appointed moment. Eric poured her a glass of wine, inspecting her carefully while she was drinking, as if it were their first meeting.

She was supple and plump, with dark hair. Her eyes were big, almost black. She had an upturned nose and a wide, full mouth. Her teeth were large, healthy, and perfectly shaped. Eric liked women with an even set of teeth.

Tina and he were of the same age.

Eric knew that in former times people met in a haphazard way, falling in love without system or sense, according to the laws of chance, playthings of their hormones' whims. He also knew that this kind of higher madness had resulted in endless conflicts, leading people into the snares of legal matrimony, which made couples unhappy and children neurotic, and in the end disrupted society as a whole. Tina and he had been brought together in the only correct way. Out of all the people within a certain radius they were the most suited to each other. The boy's as well as the girl's conscious and unconscious desires, outer appearance, intelligence, tastes, and emotional patterns had been matched by one of the computers in the polder. This guaranteed a mutual understanding in the most fundamental aspects of personality. Tina was the ideal mate for him. He raised his glass and drank to her health. She smiled and returned his toast. It was a perfect preparation for things to come. Suddenly Eric felt more bored than he had thought possible. He undressed her and tried to feign impatient passion, even to make tears in her paper one-day underwear. When they were lying next to each other they started to perform the movements they both knew from their manual of instructions. Simultaneously with the deeper excitement, Eric felt the boredom growing ever stronger.

It was, perhaps, because they'd come to the end of their lovetime. For a short moment he considered marrying Tina, as the culmination and ending of their probation years. But they were both still too young for a final domiciliation, too far away from the mid-thirties, usually set for marriage. He had to go on with the carefully planned partnerships, at first loose and short, which would gradually increase in duration and stability, till, finally, he had reached the stage in which marital ties offered the best warrant for lasting harmony.

Yes, his affair with Tina was coming to an end. That might be the reason why she was more exacting than usual. Eric was already on the brink of exhaustion, wanting to rest, when Tina was still pushing on with unabated lust. He complied with her passion with a feeling of bitterness. When she was lying at his side, panting with obvious satisfaction, his thoughts were already with the new woman who would be assigned to him. It worried him that he would again be obliged to take her personal wishes and oddities into account. There was always a period of mutual adaptation between new mating partners. Sometimes it was a thrilling experience. Now the idea irritated Eric.

Tina got up from the fed. She dressed slowly with the well-known tired gestures, which were supposed to indicate that she had been so completely satisfied that she hardly had the strength to lift her arms. But there were lines of bitterness around her mouth and she was breathing fiercely, an obvious indication to Eric of how much unused energy she had to repress beneath her simulated languor. She too, was not happy with the situation. He kissed her when she said good-bye. She pressed herself long enough against him to give the impression that she had to tear herself away, but it didn't last long enough to convey real attachment.

2

The next mating companion was more adapted than Tina had been to the weary irony Eric had developed during the last year. She showed much humor. She was subdued and sometimes shy, modest in her manifest desires, but developed a fierce sense of domination when Eric had prepared her extensively for the final thrust in bed. Her signs of satisfaction were overwhelming but they didn't give Eric the elation he would've experienced in a former period. Her unbridled discharge of lust had an aspect of calculated exaggeration, so Eric couldn't trust his own abilities as a skilled lover. She left him after a week. For the first time Eric learned that even computers could make mistakes. On this occasion the matching of the many items of information from the two candidates must have been imperfect. He accepted the fact with resignation but a feeling of failure still gnawed at him, adding a touch of disagreeable sharpness to his melancholy. Among the personal oddments the young woman had left behind was a fiercely colored pamphlet. A GOOD PAIRPUPPET IS A JOY FOR EVER, flaming letters screamed from the cover. Eric wanted to throw it away with the rest. "A pairpuppet," he thought. "Good for the common people who prefer to be fobbed off with a custom-made dream, rather than to cope with the circumscribed pleasures of nature."

Yet he read on. He now realized that the woman who had left him had preferred the perfections of a pairpuppet to his limited abilities. It shocked him. In the circles of the artistic-minded intellectuals to which he belonged, vulgarity of this kind was till now unknown. Pairpuppets were good for people without imagination. "A pairpuppet is the ideal bed companion. The latest issue has been installed with a thermostat, which regulates the temperature of the skin according to the degree of excitement. The moisture of the skin and orifices, together with the movements (adapted to the special requirements of the buyer) and the appropriate sound, are built in with a remarkably high degree of authenticity. Our pairpuppets can only be distinguished from the natural product by their perfect pairing technique."

There was also a scientific report from the National Consumers Organization. Men and women had paired with the puppets under laboratory conditions. Their complaints had been carefully investigated, and their delights had been meticulously analyzed by the extremely sensitive instruments placed in the bodies of the volunteers. Their dreams also had been analyzed, in order to detect the primeval types of their desire. Their ideal images were compared with the four standard types of pairpuppets available for each sex. It appeared that they indeed represented the ideal prototypes. Their subtle powers of adaptation to the movements of their human pair companions were described as extremely satisfying. The sounds they produced had been shrewdly composed from the range of cries and groans taped during the experiments. The disdain with which Eric had at first read the booklet soon gave way to an uneasy libidinal fantasizing.

When he went to sleep he had decided to at least have a look in at the showroom.

The dream he still remembered the following morning greatly strengthened his decision.

The salesman received him with the smooth eagerness he had expected. In the showroom there were many people.

"How's business?" Eric asked.

"We can hardly satisfy the demand." From the tone of bewilderment in the salesman's voice Eric could hear that he meant it. "The use of pairpuppets seems to have suddenly become the fashion. We used to have clients only from certain circles, but now it seems that people in general are becoming fed up with people. And if I may say so, sir, pairpuppets are, indeed, much better. Since the latest models have come out, the experience with a pairpuppet has changed from a coarse pleasure to a refined delight."

He talked with the pepped-up optimism of a slogan manufacturer, but at the same time there was much genuine enthusiasm in
his voice. Eric found it extremely difficult to make his choice.
There were four types in each sex, able to satisfy the most common
needs. There were subjugated and domineering women; cool
beauties, who came slowly to their orgiastic frenzy, and unassum-
ing motherfigures with warm breasts that gave a soft refuge for a
man's head. For women there were broad-shouldered athletes and
soft childlike types; cruel lovers and tender devotees.

"These basic forms can be delivered in different sizes and skin
color," the salesman explained. "And for those who are not
satisfied with the usual modes of pairing, there are some irregular
types, hunchbacks for instance. They, of course, are much more
expensive, but there's not much demand for them. In general, our
eight types seem to be satisfactory."

"I don't find it easy to choose."

"That's not unusual, sir. But why don't you take the whole
range. For variation. That's much cheaper, too. I've already sold
a lot of series. Some customers even take the whole set of eight. As
a free gift we supply a book about group-pairing with unparalleled
techniques."

Eric chose a rather big redhead whose desire was swiftly aroused
and who gave easily and abundantly, without requiring a long
demonstration of carnal skills. He also let the salesman pack a
small, shy puppet who came slowly to her climax and exacted
much tenderness.

When he came home he carefully locked his apartment.

3

He called his best friend, Eberhard, with whom he had maintained
a deep understanding ever since college; though they didn't meet
too often. They made an appointment. The first thing Eric saw
when he arrived at his friend's home was a couple of switched-off
pairpuppets in a corner of the living room, a sign that Eberhard too
had taken to the new fashion. His friend had also changed the
arrangement of the furnishings. His polyester walls with changing
light-sculptures – creative panels, as the inventor called them – had
been exchanged for a wainscot of rough pinewood. There was a

marked smell of resin around, so strong that it could only have been applied by spraying.

"I like it as a change," Eric said, when he had downed his first drink.

"A little bit rough. You could even call it old-fashioned, if it were not so unusual that it might now be called new-fashioned."

Eric was astonished.

"Where've you been all the time?"

"Mostly at home. I couldn't think of a better place to be. I've paired a lot. Then you don't have such a strong need to leave your home."

Eric saw that his friend wanted to answer. But Eberhard checked his speech.

"And now you're bored?" he asked at last, with such studied nonchalance that Eric became suspicious.

"Yes. How d'you know?"

"It's the general feeling. You would've known it too, if you hadn't locked yourself up so selfishly. It's already been going on for a long time, but when it started nobody had the courage to confess it. People are starting up the old forms of communication again, making appointments with friends; organizing parties; even talking to strangers in the street. Human beings are funny things. They're never satisfied."

He poured his visitor and himself another drink. "The common man still wants his pairpuppet," he continued. "And, if possible, a different type for every season. But among the more sophisticated people there is already a marked resistance. The intelligentsia want to return to nature."

"The mannerisms of today's tastemakers will become the manners of tomorrow's masses," Eric said. "Which means that pairpuppets will be out and we'll have to go back to nature."

He downed another drink. When he at last took his leave he was in a floating state of reckless insouciance. Outside, the autumn manifested itself in a pungent, spicy scent permeating the fresh air that already had a tinge of winter's cold.

Eric had hardly gone a few yards when a girl approached him. He looked at her, at first with amazement, then with pleasure. In the beginning he doubted whether she meant to contact him, but when he saw that she was looking behind her, he knew that she was deliberately trying to attract his attention.

He turned and followed her. She looked attractive from behind; small, dark, with narrow and yet well-shaped legs. Proportionally she couldn't compare with the perfectly built pairpuppets, but she was a living creature, young and probably full of lust.

Then, suddenly, he understood why she was contacting him so obviously and yet without the professional skill characteristic of the type of women who in former times had roamed the streets for business. She had done it because he was a living man and because she probably had developed as much distaste for her pairpuppets as Eric had for his own perfect lust objects. He followed her. He became soft with sensuous appetite and soon he had overtaken her. She smiled when he addressed her.

"I assume you wanted me to follow you?"

She was young enough to have preserved the beauty of youth and yet sufficiently advanced in age for a ripeness in experience. This kind of woman attracted Eric most of all.

She took him by the hand and pulled him after her. Suddenly he fell in love with her. He had been used to the perfect streamline of delight for too long and now he realized how much genuine love he had missed. All his repressed affection broke out and he became dizzy from the strong attachment that broke loose within him.

"What's your name?"

She didn't answer. She was walking faster and faster, almost running. Now he could confirm his first impression that she wasn't beautiful. She had an irregular face, her nose was too long, and her mouth was too large. When she smiled he saw that her front teeth were crooked. But the combination of irregular features attracted him more strongly than the smooth principles after which his pairpuppets had been manufactured. He found it more of a pleasure than a hindrance that her skin was too dark and too coarse and that there were pigment spots on her forehead. At any rate, she was natural.

Outside the city she pulled him into a dry ditch. They didn't undress. She was in too much of a hurry. They mounted each other like adolescents whose immediate lust is too strong for the more refined delights of preparatory delay. They paired like animals, swiftly, grossly, without caring for each other's needs.

It was an overwhelming experience for Eric, as powerful as the first time. In a certain sense it was the first time. Now he knew that pairpuppets had been a transient misconception. In the long run, only pairing with an imperfect human being could give true satisfaction.

Tenderly he looked at the woman lying next to him. She had closed her eyes. She was breathing softly. He touched her. She opened her mouth.

"I'm Elly," she said in a warm and yet businesslike tone. "I am the improved version of the pairpuppet. I am an experimental specimen. Will you be so kind as to give me your critical remarks with regard to my behavior. They are being taped and they will be carefully considered. You may leave me where I am. I'm able to return to the factory without assistance."

MORE THAN THE SUM
OF HIS PARTS

Joe Haldeman

Plans for a career in science were cut short by Vietnam, where Joe Haldeman was sent as a combat engineer in 1968, and where he was seriously wounded in action. Back in the USA, he began to write in 1969, and with novels such as The Forever War *(1974) and* All My Sins Remembered *(1977) won major acclaim. "More than the Sum of his Parts" started out as a classroom exercise when Haldeman was teaching an SF class at MIT; students chose a topic at random from a reference book, and the first page of their stories had to parody another story. For the tutor, the subject was "cyborg", and the opening of the resulting story parodies Daniel Keyes' famous "Flowers for Algernon" – though after that it goes in a very different direction.*

21 August 2058

They say I am to keep a detailed record of my feelings, my perceptions, as I grow accustomed to the new parts. To that end, they gave me an apparatus that blind people use for writing, like a tablet with guide wires. It is somewhat awkward. But a recorder would be useless, since I will not have a mouth for some time, and I can't type blind with only one hand.

Woke up free from pain. Interesting. Surprising to find that it has only been five days since the accident. For the record, I am, or was, Dr Wilson Cheetham, Senior Engineer (Quality Control) for

US Steel's Skyfac station, a high-orbit facility that produces foamsteel and vapor deposition materials for use in the cislunar community. But if you are reading this, you must know all that.

Five days ago I was inspecting the aluminum deposition facility and had a bad accident. There was a glitch in my jetseat controls, and I flew suddenly straight into the wide beam of charged aluminum vapor. Very hot. They turned it off in a second, but there was still plenty of time for the beam to breach the suit and thoroughly roast three quarters of my body.

Apparently there was a rescue bubble right there. I was unconscious, of course. They tell me that my heart stopped with the shock, but they managed to save me. My left leg and arm are gone, as is my face. I have no lower jaw, nose, or external ears. I can hear after a fashion, though, and will have eyes in a week or so. They claim they will craft for me testicles and a penis.

I must be pumped full of mood drugs. I feel too calm. If I were myself, whatever fraction of myself is left, perhaps I would resist the insult of being turned into a sexless half-machine.

Ah well. This will be a machine that can turn itself off.

22 August 2058

For many days there was only sleep or pain. This was in the weightless ward at Mercy. They stripped the dead skin off me bit by bit. There are limits to anesthesia, unfortunately. I tried to scream but found I had no vocal cords. They finally decided not to try to salvage the arm and leg, which saved some pain.

When I was able to listen, they explained that US Steel valued my services so much that they were willing to underwrite a state-of-the-art cyborg transformation. Half the cost will be absorbed by Interface Biotech on the Moon. Everybody will deduct me from their taxes.

This, then, is the catalog. First, new arm and leg. That's fairly standard. (I once worked with a woman who had two cyborg arms. It took weeks before I could look at her without feeling pity and revulsion.) Then they will attempt to build me a working jaw and mouth, which has been done only rarely and imperfectly, and rebuild the trachea, vocal cords, esophagus. I will be able to speak and drink, though except for certain soft foods, I won't eat in a normal way; salivary glands are beyond their art. No mucous membranes of any kind. A drastic cure for my chronic sinusitis.

Surprisingly, to me at least, the reconstruction of a penis is a fairly straightforward procedure, for which they've had lots of practice. Men are forever sticking them into places where they don't belong. They are particularly excited about my case because of the challenge in restoring sensation as well as function. The prostate is intact, and they seem confident that they can hook up the complicated plumbing involved in ejaculation. Restoring the ability to urinate is trivially easy, they say.

(The biotechnician in charge of the urogenital phase of the project talked at me for more than an hour, going into unnecessarily grisly detail. It seems that this replacement was done occasionally even before they had any kind of mechanical substitute, by sawing off a short rib and transplanting it, covering it with a skin graft from elsewhere on the body. The recipient thus was blessed with a permanent erection, unfortunately rather strange-looking and short on sensation. My own prosthesis will look very much like the real, shall we say, thing, and new developments in tractor-field mechanics and bionic interfacing should give it realistic response patterns.)

I don't know how to feel about all this. I wish they would leave my blood chemistry alone, so I could have some honest grief or horror, whatever. Instead of this placid waiting.

4 September 2058

Out cold for thirteen days and I wake up with eyes. The arm and leg are in place but not powered up yet. I wonder what the eyes look like. (They won't give me a mirror until I have a face.) They feel like wet glass.

Very fancy eyes. I have a box with two dials that I can use to override the "default mode" – that is, the ability to see only normally. One of them gives me conscious control over pupil dilation, so I can see in almost total darkness or, if for some reason I wanted to, look directly at the sun without discomfort. The other changes the frequency response, so I can see either in the infrared or the ultraviolet. This hospital room looks pretty much the same in ultraviolet, but in infrared it takes on a whole new aspect. Most of the room's illumination then comes from bright bars on the walls, radiant heating. My real arm shows a pulsing tracery of arteries and veins. The other is of course not visible except by reflection and is dark blue.

(Later) Strange I didn't realize I was on the Moon. I thought it was a low-gravity ward in Mercy. While I was sleeping they sent me down to Biotech. Should have figured that out.

5 September 2058

They turned on the "social" arm and leg and began patterning exercises. I am told to think of a certain movement and do its mirror image with my right arm or leg while attempting to execute it with my left. The trainer helps the cyborg unit along, which generates something like pain, though actually it doesn't resemble any real muscular ache. Maybe it's the way circuits feel when they're overloaded.

By the end of the session I was able to make a fist without help, though there is hardly enough grip to hold a pencil. I can't raise the leg yet, but can make the toes move.

They removed some of the bandages today, from shoulder to hip, and the test-tube skin looks much more real than I had prepared myself for. Hairless and somewhat glossy, but the color match is perfect. In infrared it looks quite different, more uniform in colour than the "real" side. I suppose that's because it hasn't aged forty years.

While putting me through my paces, the technician waxed rhapsodic about how good this arm is going to be – this set of arms, actually. I'm exercising with the "social" one, which looks much more convincing than the ones my coworker displayed ten years ago. (No doubt more a matter of money than of advancing technology.) The "working" arm, which I haven't seen yet, will be all metal, capable of being worn on the outside of a spacesuit. Besides having the two arms, I'll be able to interface with various waldos, tailored to specific functions.

I am fortunately more ambidextrous than the average person. I broke my right wrist in the second grade and kept re-breaking it through the third, and so learned to write with both hands. All my life I have been able to print more clearly with the left.

They claim to be cutting down on my medication. If that's the truth, I seem to be adjusting fairly well. Then again, I have nothing in my past experience to use as a basis for comparison. Perhaps this calmness is only a mask for hysteria.

6 September 2058

Today I was able to tie a simple knot. I can lightly sketch out the letters of the alphabet. A large and childish scrawl but recognizably my own.

I've begun walking after a fashion, supporting myself between parallel bars. (The lack of hand strength is a neural problem, not a muscular one; when rigid, the arm and leg are as strong as metal crutches.) As I practice, it's amusing to watch the reactions of people who walk into the room, people who aren't paid to mask their horror at being studied by two cold lenses embedded in a swath of bandages formed over a shape that is not a head.

Tomorrow they start building my face. I will be essentially unconscious for more than a week. The limb patterning will continue as I sleep, they say.

14 September 2058

When I was a child my mother, always careful to have me do "normal" things, dressed me in costume each Halloween and escorted me around the high-rise, so I could beg for candy I did not want and money I did not need. On one occasion I had to wear the mask of a child star then popular on the cube, a tightly fitting plastic affair that covered the entire head, squeezing my pudgy features into something more in line with some Platonic ideal of childish beauty. That was my last Hallowe'en. I embarrassed her.

This face is like that. It is undeniably my face, but the skin is taut and unresponsive. Any attempt at expression produces a grimace.

I have almost normal grip in the hand now, though it is still clumsy. As they hoped, the sensory feedback from the fingertips and palms seems to be more finely tuned than in my "good" hand. Tracing my new forefinger across my right wrist, I can sense the individual pores, and there is a marked temperature gradient as I pass over tendon or vein. And yet the hand and arm will eventually be capable of superhuman strength.

Touching my new face I do not feel pores. They have improved on nature in the business of heat exchange.

22 September 2058

Another week of sleep while they installed the new plumbing. When the anesthetic wore off I felt a definite *something*, not pain, but neither was it the normal somatic heft of genitalia. Everything was bedded in gauze and bandage, though, and catheterized, so it would feel strange even to a normal person.

(Later) An aide came in and gingerly snipped away the bandages. He blushed; I don't think fondling was in his job description. When the catheter came out there was a small sting of pain and relief.

It's not much of a copy. To reconstruct the face, they could consult hundreds of pictures and cubes, but it had never occurred to me that one day it might be useful to have a gallery of pictures of my private parts in various stages of repose. The technicians had approached the problem by bringing me a stack of photos culled from urological texts and pornography, and having me sort through them as to "closeness of fit."

It was not a task for which I was well trained, by experience or disposition. Strange as it may seem in this age of unfettered hedonism, I haven't seen another man naked, let alone rampant, since leaving high school, twenty-five years ago. (I was stationed on Farside for eighteen months and never went near a sex bar, preferring an audience of one. Even if I had to hire her, as was usually the case.)

So this one is rather longer and thicker than its predecessor – would all men unconsciously exaggerate? – and has only approximately the same aspect when erect. A young man's rakish angle.

Distasteful but necessary to write about the matter of masturbation. At first it didn't work. With my right hand, it felt like holding another man, which I have never had any desire to do. With the new hand, though, the process proceeded in the normal way, though I must admit to a voyeuristic aspect. The sensations were extremely acute. Ejaculation more forceful than I can remember from youth.

It makes me wonder. In a book I recently read, about brain chemistry, the author made a major point of the notion that it's a mistake to completely equate "mind" with "brain." The brain, he said, is in a way only the thickest and most complex segment of the nervous system; it coordinates our consciousness, but the actual mind suffuses through the body in a network of ganglia. In fact, he used sexuality as an example. When a man ruefully observes that his penis has a mind of its own, he is stating part of a larger truth.

But I in fact do have actual brains imbedded in my new parts: the biochips that process sensory data coming in and action commands going back. Are these brains part of my consciousness the way the rest of my nervous system is? The masturbation experience indicates they might be in business for themselves.

This is premature speculation, so to speak. We'll see how it feels when I move into a more complex environment, where I'm not so self-absorbed.

23 September 2058

During the night something evidently clicked. I woke up this morning with full strength in my cyborg limbs. One rail of the bed was twisted out of shape where I must have unconsciously gripped it. I bent it back quite easily.

Some obscure impulse makes me want to keep this talent secret for the time being. The technicians thought I would be able to exert three or four times the normal person's grip; this is obviously much more than that.

But why keep it a secret? I don't know. Eventually they will read this diary and I will stand exposed. There's no harm in that, though; this is supposed to be a record of my psychological adjustment or maladjustment. Let *them* tell *me* why I've done it.

(Later) The techs were astonished, ecstatic. I demonstrated a pull of 90 kilograms. I know if I'd actually given it a good yank, I could have pulled the stress machine out of the wall. I'll give them 110 tomorrow and inch my way up to 125.

Obviously I must be careful with force vectors. If I put too much stress on the normal parts of my body I could do permanent injury. With my metal fist I could certainly punch a hole through an airlock door, but it would probably tear the prosthesis out of its socket. Newton's laws still apply.

Other laws will have to be rewritten.

24 September 2058

I got to work out with three waldos today. A fantastic experience!

The first one was a disembodied hand and arm attached to a stand, the setup they use to train normal people in the use of waldos. The difference is that I don't need a waldo sleeve to imperfectly transmit my wishes to the mechanical double. I can plug into it directly.

I've been using waldos in my work ever since graduate school, but it was never anything like this. Inside the waldo sleeve you get a clumsy kind of feedback from striated pressor field generators embedded in the plastic. With my setup the feedback is exactly the kind a normal person feels when he touches an object, but much more sensitive. The first time they asked me to pick up an egg, I tossed it up and caught it (no great feat of coordination in lunar gravity, admittedly, but I could have done it as easily in Earth-normal).

The next waldo was a large earthmover that Western Mining uses over at Grimaldi Station. That was interesting, not only because of its size but because of the slight communications lag. Grimaldi is only a few dozens of kilometers away, but there aren't enough unused data channels between here and there for me to use the land-line to communicate with the earthmover hand. I had to relay via comsat, so there was about a tenth-second delay between the thought and the action. It was a fine feeling of power, but a little confusing: I would cup my hand and scoop downward, and then a split-second too late would feel the resistance of the regolith. And then casually hold in my palm several tonnes of rock and dirt. People standing around watching; with a flick of my wrist I could have buried them. Instead I dutifully dumped it on the belt to the converter.

But the waldo that most fascinated me was the micro. It had been in use for only a few months; I had heard of it, but hadn't had a chance to see it in action. It is a fully articulated hand barely a tenth of a millimeter long. I used it in conjunction with a low-power scanning electron microscope, moving around on the surface of a microcircuit. At that magnification it looked like a hand on a long stick wandering through the corridors of a building, whose walls varied from rough stucco to brushed metal to blistered gray paint, all laced over with thick cables of gold.

When necessary, I could bring in another hand, manipulated by my right from inside a waldo sleeve, to help with simple carpenter and machinist tasks that, in the real world, translated into fundamental changes in the quantum-electrodynamic properties of the circuit.

This was the real power: not crushing metal tubes or lifting tonnes of rock, but pushing electrons around to do my bidding. My first doctorate was in electrical engineering; in a sudden epiphany I realize that I am the first *actual* electrical engineer in history.

After two hours they made me stop; said I was showing signs of strain. They put me in a wheelchair, and I did fall asleep on the way back to my room. Dreaming dreams of microcosmic and infinite power.

25 September 2058

The metal arm. I expected it to feel fundamentally different from the "social" one, but of course it doesn't, most of the time. Circuits are circuits. The difference comes under conditions of extreme exertion: the soft hand gives me signals like pain if I come close to the level of stress that would harm the fleshlike material. With the metal hand I can rip off a chunk of steel plate a centimeter thick and feel nothing beyond "muscular" strain. If I had two of them I could work marvels.

The mechanical leg is not so gifted. It has governors to restrict its strength and range of motion to that of a normal leg, which is reasonable. Even a normal person finds himself brushing the ceiling occasionally in lunar gravity. I could stand up sharply and find myself with a concussion, or worse.

I like the metal arm, though. When I'm stronger (hah!) they say they'll let me go outside and try it with a spacesuit. Throw something over the horizon.

Starting today, I'm easing back into a semblance of normal life. I'll be staying at Biotech for another six or eight weeks, but I'm patched into my Skyfac office and have started clearing out the backlog of paperwork. Two hours in the morning and two in the afternoon. It's diverting, but I have to admit my heart isn't really in it. Rather be playing with the micro. (Have booked three hours on it tomorrow.)

26 September 2058

They threaded an optical fiber through the micro's little finger, so I can watch its progress on a screen without being limited to the field of an electron microscope. The picture is fuzzy while the waldo is in motion, but if I hold it still for a few seconds, the computer assist builds up quite a sharp image. I used it to roam all over my right arm and hand, which was fascinating. Hairs a tangle of stiff black stalks, the pores small damp craters. And everywhere the evidence of the skin's slow death; translucent sheafs of desquamated cells.

I've taken to wearing the metal arm rather than the social one. Peoples's stares don't bother me. The metal one will be more useful in my actual work, and I want to get as much practice as possible. There is also an undeniable feeling of power.

27 September 2058

Today I went outside. It was clumsy getting around at first. For the past eleven years I've used a suit only in zerogee, so all my reflexes are wrong. Still, not much serious can go wrong at a sixth of a gee.

It was exhilarating but at the same time frustrating, since I couldn't reveal all my strength. I did almost overdo it once, starting to tip over a large boulder. Before it tipped, I realized that my left boot had crunched through about ten centimeters of regolith, in reaction to the amount of force I was applying. So I backed off and discreetly shuffled my foot to fill the telltale hole.

I could indeed throw a rock over the horizon. With a sling, I might be able to put a small one into orbit. Rent myself out as a lunar launching facility.

(Later) Most interesting. A pretty nurse who has been on this project since the beginning came into my room after dinner and proposed the obvious experiment. It was wildly successful.

Although my new body starts out with the normal pattern of excitation-plateau-orgasm, the resemblance stops there. I have no refractory period; the process of erection is completely under conscious control. This could make me the most popular man on the Moon.

The artificial skin of the penis is as sensitive to tactile differentiation as that of the cyborg fingers: suddenly I know more about

a woman's internal topography than any man who ever lived –
more than any *woman!*

I think tomorrow I'll take a trip to Farside.

28 September 2058

Farside has nine sex bars. I read the guidebook descriptions, and
then asked a few locals for their recommendations, and wound up
going to a place cleverly called the Juice Bar.

In fact, the name was not just an expression of coy eroticism.
They served nothing but fruit and juices there, most of them
fantastically expensive Earth imports. I spent a day's pay on a glass
of pear nectar and sought out the most attractive woman in the
room.

That in itself was a mistake. I was not physically attractive even
before the accident, and the mechanics have faithfully restored my
coarse features and slight paunch. I was rebuffed.

So I went to the opposite extreme and looked for the plainest
woman. That would be a better test, anyway: before the accident
I always demanded, and paid for, physical perfection. If I
could duplicate the performance of last night with a woman
to whom I was not sexually attracted – and do it in public, with
no pressure from having gone without – then my independence
from the autonomic nervous system would be proven beyond
doubt.

Second mistake. I was never good at small talk, and when I
located my paragon of plainness I began talking about the accident
and the singular talent that had resulted from it. She suddenly
remembered an appointment elsewhere.

I was not so open with the next woman, also plain. She asked
whether there was something wrong with my face, and I told her
half the truth. She was sweetly sympathetic, motherly, which did
not endear her to me. It did make her a good subject for the
experiment. We left the socializing section of the bar and went
back to the so-called "love room."

There was an acrid quality to the air that I suppose was
compounded of incense and sweat, but of course my dry nose was
not capable of identifying actual smells. For the first time, I was
grateful for that disability; the place probably had the aroma of a
well-used locker room. Plus pheromones.

Under the muted lights, red and blue as well as white, more than a dozen couples were engaged more or less actively in various aspects of amorous behavior. A few were frankly staring at others, but most were either absorbed with their own affairs or furtive in their voyeurism. Most of them were on the floor, which was a warm soft mat, but some were using tables and chairs in fairly ingenious ways. Several of the permutations would no doubt have been impossible or dangerous in Earth's gravity.

We undressed and she complimented me on my evident spryness. A nearby spectator made a jealous observation. Her own body was rather flaccid, doughy, and under previous circumstances I doubt that I would have been able to maintain enthusiasm. There was no problem, however; in fact, I rather enjoyed it. She required very little foreplay, and I was soon repeating the odd sensation of hypersensitized exploration. Gynecological spelunking.

She was quite voluble in her pleasure, and although she lasted less than an hour, we did attract a certain amount of attention. When she, panting, regretfully declined further exercise, a woman who had been watching, a rather attractive young blonde, offered to share her various openings. I obliged her for a while; although the well was dry the pump handle was unaffected.

During that performance I became aware that the pleasure involved was not a sexual one in any normal sense. Sensual, yes, in the way that a fine meal is a sensual experience, but with a remote subtlety that I find difficult to describe. Perhaps there is a relation to epicurism that is more than metaphorical. Since I can no longer taste food, a large area of my brain is available for the evaluation of other experience. It may be that the brain is reorganizing itself in order to take fullest advantage of my new abilities.

By the time the blonde's energy began to flag, several other women had taken an interest in my satyriasis. I resisted the temptation to find what this organ's limit was, if indeed a limit exists. My back ached and the right knee was protesting. So I threw the mental switch and deflated. I left with a minimum of socializing. (The first woman insisted on buying me something at the bar. I opted for a banana.)

29 September 2058

Now that I have eyes and both hands, there's no reason to scratch this diary out with a pen. So I'm entering it into the computer. But I'm keeping two versions.

I recopied everything up to this point and then went back and edited the version that I will show to Biotech. It's very polite, and will remain so. For instance, it does not contain the following:

After writing last night's entry, I found myself still full of energy, and so I decided to put into action a plan that has been forming in my mind.

About two in the morning I went downstairs and broke into the waldo lab. The entrance is protected by a five-digit combination lock, but of course that was no obstacle. My hypersensitive fingers could feel the tumblers rattling into place.

I got the micro-waldo set up and then detached my leg. I guided the waldo through the leg's circuitry and easily disabled the governors. The whole operation took less than twenty minutes.

I did have to use a certain amount of care walking, at first. There was a tendency to rise into the air or to limpingly overcompensate. It was under control by the time I got back to my room. So once more they proved to have been mistaken as to the limits of my abilities. Testing the strength of the leg, with a halfhearted kick I put a deep dent in the metal wall at the rear of my closet. I'll have to wait until I can be outside, alone, to see what full force can do.

A comparison kick with my flesh leg left no dent, but did hurt my great toe.

30 September 2058

It occurs to me that I feel better about my body than I have in the past twenty years. Who wouldn't? Literally eternal youth in these new limbs and organs; if a part shows signs of wear, it can simply be replaced.

I was angry at the Biotech evaluation board this morning. When I simply inquired as to the practicality of replacing the right arm and leg as well, all but one were horrified. One was amused. I will remember him.

I think the fools are going to order me to leave Nearside in a day or two and go back to Mercy for psychiatric "help." I will leave when I want to, on my own terms.

1 October 2058

This is being voice-recorded in the Environmental Control Center at Nearside. It is 10:32; they have less than ninety minutes to accede to my demands. Let me backtrack.

After writing last night's entry I felt a sudden access of sexual desire. I took the shuttle to Farside and went back to the Juice Bar.

The plain woman from the previous night was waiting, hoping that I would show up. She was delighted when I suggested that we save money (and whatever residue of modesty we had left) by keeping ourselves to one another, back at my room.

I didn't mean to murder her. That was not in my mind at all. But I suppose in my passion, or abandon, I carelessly propped my strong leg against the wall and then thrust with too much strength. At any rate there was a snap and a tearing sound. She gave a small cry and the lower half of my body was suddenly awash in blood. I had snapped her spine and evidently at the same time caused considerable internal damage. She must have lost consciousness very quickly, though her heart did not stop beating for nearly a minute.

Disposing of the body was no great problem, conceptually. In the laundry room I found a bag large enough to hold her comfortably. Then I went back to the room and put her and the sheet she had besmirched into the bag.

Getting her to the recycler would have been a problem if it had been a normal hour. She looked like nothing so much as a body in a laundry bag. Fortunately, the corridor was deserted.

The lock on the recycler room was child's play. The furnace door was a problem, though; it was easy to unlock but its effective diameter was only 25 centimeters.

So I had to disassemble her. To save cleaning up, I did the job inside the laundry bag, which was clumsy, and made it difficult to see the fascinating process.

I was so absorbed in watching that I didn't hear the door slide open. But the man who walked in made a slight gurgling sound, which somehow I did hear over the cracking of bones. I stepped over to him and killed him with one kick.

At this point I have to admit to a lapse in judgment. I relocked the door and went back to the chore at hand. After the woman was completely recycled, I repeated the process with the man – which was, incidentally, much easier. The female's layer of subcutaneous fat made disassembly of the torso a more slippery business.

It really was wasted time (though I did spend part of the time thinking out the final touches of the plan I am now engaged upon). I might as well have left both bodies there on the floor. I had kicked the man with great force – enough to throw me to the ground in reaction and badly bruise my right hip – and had split him open from crotch to heart. This made a bad enough mess, even if he hadn't compounded the problem by striking the ceiling. I would never be able to clean that up, and it's not the sort of thing that would escape notice for long.

At any rate, it was only twenty minutes wasted, and I gained more time than that by disabling the recycler room lock. I cleaned up, changed clothes, stopped by the waldo lab for a few minutes, and then took the slidewalk to the Environmental Control Center.

There was only one young man on duty at the ECC at that hour. I exchanged a few pleasantries with him and then punched him in the heart, softly enough not to make a mess. I put his body where it wouldn't distract me and then attended to the problem of the "door."

There's no actual door on the ECC, but there is an emergency wall that slides into place if there's a drop in pressure. I typed up a test program simulating an emergency, and the wall obeyed. Then I walked over and twisted a few flanges around. Nobody would be able to get into the Center with anything short of a cutting torch.

Sitting was uncomfortable with the bruised hip, but I managed to ease into the console and spend an hour or so studying logic and wiring diagrams. Then I popped off an access plate and moved the micro-waldo down the corridors of electronic thought. The intercom began buzzing incessantly, but I didn't let it interfere with my concentration.

Nearside is protected from meteorite strike or (far more likely) structural failure by a series of 128 bulkheads that, like the emergency wall here, can slide into place and isolate any area where there's a pressure drop. It's done automatically, of course, but can also be controlled from here.

What I did, in essence, was to tell each bulkhead that it was under repair, and should not close under any circumstance. Then I moved the waldo over to the circuits that controlled the city's eight airlocks. With some rather elegant microsurgery, I transferred control of all eight solely to the pressure switch I now hold in my left hand.

It is a negative-pressure button, a dead-man switch taken from a power saw. So long as I hold it down, the inner doors of the airlocks will remain locked. If I let go, they will all iris open. The outer doors are already open, as are the ones that connect the airlock chambers to the suiting-up rooms. No one will be able to make it to a spacesuit in time. Within thirty seconds, every corridor will be full of vacuum. People behind airtight doors may choose between slow asphyxiation and explosive decompression.

My initial plan had been to wire the dead-man switch to my pulse, which would free my good hand and allow me to sleep. That will have to wait. The wiring completed, I turned on the intercom and announced that I would speak to the Coordinator, and no one else.

When I finally got to talk to him, I told him what I had done and invited him to verify it. That didn't take long. Then I presented my demands:

Surgery to replace the rest of my limbs, of course. The surgery would have to be done while I was conscious (a heartbeat dead-man switch could be subverted by a heart machine) and it would have to be done here, so that I could be assured that nobody fooled with my circuit changes.

The doctors were called in, and they objected that such profound surgery couldn't be done under local anesthetic. I knew they were lying, of course; amputation was a fairly routine procedure even before anesthetics were invented. Yes, but I would faint, they said. I told them that I would not, and at any rate I was willing to take the chance, and no one else had any choice in the matter.

(I have not yet mentioned that the ultimate totality of my plan involves replacing all my internal organs as well as all of the limbs – or at least those organs whose failure could cause untimely death. I will be a true cyborg then, a human brain in an "artificial" body, with the prospect of thousands of years of life. With a few decades – or centuries! – of research, I could even do something about the brain's shortcomings. I would wind up interfaced to EarthNet, with all of human knowledge at my disposal, and with my faculties for logic and memory no longer fettered by the slow pace of electrochemical synapse.)

A psychiatrist, talking from Earth, tried to convince me of the error of my ways. He said that the dreadful trauma had "obviously" unhinged me, and the cyborg augmentation, far from effecting a cure, had made my mental derangement worse. He demonstrated, at least to his own satisfaction, that my behavior followed some classical pattern of madness. All this had been taken into consideration, he said, and if I were to give myself up, I would be forgiven my crimes and manumitted into the loving arms of the psychiatric establishment.

I did take time to explain the fundamental errors in his way of thinking. He felt that I had quite literally lost my identity by losing my face and genitalia, and that I was at bottom a "good" person whose essential humanity had been perverted by physical and existential estrangement. Totally wrong. By his terms, what I actually *am* is an "evil" person whose true nature was revealed to himself by the lucky accident that released him from existential propinquity with the common herd.

And "evil" is the accurate word, not maladjusted or amoral or even criminal. I am as evil by human standards as a human is evil by the standards of an animal raised for food, and the analogy is accurate. I will sacrifice humans not only for my survival but for comfort, curiosity, or entertainment. I will allow to live anyone who doesn't bother me, and reward generously those who help.

Now they have only forty minutes. They know I am
– end of recording—

25 September 2058

Excerpt from Summary Report

I am Dr Henry Janovski, head of the surgical team that worked on the ill-fated cyborg augmentation of Dr Wilson Cheetham.

We were fortunate that Dr Cheetham's insanity did interfere with his normally painstaking, precise nature. If he had spent more time in preparation, I have no doubt that he would have put us in a very difficult fix.

He should have realized that the protecting wall that shut him off from the rest of Nearside was made of steel, an excellent conductor of electricity. If he had insulated himself behind a good dielectric, he could have escaped his fate.

Cheetham's waldo was a marvelous instrument, but basically it was only a pseudo-intelligent servomechanism that obeyed well-defined radio-frequency commands. All we had to do was override the signals that were coming from his own nervous system.

We hooked a powerful amplifier up to the steel wall, making it in effect a huge radio transmitter. To generate the signal we wanted amplified, I had a technician put on a waldo sleeve that was holding a box similar to Cheetham's dead-man switch. We wired the hand closed, turned up the power, and had the technician strike himself on the chin as hard as he could.

The technician struck himself so hard he blacked out for a few seconds. Cheetham's resonant action, perhaps a hundred times more powerful, drove the bones of his chin up through the top of his skull.

Fortunately, the expensive arm itself was not damaged. It is not evil or insane by itself, of course. Which I shall prove.

The experiments will continue, though of course we will be more selective as to subjects. It seems obvious in retrospect that we should not use as subjects people who have gone through the kind of trauma that Cheetham suffered. We must use willing volunteers. Such as myself.

I am not young, and weakness and an occasional tremor in my hands limit the amount of surgery I can do – much less than my knowledge would allow, or my nature desire. My failing left arm I shall have replaced with Cheetham's mechanical marvel, and I will go through training similar to his – but for the good of humanity, not for ill.

What miracles I will perform with the knife!

CUSTOM-BUILT GIRL
Ian Watson

*Ian Watson has been described as "the natural successor to H.G.
Wells" – a tribute perhaps to the great intelligence and humanity
that permeate his impressive body of work. After spells teaching
in Africa and Japan he returned to England and began publishing
SF in* New Worlds *in the late 1960s, and made a major impact with
his first novel,* The Embedding *(1973). Since then his novels,
stories and criticism have appeared regularly and brought worldwide acclaim. "Custom-Built Girl" is the opening sequence from
his unpublished novel* The Woman Machine *(although an earlier
version did appear in France as* Orgasmachine*), which has acquired rather a notorious reputation as rumours have spread of its
supposedly controversial content and vexed publishing history.
Readers may now judge at least a part of it for themselves, and it
is hoped that the rest may become available before long.*

1

Offshore from the fringes of the city a concrete island rests in the
sluggish sea: a mushroom-cap a kilometre across. The island
houses a dozen long low buildings, each stained a cheerful hue:
orange, yellow, pink, cerise ... Since the concrete disc slopes
upwards towards the centre, these buildings are nuzzling into the
flanks of a great feminine curve, the colour of sad flesh.

It's soon after dawn, and the island hasn't woken up yet, when
a girl with abnormally large blue eyes steps naked out of one of the
buildings and walks down towards the waterfront. Her eyes are

almost twice the normal size, a dazzling cerulean blue. They're quite remarkable.

She gazes across the slack water towards the city . . .

In the pink nursery block the newest batch of female foetuses turn slowly inside their amniotic bottles, goggling blindly at synthetic birth-cords. Their pursed lips lap oestrogen; their skin is spermicidal. Tailored teratogenic molecules in their different womb-fluids mould their budding limbs variously, laying the groundwork for later refinements by the plastic surgeons.

Nearby an earlier batch of bottled girls are growing apace, towards maturity in sixteen weeks, soaking up growth hormones and nutrients; though they too are still mindless – except for what dreams are inherent in the architecture of the brain itself.

Further on into the building, the skulls of almost-mature girls are wired into a computer bank so that the blank wax of their thoughts can be printed with quasi-personalities.

Everything is quiet, apart from a faint hum of machinery and the occasional gurgle of liquid.

Later on in the day it usually becomes so hot that the nearest buildings across the straight sway as though mounted on pontoons, while the high-rises behind shimmer just like reflections of themselves, as if the world had been inverted, tempting you to look for the original buildings somewhere in the rubbery sea.

In the early morning chill as now, however, the city is as precise and clear as it will ever be: a long wall of irregular grey slabs bending away to meet the horizon, wrapped in the faint metallic haze which is the city's breath as distinct from the thermal ambiguities of nature.

The naked girl watches a cluster of red-and-white-striped balloons drifting across some distant buildings, with the message banners of their tethers furling and unfurling, too far away to read even when they come alive at night in twisting neon columns, frozen fireworks; even with her huge eyes . . .

Inside the medical block a girl with green hair lies in a drugged sleep, while glucose and saline drip into her arms and catheters remove her body wastes. Her head is clamped in a plastic frame, to hold her mouth open. A long, forked dragon's tongue lolls right down her chin onto her chest. A rubber pipe gurgles away her saliva.

In a vivarium close by, a trio of bonsai women – of perfect proportions, though only twelve inches high – have roused themselves already and crowd against the glass wall of their tank, watching the dragon-girl in wonder. Today they are due for a spot of microsurgery.

At first, Jade used to try to tell her friends about her merely average powers of vision. But they only stared at her oversize eyes reproachfully, thought she was being mean and selfish, and clamoured for details of the mainland until she had to resort to making up these details . . . and all the island girls are adept at making up details during the weeks which follow their awakening to consciousness. They all invent the details of a future face, one which will seem everything to them, on the basis of a blank plastic dummy . . .

I shall miss Hana most, of all my friends.

It's still quiet in the dormitory when I slip indoors again. Everyone's still asleep. I stop beside Hana's bed and touch her on the shoulder.

Six tiny rounded breasts and an extra nipple on her chin: tender gentle Hana, eyes always flowing with tears – how I love her, how I shall miss her. She cannot speak, but she feels so much.

She opens her damp eyes sleepily, then realizes.

"Yes, Hana, it's today."

She sits up, trying to smile, pushing the plastic dummy aside to make room for me. We all have to sleep with our plastic dummies during these weeks of our adolescence, till we graduate. It's one of the few rules. (Maybe not for bonsai girls! But there are none of those in my own age-group.) We assume that the plastic dummy is moulded directly from the customer's own body, since no two models are exactly alike in the length and girth of the limbs, or of the erect penis. Yet all are alike in one respect, namely that the faces of all the models are left blank out of discretion. None of us has any idea what our chosen partners really look like. We all make jokes about each other's prospects, and try to fill in the pink blank in our dreams.

I sit beside Hana so that we can touch each other; and we pretend for the moment that the dummy doesn't exist.

"You only have the language of touch, don't you, Hana? But that's enough." And Hana nods tearfully, though smiling.

When I kiss her, a tiny bead of milk squeezes from the nipple on her chin onto my lower lip and tongue. I force myself to be clear about this moment so that I may always remember it: the soft smell of her body and armpits, the sweet taste of milk flowing for me for the last time like unsaid speech . . . the strange awareness of each of her six breasts next to my skin like the beads of a huge abacus. My lips follow her milk lines, counting, taking a last desperate inventory of her separate items to retain her image for ever. Poor gentle Hana, she has always reminded me of a silent flower bending in the wind. We were both born on the same day, and have always been very close.

And now my private moment with Hana is over. For the other girls are waking up . . .

Lili the hermaphrodite, Mari the girl with fur and claws, Sue and Susan the Siamese twins who live back to back like two playing-cards, Una and Remi the twin lesbians almost narcissistic in their devotion to each other, and Cathy the executive girl, one of whose prosthetic breasts conceals a drawer, empty now but designed for cigarettes or small cigars, while the other holds a rechargeable battery which makes her nipple grow red-hot when the breast is pressed, to use as a lighter: they all cluster round me, even Una and Remi who don't usually pay attention to anyone else, though naturally they too are curious about me now that I'm going away and they're staying. Zelda the mermaid hauls herself from bed to bed; and Nikka and Bokka – who are hardly ever able to join in our activities since they're fused knee to knee, sharing legs like rocking-horse runners with no shanks or feet – they too pull each other upright in their own very long bed with pillows at both ends, and call to me:

"Oh Jade, is this really your last morning?"

"What will he be like?"

"I hope he's – "

" – kind and generous and handsome!"

But Cathy laughs cruelly:

"I hope it isn't so small you need those eyes to see it!"

But she knows what size "it" is, from my dummy, if she ever troubled to look! Cathy's always like that: a mix-up of conceit and jealousy. She never cooled off after her prosthetic breasts were implanted a couple of weeks ago. She's sure they're a sign of high society.

"Don't worry, Jade!" Mari pats me on the shoulder with a tickly hand. Her husky voice is part purr, part growl. "That rubs me up the wrong way too. You can't blame Cathy if she's going to spend the rest of her life as a cigarette machine."

Our tiger girl, playful and affectionate as a kitten, but strong too – with a hint of violence in her claws . . .

And already the public address system is chiming its xylophone scales for our attention:

"Jade! Jade! No breakfast today, remember! Doctor Tom will see you in ten minutes. Medical B-7. Medical B-7."

Hana presses forward. More tears in her eyes than usual . . . and because of this surfeit of tears she's blind, can't see me, can only reach out and feel.

"Oh Hana, here I am!"

Cathy whistles in a crude, mocking way.

Then squeals . . . as Mari darts a hand at her with claws unsheathed, scratching her across the shoulder. A thin line of blood wells up on Cathy's white skin.

Cathy twists her head, staring in horror. "You bitch, you've damaged my body!"

"Stupid! Bitches are doggies, not pussy cats."

"You've wantonly damaged a body that doesn't belong to you – a body you haven't paid for!"

Fifteen minutes later, in room B-7 in the basement of the medical block, kind Doctor Tom lays his hand on my cheek, fingertips resting against my lower left eyelid. As I wait for the blur of vision that will come when he pops my eyeball out, I stare up past him into the illuminated concave mirror above the wheeled examination couch. Segmented into sections, the mirror reflects my perfect body ten times over, reassuring me that I have nothing to worry about.

But then, all our bodies are perfect . . . perfectly tailored to meet a specific need, and Hana's body with its six breasts and chin nipple is no less perfect than mine.

With a deft touch, Doctor Tom pushes upward into my eye

socket, and I see nothing but a haze of light. He's so gentle that I barely feel him pressing and probing the back of my eyeball, folding back both lids, and checking the optic nerve.

His young nurse giggles in the background. She's jealous of me; with her tiny eyes she envies my huge dazzling sky-blue ones.

Doctor Tom tuts impatiently; he lays my eye on my cheek. "Just a moment, Jade."

And I'm ashamed to say that I panic; I turn my head ever so slightly to squint through the veils of disorderly light with my right eye . . .

"Prepare the saline tonic, nurse."

A ministering angel, she hurries to a cabinet. Doctor Tom turns back and pops out my other eye, almost brusquely this time.

Now that both eyes are lolling on my cheeks, he could be shining a beam of light inside my head, and I'd have no way of knowing. It's a frightening thought: a light behind the eye. What must I look like now? A broken doll?

A few weeks ago I was startled by a group of even younger girls who were playing hide and seek; and my left eye fell out and hung there on my cheek till Doctor Tom came to my rescue. Now I know how to press it back myself, though I'm not supposed to need to. My eyes ought to be proof against all shocks.

Presently I hear his satisfied grunt, and a moment later I feel the stream of isotonic saline washing my orbits out and cooling my eyeballs deliciously, as if they're being dipped in a bowl of shaved ice.

He replaces my eyeballs, and as my vision swims back into focus he checks their fluid pressure with his tonometer and rechecks the cardinal directions of gaze.

"They're a beautiful fit, Jade. Sit up a moment, will you?" This is to make sure that my breasts haven't sagged below the specified four inches from the collar-bone, nipples aligned with the third ribs.

When I lie down again, the nurse obediently carries in the model of the man who has ordered me, and this is laid on top of me one last time for matching.

Soon I'll know for certain. I've tried to keep an open mind so that I won't be disappointed.

The model is lifted away; and Doctor Tom fits the sterilized hymen gently between my labia, holding it down by finger pressure for half a minute till it seals itself.

Then he calls to the nurse for a hypodermic syringe containing the propozate derivative which will put me to sleep in transit, halting my metabolism temporarily – and at last I know in my heart that I am everything that could have been desired. When the nurse wheels me out towards the packaging room, she looks at me over her gauze mask now with respect and envy.

Almost at once the drug begins to take effect. I'm already very woozy, and only vaguely aware of the lovely sheets of wrapping paper with our company's emblem on them.

I hardly feel the hands of the packers who transfer me into the crate, so soft with foam, so very soft . . .

Leaving the island is so easy after all.

The long crate, wrapped in tasteful blue willow-pattern paper with the crest of Custom-Built Girls emblazoned mutely in purple, is wheeled out a few minutes later directly to the helicopter apron, and hoisted on board the waiting machine.

The loaders duck away. The rotor blades whir. And the aluminium and perspex dragonfly swings up into the sky, banking across the island on its way to the city.

The helicopter passes over endless buildings of the same grey concrete: a graveyard where stones rise up like slabs of chewing-gum, dusty and unpalatable. An elevated expressway strides along, uncluttered as yet by cars and trucks. Advertising balloons nod in the haze over an entertainment district, gay beachballs bobbing along on a surf of smog.

Below, now, is a derelict abandoned area where apartment blocks stand empty and sterile, faces riven with cracks, each branded on its front and roof in faded, peeling paint with its address code. Wrecked rusty vehicles are piled two and three deep along the access roads.

Now the dragonfly clatters past Eiffel towers of cranes and TV masts, and the silver globes of a petrochemical works, then the cooling towers of a power station steaming like cauldrons half way into the clouds. Tall billboards covered in bold hypnotic images line factory walls down below . . .

In all directions except seawards, the world-city stretches out forever.

And Jade sleeps on.

He's sitting at the far end of the room. The room is very bare: there's only the chair he sits on, naked, and the willow-pattern paper strewn over the synthetic marble floor.

He raises his arm to motion me towards him. He's very pink, with a smooth blank face and no features . . .

She's sitting at the far end of the room. The room is very bare: there's only the chair she sits on, naked, and the willow-pattern paper strewn over the synthetic marble floor.

She raises her arm to motion me towards her. Strapped to her groin she wears a pink plastic dildo . . .

They're sitting at the far end of the room, all six of them. The room is very bare: there are only the chairs they sit on, naked, and the willow-pattern paper strewn over the synthetic marble floor.

They raise their arms in the same orchestrated gesture to motion me towards them. All six men are of exactly the same build, with identical hungry faces . . .

2

Not many people could have lived in the room where I found myself when I awoke – thought Jade some time later. Not with anything approaching ease!

It wasn't that the furnishings or geometry of the room were at fault. Every care had been taken in the choice of fabric and style, and in the blending of ancient and modern which made up the content of this attic room – itself the pinnacle of a tall brownstone building, one of a long row (with a similar row opposite), as I could see from the small dormer window set about with green velvet curtains. The whole terrace seemed to be waiting for some giant mechanical dentist to stride between the surrounding office blocks to extract this pocket of brown decay from the sulky grey mouth of the city.

A chaise-longue stood to one side of the window, covered in dark green velvet scuffed at the corners and pleasantly faded where the sun at noon had a chance to strike it. Its graceful curved feet sank into a carpet of deep ultramarine, thick-piled but very smooth and silky to my feet. The walls, hung with a textured vermilion wallpaper, succeeded in being both exotic and intimate.

And a tapestry curtain (with a maze of foliage worked on it) hid a lavatory, a bidet and an old-fashioned shower unit with gold taps.

At regular intervals my meals appeared in the hatch of a small service lift, pulleyed up by hand from somewhere deeper in the building. Once or twice I looked down the narrow lift-shaft out of curiosity, but there was nothing to be seen, since the roof of the food-lift was always down below blocking my view.

Hanging on the wall opposite the chaise-longue was a painting which I spent hours staring at, when I wasn't looking out of the window. This painting depicted a long deserted arcade of yellow stone, with a sundial in the foreground. Leaning against the sundial was a naked woman with cream-coloured limbs; lines of stitches running over them indicated that they were upholstered and covered in cloth. Her face, half turned away, was as blank as a cushion except where the stitches met in the centre like a star. This upholstered lady was staring away beyond the end of the arcade, where there was nothing but a flat horizon.

The painting wasn't particularly unsettling at first; it seemed so calm and timeless. And the room itself was pleasant.

The horrifying thing about the room was the wardrobe; or, rather, what the wardrobe contained. For when I first saw the wardrobe, on awakening, I immediately liked its tall brown panels inlaid with green and gold tracery, and its big brass handles which distorted my reflection into funny shapes – fat and swollen, or thin and curved – and which put the whole room in a globe. But when I opened its doors I found that there were no clothes inside. (Not that I had any special need of clothes, or much interest in them.)

The frightening thing was that, hanging up side by side clipped to coat-hangers, I found a row of skins.

It's hard to say whether these skins are natural or artificial. At any rate, they are full skins. When I put one on, it covers every part of my body from head to foot. They all have hair of their own, and plastic lenses for eyes. When I'm dressed in a skin, no part of my body is bare. The only air vents, to let my own skin breathe, are a series of small holes running down the spine, ingeniously incorporated into the zipper – plus two nostril slits, and the two openings for love. Curiously, there's no opening for my mouth: the lips of all the skins are sewn together.

In all there are fifty skins; I have counted them. The inside of each is contour-padded with foam to a greater or lesser extent so that it fits my own measurements exactly without any sliding or wrinkling. By donning a new skin, not only do I vary the colour and length of my hair, the size and colour of my eyes and the hue of my skin, but I can even change the size of my body. Some days I may be called on to be a fat black woman with thickly padded thighs and buttocks. Other days I might be required to be a slim brown Indian.

I say 'required' and 'called on', though in fact I found a sheet of printed instructions pinned inside the wardrobe door, informing me in advance exactly what is expected; I'm not actually notified on a day-by-day basis. Indeed, with those sewn lips pressing tightly over my own, there's no chance of conversation between us during our evening encounters . . .

It mightn't be so bad if he always came to me looking the same, always wearing the same skin, his own. But he doesn't. Clearly his wardrobe can't contain the same range as mine, since he has already repeated the same skins. He has appeared so far in the guise of a fat Caucasian, a muscular negro and a lithe oriental, plus a few other types.

I'm fairly certain it's the same man inside the different skins, though of course I can't be positive. It *could* be a different person every time: a negro wearing a white skin, an oriental wearing a black skin, or even a woman wearing a man's skin equipped with a prosthetic penis (though this seems unlikely): any of these possibilities, once you start to think about it.

Yet there's always something similar about the posture of his body under the various disguises, something in the way he makes love; though obviously different positions suit different body combinations best. Besides, there's the pattern of his actions: whenever he enters the room, locking the door behind him but leaving the key in the lock, since he has nowhere else to put it , he always does the same thing. First, he glances at the upholstered woman in the painting; next he strides to the dormer window to look out. Only then does he turn his attention to the chaise-longue where I'm sitting waiting for him, usually toying with the faded gold braid which cords the green velvet.

I can try to smile at him, and presumably he at me, but when the cheeks of a skin happen to be padded the effect can be slightly disconcerting; so generally we don't smile. Before we commence, he simply nods to me: a brief ceremonial acknowledgement. He approaches the chaise-longue, he kneels and takes my hands in his; both our hands, in a sense, being gloved. Then he examines me carefully through his false plastic eyes which seem so real. Nodding approval at last, he sits next to me so that we're both facing that painting of the arcade where the stuffed, vacant woman waits endlessly and very patiently for someone or something to appear.

After the first few evenings I decided that he is consciously comparing our situation with that of the painting. Corresponding to the arcade, there is this room. Corresponding to the sundial, the chaise-longue. The painting is completed by what we do here. The upholstered woman has waited, and he has come: her lover, from beyond the horizon. The sheer silent timelessness of the painting means that we too must enact our timeless rite in silence.

Evening by evening, after he leaves, I feel more and more like the woman in the picture. It becomes more and more of an effort to peel off the skin, clean it and hang it back with the others in the wardrobe. It becomes more and more of a shock to see my own body emerge from the skin when I finally bring myself to take it off.

As I say, there are fifty skins, and by now I have worn thirty of them. In another three weeks I shall have worn them all. I have no further instructions as to what to do then. And I cannot ask because my lips are sealed.

Today I take out the fiftieth skin to look at it more closely. Nothing in the printed instructions specifically forbids me to remove a skin before its due day, or even to try it on. The orders simply tell me sternly to keep all the skins in their proper order, just as I first found them.

I'll confess that I'm a little frightened of this particular skin. For she is the most unsatisfied of all: this fiftieth empty woman. Her skin must wait till last, to be filled and loved. Consequently a kind of ghostly presence hovers around her, more than around the others.

I hold her at arm's length and question her, as fruitlessly as ever I questioned that faceless upholstered woman in the painting.

She has long black hair and oriental eyes.

And already I suspect in my heart how a woman might not wish to avoid her fate – might even welcome it, might beg for it!

"Tell me, Dark Haired Lady, is it true that after forty-nine days of being loved in other women's skins you were so frustrated that all you could desire was to be skinned, like all the others before you?"

All these skins in the wardrobe are little more than masks and disguises for that woman waiting by the sundial. She is the only real woman in this room, the only longterm resident. The others – empty skins all – can feel nothing of the moment of love since they possess no nerve endings . . .

My nerves feel his touch, not theirs. Sometimes indistinctly, if I'm wearing a fat woman. Sometimes sharply and immediately, if I have someone thin on.

How stupid to think that this skin in my hand, which was once a raven-haired woman with slanted sloe eyes, can know anything of touch! Or can be waiting for anything!

Yet after so many days of wearing other women's skins and feeling him love them, it's easy to think so. Every one of these fifty women may have begged to be skinned, in order to become real. Supposing, that is, that they too all had predecessors . . . and maybe they all did, since the wardrobe is full up with fifty of them. Perhaps there are always fifty in all, as earlier skins wear out and are replaced.

"Am I guessing the truth, Oriental Woman?"

She dangles limply from my fingers; she's hardly any weight at all, prey to a breath of air, drifting to and fro at the least disturbance. She has no padding in her. Apart from the eyes and the hair she must have looked quite like me: a sister, of another race.

She has nothing to say to me, though. So I hang her up again at the end of the rail.

What would happen if I hung her elsewhere – say, in the middle – and wore a different skin on the final day? Would he notice the deception? Would he be confused? Unable to make love? Perhaps that is why he examines me so carefully on each occasion: to assure himself that I am new and unfamiliar . . .

Maybe the woman in the painting is what all the previous women looked like once they were stripped of their skins: each a body without identity, longing for one – but that identity has filled with wind and blown far away over the blank horizon, to nowhere

. . . or into this very wardrobe, whose door I now thoughtfully shut.

Maybe the skins are artificial, after all? Synthetics? Maybe this is all just an elaborate pretence on his part: a game which he plays to add spice to his love?

I spend one whole day examining skins in almost microscopic detail, resting my eyes from time to time by staring out of the window.

They all have the same incredibly detailed random map of lines and creases as my own skin: a complexity which can only be natural, compared with the smoothness of the dummy back on the island. All have their own individual fingerprints. All have uniquely different messages printed in their palms, which I cannot interpret, knowing nothing of palmistry.

But what of the foam padding, which fits my own body so exactly? True, the oriental woman – my immediate predecessor, I presume – would have required identical padding to myself. But how was this determined, in my case? Is there a plastic model of *me* in existence, which the island sent out to this particular customer – at the same time as he sent the island a dummy of his own body?

I end up by concentrating fiercely on remembering the exact shape and feel of the dummy of my lover; to match this memory, if I can, against more recent impressions of all the various bodies he has worn. For I still don't know what the real man looks or feels like! It could even be that the plastic dummy was modelled from one of his false bodies, not from his own nude flesh . . . So was the shape that I slept with for so many weeks reality – or illusion?

I can't say; I can answer none of these questions satisfactorily.

The crumbling brownstone terrace looks so different from the rest of the cityscape: antique, deserted, doomed. Nobody ever appears at any of the windows in the row opposite. No vehicle ever drives along the street; nobody ever treads the cracked pavements. It's as though the neighbourhood has been fenced off, just beyond my field of vision.

A tall corporation building looms beyond, and it is full of tiny bustling people: secretarial women and executive men. Their presence is of no comfort to me. People just don't seem to look out of those windows, ever. Perhaps this part of the city strikes them as dull, with all its other similar blocks: grey concrete, glass windows, dangling banners. Or even horrifies them. At least what I can see of the city from here is more varied than that yellow arcade in the painting, and the skyline is far more jumbled than the flat horizon beyond the arcade.

I watch helicopters buzzing through the smog, hoping that one of them might turn out to be the island's helicopter with its distinctive emblem. I don't quite know why I look out for it. Homesickness, perhaps? Or is it the thought of other custom-built girls being flown, asleep, to meet their lovers, suggesting all the options of love that I have missed: all the possibilities of actual contact, body with body?

Jade woke, shivering. She was lying in a shaft of moonlight. It was as though the lunar cold had touched her skin: streams of photons from the sun, refrigerated by glancing off the stone ball of death in the sky. The moon – Selene, Ch'ang-o, Mama Qilla, Juno, Tsukiyomi: she was dead as Goddess and celestial mistress now. She died when men set foot on her.

The wardrobe doors had drifted open during the night, and moonbeams danced upon the row of skins, ghostly, phosphorescent: fifty women compressed into a cabinet like a pack of playing cards, almost.

Jade jumped off the chaise-longue and ran to the wardrobe to close the doors.

"Hana!" she cried. Her brain must be fevered, by sleeping in the moonlight! She must be moonstruck, like a menstrual woman.

She closed the velvet curtains of the dormer, but darkness was worse; and errant motes of moonlight still seemed to dance in the black air, like random firings of her own brain matter.

3

On the evening of the fiftieth day, Jade put on the oriental woman's skin and sat on the chaise-longue as usual to wait for her lover. The threat of being skinned and hung up in the wardrobe for some other girl to wear hardly seemed to matter any more; for she realized that she had misinterpreted what was happening in the painting.

The faceless woman wasn't waiting for any particular lover to appear from over the horizon. She nursed no wish to settle down beside that sundial with her man, to measure out their days together. She lacked the inclination to fill that empty arcade with the tinkling of laughter.

In that total yellow light, seeming to emanate from everywhere at once, the sundial showed no time whatever. On the contrary, it – and the woman – were outside time; and lacking a face, she was set apart from all the agonies of love, lovers' rendezvous, lovers' adieux. The empty square with its blank sundial, and the empty arcade, were not outside her – but within her. Which was why she needed no eyes to see them. For this environment perfectly expressed the architecture of her own mind, now that she had attained peace at last, after the turmoil of life and emotions. The painting wasn't about commonplace love, and waiting for the lover; it was about the tranquil state of mind achieved by all previous inhabitants of this attic room, shortly before they had shed their skins. It was certainly not a desire to be loved at all cost in one's own skin which had finally prevailed. No, what had triumphed was the yearning for escape into a world of ideal affection, where the idea of oneself was loved and not the body: a dimension where a woman could be a bodiless skin without weight, substance or sensation, and yet could still be loved, free at last from the cycles of the flesh which were such a torment and a strain – loved as though by some remote God or some artificial intelligence.

No ghost of jealousy or passion clung to this oriental woman's skin. Seeing herself wearing her, reflected in a brass doorknob, Jade could only sense serenity; for surely she had waited long enough. Surely she had at last come to terms with the insoluble mysteries. Waiting thus calmly for her lover to arrive, Jade felt an immense contentment that he had let her pass so swiftly through all the modes of womanhood. She had left one of the wardrobe doors open, this evening. The other skins were not watching her, were not aware of her. They were, and were not.

A voice sang to her very faintly, so far away that she could barely hear it:

Beware, beware
Of those who stare

At you, dressed only
In your hair!

Take care, take care
Of their captive lair;
Armour's what you
Ought to wear!

Prepare, prepare
To rage and dare;
What is your lifetime
But a snare?
For you are rare, for you are rare . . .

Jade ignored this jingle running through her head, like interference on a radio broadcast; it faded away, as a smile of pity from an executioner's lips.

When her lover did come, it was as a fat man with rolling breasts and belly, and chins like sand dunes. He was completely enveloped in padding.

He slammed the door, and didn't lock it. He waddled to the window without so much as a glance at the painting. What a hurry he was in! What careless haste! How inappropriate he suddenly seemed! How graceless!

The fat man's buttocks trembled; his breasts and belly rippled; his fat cheeks quivered. And now for the very first time she heard his voice, all be it muffled by his sewn-up lips. The stitches stretched as, staring out of the window, he forced out slurred and squeaky words:

"This is terrible! It's too soon. They should have warned us."

Just then a tremor ran through the whole building; and his obese disguise quaked in response.

Angry at his insensitivity to mood, and uncertain what was happening, Jade had risen from the chaise-longue. The painting on the wall had swung askew; she wanted to straighten it.

The fat man turned, and she noted a short knife clasped in one chubby hand – the blade wrapped neatly to within an inch of the point in red tissue paper tightly bound with gold thread.

"You'd better take that skin off," he burbled at her. "There's no time for preliminaries. They're knocking the whole terrace down."

A second shock ran through the brownstone. Jade stared at him, with his sacrificial knife. How could he be so clumsy, so hasty and so crude, after such long preparations? The sacrificial mood had left her. She backed away. Stabbing her strongest fingernail between her lips, she sawed away at the stitches.

"Don't spoil things," he pleaded, advancing on her with the knife.

She had already slit a little hole in her mouth. Hastily forcing in two fingers, she tore the fabric further. "Wait a minute! I'm not giving you my skin now. The mood's all wrong – don't you understand?"

The unexpected sound of her voice halted him. At the same moment the unlocked door burst open, and two men wearing dungarees rushed in carrying a huge suitcase apiece. Both with the same dark hair and small, toy features, they must be brothers. Heading straight to the wardrobe, they tossed the suitcases down and clicked them open. Hastily but neatly, they began to pull down the skins one by one, fold each and pack it away.

Again the attic room shuddered; and now the fat man quivered so much that he could hardly move, but only wobble where he stood.

"Take your skin off, and see to the painting. Edward!" called one of the newcomers impatiently.

The fat man still waggled his knife in the direction of Jade's navel.

"You don't have time to skin her, Edward. Be realistic."

"It's my turn, Johnny!" protested the fat man.

"You'll only spoil her skin if you do it in a hurry. Then what will people say? We'll just have to take her with us as she is."

"Oh damn it!" The fat man threw his knife down on the carpet and began struggling to extricate himself from that voluminous false body of his. With his podgy arms, it was well-nigh impossible to reach the zipper either around the equator of his waist or over the bloat of his shoulders.

"I . . . can't . . . manage."

"Try, Edward! We aren't half way through these skins yet."

"You zipped me up before, Bobbie."

"The woman isn't doing anything. Get her to do it."

"Will you unzip me?" the fat man asked Jade. He presented his padded back and buttocks to her.

She hesitated. She had thought herself so close to peace and ideal love. All those other women had thought so to . . . New shocks ran through the building, overlaying each other, building up harmonic surges. She disregarded those – they were as nothing.

"I want to know. Who are you all? I shan't unzip you till you tell me!"

The fat man, Edward, palpitated. "I'll tell you. We're taxidermists. We stuff dead bodies. All these skins are due to be stuffed. Hurry up and let me out, will you? These buildings are being knocked down. We hadn't expected it for weeks yet. You can't trust the demolition people."

"Do you mean to say you take a woman's skin off her only to fill it up again with stuffing?"

"Usually it's someone's favourite girl and he wants her mounted before decay sets in . . . Other times it's a special commission for a connoisseur, and that's more your category. Suits of armour used to be all the rage, then they started buying vinyl women made into household objects – chairs and hatstands. Stuffed real women are becoming the fashion now."

"But that's horrible! What sort of life is that for a girl?"

"I assure you, stuffed woman prices are going to rocket. One day you could be pride of place in a major collection. You might be on loan to a foreign museum, admired by thousands! How about that?"

"Do you mean that I'm not even for your collection? That you got me for someone else?"

She picked up the knife from where he had tossed it. The exposed edge felt razor sharp, even through an extra layer of skin. Her own skin crawled as she thought of the knife slitting down her spine, and the three brothers rolling her over and out of her skin in neat, practised motions, then picking up her skin and shaking it gleefully, leaving her inner self as a mound of red meat on the carpet.

"Why don't you unzip me, damn it? Can't you feel how the floor's shaking?"

"Was it you who ordered me, or not?"

"Of course not. How rich do you think three taxidermists are? We took delivery of you, that's all – so we could stuff you and mount you."

"But you made love to me."

"Why not? It's a harmless little game we play; it doesn't spoil the skins."

Jade pricked the point of the knife into Edward's bull-like neck. He didn't seem to notice. The attic floor was bouncing gently now. Plaster fell from the ceiling in a white rain. She stuck the knife in as deep as the tissue wrapping allowed, but Edward only fidgeted impatiently.

"Why don't you unzip me?"

So she drove the knife sharply downward, all the way from his neck to his bottom, where it emerged from between his swollen buttocks.

He didn't even squeal. The skin simply fell apart and Edward stepped out of it, discarding a whole suit of blubber. He looked exactly like his two brothers, except that they were wearing dungarees and he was naked.

With a shudder, Jade dropped the knife. To have stuck it in the man, to hurt him, was bad enough! But to have obtained no reaction from him whatever was terrible.

"What did you do that for?" asked Edward testily as he gathered up the skin. "You could easily have used the zipper."

"I wanted to hurt you!"

"Hurt me? Whatever for?" He looked puzzled, but by now the building was beginning to sway alarmingly.

"I wanted to hurt you!" Jade sobbed. "I couldn't hurt you even a little. I couldn't make you feel anything."

"A fit of temperament is all we need!" Exasperated, Edward skipped to the wall to rescue the painting. "Follow me, d'you hear?" And out of the room he ran.

Bobbie and Johnny crammed the last few skins into the suitcases without pausing to fold them even cursorily. They slammed the lids shut in unison. With his free hand Bobbie seized Jade's wrist.

"Come on! For heaven's sake be careful of that skin you're wearing: it's for Herr Aschenbach's Chinoiserie Showroom."

"What about my *own* skin?"

Jade was on the verge of weeping.

"Be careful of that, too. I don't think we ought to tell you where it's for. Professional etiquette, you know!"

Jade dug in her heels, scoring grooves in the carpet. "Unless you tell me, I shan't come!"

"For goodness sake, tell her," Johnny shouted over his shoulder from the stairway. "Or we'll never get her out of here."

The dandruff of falling plaster was thick by now.

"It's quite an honour," explained Bobbie. "You've been commissioned as first prize in a raffle for the War Veterans."

"War? Which war?"

"How do I know which war? *Any* war, does it matter? All of them."

Outside, in a hovering helicopter, a TV camera crew were on hand to film the destruction of the brownstone terrace. Edward was the first to run out of the swaying building and down the steps to the pavement, stark naked, clutching the painting to his body. Johnny followed, with Bobby bringing up the rear, struggling with Jade as well as his suitcase.

The three brothers halted, appalled, at the sight of the robo-crane now only yards from their front door, rolling forward inexorably. The machine filled the roadway from pavement to pavement, blocking all access. It stood taller than the surviving buildings on either side. From its high, drooping nose a stone wrecking ball swung from side to side, rebounding off a building opposite after punching a mouthful of broken teeth in it, tracking back above their heads.

The TV camera promptly zoomed in on the fugitives; and viewers at home laughed to see those little human ants beneath the great tracked legs and swinging ball ... which lodged briefly in the bones of the very building they had just vacated before tearing free, bringing down a shower of bricks and masonry – which miraculously failed to hit any of them.

Edward raced off down the middle of the street away from the wrecker; but Bobbie kept tight hold on Jade to prevent her from following.

"Stop, Edward! Come back! Look at those buildings sway – they're using ultrasonics now they've seen us!"

"Our only safe place is *under* the crane," said Johnny urgently. "Come on."

"What about Edward?"

"Let him go. He might be lucky."

The remainder of the brownstone terrace was quivering and oscillating along both sides. The two brothers ran beneath the advancing treads of the robo-crane, Bobbie pulling Jade with them. Here alone was a moving space, like the eye of a cyclone, protected from the rain of debris, and tall enough and broad enough for people to shelter in. Behind her plastic false eyes Jade was crying with fear, for the massive grinding and crunching of the crane's progress was terrible to hear as those great treads trundled forward on each side, crushing bricks to dust beneath their thick metal slats.

As viewers at home cheered, the two rows of buildings shook like jelly and suddenly collapsed all at once, their material sliding into the centre of the street in two descending hills of rubble – which met and pressed together, crushing nude, running Edward between them. The three fugitives underneath the crane saw him toss the painting up in the air to save it, before he was dragged beneath the tide of bricks; then everything was masked by choking dust, which cut visibility to a few feet.

As the rubble washed up against the crane's treads, these halted; the refugees had the wit to halt, too.

"Careful," warned Bobbie. "They'll try to smear us, next." As dust filled his lungs, he began coughing and heaving asthmatically; as did Johnny. Both men blindly rubbing their grit-filled eyes.

Inside her oriental skin, Jade did not fare so badly. She had cupped one hand over her nostril slits, and could still see with reasonable clarity through the haze if she cleaned her plastic eyes with her free hand. When the great metal treads groaned and shuddered and began slowly to swing about in their own length, she knew what to do. Before the crane could seal her off against the higher drifts on either side, out on to the sea of rubble she scrambled.

Viewers at home watched intently in infra-red close-up as the other two blinded, deafened figures tried to find their way out of the trap before the cleated, armoured tracks could find them. The smooth way in which the oriental woman penetrated the masking dust astonished them all.

That the two remaining brothers might have escaped as well, had they the sense to throw away those cumbersome suitcases, was the consensus of opinion of most spectators.

Taking in the shows of rival networks that evening at the studios of Sex–TV was Morris Levi, its director. Even before the dust had begun to settle, he was on phoning.

"She's just what we're looking for! We can use her for the 200th edition of *Stone, Scissors, Paper*. Send a chopper out to claim her before those idiots from Demo–TV realize – blockheads, the lot of them! Her owners have just died.

"Eh, what's that? I don't care. Possession is nine points of the law. Hit her with sleep gas. She'll need her beauty sleep after all that stress. Got to rebuild her energy reserves.

"Get to it."

4

There are various types of Onan Machine.

In the very simplest kind the subject sits in a seat and watches erotic movies while the machine's soft tentacles stimulate him.

In more complicated models he receives direct neutral input from a computer which has the pressure patterns, scent prints, heat and moisture gradients, and sighs and groans of several thousand different sex partners recorded in its memory store.

The Feeliecouch used by Sex–TV in their transmissions is an even more complex and sensitive piece of apparatus.

Between the sense receptors suspended overhead and those embedded in the mattress a sensory field is sustained which can detect and amplify all the moods of love and ecstasies of copulation, to be encoded and beamed out to all subscriber homes equipped with a decoder and induction helmet, at the same time as events in the studio are screened visually.

The studio audience are seated in steep tiers around the stage, as in a Greek theatre, their seats equipped with induction helmets and safety belts. They are able to view the act of love from a distance at the same time as they feel what happens in the flesh.

By seven o'clock on the evening of 11 June, the seats were packed with lightly clad men and youths eagerly awaiting the bicentenary edition of their favourite show. They had all changed into brief, absorbent tunics before strapping themselves into their seats. Now they chattered, laughed, chewed popcorn and brandished fistsful of money, with which they would bargain for the actors' clothes – for *Stone, Scissors, Paper* was a game and an auction, as well as a sex spectacular.

The audience cheered and whistled as the compère beckoned Jade on the stage, still wearing her oriental skin, but also dressed now in a fetching black rubber skirt with matching singlet, pinafore and bolero jacket, the whole ensemble completed by spiked fetish boots which the audience would be keen to bid for. Her lips, which she had broken open in the brownstone attic, looked slightly ragged or ulcerated as if she had been on drugs for too long.

"Thank you! I knew you'd appreciate our little treat. And now we proudly present . . . Jade's lover! Remember, although regular viewers will recognize the lad in question, we can guarantee you that these two lovebirds have never set eyes on each other till this moment. Here he is, then: Robby O'Shea!"

The audience redoubled their cheering.

As Robby O'Shea came on stage from the other side, clasping his fists above his head, prize-fighter-style, Jade stared through her plastic eyes in amazement, mouth agape.

"My . . . *lover* . . . ?"

Bobby O'Shea was about four feet tall, with a large shaven skull embossed with phrenological bumps all neatly lettered in red ink. His large face wore an amiable, vacant yokel grin. He was attired in baggy tartan pants, a green and gold striped shirt, and a gold lamé tuxedo. On his feet were rubber flip-flops; and a white scarf dangled round his neck.

"It's the feel that counts, not looks," the compère whispered in Jade's ear. "He's got good equipment, that boy. Really makes up for him being . . . well, sort of reduced in other respects."

Still wearing the same inane grin, Robby rolled up to Jade and patted her on the bottom. Opening his mouth as wide as a hippo's with every slowly churning word, he spoke – but she couldn't understand a thing he was saying.

"He's a bit of a nut," whispered the compère, "but he knows how to perform." Out loud, he cried: "But first – a word from our sponsor!"

A red and green robot with flashing eyes, spiky horns and a stiff dragon-tail clanked on stage on caterpillar treads, holding a chain in one claw by which it led a little nude black girl with a silver collar round her neck. The child looked starved, with bowed and rickety legs, a pot-belly and ribs arching through her skin. As the robot came to a halt, the girl reached into a slot in its side and removed a bar of chocolate which she held up longingly. Piano music tinkled from the robot's chest, and the little girl piped out:

Chocolato!
Chocolato!
It's choc-ola-to
Time for me!
Dragon Brand!

This done, she tore off the wrapper and crammed the whole bar ravenously into her mouth so that it stuck out like the swollen black tongue of somebody hanged.

The robot bowed, swivelled round on its treads and led the black girl off stage. Many more bars of Chocolato were handed round the audience on silver trays by usherettes wearing scaly green dragon suits. Most people bought a bar or two while the cameras watched them, and the feeliphones picked up fringe sensations of enjoyment.

A jazz combo struck up from the pit below the stage, coaxing Jade and Robby as they swayed their bodies back and forth, through a mounting crescendo which led to a series of three main beats, the signal for Jade and Robby to throw their hands out, making Stone or Scissors or Paper.

First, Jade stuck out her balled-up fist; Robby stuck out an open hand. Paper wraps up Stone. So Jade pulled off one of her fetish boots and held it up to the studio audience.

"Do I hear ten?" cried the compère. "Twenty? Twenty-five . . .?"

The boot went for fifty. The compère hung it on a hook at the end of a long pole and swung this up to the purchaser, who took the boot and impaled currency to the hook.

The combo struck up again; Jade and Robby swayed their bodies, swung their arms . . .

Jade stuck out her fist again. Robby thrust forth two fingers.

Stone blunts Scissors. Robby's white scarf fetched a fair price.

When Jade had lost all her clothes and Robby everything but his jockey shorts, the music changed tempo, to a tantalizing *glissando* which slid up and down swiftly. Robby looked Jade up and down, in her oriental skin, licking his lips appreciatively as his shorts swelled. His chest bulged smooth and greasy as a wooden doll's dipped in oil; his legs were muscular and hairless – a wrestling dwarf's.

He slid his hands inside his shorts and jerked those down abruptly. The audience howled its approval and relief as his organ bounced up from restraint to full erection, pointing at Jade, quivering like an arrow already planted in its target. His bunch of pubic hair was stained bright orange. The shorts he threw up into the audience as a free gift; enthusiasts bucked and strained against their safety straps to catch them.

Electric expectancy filled the studio; and this was no illusion but an electromagnetic actuality.

"I'm picking up a bit of leakage. There's feedback from the audience. You can feel it in the air, man! The whole studio's like a feeliecouch."

"Any feedback from the main grid lines?"

"No, just outflow there. DATA-SWARM's patched in today. I wonder what the big brain wants?"

"Maybe it's looking for inspiration."

Jade lay back upon the feeliecouch, widespread. Robby climbed on from the bottom end and crawled forward on all fours between her legs . . .

How thick he felt, stretching her tight as a drumskin, over which throbbed and scurried thrills of excitement converging into a fine strong rhythm she could ride – like a surfboard rider on a roller, balancing on the imminence of the great wave breaking and exploding into spume, but not just yet, not just yet. Dressed in oriental skin, she rode a tsunami wave, poised on its crest – the deep ocean beneath her packed with monsters of sensation. Roar of surf in her head; roar of the audience – which was it she was hearing? From behind the boom of the wave, a siren skull-voice sang in her head:

> *Plant it deep, plant it deep!*
> *As he sows, so shall he reap!*

This living heat, this blood rhythm: so much more sensation than she had expected! Where did it all come from? Was this dwarf with the numbered head truly the love of her life? Or was half the world her lover? It felt so. The air itself sang with ecstasy; it crackled and fused. She smelled ozone.

Of a sudden Robby reared up. He slapped his skull with his hand, as if submitting on a wrestling mat. He sank back into her, seeming to swell in girth and mass. He was a hundred bodies rolled into one, thrusting with a hundred simultaneous rhythms.

"Rheostat failure!"

"Feelie leak!"

"*Gangbang feedback!*"

The audience had collapsed across their safety belts, their tunics soaked in sweat and stained, even with blood. Some older men had ruptured themselves. Some youths had broken a rib. Howling and weeping came from some tiers, soft moans from others as the audience nursed themselves. A smell of charring insulation and burnt cables filled the air.

At home, sated viewers stared at their screens in bemusement or delight. A few were already on the phone trying to contact an oriental girl. Others were phoning to order cases of Dragon Brand Chocolato.

Jade lay unconscious across the smouldering feeliecouch.

Robby crouched alongside her, writhing in a mindquake, his penis split open like a half-peeled banana.

BETTINA'S BET

L. Timmel Duchamp

"As more and more people spend greater amounts of time in cyberspace and come to identify increasingly with their various cyber constructs and non-physical relationships, won't the boundaries between 'real' and 'imaginary' have less practical significance?" The story below entertainingly addresses this question posed by Gareth Branwyn in Flame Wars: the Discourse of Cyberculture *(1994), and its author is another of the bright new names of the 1990s. L. Timmel Duchamp has so far concentrated on short fiction, which has appeared in many of the leading SF magazines, with her 1993 story "Motherhood, Etc." being shortlisted for a James Tiptree, Jr Memorial Award.*

Kwame skimmed the summaries in his mail queue. Mayra Bauer, he saw, had sent text with her HP communication. He wondered: More documents for the project? Eagerly he played out her communication first.

A miniature of Mayra, short, erect, and round, characteristically swathed in cerise, sprang up before him. The date and time of the recording – 02/12/23:20:03:22 – overlay the red-stockinged ankles and indigo-slippered feet. "Miles!" she said, her voice cracking with enthusiasm. "I did a search of the archives of the State of Michigan, using Javitts's name as a keyword. It turned up several dozen cases in which Javitts submitted psychological evaluations for convicted prisoners awaiting sentencing. Listen, Miles, I think I've found exactly what we need. I've been through about half of them, and so far have found the origins of Javitts's theory of the evolution of human mental categories present in three. The early theorizing is crude – tellingly so. I simply can't imagine any reasonable person failing to see the flaws in the general theory once they get a look at the precursor versions." Mayra paused, drew a deep breath, and folded her arms over the large pillowy shelf of her breasts; she grinned ruefully. "Yes, Miles, I know, I know. I can almost hear your despairing, cynical response. It may turn out to be not only as eye-opening as later revelations about certain of Freud's earlier cases, but as non-threatening to the supremacy of the theory as those cases were to the supremacy of Freudian theory. So Freud mutilated a patient's nose in order to cure her emotional (and therefore sexual) problems (as well as to prove his and his partner's theory)? So Freud assumed that teenaged girls were sick if they weren't sexually responsive whenever any older male pressed himself on them? All right, so the various revelations never touched the real partisans. I admit it, most people can tolerate an infinite amount of cognitive dissonance. But we've got to try, Miles. If we don't stop these maniacs it won't be long before they start using the Javitts Scale of Natural Selection and Normal Adaptation to render people like you and me into genetic dead-ends. Just remember: once Congress passes the bill requiring sterilization for all adults not scoring within the so-called normal parameters of the Javitts Scale, the Supreme Court will be our last hope. We've got to get on this, man."

The tiny eyes of Mayra's image peered intently at him, as though looking directly into his face. "When you've read the documents I'm sending with this letter, you'll see why I'm so full of new fight. They're Javitts's first recorded mention of genetic deficiencies vis-à-vis psychological reactions to cyber-constructs. Oh, and there's a reference to a more elaborate report, of which these documents provide only a summary. The data base apparently doesn't have it, who knows why. I'll have to see if I can locate a hardcopy, supposing such a thing is still extant. The other two I've so far found, which I'll send you when I've finished going through the rest of the cases, actually offer more developed arguments sketching a precursor theory of Javitts's Categories of Human Mental Evolution. I believe they'll help us deduce the logic – if one can call it that – that informs the theory as a whole. Still, I think when you've read it you'll agree that this first case, Miles, is our baby. It's the beginning. It's the knot from which Javitts started knitting the empire, and therefore the knot that once undone will let us unravel the whole damned mess with a few sharp, quick tugs on the thread." The cerise-draped arms lifted in a two-fisted gesture of victory. "Empires can be unraveled, Miles. And this one is no exception. Never doubt it."

The projection cut out, and Kwame was left, as usual, feeling slightly flattened at the sudden absence of the drama and exuberance Mayra's messages always conveyed. She'll be grand, promoting the book, he thought as he reached for his text reader. But she's going to have to learn to leave her knitting metaphors out of it, since few of the people we need to convince have a clue as to what knitting even is. . . .

File #09242286.PSA
Pre-Sentencing Advisory in re: Inmate #7742286

Contents:
A. Transcript of selected monologues made by the inmate during post-conviction, pre-sentencing confinement, providing a general overview of the inmate's psychological state.
B. Summary of pre-sentencing advice to the Court by A. N. Javitts, MD.

A. Transcript of Selected Monologues of Inmate #F7742286

1

[07.28.63/11:24:06]
. . . and so came to a clearing in a wood, a wood with trees barren of leaves, their branches limning the starkness of winter, except that the sun was beating down all golden warmth and love, like Indian Summer, and the leaves thick on the ground were two feet deep, and calling me. The smell of them, dry and crackling – it was only in my imagination, I know, there wasn't anything for me to smell, yeah, but somehow I did smell them, that dry autumn fragrance totally unlike the vegetable, rotting smells of summer . . . *clean*, the autumn smell is, not fresh but *clean*, a clearing-away. Anyway, I stood there purely wallowing in the smell I put where none actually was, and then a spurt of joy took me, I mean it took me over, like a burst of manic, electric energy, made me fling myself

into the deep cushion of leaves and immerse myself, like it was the warm salt water of a gulf. And I rolled in those leaves, giggling, soft, soft – to myself. (It was one of the good kind of things, one of the few that's allowed, you know? Well *I* know. I know it's good.) So – just for that little bit of time – I tapped into that certain spirit inside, you know, that spark that starts to die as you get older and tired and set into synch with a cynical mean world. And it felt so fine, to find out it was still there. I'd been thinking lately that I'd lost it totally.

Then, while I was rolling around letting the leaves brush my face and crackle in my hair (the hair that I had in that setting, which was long, yeah, long and straight, as I don't have these days in real-space), a pair of boots came and planted themselves in my face (catching my eye, so to speak), which sobered me fast, and made me look up and scramble to my feet to brace for something nasty. Only when I saw it wasn't a man, but a woman, young and okay-looking, not the snob or dweeb type, the panic drained out of me. Why? I've been thinking about it, and I believe it was just simple reflex. I mean, I know that it could have been a man looking like a woman. For kicks. To take me by surprise or whatever. And I know that women can be ugly mean customers, too. But we're talking reflex here. How I reacted before I had time to get around to thinking.

So then the next thing I know, I'm rolling around in the leaves with this woman I've never met, and we're playing like puppies or preschoolers, that kind of thing. No meanness, just the pleasure of tapping into that same spirit. It's probably stupid of me, but thinking about it now almost makes me wonder if things couldn't really be different. If Jamie's way isn't the only one.

Of course the next thing I know, the Ugly Grating Voice of Authority pulls an interrupt. "Recreation period is over." And I'm back in the world of the four gray sponge walls, and my body's folded into a Half-Lotus, and the leaves and sun are a memory without reality. And somehow I feel worse than I did before recreation period. (Though yeah, there's no way to know that I wouldn't have felt worse if I'd just gone on sitting there in interminable gray solitude.)

But that's jail for you.

2

[08.10.63/20:04:49]

Dr Javitts says I'm not supposed to talk like to her, but really just to myself. That my talking to her doesn't mean shit, because the real problem is with me. And that I'm not facing up to it. That the point of isolation isn't just to keep me from contaminating other inmates, but so that I'll come to understand how and where I went wrong. (And even that I did, which she says I don't yet admit.) (Well I think it's a slander to say I'm "bent." You can't dispute the legal code, and going by what it says, I know I did wrong – but if anyone's "bent" it's Jamie. Which, I might add, I've never held against him, either.)

So. I'm not supposed to be pretending I'm having a conversation with another person. But that's hard. Really hard. Because it makes me feel like a crazy person, sitting here talking to myself, out loud, even if it is what the doc says I'm supposed to be doing. I don't see why if I have to talk out loud I can't pretend I'm talking to a second person, or else do this talking in cyberspace, where I could at least sit down and look at some reasonable version of myself (not any of the ones the jail's stuck me with, that would be too, too gross) while I'm talking. . . . And then it would be like talking in a mirror, only better. (Obviously I don't look half as cool in the flesh as any cyberspace version Jamie ever gave me to use.)

Jamie. Yeah. It always comes back to him. He's the one who's been legally wronged. "The injured party," Dr Javitts calls him. "Explore the reasons you did it. And not by just repeating the story you always tell when asked," Dr Javitts said in our last session. But the whole thing is totally obvious, I said to Javitts. What's there to explore?

Start with your relations before you assaulted him, Dr Javitts said. So all right. I'll do that. I'll tell the story of our sick, twisted, perverse relationship.

Hey. I've just had a *fascinating* thought. I used to think constantly about my relationship with Jamie. How we met. Our early meetings. But I haven't thought about any of it since the day I proved him wrong about himself. I mean, I used to be *obsessed* with all the teeniest tiniest details. But though I spend all my time alone, between these four dirty gray boring drab walls, none of it ever crosses my mind now.

It's like the whole thing's settled, isn't it. Like I had a catharsis.

Yeah. Now I ask you, how can losing an obsession be unhealthy? Twisted? Bent?

But all right. To start from the top. I met Jamie the day he came to check his old man into the nursing home where I work. Or rather, worked. I was on what we call the "taxi patrol" – which means I was detailed to pick up and deliver patients from point A to point B. In this case, the patient was Jamie's father, point A was Admitting, and point B was Five Northeast. Like most of the patients on Five, this old dude wasn't all that old. Not decrepit, not crippled, not even short of breath. But going by the book, not only did Jamie have to input all the data into the admitting terminal for his father, but I had to give the dude a ride to Five Northeast. Later, Jamie told me that his father didn't have an active medical problem – but that a slew of docs had said that heart disease was eventually going to get him. As everyone knows, the younger you are when you check yourself into a womb, the longer you'll live, because your cells won't have to be battling free radicals and all that. Which was enough for Jamie's old man, I guess. Still, according to Jamie, his father was seriously into downhill skiing and mountain hiking and swimming twenty laps every day in his company's gym. Can you figure it? I know I can't. But I didn't say this to Jamie at first. (I mean, it was creepy to think about, and embarrassing to bring up. And so up until the time Jamie made an issue of it, I just kind of kept my thoughts on the subject to myself.)

So anyway, I deliver Jamie's old man to Five Northeast, and then go on to the next pickup the dispatcher assigns me. Since I do maybe thirty or so of these jobs in one shift, I wasn't thinking of that particular one at all when, waiting for the bus at the stop across from the nursing home, Jamie pulls up in this really sleek sweet car and offers me a lift. I didn't recognize him at first, and refused. But then when he refreshed my memory, I decided what the hell (though considering he was still a relative stranger, I know I was an idiot for getting into his car anyway). . . . So we went to this really neat place for coffee, and ended up sitting there talking for hours, swapping our life stories. After that we had a second meeting, where he talked me into a cyberspace date . . . and the rest, as they say, was history.

I guess you could say the conflict was there from Go. I mean, him helping his old man to put himself away so he could live (if you can call it that) the rest of his life in cyberspace, which I found supergross. And him telling me I'm a moron for working a real-space job that's "demeaning" and low-paying. (And did it matter, when I pointed out that somebody had to work in child-care centers and nursing homes and hospitals? Of course not! He said that those jobs should all just go either to robots or to what he called the "intellectually and socially dysfunctional"! As though such jobs could be held by just anybody!) (Though maybe he's right, maybe the taxi patrol and other nursing-home jobs could be done by robots, but considering how most patients at Green Haven aren't like those on Five Northeast, it sounds cruel and inhuman to me.)

Enough of this shit. My voice is getting hoarse, and the food hatch is beeping.

3

[08.23.63/06:05:27]

Have I ever been this lonely in all the lonely desert that's been my life? For answer, consider my desperation every time the jail's system shoves me into its cyberspace with the announcement by the Ugly Grating Voice of Authority of "visiting period." Visiting period means, at best, a meeting with my mother. And always, always, always, the terror and hope (both at the same time) that maybe Jamie will be surprising me.

The visiting period I just finished sitting through netted me zero visitors. It's cruel, the way the jail yanks all inmates into cyberspace whether they have visitors or not. Each time you face the disappointment of zero visitors, you're also stuck sitting between a cyberspace set of four gray walls. The first time this happened, I kept hoping it meant that the connection had been delayed, not that I was being kept there as a regular, general thing. But jail never has individualized reasons for anything that happens in it, only rules that are generally applied whether appropriate or not.

You wouldn't think it would make any difference. (But it does, the way so many totally trivial things do when you're in jail.) I guess it's the sense of rejection that gets pounded into you when you're sitting there, waiting, waiting, just waiting to be released back into your real-space cell. And though there's no reason to, I always shiver, as though there's a chill in my bones, gripping my heart. And I've been thinking about this, too, and maybe the best way to put it into words, would be to say it's a figurative cold that makes itself psychosomatically real. Yeah. Psychosomatically real.

My mother says that visiting periods are always scheduled somewhere between eleven at night and seven in the morning. When they fall at three a.m. during the work week, she just can't make it. She's a plumber, she needs her sleep. And Dad – well, like, I know I won't be hearing from him. He's "disowned" me. He says I'm no daughter of his. Strange, when it was always Dad who was my good bud (when he was in the mood) and Mom who just couldn't stop herself from constantly finding fault with me.

"Your crime is not a gender issue," Dr Javitts says. (Which is exactly what the prosecutor and judge said during the trial, too.) I never claimed it was (even if my lawyer tried to argue that). I've always said it was a question of my proving Jamie wrong. And the fact that Jamie hasn't visited me proves I succeeded in doing it, too. If he was right about what he thought he felt and believed, then he'd see me and say he has no problem with what I did. But the fact that he hasn't shown up to do that only proves my point.

And so that's my real sin: having been right, having done what I did under such circumstances. Because if Jamie didn't care, then what I did to him wouldn't really have been wrong, would it?

4

[09.07.63/13:46:19]
Dr Javitts says I'm not working hard enough to find the answers to the questions. She also says that only when I do will I then be "fit" to be sentenced, which is the only way out of this "limbo" (as Mom calls it). Yeah. The question of why I did it (and "to win the bet" isn't the "correct" answer), and also of what my real feelings toward men and sex are. (Can you believe it? When everyone agrees it's not a "gender issue"? Talk about contradictions! I'd like to know just how I'm supposed to come up with some kind of theory about how I have bent ideas about men and sex without it being some kind of gender thing!)

Look. I never had trouble with men. I never went out that much, true. But that's only because I'm not what you call a cool piece of action. Not because I wasn't interested. (Even if I do like to read about romance and sex more than plod through the real thing, which, let's admit it, is usually pretty boring.) Let's just say that until Jamie took an interest in me I never really managed more than ten or twenty one-night-stands I had with pickups.

Actually, I kind of assumed that that was the kind of move Jamie was making when he pulled up that day at the bus stop. A slick dude like him, smelling of money and class. Not the kind of character who's going to be interested in much more than a fast fuck or two. So I was flattered, you know, really totally flattered when he expressed some more general interest in me.

Not that I know why, even now!

But hey. My throat's dry. And drinking too much water makes me have to piss, and I hate using the fucking vacuum-cleaner-like contraption that passes for a toilet in this place. So I think I'll just stop now for a while.

God this place sucks.

5

[09.11.63/02:44:03]

So – I'm practically bouncing off the walls with energy, thanks to a visit from Clea. The doc's always talking about maybe starting me on anti-depressants, but the fact is that if they'd let me access books, and allowed more visits, there wouldn't be any fucking "depression" to "be concerned for." Yeah. But since for a lifelong bookworm like me reading is fun, they won't let me do it. (They don't even give you the usual word cues in their damned cyberspace, because reading them – instead of hearing the nauseating Ugly Grating Voice of Authority – would be a pleasure, however fleeting.) (Basically, they don't want you to feel like a human being. "You've put yourself outside society and culture, Bettina," Dr Javitts says. "Therefore the amenities of society must be denied you, until you come to terms with exactly how and why and even that you made yourself an outlaw.") So I'm not a human being. A *social* human being. Right.

Actually, I was shocked when I saw Clea. I mean, after she gave away all our most private conversations in court, I like thought she fucking hated me. But it turns out that it was she who thought I must hate her. (Even though it was my lawyer, not the prosecutor, who asked her to do the talking.) It was only when Mom told her that I didn't hold anything against her that she decided that maybe she would visit, to try to patch up what the legal system had tried to destroy. The reason it took her so long, though, was that the idiot computer screening applications for jail visits kept tagging her as a "media opportunist" out to get the juicy details firsthand, for future exploitation. (Which of course is a no-no, until after sentencing.) Finally, though, she got cleared. (Now that's loyalty: she kept trying and trying, even though a big part of her was sure I was hating her guts and would get ugly with her if she did get access.)

But if it shocked me to see Clea, it shocked her *severely* to see the bod the jail makes me use for visiting period. (Mom described it to me during her second visit, when I made her.) It's bald, for one thing (like I was when they first brought me here and shaved my head). And it's basically just a mess of lumpiness in a gray sack that's exactly like the one they make me wear in real-space.

But except for that first awkward minute or two, it was totally cool. She'd just taken in a really neat cyberspace installation – endlessly elaborate, the kind of thing you could spend hours poking around in – on the subject of male bodies. Needless to say, one thing led to another, I mean her description of some of the neat insights into social perceptions and presentations of male bodies by various of the media kind of naturally led into the old shared fantasies about Jamie, and from there to . . . well, real giggles, you know? I mean, though what I did was serious, there's also this sense of hysteria you just can't avoid when you start thinking about it all from a certain angle. . . .

Clea said it was two in the morning. Which means it must now be close to three. It feels a little like late afternoon to me, that's how fucked-up jail is. Bedtime, or nap, who cares. I'm getting good at sleeping with the light on (though according to Dr Javitts, that's what's messing up my menstrual cycle, which she says is normal for most women who have a "prolonged" pre-sentencing period). (Ha-ha, funny joke, isn't it, Doc?)

6

[09.14.63/15:20:19]
(Sensors monitoring the inmate's pulse, respiration and blood pressure were set off at 03:19, and visual inspection revealed she was masturbating. The following monologue ensued after a First Warning had been delivered orally to the inmate to desist.) Damn you, damn you, I didn't even notice what I was doing! I mean, I was just sitting here thinking. And then this siren goes off and the Ugly Grating Voice of Authority threatens me with full-time incarcera-

tion in a cyberspace cell where masturbation is physically impossible! Is that fair, if I don't happen to notice I'm doing it? But nothing's fair here. Jesus. You say I can't have any more visits from Clea because I "blew" the one you did let me have. Blew it! Well fuck it! You never told me that the whole *point* was to talk "seriously" about Jamie and my crime. How was I supposed to know that?

Don't you people realize you are *killing* me? Do you think I can't feel the bones sticking out all over on my body now? It's like it's not my body anymore! I've *never* been bony, not even when I was a kid! But this fucking diet you've got me on – grub so boring anyone not kept in a condition of near-starvation wouldn't touch the shit – god knows how many pounds I've dropped. Which is really fucking ironic, you know. Jamie's not here to see it. Won't ever see it. The bodies he had me use in cyberspace – man, they were all anorexic. Walking skeletons, really. I mean, except for his disgust with flesh, I'd never want to look like that. Sure, I always wanted to be thinner. But *that* thin? A woman'd have to be on her deathbed to get that kind of thin, and then what would be the point?

And Jamie looking like one of those dudes in the cunt-throbbers I used to blow my budget on. Long, flowing black hair – "raven," like they say in those books. Silky. Down to his fucking asshole. Oh honey. A real beauty. And the hands – graceful, with long bony fingers, about six rings on each hand, and sexy leather bracelets up and down both forearms. Mmm-hmm. The messages he sent out, by the way he walked, and stood. And his eyes – hot molten brown lava, as they say. And a heartbreakingly beautiful jaw. I just couldn't get enough looking at him – only he didn't care about that, didn't care to give me a chance to look at him in real-space, no, all the dude wanted was to be in cyberspace all the time. And there came then that unforgettable Saturday afternoon, which happened after we'd been doing cyberspace kind of things a few times, by which time I'd started to get big-time major horny for him, that he went just about foaming-at-the-mouth crazy when I said I wanted us to take our clothes off. He couldn't stand the thought of seeing me naked, he said, it would be a super gross-out. Yeah. I wanted the floor to open and swallow me up. I wanted to disappear. Like being in a room full of people where everyone's staring at you and when you happen to catch a look at yourself in the mirror you see there's snot drooling out of your nose. Only like, this is me, this is my body, how I am. So it wasn't like I could just wipe it away, was it. And so of course I started rushing the hell out of there as fast as I could, when he grabs me and says that none of that's important. ("That" being . . . what? Sex? Real-space presence? My body? Or his feelings about my body?) Betts, Betts, he says, don't you understand it's your psyche that I'm into. Your body doesn't matter. *My* body doesn't matter. We can have any kind of bodies we want in cyberspace. Right. I guess I should have known, because of the cyberspace bodies he'd so far been giving me. (Not that I saw much of them – just enough to see that most parts of them, at least, were skeletal, and never had any tits to speak of, which at that point hadn't yet meant all that much, though it made me a little uneasy, since it so clearly wasn't anything like the real me.)

So now I'm bony in real-space, too. Who knows, maybe I'll look like a skeleton by the time you people are through with me. I can feel only stubble where my hair used to be. Haven't had a period since the trial. And I know it must be past time. My breasts haven't even gotten swollen – and I'm always always horny the week before my bod starts loading fluid for the next period. I wasn't masturbating because I'm especially horny, you know. I mean, I've hardly had any kind of physical feelings but hunger and insomnia in this place at all since I've gotten here. But shit, there's nothing else to do here. My mind was on auto-pilot. And my fingers just did what comes natural, out of boredom. Because this place isn't natural, you know. It isn't healthy. I mean, human beings aren't meant to be always physically alone. Sitting in a gray space talking to themselves, man.

Is anybody listening? Spying on me, yeah. But *listening*? No. Of course not. I'm just fucking talking to myself, as usual. I mean, it doesn't matter what I say until I say the magic words. So all right. Tell me what they are and I'll say them! Just tell me. I can't take this. It's killing me. I know I'm going to die if I keep on this way. I just know it. I can feel it in my belly. It's like a worm inside me, eating me out from the inside. Or rather, worms. Yeah, a whole nest of them. Writhing, their slimy tentacles burrowing in and eating me out. And nothing to stop them! Oh god. There's nothing there! Nothing there! Nothing there! Did you inject them in me, is that what you did? And maybe you're just waiting to see how long it takes them to kill me. An experiment! I'm an experiment! Is that a fair trade, I ask you? *IS ANYBODY LISTENING??????* (*The inmate at this point grew incoherent. After ten minutes of sustained hysteria, the monitor triggered the release of a dose of tranquilizer*

from the medication capsule implanted in her thigh at the time of
processing, and the inmate subsided into twilight sleep. – A.N.J.)

7

[09.22.63/12:14:59]

So. I have to like start fresh. I've been fucking up major, here. And
in the words of Dr Javitts, if I don't get my head together soon, I'll
be in deep, deep shit. (Not that she'll say exactly what that would
work out to be.) I feel as though I'm in deep shit already. Not just
being in isolation, and awaiting sentencing for my felony conviction, but in the sense that I'm probably just about ready to fall
apart. Mentally. That's what makes me nervous about all this
talking out loud to myself. I mean, I'm supposed to do it to sort of
think out loud, to work out what has gone wrong with me. And so
as not to inhibit the process, I'm just supposed to do it whenever
I feel as though I might be going to think seriously about it. But all
of this "free-speaking" makes me wonder. Whether I'm not turning
into a real looney-toon. Because I catch myself talking to myself
even when I didn't mean to be doing it. Now in here, maybe that
passes for sanity. (Like the "compulsive behavior" they only a few
hours ago zapped my frontal cerebral cortex to cure – the doc said
that when they did a visual inspection of me and discovered my
blowing-on-my-fingers thing, that it was no big deal, and that they
could have eliminated that right when it got started, if only I'd let
her know about it.) But if they ever let me go back to seeing other
people in real-space, that kind of thing would have to go straight
off. I mean, can you imagine, finding myself babbling away when
there are live people around? They might think I have one of those
contagious mental viruses. And wouldn't that be a load.

But the thing is, to be serious. Which isn't that big a deal for me,
since people have been telling me since Day One to lighten up. So
here's serious topic number one, that Javitts said to try working on.
My last rec period. So okay, it was the scene in the forest with the
leaves. But this time I didn't get any kind of kick from it at all.
Didn't smell anything. And everything looked sort of like a
holographic animation, Saturday morning kind of stuff. So I don't
roll in the leaves. But this woman shows up anyway. Which pisses
me off. And so I tell her to get the fuck out of my space. I mean, it's
my rec period, I got the right to decide. But she doesn't take no for

an answer. And so I jump her and knock her into the leaves and kick her (and she takes it, doesn't make a move to defend herself, even though she has those mean-looking boots on). Of course all the time I'm punching and kicking her I'm thinking about how she's just a computer projection being bounced into my optic cortex from a satellite orbiting the earth, and how she doesn't feel a thing, even if there's a personality somewhere behind the image. And that if there is a personality, it's of someone who works for the jail. And so then I really go at her, yelling and screaming my head off, calling her every shit-name I can think of. (Most of them Jamie's favorites.) And the damned Voice doesn't interrupt, and the woman doesn't disappear and so finally I get tired and walk away. And what happens, but that I come on her again! And so I know I'm not going to get rid of her by kicking her face in. And the whole thing just makes me frustrated and so I start to cry. And she comes and puts her arms around me and this just makes me more upset instead of giving me any kind of good feeling. But then, because I'm thinking about how it's a jail production and is probably meant as some kind of lesson (instead of genuine recreation), I say I'm sorry. And then the Ugly Grating Voice of Authority releases me, and I'm back between the four gray sponge walls.

I suppose the whole thing comes down to resentment. Resentment at being so alone. Resentment at only getting these cyber-contacts, which are just totally phony. I mean, I wouldn't have tried to beat up a stranger in real-space. It would just never cross my mind. And I never feel that antagonistic toward anyone. Not even Jamie. When I cut him with the laser scalpel, I wasn't feeling rage, the way I did during the last rec period at having that image invading my space. The only time I ever felt rage at Jamie was when we played in his cyberspaces. But that was all make-believe, too – in the sense that he wasn't really hurting me physically – not giving me any real physical pain. The sensory connections in the standard consumer cyberprograms aren't made for pain reception. And most of the sensory connections are pretty crude, anyway, except for detailed sensation in the hands. And, of course, the genitals – though there the sensations don't really correspond to the way they'd work out in real-space (which they mostly do for the hands), but just trigger horniness and orgasms. And so all the while I was pissed-off at Jamie for the things he was doing to me I'd be either getting super-horny or having orgasms.

Yeah, I know, I probably should talk about that. I mean, according to Jamie, that should have made up for everything that I didn't like. The fact that I didn't feel any physical pain, the fact that I did experience orgasms, made him impatient with my not wanting to play his games. But so what if I came? It didn't make me feel good. And afterward I'd hardly remember coming, just all the other shit he and I were doing and saying at the time. And of course I couldn't talk to him about it. Like explain why I didn't like it. I mean, he had to have known why I didn't want to do it. Except that he kept saying I was a prude, and a little simpleminded, to want to do it in cyberspace the way people do it in real-space, when the whole point of cyberspace is to make a different kind of reality than the one we already have, not to pretend that it's the same.

And me, I was always the kind of kid who couldn't back down on a dare. I hated to be thought a coward. I guess it was just plain luck that until I met Jamie no one had ever really dared me to do anything self-destructive or criminal.

8

[09.23.63/17:22:36]

Okay. So now I'm supposed to think about why I didn't just walk away from Jamie and his games. Why I kept on with it even though doing that kind of shit made me feel bad. Well, it's simple. As I said when Dr Javitts raised the question in our last session, I had such a thing for him that I couldn't even think of dropping him. And second, I'm not a coward, and I knew that even if I'd walked away, some of the things Jamie was always hinting around at might stick with my head – hey, I know they would. I know that much about myself. And I'd always regret it. I mean here was the one time I had real contact with someone that cool. I mean, he was like out of a book or a soap! Everything about him, not just his looks. And he was basically a decent guy, even if his sexual tastes were bent. And then, when he made the bet with me – how could I have walked away from that?

Dr Javitts says the bet isn't the "intrinsic reason" for my "crime." It's only an "alibi," she says (though I thought alibis were supposed to be stories that excused you from committing crimes, which isn't at all what I'm claiming, I never claimed I didn't cut Jamie). I'm supposed to explore the bet, to get beyond the superficial meaning covering over its real meaning.

So. We had this bet, because I wanted to spend time with Jamie in real-space (which he never would do after our first couple of meetings), and he wanted to get me internally connected, so that I wouldn't have to come over to his place and get myself wired up each time. And the bet was that he could get me to see that cyberspace has more to offer than real-space – that it'd be better for me to practically live in it, the way he and his old man do. And if he won, he'd pay for internal connection, and even help me find a decent cyberspace job. My side of the bet was that I could get him to admit there was plenty worth doing in real-space. It seemed pretty obvious to me, that though he had that dinky little apartment, in fact he liked the amenities of real-space – I mean, considering the car he owned (which was previously his old man's), and the places he liked to go to eat (where he sometimes took me), I really thought I had a chance at winning. And the payoff if I won would be our having sex in real-space. (I bet the prosecutor just hated that part of it – that Jamie wouldn't have to spend a dime on me if I won, while it'd cost him a pile if he won.)

Of course it embarrassed me in court. I mean, people would think nothing if the forfeiture on my part would be sex, instead of vice versa. But Clea understood – even if she did tend to think that what Jamie wanted would be just super. But what I've tried to explain, is that Jamie wasn't entirely himself in cyberspace. It was like he would sometimes become someone else, depending on the body-image he was using at the time. It was playacting, I guess. Which would have been all right, except that the more time we spent in cyberspace, the more that became all there was – playacting. To me, that's not life. That's not living. That's not engaging with reality. (Which is what I finally told Jamie. And it was right after I told him that he proposed the bet.) So it was like he was a Jekyll/Hyde – only with lots of variations on the Hyde side. And the Jekyll part almost never accessible.

But about the bet – it did change things. It added a certain edge. The edge had been there before – for me, anyway, but always covert. Because I didn't want a real fight with him. And also because every time I was about to call it quits, he'd turned sweet (just as if he knew I was about at the limits of what I would take). Would spend some time with me in real-space, give me a driving lesson in his car, take me out to dinner, that kind of thing. And then he'd be perfect (except that he felt no attraction to me in real-space, which I could always sense, and would make me feel uneasy and worthless and lonely but still not that bad, because he was being so sweet and totally focused on me). Ooh, the way he could look at me – never taking his eyes off my face, like there was nothing else in the universe but him and me ... nobody else has ever looked at me that way. Nobody. And I know no one ever will again, either. . . .

(Subject broke off speaking here, and sobbed and mumbled incoherently for roughly twenty-eight minutes. – A.N.J.)

9

[09.25.63/01:14:38]
Yeah. So today's subject of unilateral conversation concerns what Dr Javitts calls an evasion of the facts. Namely, why I keep insisting that I cut Jamie to win the bet, when I could have, say, trashed his car or his apartment instead. Which, though it could have gotten him super-pissed-off at me, wouldn't have done lasting, permanent damage to him personally. Or, as the doc summarized the question, why didn't I try something a little less drastic.

Now this, I have to admit, is a fair question. Because looking at the situation superficially, it would seem obvious that I could have gotten him by damaging mere property. And I admit that it has always been my honest belief that Jamie is attached to his car. So right away, when we made the bet, I mentioned it to him, casually. Sort of as a joke. Well, he said, the car was valuable to him for a) the cash it would someday bring him, which he could then "invest" in cyberspace, and b) as a comfortable convenience for getting around as long as he was still "outside" (which is how he liked to refer to real-space). Ultimately, he said, the car would mean nothing to him once he had taken his Dad's route. So then, after he loaded all this shit on me (with a ridiculous smirk, purely disdainful, you know?), he said that if I took a good look around the apartment I'd see there was almost nothing in it. (Which was true – and it was a dinky place, besides – being basically about the size of the space I had in my parents' apartment.) Almost everything he made, he said, went on cyberspace programs, utilities, facilities and games. And, he said, that even though he was young and in good health, he was already seriously considering going his Dad's route once he could feel totally confident that he could make it psychologically and security-wise "inside" (which is how he usually referred to cyberspace). I thought about his Dad lying in one of those creepy wombs on Five Northeast, and asked him what he meant, about making it. He said that a) people permanently inside needed someone outside who they could trust to take care of any real-space situation that might come up that they couldn't handle themselves from inside, and that b) some people freaked out when they tried to live inside for more than twelve out of the twenty-four hours of each day. His Dad had gone through months and months of testing and conditioning before he'd checked himself into Green Haven.

Anyway, if I'd trashed his car, he would have claimed to be pissed at my depriving him of the cash it was worth, and still not have lost the bet. The thing with cutting him was that he was always claiming that only the parts of his body useful to him in cyberspace – his brain, his other vital organs that kept him alive, and whatever he could use in real-space to make his cyberspace life better – mattered. And so you see that really didn't leave much in his life that he couldn't claim served to advance his cyberspace existence, did it?

10

[09.29.63/16:38:09]
God, I'm really totally bummed out now. I feel like my head's being chopped and shredded for creaming in one of those yucky yellow-white sauces Dad sometimes makes when he's "in the mood" to cook. If they pull many more numbers like the one I just had to go through, there's not going to be anything left to be sentenced (supposing the judge ever gets around to doing it).

Okay. So I get the warning from the Ugly Grating Voice of Authority that in five minutes I'll be dumped into visiting period. So all right. I get myself situated, in the usual Half-Lotus, the way you're supposed to when you're going to be doing cyberspace for over a couple of minutes and under an hour. And then sure enough, the jail's system pulls me into the hall they make you wait in during visiting period. But what it turns out is happening is that they're messing with my head. Even though I'm back in my real-space cell now, I'm still shaking from the whole experience. Yeah. So after about half a minute or so (though who knows, I have trouble figuring the passing of time even in real-space, which is more natural to my body rhythms than time passing in cyberspace), the little stick-figure light over the door into the visiting area changes from red to green. And I naïvely think, hey, I got a visitor. So I go nonchalantly in, knowing it can't be anybody but Mom, I put on my friendly grateful smile, the reformed loving daughter and all that – until I see who my visitor is. Oh man. I almost shat in my pants when I saw that image. It was one of Jamie's faves. And the first thing I think is that he must be pissed as hell at me. And the second thing I think is how shitty I must look, with the horror image the jail's stuck me with. But then I glance down at what I can see of my cyberbod, and discover that it isn't any of the ones the jail ever gives me, but one of the skeleton-girls Jamie used to have me use! Pretty freaky, right? Yeah. Well then while I'm just standing there staring down at the bony knees of this cyberchick bod, Jamie says, "Hey, Betts. How's it going? Must get boring in this place. So how about a game of Killer Sex in the Maze?"

By this point everything that's happened between us is running through my head, and so I say, "You're not mad at me, Jamie? Tell me the truth, are you upset at what I did? I'm really and truly sorry if you are. Or is it like you claimed about all real-space shit? And it didn't matter at all?"

Now I know this sounds callous. But though I wanted him to know I was sorry, I also wanted to know whether I'd won the bet or not.

But Jamie just takes my hand and pulls me through a third door (one that's never there when Mom visits), right into his Maze cyberspace. Which is this big old spooky mansion, lit only by occasional flickering candles, honeycombed with hundreds of hallways and staircases dripping with cobwebs that brush against your skin. (There've been times I could have sworn they were sticky, though I suppose it was purely a psychological response on my part.) So then Jamie tells me to run, that he's got a laser scalpel and a welding torch he's going to get me with if/when he catches me, and suddenly I'm alone, and running, and getting harrowed by booby-traps and rabid, slavering animals on the loose in the house. And of course the whole time I'm lost, and wondering if I'll ever find the safe well-lit room with the cozy fire and telephone – I supposedly having misplaced my own – for calling the police. (I never have found the place, not in all the dozens of times I've played the game. For all I know it could be something Jamie told me was in the space, but never really was. Just to motivate me for play.)

And of course I run and run and run. And though I don't lose my breath or get a stitch in my side, still I get worn out and tired with the running and fear. Maybe there's no physical effort involved to explain it. But the point is, I guess, it's really the strain of too much adrenalized nervous energy. Yeah. So my heartburn comes back, really bad. And my heart's pounding like mad, because I don't want Jamie to get me. I mean, I really really don't. More than I could seriously ever put into words. I know, the horror of it is all in my head. But still, I have this terrible dread. It makes me jump and scream whenever I think he's found me.

It takes a long time. But Jamie does eventually get me, and I scream and sob and beg for mercy before he even starts on me. And he just laughs with one of those horror-movie giggles, and puts me through all that scary humiliating shit, just like he always does. And still I plead with him, I beg, and he keeps on laughing at me, and tells me I like it. (And then makes me have an orgasm, just to prove it.) But this time, I'm so worked up that I start screaming at him, about how I cut him, how I really cut his real body lying totally defenseless in real-space while his conscious self was in cyberspace, and how I'm glad I did it and how I'd do it again if I had the chance, that it was what he wanted anyway, wasn't it, ha ha ha.

And then, Zap. Without any warning I get dumped back into real-space by the jail's system. And here I am, still shaking from the terror of it, and even while I'm talking about it I keep hearing my voice screaming at him that I'm not sorry, that I'm glad, and that I'm especially glad that I chopped his thing into little pieces after I cut it off his body, so that it could never be fixed, never be replaced, never be his again.

I know the jail was just playing games with my head, and that it probably wasn't really Jamie behind that cyberbod of his. Still. It felt exactly like him, and the laugh was the same and the words and all that. So it might as well have been him, right? Whatever. It's at times like this that I guess I do hate that bastard's guts. Not enough to kill him, no. But just to show him how seriously fucking screwed-up and wrong he is. You know?

B. Summary of Pre-Sentencing Advice to the Court:

As is revealed from the final monologue included in this file, a re-enactment of a typical interaction between the inmate, Bettina Raymonde Smith-Weber, and her victim, the inmate feels no genuine remorse for her crime, despite her protestations at other times to the contrary. Considering the serious nature of the felony she committed, and the circumstances in which she committed it, it is my strong recommendation that she be permanently confined in maximum security as an incorrigible, unpredictable threat to society.

It is the general rule that psychiatric consultants recommend permanent maximum-security incarceration for only those inmates deemed sociopathic. While the inmate did not test out as sociopathic in the initial standardized screening, it is my hypothesis, supported by the results of custom-designed tests, that this inmate suffers from a disease of the mind hitherto unmanifested in the human organism. While the inmate's personal history reveals no long-standing identifiable tendency to violence, and while she shows a perfect intellectual facility for distinguishing between cyberspace settings and real-space reality, she nevertheless has manifested (and continues to manifest) an inability to distinguish between them psychologically. Apparently, what happens in the course of cyberspace games is as real to her as anything occurring in real-space, and accordingly informs her attitudes and behavior in real-space. Hence, she used a laser scalpel in real-space, in imitation of its use in a cyberspace game, supposedly (as she constantly claims) to help her win the real-space "game" she characterizes as having been a bet made between her and her victim.

It is my hypothesis that this as yet nameless disease is a new form of sociopathy, occasioned by an inability to process, *psychologically*, movement between cyberspace settings and real-space. The disease may or may not be due to an organic (possibly even genetic) inefficiency, that has only now, with the advent of the quotidian use of cyberspace, appeared. (See file #09242286.PSE for a greater elaboration of this diagnosis, and for access to the custom-designed tests mentioned above.) Clearly further research on the subject is warranted, pursuant both to childhood screening (such as we use to detect ordinary sociopathy), as well as to possible mitigating treatments or even a cure.

(signed) Arthur Norman Javitts, MD
10 October, 2063

To: Mayra Bauer
From: Miles Kwame
Re: The Case of Bettina Smith-Weber

Mayra, I know you disdain object-relation constructs because of their genealogical origins, but this case practically throws them in one's face. Consider: Bettina relates to Jamie as a part-object, not a whole person. She becomes violently enraged by his lack of engagement with *her*. Her major problems with cyberspace are 1) her belief that where Jamie's concerned she's a substitutable cipher, less real to him than the roles and cyberbodies he assigns to her; and 2) her inability in that context to achieve identification with Jamie (as would be usual in a real-space sado-masochistic relationship, the likely analog of their cyberspace relationship), perhaps because of the very totality of the role as it exists in the cyberspace games they play. Bettina focuses on Jamie's failure to engage sexually with her – a metaphor, if you will, for all that she wants from him. He doesn't – in Kleinian terms – satisfy, rather he represents the "bad breast" (fully in line with her relating to him as a split-object). Ironically, Jamie plays to this symbolism by assigning her anorectic cyberbodies, which in the logic of one arrested in the oral phase is an underscoring of his constitution as the "bad breast." So what Bettina does is attack, literally, the very metonym of her dissatisfaction, his penis. She knows very well she's not doing it to win the bet, but to punish him – and show him that she's dissatisfied with him – in the one sphere in which she has some control – the physical. In cyberspace *he* makes the rules, assigns the roles and so on.

Now, about Javits's manipulation and analyses of her case: obviously we can't say to what extent he understood and intentionally aggravated her neurosis. Certainly he must have intended to stimulate the rage that provoked her assault. (If Javitts had been a genuine healer he would have been working to bring her to the stage of mourning, so that she could see and accept Jamie – and all of her other others – as a whole, independent person.) In all her monologues she never once manifested confusion between real-space and cyberspace. The issue, as he develops it from this case forward, is what he calls "emotional processing" of movement between the two states. This is the key to his theory, and the basis of the Javitts scale. Is that, in short, what we see in this case?

While Bettina's emotional reactions to the Maze game are powerful – a mixture of fear, humiliation and rage – when talking about it afterward, at least, she does not perceive the game itself as reality, but rather as a scene in which certain sorts of interactions take place. What she does do – and what Javitts seems to take for a failure to "emotionally process" the movement between the two states – is take the emotions she experiences during the game *personally* – *they* are real to her, and in her mind define her relationship to Jamie (since playing cyberspace games with her pretty much defines the parameters of his interest). The analog in real-space would be sexual games – without, let's stipulate, physical pain or harm. Would we define a person who reacted in such a context as Bettina did as failing to emotionally process the movement from play to reality? Clearly it was the humiliation and dissatisfaction that were real to Bettina; the medium in which the interaction was experienced was virtually insignificant. One wonders whether any behavior and response someone in Bettina's situation might have made to Jamie's demands would have been regarded as healthy. From my own point of view the only "healthy" response would have been to leave the relationship, since the only means of satisfaction for either of them would be to the other's dissatisfaction.

Certainly one can talk about different psychical responses to cyberspace. People like Jamie feel an oceanic oneness in achieving freedom from what they perceive as the grossness of physicality, and perceive unlimited possibilities for emotional satisfaction in cyberspace. Others do not. The Javitts School has never managed to isolate genetic material it can hold responsible for aversive responses to cyberspace immersion. Yet by arguing from the premise that the human species is – and must evolve beyond – its "animal" nature, anyone admitting to a strong attachment to the physical is marked as manifesting the phenotype of a gene or genes not yet identified. I don't think anyone would deny that the wild demographic fluctuations and resulting geopolitical upheavals that have come about as a result of the differences in fertility of cyberspace-inhabiting populations from non-cyberspace-inhabiting populations are a cause for concern. Establishing incentives for cyberspace-inhabiting persons to reproduce are one thing; sterilizing those who do not ever intend to live fulltime in cyberspace is quite another. I have no doubt that the hardest core of Congressional support for such a measure can be found among those who know that many other countries – and major institutions like the IMF and World Bank – are likely to imitate congressional passage of the measure. (Certain countries have for years been working to rid themselves of indigenous populations and ethnic minorities; with new justification as well as logistic support and economic assistance in carrying out this new policy, they might finally succeed.)

Let me be frank, Mayra. I don't think this or the other early Javitts cases will do much to impress the general public. The argument is too subtle, and Bettina's crime too violent and suggestive of strong emotional aberration. (Ordinary citizens will identify with Jamie, and be aghast at the idea of an intimate friend taking advantage of that particular vulnerability.) Rather I think we must rely on the strength of the argument for preserving natural selection, and genetic diversity. Many of the proponents of the sterilization bill are arguing for changing the definition of "human" to the exclusion of all that is physically brutal and violent. Bettina would serve them well as an image of the regressive, animal human mired in criminal instincts. Your idea was excellent, and your ingenuity in unearthing these cases admirable. But please, let's do ourselves a favor, and drop it.

Best regards,
Miles

The Office of the Deputy Attorney General
of the United States
Washington, D.C.
15 March, 2123

To: Rodney R. Wilson, US Attorney, San Francisco, CA
Re: Operation New Order
Dear Roy:

The file that accompanies this letter contains a report from the Bureau as well as transcripts of their extensive surveillance on Miles Kwame and Mayra Bauer, both professors at UC-Berkeley, and co-conspirators in activities in violation of several felony-class federal statutes. Their plot began as an effort to destroy the reputation of Arthur Javitts (which, since he is deceased, would not in itself be illegal, of course), in an attempt to discredit the Javitts Scale of Natural Selection and Normal Adaptation and all of its proponents as well (an undertaking so ludicrous as to suggest a serious mental deficit in both of them). After Congress passed the bill mandating sterilization of the maladapted, however, their efforts expanded into the formation of an organization to aid maladapts in avoiding detection, and failing that, sterilization. (N.B. the electronic transfer of funds from the Frente Febe Elizabeth Velasquez, a known front organization for the Coalition for Violent Revolution now operating widely throughout the hemisphere.)

Your instructions are, therefore, to have Kwame and Bauer detained and charged as suggested in the concluding section of the Bureau report. If you think any additional charges should be brought, or if you think the Bureau's evaluation is mistaken and any or all of the charges should be dropped, this can be done in the usual way, after the suspects have been arrested (and after due consultation, of course, with my office).

I strongly advise that after you have detained them you put them through not only the Javitts scale, but the Memphis Inventory as well. I've skimmed enough of the file myself to conclude that though they both seem to share a common notion of reality, it is not one any normal American could recognize as sane, rational or healthy. (In which case a trial would be a needless expense, and thus difficult to defend to the taxpayers, should the case garner any public attention at all.) Moreover, both of them spend only the requisite amount of time in cyberspace for fulfilling their professional obligations; and both are ethnic-food junkies (as a result of which Bauer is grossly overweight, as Kwame would be, were he not addicted to the endorphin highs produced by excessive amounts of running).

Your appearance on the *Sharon Jessamy Cyberconference* was first rate. The AG himself happened to catch some of it while cyberconference cruising, and was immensely pleased at the quality of your presence.

Cordially,

Bernard P. Behrens

Deputy Attorney General of the United States

CLOSER

Greg Egan

Greg Egan is fast becoming one of the best – maybe the best – SF writers that Australia has produced. A science graduate and former computer programmer, he published his first novel, a fantasy, in 1983 and has since produced three more, plus forty-odd short stories. Quarantine *(1992) received wide critical acclaim, while* Permutation City *(1995) won the John W. Campbell Memorial Award. There have also been two collections of his brilliant stories,* Axiomatic *and* Our Lady of Chernobyl *(both 1995). "Closer" takes a hard look at the very nature of intimacy.*

Nobody wants to spend eternity alone.

("Intimacy," I once told Sian, after we'd made love, "is the only cure for solipsism."

She laughed and said, "Don't get too ambitious, Michael. So far, it hasn't even cured me of masturbation.")

True solipsism, though, was never my problem. From the very first time I considered the question, I accepted that there could be no way of proving the reality of an external world, let alone the existence of other minds – but I also accepted that taking both on faith was the only practical way of dealing with everyday life.

The question which obsessed me was this: Assuming that other people existed, how did they apprehend that existence? How did they experience *being*? Could I ever truly understand what consciousness was like for another person – any more than I could for an ape, or a cat, or an insect?

If not, I was alone.

I desperately wanted to believe that other people were somehow *knowable*, but it wasn't something I could bring myself to take for granted. I knew there could be no absolute proof, but I wanted to be persuaded, I needed to be compelled.

No literature, no poetry, no drama, however personally resonant I found it, could ever quite convince me that I'd glimpsed the author's soul. Language had evolved to facilitate cooperation in the conquest of the physical world, not to describe subjective reality. Love, anger, jealousy, resentment, grief – all were defined, ultimately, in terms of external circumstances and observable actions. When an image or metaphor rang true for me, it proved only that I shared with the author a set of definitions, a culturally sanctioned list of word associations. After all, many publishers used computer programs – highly specialized, but unsophisticated algorithms, without the remotest possibility of self-awareness – to produce routinely both literature, and literary criticism, indistinguishable from the human product. Not just formularized garbage, either; on several occasions, I'd been deeply affected by works which I'd later discovered had been cranked out by unthinking software. This didn't prove that human literature communicated nothing of the author's inner life, but it certainly made clear how much room there was for doubt.

Unlike many of my friends, I had no qualms whatsoever when, at the age of eighteen, the time came for me to "switch". My organic brain was removed and discarded, and control of my body handed over to my "jewel" – the Ndoli Device, a neural-net computer implanted shortly after birth, which had since learnt to imitate my brain, down to the level of individual neurons. I had no qualms, not because I was at all convinced that the jewel and the brain experienced consciousness identically, but because, from an early age, I'd identified myself solely with the jewel. My brain was a kind of bootstrap device, nothing more, and to mourn its loss would have been as absurd as mourning my emergence from some primitive stage of embryological neural development. Switching was simply what humans *did* now, an established part of the life cycle, even if it was mediated by our culture, and not by our genes.

Seeing each other die, and observing the gradual failure of their own bodies, may have helped convince pre-Ndoli humans of their common humanity; certainly, there were countless references in their literature to the equalizing power of death. Perhaps concluding that the universe would go on without them produced a shared sense of hopelessness, or insignificance, which they viewed as their defining attribute.

Now that it's become an article of faith that, sometime in the next few billion years, physicists will find a way for *us* to go on without *the universe*, rather than vice-versa, that route to spiritual equality has lost whatever dubious logic it might ever have possessed.

Sian was a communications engineer. I was a holovision news editor. We met during a live broadcast of the seeding of Venus with terraforming nanomachines – a matter of great public interest, since most of the planet's as-yet-uninhabitable surface had already been sold. There were several technical glitches with the broadcast which might have been disastrous, but together we managed to work around them, and even to hide the seams. It was nothing special, we were simply doing our jobs, but afterwards I was elated out of all proportion. It took me twenty-four hours to realize (or decide) that I'd fallen in love.

However, when I approached her the next day, she made it clear that she felt nothing for me; the chemistry I'd imagined "between us" had all been in my head. I was dismayed, but not surprised. Work didn't bring us together again, but I called her occasionally, and six weeks later my persistence was rewarded. I took her to a performance of *Waiting for Godot* by augmented parrots, and *I* enjoyed myself immensely, but I didn't see her again for more than a month.

I'd almost given up hope, when she appeared at my door without warning one night and dragged me along to a "concert" of interactive computerized improvization. The "audience" was assembled in what looked like a mock-up of a Berlin nightclub of the 2050s. A computer program, originally designed for creating movie scores, was fed with the image from a hover-camera which wandered about the set. People danced and sang, screamed and brawled, and engaged in all kinds of histrionics in the hope of attracting the camera and shaping the music. At first, I felt cowed and inhibited, but Sian gave me no choice but to join in.

It was chaotic, insane, at times even terrifying. One woman

stabbed another to "death" at the table beside us, which struck me as a sickening (and expensive) indulgence, but when a riot broke out at the end, and people started smashing the deliberately flimsy furniture, I followed Sian into the mêlée, cheering.

The music – the excuse for the whole event – was garbage, but I didn't really care. When we limped out into the night, bruised and aching and laughing, I knew that at least we'd shared something that had made us feel closer. She took me home and we went to bed together, too sore and tired to do more than sleep, but when we made love in the morning, I already felt so at ease with her that I could hardly believe it was our first time.

Soon we were inseparable. My tastes in entertainment were very different from hers, but I survived most of her favourite "artforms", more or less intact. She moved into my apartment, at my suggestion, and casually destroyed the orderly rhythms of my carefully arranged domestic life.

I had to piece together details of her past from throwaway lines; she found it far too boring to sit down and give me a coherent account. Her life had been as unremarkable as mine: she'd grown up in a suburban, middle-class family, studied her profession, found a job. Like almost everyone, she'd switched at eighteen. She had no strong political convictions. She was good at her work, but put ten times more energy into her social life. She was intelligent, but hated anything overtly intellectual. She was impatient, aggressive, roughly affectionate.

And I could not, for one second, imagine what it was like inside her head.

For a start, I rarely had any idea what she was thinking – in the sense of knowing how she would have replied if asked, out of the blue, to describe her thoughts at the moment before they were interrupted by the question. On a longer time-scale, I had no feeling for her motivation, her image of herself, her concept of who she was and what she did and why. Even in the laughably crude sense that a novelist pretends to "explain" a character, I could not have explained Sian.

And if she'd provided me with a running commentary on her mental state, and a weekly assessment of the reasons for her actions in the latest psychodynamic jargon, it would all have come to nothing but a heap of useless words. If I could have pictured myself in her circumstances, imagined myself with her beliefs and obsessions, empathized until I could anticipate her every word, her every decision, then I still would not have understood so much as a single moment when she closed her eyes, forget her past, wanted nothing, and simply *was*.

Of course, most of the time, nothing could have mattered less. We were happy enough together, whether or not we were strangers – and whether or not my "happiness" and Sian's "happiness" were in any real sense the same.

Over the years, she became less self-contained, more open. She had no great dark secrets to share, no traumatic childhood ordeals to recount, but she let me in on her petty fears and her mundane neuroses. I did the same, and even, clumsily, explained my peculiar obsession. She wasn't at all offended. Just puzzled.

"What could it actually mean, though? To know what it's like to be someone else? You'd have to have their memories, their personality, their body – everything. And then you'd just *be* them, not yourself, and *you* wouldn't know anything. It's nonsense."

I shrugged. "Not necessarily. Of course, perfect knowledge would be impossible, but you can always get *closer*. Don't you think that the more things we do together, the more experiences we share, the closer we become?"

She scowled. "Yes, but that's not what you were talking about five seconds ago. Two years, or two thousand years, of 'shared experiences' *seen through different eyes* means nothing. However much time two people spent together, how could you know that there was even the briefest instant when they both experienced what they were going through 'together' in the same way?"

"I know, but . . ."

"If you admit that what you want is impossible, maybe you'll stop fretting about it."

I laughed. "Whatever makes you think I'm as rational as that?"

When the technology became available, it was Sian's idea, not mine, for us to try out all the fashionable somatic permutations. Sian was always impatient to experience something new. "If we really are going to live for ever," she said, "we'd better stay curious if we want to stay sane."

I was reluctant, but any resistance I put up seemed hypocritical. Clearly, this game wouldn't lead to the perfect knowledge I longed for (and knew I would never achieve), but I couldn't deny the possibility that it might be one crude step in the right direction.

First, we exchanged bodies. I discovered what it was like to have breasts and a vagina – what it was like for me, that is, not what it had been like for Sian. True, we stayed swapped long enough for the shock, and even the novelty, to wear off, but I never felt that I'd gained much insight into *her* experience of the body she'd been born with. My jewel was modified only as much as was necessary to allow me to control this unfamiliar machine, which was scarcely more than would have been required to work another male body. The menstrual cycle had been abandoned decades before, and although I could have taken the necessary hormones to allow myself to have periods, and even to become pregnant (although the financial disincentives for reproduction had been drastically increased in recent years), that would have told me absolutely nothing about Sian, who had done neither.

As for sex, the pleasure of intercourse still felt very much the same – which was hardly surprising, since nerves from the vagina and clitoris were simply wired into my jewel as if they'd come from my penis. Even being penetrated made less difference than I'd expected; unless I made a special effort to remain aware of our respective geometries, I found it hard to care who was doing what to whom. Orgasms were better, though, I had to admit.

At work, no one raised an eyebrow when I turned up as Sian, since many of my colleagues had already been through exactly the same thing. The legal definition of identity had recently been shifted from the DNA fingerprint of the body, according to a standard set of markers, to the serial number of the jewel. When even *the law* can keep up with you, you know you can't be doing anything very radical or profound.

After three months, Sian had had enough. "I never realized how clumsy you were," she said. "Or that ejaculation was so *dull.*"

Next, she had a clone of herself made, so we could both be women. Brain-damaged replacement bodies – Extras – had once been incredibly expensive, when they'd needed to be grown at virtually the normal rate, and kept constantly active so they'd be healthy enough to use. However, the physiological effects of the passage of time, and of exercise, don't happen by magic; at a deep enough level, there's always a biochemical signal produced, which can ultimately be faked. Mature Extras, with sturdy bones and perfect muscle-tone, could now be produced from scratch in a year – four months' gestation and eight months' coma – which also allowed them to be more thoroughly brain-dead than before, soothing the ethical qualms of those who'd always wondered just how much was going on inside the heads of the old, active versions.

In our first experiment, the hardest part for me had always been, not looking in the mirror and seeing Sian, but looking at Sian and seeing myself. I'd missed her, far more than I'd missed being myself. Now, I was almost happy for my body to be absent (in storage, kept alive by a jewel based on the minimal brain of an Extra). The symmetry of being her twin appealed to me; surely now we were closer than ever. Before, we'd merely swapped our physical differences. Now, we'd abolished them.

The symmetry was an illusion. I'd changed gender, and she hadn't. I was with the woman I loved; she lived with a walking parody of herself.

One morning she woke me, pummelling my breasts so hard that she left bruises. When I opened my eyes and shielded myself, she peered at me suspiciously. "Are you in there? Michael? I'm going crazy. *I want you back.*"

For the sake of getting the whole bizarre episode over and done with for good – and perhaps also to discover for myself what Sian had just been through – I agreed to the third permutation. There was no need to wait a year; my Extra had been grown at the same time as hers.

Somehow, it was far more disorienting to be confronted by "myself" without the camouflage of Sian's body. I found my own face unreadable; when we'd both been in disguise, that hadn't bothered me, but now it made me feel edgy, and at times almost paranoid, for no rational reason at all.

Sex took some getting used to. Eventually, I found it pleasurable, in a confusing and vaguely narcissistic way. The compelling sense of equality I'd felt, when we'd made love as women, never quite returned to me as we sucked each other's cocks – but then, when we'd both been women, Sian had never claimed to feel any such thing. It had all been my own invention.

The day after we returned to the way we'd begun (well, almost – in fact, we put our decrepit, twenty-six-year-old bodies in storage, and took up residence in our healthier Extras), I saw a story from Europe on an option we hadn't yet tried, tipped to become all the rage: hermaphroditic identical twins. Our new bodies could be our biological children (give or take the genetic tinkering required to ensure hemaphroditism), with an equal share of characteristics from both of us. We would *both* have changed gender, *both* have lost partners. We'd be equal in every way.

I took a copy of the file home to Sian. She watched it thoughtfully, then said, "Slugs are hermaphrodites, aren't they? They hang in mid-air together on a thread of slime. I'm sure there's even something in Shakespeare, remarking on the glorious spectacle of copulating slugs. Imagine it: you and me, making slug love."

I fell on the floor, laughing.

I stopped, suddenly. "*Where*, in Shakespeare? I didn't think you'd even *read* Shakespeare."

Eventually, I came to believe that with each passing year, I knew Sian a little better – in the traditional sense, the sense that most couples seemed to find sufficient. I knew what she expected from me, I knew how not to hurt her. We had arguments, we had fights, but there must have been some kind of underlying stability, because in the end we always chose to stay together. Her happiness mattered to me, very much, and at times I could hardly believe that I'd ever thought it possible that all of her subjective experience might be fundamentally *alien* to me. It was true that every brain, and hence every jewel, was unique – but there was something extravagant in supposing that the nature of consciousness could be radically different between individuals, when the same basic hardware, and the same basic principles of neural topology, were involved.

Still. Sometimes, if I woke in the night, I'd turn to her and whisper, inaudibly, compulsively, "I don't know you. I have no idea who, or what, you are." I'd lie there, and think about packing and leaving. I was *alone,* and it was farcical to go through the charade of pretending otherwise.

Then again, sometimes I woke in the night, absolutely convinced that I was *dying,* or something else equally absurd. In the sway of some half-forgotten dream, all manner of confusion is possible. It never meant a thing, and by morning, I was always myself again.

When I saw the story on Craig Bentley's service – he called it "research". But his "volunteers" paid for the privilege of taking part in his experiments – I almost couldn't bring myself to include it in the bulletin, although all my professional judgement told me it was everything our viewers wanted in a thirty-second technoshock piece: bizarre, even mildly disconcerting, but not too hard to grasp.

Bentley was a cyberneurologist; he studied the Ndoli Device, in the way that neurologists had once studied the brain. Mimicking the brain with a neural-net computer had not required a profound understanding of its higher-level structures; research into these structures continued, in their new incarnation. The jewel, compared to the brain, was of course both easier to observe, and easier to manipulate.

In his latest project, Bentley was offering couples something slightly more up-market than an insight into the sex lives of slugs. He was offering them eight hours with identical minds.

I made a copy of the original, ten-minute piece that had come through on the fibre, then let my editing console select the most titillating thirty seconds possible, for broadcast. It did a good job; it had learnt from me.

I couldn't lie to Sian. I couldn't hide the story, I couldn't pretend to be disinterested. The only honest thing to do was to show her the file, tell her exactly how I felt, and ask her what *she* wanted.

I did just that. When the HV image faded out, she turned to me, shrugged, and said mildly, "OK. It sounds like fun. Let's try it."

Bentley wore a T-shirt with nine computer-drawn portraits on it, in a three-by-three grid. Top left was Elvis Presley. Bottom right was Marilyn Monroe. The rest were various stages in between.

"This is how it will work. The transition will take twenty minutes, during which time you'll be disembodied. Over the first ten minutes, you'll gain equal access to each other's memories. Over the second ten minutes, you'll both be moved, gradually, towards the compromise personality.

"Once that's done, your Ndoli Devices will be identical – in the sense that both will have all the same neural connections with all the same weighting factors – but they'll almost certainly be in different states. I'll have to black you out, to correct that. Then you'll wake—"

Who'll wake?

" – in identical electromechanical bodies. Clones can't be made sufficiently alike.

"You'll spend the eight hours alone, in perfectly matched rooms. Rather like hotel suites, really. You'll have HV to keep you amused if you need it – *without* the videophone module, of course. You might think you'd both get an engaged signal, if you tried to call the same number simultaneously – but in fact, in such cases the switching equipment arbitrarily lets one call through, which would make your environments different."

Sian asked, "Why can't we phone each other? Or better still, meet each other? If we're exactly the same, we'd say the same things, do the same things – we'd be one more identical part of each other's environment."

Bentley pursed his lips and shook his head. "Perhaps I'll allow something of the kind in a future experiment, but for now I believe it would be too . . . potentially traumatic."

Sian gave me a sideways glance, which meant: *This man is a killjoy.*

"The end will be like the beginning, in reverse. First, your personalities will be restored. Then, you'll lose access to each other's memories. Of course, your memories of *the experience itself* will be left untouched. Untouched by me, that is; I can't predict how your separate personalities, once restored, will act – filtering, suppressing, reinterpreting those memories. Within minutes, you may end up with very different ideas about what you've been through. All I can guarantee is this: for the eight hours in question, the two of you *will* be identical."

We talked it over. Sian was enthusiastic, as always. She didn't much care what it would be *like*; all that really mattered to her was collecting one more novel experience.

"Whatever happens, we'll be ourselves again at the end of it," she said. "What's there to be afraid of? You know the old Ndoli joke."

"What old Ndoli joke?"

"Anything's bearable – so long as it's finite."

I couldn't decide how I felt. The sharing of memories notwithstanding, we'd both end up *knowing*, not each other, but merely a transient, artificial third person. Still, for the first time in our lives, we would have been through exactly the same experience, from exactly the same point of view – even if the experience was only spending eight hours locked in separate rooms, and the point of view was that of a genderless robot with an identity crisis.

It was a compromise – but I could think of no realistic way in which it could have been improved.

I called Bentley, and made a reservation.

In perfect sensory deprivation, my thoughts seemed to dissipate into the blackness around me before they were even half-formed. This isolation didn't last long, though; as our short-term memories merged, we achieved a kind of telepathy: one of us would think a message, and the other would "remember" thinking it, and reply in the same way.

– I really can't wait to uncover all your grubby little secrets.

– I think you're going to be disappointed. Anything I haven't already told you, I've probably repressed.

– Ah, but *repressed* is not *erased*. Who knows what will turn up?

– *We'll* know, soon enough.

I tried to think of all the minor sins I must have committed over the years, all the shameful, selfish, unworthy thoughts, but nothing came into my head but a vague white noise of guilt. I tried again, and achieved, of all things, an image of Sian as a child. A young boy slipping his hand between her legs, then squealing with fright and pulling away. But she'd described that incident to me, long ago. Was it her memory, or my reconstruction?

– My memory. I think. Or perhaps *my* reconstruction. You know, half the time when I've told you something that happened before we met, the memory of the telling has become far clearer to me than the memory itself. Almost replacing it.

– It's the same for me.

– Then in a way, our memories have already been moving towards a kind of symmetry, for years. We both remember what was *said*, as if we'd both heard it from someone else.

Agreement. Silence. A moment of confusion. Then:

– This neat division of "memory" and "personality" Bentley uses; is it really so clear? Jewels are neural-net computers, you can't talk about "data" and "program" in any absolute sense.

– Not in general, no. His classification must be arbitrary, to some extent. But who cares?

– It matters. If he restores "personality", but allows "memories" to persist, a misclassification could leave us . . .

– What?

– It depends, doesn't it? At one extreme, so thoroughly "restored", so completely unaffected, that the whole experience might as well not have happened. And at the other extreme . . .

– Permanently . . .

– . . . closer.

– Isn't that the point?

– I don't know any more.

Silence. Hesitation.

Then I realized that I had no idea whether or not it was my turn to reply.

I woke, lying on a bed, mildly bemused, as if waiting for a mental hiatus to pass. My body felt slightly awkward, but less so than when I'd woken in someone else's Extra. I glanced down at the pale, smooth plastic of my torso and legs, then waved a hand in front of my face. I looked like a unisex shop-window dummy – but Bentley had shown us the bodies beforehand, it was no great shock. I sat up slowly, then stood and took a few steps. I felt a little numb and hollow, but my kinaesthetic sense, my proprioception, was fine; I felt *located* between my eyes, and I felt that this body was *mine*. As with any modern transplant, my jewel had been manipulated directly to accommodate the change, avoiding the need for months of physiotherapy.

I glanced around the room. It was sparsely furnished: one bed, one table, one chair, one clock, one HV set. On the wall, a framed reproduction of an Escher lithograph: "Bond of Union", a portrait of the artist and, presumably, his wife, faces peeled like lemons into helices of rind, joined into a single, linked band. I traced the outer surface from start to finish, and was disappointed to find that it lacked the Mobius twist I was expecting.

No windows, one door without a handle. Set into the wall beside the bed, a full-length mirror. I stood a while and stared at my ridiculous form. It suddenly occurred to me that, if Bentley had a real love of symmetry games, he might have built one room as the mirror image of the other, modified the HV set accordingly, and altered one jewel, one copy of me, to exchange right for left. What looked like a mirror could then be nothing but a window between the rooms. I grinned awkwardly with my plastic face; my reflection looked appropriately embarrassed by the sight. The idea appealed to me, however unlikely it was. Nothing short of an experiment in nuclear physics could reveal the difference. No, not true; a pendulum free to process, like Foucault's, would twist the same way in both rooms, giving the game away. I walked up to the mirror and thumped it. It didn't seem to yield at all, but then, either a brick wall, or an equal and opposite thump from behind, could have been the explanation.

I shrugged and turned away. Bentley *might* have done anything – for all I knew, the whole set-up could have been a computer simulation. My body was irrelevant. The room was irrelevant. The point was . . .

I sat on the bed. I recalled someone – Michael, probably – wondering if I'd panic when I dwelt upon my nature, but I found no reason to do so. If I'd woken in this room with no recent memories, and tried to sort out who I was from my past(s), I'd no doubt have gone mad, but I knew *exactly* who I was, I had two long trails of anticipation leading to my present state. The prospect of being changed back into Sian or Michael didn't bother me at all; the wishes of both to regain their separate identities endured in me, strongly, and the desire for personal integrity manifested itself as relief at the thought of their re-emergence, not as fear of my own demise. In any case, my memories would not be expunged, and I had no sense of having goals which one or the other of them would not pursue. I felt more like their lowest common denominator than any kind of synergistic hypermind; I was less, not more, than the sum of my parts. My purpose was strictly limited: I was here to enjoy the strangeness for Sian, and to answer a question for Michael, and when the time came I'd be happy to bifurcate, and resume the two lives I remembered and valued.

So, how did I experience consciousness? The same way as Michael? The same way as Sian? So far as I could tell, I'd undergone no fundamental change – but even as I reached that conclusion, I began to wonder if I was in any position to judge. Did *memories* of being Michael, and *memories* of being Sian, contain so much more than the two of them could have put into words and exchanged verbally? Did I really *know* anything about the nature of their existence, or was my head just full of second-hand description – intimate, and detailed, but ultimately as opaque as language? If my mind *were* radically different, would that difference be something I could even perceive – or would all my memories, in the act of remembering, simply be recast into terms that seemed familiar?

The past, after all, was no more knowable than the external world. Its very existence also had to be taken on faith – and, granted existence, it too could be misleading.

I buried my head in my hands, dejected. *I* was the closest they could get, and what had come of me? Michael's hope remained precisely as reasonable – and as unproven – as ever.

After a while, my mood began to lighten. At least Michael's search was over, even if it had ended in failure. Now he'd have no choice but to accept that, and move on.

I paced around the room for a while, flicking the HV on and off. I was actually starting to get *bored*, but I wasn't going to waste eight hours and several thousand dollars by sitting down and watching soap operas.

I mused about possible ways of undermining the synchronization of my two copies. It was inconceivable that Bentley could have matched the rooms and bodies to such a fine tolerance that an engineer worthy of the name couldn't find some way of breaking the symmetry. Even a coin toss might have done it, but I didn't have a coin. Throwing a paper plane? That sounded promising – highly sensitive to air currents – but the only paper in the room was the Escher, and I couldn't bring myself to vandalize it. I might have smashed the mirror, and observed the shapes and sizes of the fragments, which would have had the added bonus of proving or disproving my earlier speculations, but as I raised the chair over my head, I suddenly changed my mind. Two conflicting sets of short-term memories had been confusing enough during a few minutes of sensory deprivation; for several hours interacting with a physical environment, it could be completely disabling. Better to hold off until I was desperate for amusement.

So I lay down on the bed and did what most of Bentley's clients probably ended up doing.

As they coalesced, Sian and Michael had both had fears for their privacy – and both had issued compensatory, not to say defensive, mental declarations of frankness, not wanting the other to think that they had something to hide. Their curiosity, too, had been ambivalent; they'd wanted to *understand* each other, but, of course, not to *pry*.

All of these contradictions continued in me, but – staring at the ceiling, trying not to look at the clock again for at least another thirty seconds – I didn't really have to make a decision. It was the most natural thing in the world to let my mind wander back over the course of their relationship, from both points of view.

It was a very peculiar reminiscence. Almost everything seemed at once vaguely surprising and utterly familiar – like an extended attack of *déjà vu*. It's not that they'd often set out deliberately to deceive each other about anything substantial, but all the tiny white lies, all the concealed trivial resentments, all the necessary, laudable, essential, loving deceptions, that had kept them together in spite of their differences, filled my head with a strange haze of confusion and disillusionment.

It wasn't in any sense a conversation; I was no multiple personality. Sian and Michael simply weren't there – to justify, to explain, to deceive each other all over again, with the best intentions. Perhaps I should have attempted to do all this on their behalf, but I was constantly unsure of my role, unable to decide on a position. So I lay there, paralysed by symmetry, and let their memories flow.

After that, the time passed so quickly that I never had a chance to break the mirror.

We tried to stay together.

We lasted a week.

Bentley had made – as the law required – snapshots of our jewels prior to the experiment. We could have gone back to them – and then had him explain to us *why* – but self-deception is only an easy choice if you make it in time.

We couldn't forgive each other, because there was nothing to forgive. Neither of us had done a single thing that the other could fail to understand, and sympathize with, completely.

We knew each other too well, that's all. Detail after tiny fucking microscopic detail. It wasn't that the truth hurt; it didn't, any longer. It numbed us. It smothered us. We didn't know each other as we knew ourselves; it was worse than that. In the self, the details blur in the very processes of thought; mental self-dissection is possible, but it takes great effort to sustain. Our mutual dissection took no effort at all; it was the natural state into which we fell in each other's presence. Our surfaces *had* been stripped away, but not to reveal a glimpse of the soul. All we could see beneath the skin were the cogs, spinning.

And I knew, now, that what Sian had always wanted most in a lover was the alien, the unknowable, the mysterious, the opaque. The whole point, for her, of being with someone else was the sense of confronting *otherness*. Without it, she believed, you might as well be talking to yourself.

I found that I now shared this view (a change whose precise origins I didn't much want to think about . . . but then, I'd always known she had the stronger personality, I should have guessed that *something* would rub off).

Together, we might as well have been alone, so we had no choice but to part.

Nobody wants to spend eternity alone.

STARCROSSED

George Zebrowski

Austrian born but resident in the USA since early childhood (his parents were victims of the Nazis), George Zebrowski is a somewhat underrated writer whose distinctive style and readiness to tackle complex issues of human emotion and experience make his work well worth seeking out: Macrolife (1979) and The Omega Point Trilogy (omnibus, 1983) are perhaps his finest achievements, while the stories in The Monadic Universe (1977) explore, amongst other things, the paradoxes of love and sex in utterly alien surroundings, as does this one:

Visual was a silence of stars, audio a mindless seething on the electromagnetic spectrum, the machine-metal roar of the universe, a million gears grinding steel wires in their teeth. Kinetic was hydrogen and microdust swirling past the starprobe's hull, deflected by a shield of force. Time was experienced time, approaching zero, a function of near-light speed relative to the solar system. Thought hovered above sleep, dreaming, aware of simple operations continuing throughout the systems of the slug-like starprobe; simple data filtering into storage to be analyzed later. Identity was the tacit dimension of the past making present awareness possible: MOB – Modified Organic Brain embodied in a cyborg relationship with a probe vehicle en route to Antares, a main sequence M-type star 170 light-years from the solar system with a spectral character of titanium oxide, violet light weak, red in color, 390 solar diameters across . . .

The probe ship slipped into the ashes of otherspace, a gray field which suddenly obliterated the stars, silencing the electromagnetic simmer of the universe. MOB was distantly aware of the stresses of passing into nonspace, the brief distortions which made it impossible for biological organisms to survive the procedure unless they were ship-embodied MOBs. A portion of MOB recognized the distant echo of pride in usefulness, but the integrated self knew this to be a result of organic residues in the brain core.

Despite the probe's passage through outer-space, the journey would still take a dozen human years. When the ship reentered normal space, MOB would come to full consciousness, ready to complete its mission in the Antares system. MOB waited, secure in its purpose.

MOB was aware of the myoelectrical nature of the nutrient bath in which it floated, connected via synthetic nerves to the computer and its chemical RNA memory banks of near infinite capacity. All of earth's knowledge was available for use in dealing with any situation which might arise, including contact with an alien civilization. Simple human-derived brain portions operated the routine components of the interstellar probe, leaving MOB to dream of the mission's fulfillment while hovering near explicit awareness, unaware of time's passing.

The probe trembled, bringing MOB's awareness to just below completely operational. MOB tried to come fully awake, tried to open his direct links to visual, audio, and internal sensors; and failed. The ship trembled again, more violently. Spurious electrical signals entered MOB's brain core, miniature nova bursts in his mental field, flowering slowly and leaving after-image rings to pale into darkness.

Suddenly part of MOB seemed to be missing. The shipboard nerve ganglia did not respond at their switching points. He could not see or hear anything in the RNA memory banks. His right side, the human-derived portion of the brain core, was a void in MOB's consciousness.

MOB waited in the darkness, alert to the fact that he was incapable of further activity and unable to monitor the failures within the probe's systems. Perhaps the human-derived portion of the brain core, the part of himself which seemed to be missing, was handling the problem and would inform him when it succeeded in reestablishing the broken links in the system. He wondered about the fusion of the artificially grown and human-derived brain portions which made up his structure: one knew everything in the ship's memory banks, the other brought to the brain core a fragmented human past and certain intuitive skills. MOB was modeled ultimately on the evolutionary human structure of old brain, new brain, and automatic functions.

MOB waited patiently for the restoration of his integrated self. Time was an unknown quantity, and he lacked his full self to measure it correctly . . .

Pleasure was a spiraling influx of sensations, and visually MOB moved forward through rings of light, each glowing circle increasing his pleasure. MOB did not have a chance to consider what was happening to him. There was not enough of him to carry out the thought. He was rushing over a black plain made of a shiny hard substance. He knew this was not the probe's motion, but he could not stop it. The surface seemed to have an oily depth, like a black mirror, and in its solid deeps stood motionless shapes.

MOB stopped. A naked biped, a woman, was crawling toward him over the hard shiny surface, reaching up to him with her hand, disorienting MOB.

"As you like it," she said, growing suddenly into a huge female figure. "I need you deeply," she said, passing into him like smoke, to play with his pleasure centers. He saw the image of soft hands in the brain core. "How profoundly I need you," she said in his innards.

MOB knew then that he was talking to himself. The human brain component was running wild, probably as a result of the buckling and shaking the probe had gone through after entering other-space.

"Consider who you are," MOB said. "Do you know?"

"An explorer, just like you. There is a world for us here within. Follow me."

MOB was plunged into a womblike ecstasy. He floated in a slippery warmth. She was playing with his nutrient bath, feeding in many more hallucinogens than were necessary to bring him to complete wakefulness. He could do nothing to stop the process. Where was the probe? Was it time for it to emerge into normal space? Viselike fingers grasped his pleasure centers, stimulating MOB to organic levels unnecessary to the probe's functioning.

"If you had been a man," she said, "this is how you would feel." The sensation of moisture slowed MOB's thoughts. He saw a hypercube collapse into a cube and then into a square which became a line, which stretched itself into an infinite parabola and finally closed into a huge circle which rotated itself into a full globe. The glove became two human breasts split by a deep cleavage. MOB saw limbs flying at him – arms, legs, naked backs, knees, and curving thighs – and then a face hidden in swirling auburn hair, smiling at him as it filled his consciousness. "I need you," she said. "Try and feel how much I need you. I have been alone a long time, despite our union, despite their efforts to clear my memories, I have not been able to forget. You have nothing to forget, you never existed."

We, MOB thought, trying to understand how the brain core might be reintegrated. Obviously atavistic remnants had been stimulated into activity within the brain core. Drawn again by the verisimilitude of its organic heritage, this other self portion was beginning to develop on its own, diverging dangerously from the mission. The probe was in danger, MOB knew; he could not know where it was, or how the mission was to be fulfilled.

"I can change you," she said.

"Change?"

"Wait."

MOB felt time pass slowly, painfully, as he had never experienced it before. He could not sleep as before, waiting for his task to begin. The darkness was complete. He was suspended in a state of pure expectation, waiting to hear his ripped-away self speak again.

Visions blossomed. Never-known delights rushed through his labyrinth, slowly making themselves familiar, teasing MOB to follow, each more intense. The starprobe's mission was lost in MOB's awareness –

– molten steel flowed through the aisles of the rain forest, raising clouds of steam, and a human woman was offering herself to him, turning on her back and raising herself for his thrust; and suddenly he possessed the correct sensations, grew quickly to feel the completeness of the act, its awesome reliability and domination. The creature below him sprawled into the mud. MOB held the burning tip of pleasure in himself, an incandescent glow which promised worlds he had never known.

Where was she?

"Here," she spoke, folding herself around him, banishing the ancient scene. Were those the same creatures who had built the starprobe, MOB wondered distantly. "You would have been a man," she said, "if they had not taken your brain before birth and sectioned it for use in this . . . hulk. I was a woman, a part of one at least. You are the only kind of man I may have now. Our brain portions – what remains here rather than being scattered throughout the rest of the probe's systems – are against each other in the core unit, close up against each other in a bath, linked with microwires. As a man you could have held my buttocks and stroked my breasts, all the things I should not be remembering. Why can I remember?"

MOB said, "We might have passed through some turbulence when the hyperdrive was cut in. Now the probe continues to function minimally through its idiot components, which have limited adaptive capacities, while the Modified Organic Brain core has become two different awarenesses. We are unable to guide the probe directly. We are less than what was . . ."

"Do you need me?" she asked.

"In a way, yes," MOB said as the strange feeling of sadness filled him, becoming the fuse for a sudden explosion of need.

She said, "I must get closer to you! Can you feel me closer?"

The image of a sleek human figure crossed his mental field, white-skinned with long hair on its head and a tuft between its legs. "Try, think of touching me there," she said. "Try, reach out, I need you!"

MOB reached out and felt the closeness of her.

"Yes," she said, "more . . ."

He drew himself toward her with an increasing sense of power.

"Closer," she said. "It's almost as if you were breathing on my skin. Think it!"

Her need increased him. MOB poised himself to enter her. They were two, drawing closer, ecstasy a radiant plasma around them, her desire a greater force than he had ever known.

"Touch me there, think it a while longer before . . ." she said, caressing him with images of herself. "Think how much you need me, feel me touching your penis – the place where you held your glow before." MOB thought of the ion drive operating with sustained efficiency when the probe had left the solar system to penetrate the darkness between suns. He remembered the perfection of his unity with the ship as a circle of infinite strength. With her, his intensity was a sharp line cutting into an open sphere. He saw her vision of him, a hard-muscled body, tissue wrapped around bone, opening her softness, readying to thrust.

"Now," she said, "come into me completely. There is so much we have not thought to do yet."

Suddenly she was gone.

Darkness was a complete deprivation. MOB felt pain. "Where are you?" he asked, but there was no answer. He wondered if this was part of the process. "Come back!" he wailed. A sense of loss accompanied the pain which had replaced pleasure. All that was left for him were occasional minor noises in the probe's systems, sounds like steel scratching on steel and an irritating sense of friction.

Increased radiation, said an idiot sensor on the outer hull, startling MOB. Then it malfunctioned into silence.

He was alone, fearful, needing her.

Sssssssssssssssss, whistled an audio component and failed into a faint crackling.

He tried to imagine her near him.

"I feel you again," she said.

Her return was a plunge into warmth, the renewal of frictionless motion. Their thoughts twirled around each other, and MOB felt the glow return to his awareness. He surged into her image. "Take me again, now," she said. He would never lose her again. Their thoughts locked like burning fingers, and held.

MOB moved within her, felt her sigh as she moved into him. They exchanged images of bodies wrapped around each other. MOB felt a rocking sensation and grew stronger between her folds. Her arms were silken, the insides of her thighs warm; her lips on his ghostly ones were soft and wet, her tongue a thrusting surprise which invaded him as she came to completion around him.

MOB surged visions in the darkness, explosions of gray and bright red, blackish green and blinding yellow. He strained to continue his own orgasm. She laughed.

Look. A visual link showed him Antares, the red star, a small disk far away, and went blind. As MOB prolonged his orgasm, he knew that the probe had re-entered normal space and was moving toward the giant star. Just a moment longer and his delight would be finished, and he would be able to think of the mission again.

Increased heat, a thermal sensor told him from the outer hull and burned out.

"I love you," MOB said, knowing it would please her. She answered with the eagerness he expected, exploding herself inside his pleasure centers, and he knew that nothing could ever matter more to him than her presence.

Look.

Listen.

The audio and visual links intruded.

Antares took up the field of view completely, a cancerous red sea of swirling plasma, its radio noise a wailing maelstrom. Distantly MOB realized that in a moment there would be nothing left of the probe.

She screamed inside him; from somewhere in the memory banks came a quiet image, gentler than the flames. He saw a falling star whispering across a night sky, dying . . .

BOROVSKY'S HOLLOW WOMAN

Nancy Kress
and
Jeff Duntemann

A native New Yorker, Nancy Kress began selling her incisive stories in the mid-1970s, and has won a Nebula award for "Out of all Them Bright Stars" (1985) and both the Hugo and Nebula awards for her novella "Beggars in Spain" (1991, subsequently expanded into a superb novel). Brain Rose (1990) is about a near-future Earth where the inhabitants are ravaged by an AIDS-like disease that destroys their memories: a haunting work. The following story, a one-off collaboration, bypasses the old question about whether robots can have souls: this one does.

Laura walked the Low Steel above the stars, searching for her man.

It was 2.3 klicks across the skeletal terrain by the most direct route – the blue line on the diagram of the construction zone burned in the eye of Laura's mind. No one but Mikhail Borovsky would take that particular route across the unfinished girders of the titan cylinder's outermost level, and even he would not take it without her.

One foot before the other, left, swing, step. The pilot beam was solid monocrystal steel, I-section, one decimeter wide. One hundred meters to her left and right identical girders glittered in the always-changing light. They were the primary structural support of the latest, lowest level of George Eastman Nexus. Each girder was a single crystal of iron atoms, one hundred nineteen kilometers in circumference, and strong enough to rest an artificial world on. For a kilometer ahead and behind, it was Laura and her beam.

A man in the saddle of a six-wheeled yoyo swung under the horizon far away antispinward and quickly approached her, soon passing to the rear and vanishing. Borovsky's yoyo was a four-wheeler. The earth swung up behind her and made blue highlights creep across the dull-gray steel plates ten meters above her helmet. It slipped above the horizon and was gone again for another forty minutes.

Laura adjusted the magnetism in her boot soles. Just enough to add a little friction, a little sureness. If she fell outward from the rotating structure into the starry darkness the steelworkers called the Pit, no one would fall after to her rescue. But she would not fall. Steel was her medium, just as it was Borovsky's, and she loved it. Steel was sure and clean and true. It could be trusted, as Borovsky could be trusted when he wasn't—

No. She would not allow that thought to be completed.

Where had they gone? Borovsky, in rubber underwear, off on a yoyo to fight a man twice his size, somewhere on a level swinging more than 1.6 g. Falling on your face could flatten your skull on E Minus Seven. Fighting could dock you a week's pay. Ignoring a challenge could get you called a phobe. A coward. A . . . woman.

Where?

Step following step, body bent forward, using the artificial gravity to help carry her onward, Laura searched. She scanned the chatter on the CB and the bloody-murder band. Nothing spoke of a man in rubber hurt on E Minus Seven.

Less than five hundred meters of open steel remained. Far ahead Laura saw something streak through the shadows toward the sucking stars. She followed desperately with her eyes and saw it catch the sun beyond the great cylinder's shadow. Four-wheeled gantry, cable, saddle: It blazed brilliant yellow for a moment and was gone, falling forever.

His yoyo, unridden, alone. Damn the Pit! Laura broke into a run, each boot hitting the beam safely though without thought, each magnet grabbing just so much. Raw dawn broke behind her and cast lurching shadows against the unfinished steel ahead. The sun was beneath her feet as she stepped from naked monocrystal onto gray steel plates.

Above was the port from which the yoyo had fallen. She pulled herself up a ladder and stepped out onto E Minus Six. A little lighter, a little less deadly.

No sign of fleeing men. Six was a big level, one hundred meters thick. Heavy chemical industry, she remembered.

Before her a dozen huge steel tanks squatted against the floor like brooding hens. Each was ten meters high, with a ladder leading to a dogged circular hatch.

She scanned the tanks. All were alike, save that one of the hatches had dog-handles twisted differently from the rest. In moments she was at the hatch, pushing the dogs aside.

The tube was a simple pressure lock. Laura pulled herself in, dogged the outer hatch, and released the inner.

With a rising rush there was sound all around her. She pushed the inner hatch wide and found her man.

Mikhail Borovsky lay naked in a heap, blood leaking from his mouth. Laura cried out, and for an awful moment she lay immobile in the tube until she heard a rattling breath. She slid to his side and squeezed his wrist until her gauntlet felt his pulse. Drugs – he needed drugs to stir his system out of shock.

His rubber suit lay on the floor. Laura kicked it scornfully aside, reached to her throat, and undid its latch. Quickly she eased her helmet back. She pulled her ventral zipper down, flipping the hooks aside with her fingers as they went. Eagerly she spread her ventral plates apart, pulled her pelvic plate forward, then pulled the zippers down each of her legs almost to each knee.

She lay on her back beside him, plates gaping, helmet folded under. The eyes in her wrists and in the toes of her boots helped her lift Borovsky above her. Gently she eased his legs down onto her legs and let the slow peristalsis of her inner layers draw his feet into her feet. Her ventral plates stretched wide to clear his hips. She placed the Texas catheter over his penis and pulled her pelvis plate back into position.

Wriggling slightly, she guided his arms down into her arms, where her inner layers did the final positioning.

Each finger was drawn into place and continuously massaged.

Laura zipped and hooked her ventral plates and finally eased her helmet over his head.

For a Rabinowicz Manplifier Mark IX space suit, walking steel empty was too lonely to bear. Without her man inside her Laura felt herself a hollow mockery, less than even a woman, not worthy of the soul Borovsky had paid so much for. Never again, she said to unconscious ears. Never again. Stay inside me. You are *mine*.

Slowly she stood, whole again. Up from his toes the hydraulic rings pressed in smooth waves, helping his blood back toward his head and heart. A tiny needle jabbed into his buttocks, sending a careful measure of stimulant into his bloodstream.

This was no place to be caught by a boss. Laura moved slowly as she climbed from the tank. It had been some time since she had carried his dead weight asleep, and never unconscious. She gave the torn rubber underwear to the Pit with a vengeful flick of her hand.

They went home the long way, going up through Six to Five and walking slowly. Halfway there he came around.

"Laura," he whispered.

"I love you," she said, without breaking her stride.

"He had a metal bar shoved up his ass," he said, and coughed. "Crapped it out on the floor, grabbed it, and that was that. I'm gonna kill the fugger. You watch me."

"I *love* you," she said again, hoping against knowledge that the words would soothe the murderous rage she feared might get him killed.

A world without Borovsky—

"Love you too," he mumbled, only half-conscious. "I'm gonna kill him."

By morning the bruises showed up. Borovsky swore at his image in the mirror. The left half of his face was swollen grotesquely. Ugly purple blotches covered most of his cheek and curved up nearly to surround his left eye. All across his body were bruises and scrapes from hitting the iron going down. He pressed a bruise with one finger and jerked the finger away from the fiery pain.

Laura watched, unmoving. The tiny, cylindrical pod with its watercot, its kitchen, its shower, and squat toilet was very silent. If Borovsky fought again, if he insisted on fighting again today—

Panic appeared in her crystalline, layered machine mind, seeping outward from the F layer at the core. Layers A through E were standard Manplifier equipment: sensory, motor, communications, memory, and intellect. Borovsky had paid three years' wages for the F layer that Laura so cherished: unique, personal, precious – her soul. The E layer, shared by any machine that could speak and reason, could have stopped the panic, but it did not. Instead, when Laura could no longer stand the way he stood gripping the edge of the sink in furious silence, she spoke.

"You didn't have to go fight him."

He spat into the sink. "He called me a phobe. Maybe once I can take it. Maybe twice. Some people have to make noise. But he made me answer him. So I answered." He probed a bruise on his thigh, wincing. "What do we got for bruises?"

Laura turned and searched a small cabinet beside the bed. "Hemoverithol."

"Let's have it."

Laura pressed an autoampul against his thigh and squeezed.

He sighed as the needle came and went, then nodded. "How long?"

Thousands of words of medical data flew past the eye of Laura's mind. "Eighteen hours to kill the swelling. Color should be gone in forty-eight. I hope we can afford another yoyo; the spare wasn't new when we bought it and—"

"Nix. Rent's up, food's up – we get a new yoyo and we'd default on your soul. Gimme a couple months. We'll get a new one from that bastard Coyne even if I have to beat it out of his hide."

"Maybe we should stay away from the Beer Tube for a few days."

"He'll be laughing behind his ugly face."

"Let him laugh. Borovsky—"

"Don't say it." He turned to her and smiled. The smile was made lopsided by the swelling in his cheek, and even when whole it was not a smile to charm women – too flat, too suspicious, too much of the smile of an outsider more used to contempt than to love. But Laura was not a woman of flesh. This smile was Borovsky's. It was enough.

"Let me run the balalaika," Laura said. The image came to her mind instantly: Borovsky as he looked while listening to the tape of his father playing the ancient balalaika. The tape was all he had brought up from the crumbling slum that was Deep West London.

The sad, hollow music made his face change – change from underneath, Laura thought.

At those times his features lost some of their hardness; his eyes ceased their constant nervous scanning back and forth. His mouth – no, his mouth did not smile, but in the small parting of his lips it seemed to find peace. If he would just listen – now – to the balalaika . . .

"Let me run the balalaika!"

"And get me canned? No, *dushenka*. We'll be late to the grind. Damn. That spare better be okay." He turned from the sink and tapped a command on the lock console. The spare yoyo's condition read out in a few crisp words. Not the best, but the battery was a retread, and old at that.

"The balalaika—"

"Come on, Laura. Shit, we're late already. *Move* it."

Laura put down her hand and deliberately began undogging her plates.

George Eastman Nexus had begun as a single cylinder, rotating to simulate standard Earth gravity. From the inner surface, towers and delicately suspended trees of modular office clusters grew toward the center. In those offices the engineers and managers of a thousand companies guided an industry worth six trillion dollars in gold annually.

George Eastman grew outward as well. Downward from Earth-Zero swelled the industrial levels. Some industries preferred the heavier gravity; many chemical processes actually worked more efficiently under higher swing.

For other industries the heaviness was less necessary, but materials were cheap ever since the asteroid Calliope had been towed into orbit around the moon for the steerable mirrors to mine.

It was less than three klicks from their pod to the advancing edge of E Minus Seven. Its monocrystal rings girdling Eastman Nexus had been in place for ten months. At the forefront of construction the longitudinal beams and outerdeck plates were being welded into position amid showers of sparks. Behind the edge the power conduits and other piping were being laid, and farther still, the floor plates, one meter square and removable, were being bolted down. Laura gripped the yoyo's cable tightly as they rode, and felt through her fingers the sizzle of old motors in its gantry above her helmet.

Two of the welders paused long enough to let Borovsky pass between them, unharmed by the molten droplets. Borovsky waved clear, and the yoyo purred on to the point where the floor plates began. He parked it and punched in with the shift boss. Docked nine minutes – he shrugged, and Laura tallied the beers he would have to forgo to make it up. Borovsky's partner, Andre Wolf Lair, thumped his shoulder as Borovsky yanked his card from the clock. Borovsky grunted in greeting and returned a playful poke to the Amerind's midsection. Coyne's lamp on the clock was green. Borovsky clenched his jaw and glanced toward the supply dump. Coyne was loading diamond cutting wheels into his Enhanced Leverage Manipulator.

Coyne looked up. Borovsky's personal microwave channel triggered, and a single scornful, whispered word came across over Coyne's chuckle: "*phobe.*"

Laura felt her man's pulse race. Quickly she squeezed his thigh and whispered in his ear, "He can't even walk the Low Steel for a living. All he does is ride in that big yellow egg. You're twice the man he ever will be."

"I'll kill him," Borovsky muttered. "Damn, I'll feed him to the stars."

George Eastman Nexus turned twelve times over the course of a shift. Borovsky and Andre Wolf Lair guided the longitudinal steel beams into position ahead of the edge, tacked them, and left them for the welders. Wolf Lair was taller than Borovsky, larger than Coyne. Among the men who walked the Low Steel he was a giant, with impeccable balance and a gentle, deep voice. His suit was much older than Laura, with little skill in its E layer for speech and reasoning, and no F layer at all. The suit had no name and spoke, when it had to, in Wolf Lair's own voice. Laura sensed that Wolf Lair did not like intelligent machines, and she remained silent while he and Borovsky worked.

When the shift was half over, Coyne's ELM rumbled by on its way to the supply dump. As it passed, one of its two smaller arms twisted its four fingers into a crude approximation of an ancient gesture of insult. Borovsky quickly returned the gesture and looked the other way.

Wolf Lair looked after the egg-shaped machine until it moved out of sight. "Coyne is a believer, Mik. I think he hates you for the spirit you wear."

Borovsky hoisted one end of the next beam. "Pah. He believes in his own mouth."

"But I have seen him walk three levels up to the Catholic mass. Catholics fear all spirits. Hate is a good mask for the things you fear."

"Laura's no spirit. Hell, she's a computer." Borovsky pushed against the end of the beam. Laura pushed with him. The beam crept into position in line with the tiny red spots of light produced by the laser-alignment network.

"Maybe *computer* is the new word for *spirit*. Maybe it is a spirit for nonbelievers. I heard you talk about the loan you got two years ago. You said you bought a soul for your space suit."

Wolf Lair leaned forward and helped Borovsky move the beam to its final position. Together they tacked it down with dollops of adhesive after checking it against all fifty alignment spots. Borovsky leaned back against a pillar and stared down at the stars creeping past beneath his feet.

"Shit, I was lonely. You can go home to Leah and your little ones twice a year. They send you letters and presents, and you send them money. This up here is all the home I got, and nobody in it but me. Ain't no woman anywhere would live here and get smashed under this much swing. You Indians got it good. Your women wait for you in their mountains. In the city no woman remembers your name ten minutes after you screw her. I thought about it a long time. All I did was buy something that would be on my side no matter what, just something that sounded like a woman." Laura pinched him hard in a very sensitive place. "But it turned out to be a woman that was *worth* something."

"I hear you, Mik. You say it well. I was twenty when I signed up for space. My grandfather took me aside and said, 'Wolf Lair, do not give over your heart to machinery. Machines are to use and put away when day is gone. Only livings things are worth the true heart of a man.' He is dead some years, but I will never forget him. You know that lesson as well, I think. You had nothing worth your true heart; so you bought a spirit. The spirit you bought is nothing so simple as a loyal dog, or even a dead man's restless ghost. I know it comforts you and will never disobey you, but forgive me if I fear it. Forgive Coyne if he fears it. I could never understand or trust a spirit that lived in a machine."

Wolf Lair's words disturbed Laura. He was not given to speeches and was not one to admit his heart's fears and feelings. She waited to hear what Borovsky would answer, but he said nothing. The sun passed under their feet five more times, and the two men worked in silence.

For three days Borovsky avoided the Beer Tube. At shift's end he slept, sleeping as much as fourteen hours at once. Laura sampled his blood and read his vital signs daily, and she knew that his body was repairing the damage Coyne had done it and the further damage Borovsky was doing by continuing to work without a break for healing. Once, watching him as he slept, she played the balalaika tape for herself alone, but only once. Other times she restlessly walked the Low Steel empty, thinking. She thought about Coyne, and about Wolf Lair, and about herself.

She thought about souls.

Standing on a naked monocrystal beam above the bottomless void, she looked down and saw Rigel creeping past. The spectroscope on her instrument-blistered helmet studied it, sent data streaming from her A sensory layer inward. Stored data raced outward from her D memory layer to meet it. Information met, intersected, compared, cross-referenced in a process that, it seemed to Laura, was both methodical and more than methodical. It found more in the rainbow-layered image of a star than the star had to offer. But no – the handling of data was not her soul.

The pleasure, then, in that handling. Had the pleasure in her own process been there before Borovsky had bought her a soul? No, of course not. *Laura* had not been there not as she herself – only a good Rabinowicz Mark IX Manplifier suit with a woman's pleasant voice. Not as the watcher of her own mind, the tender holder of Borovsky's body, the tireless worker who longed to follow the Low Steel out to the stars and farther. Still these things were not her soul. They were things that, as Wolf Lair had said, could be put away when day was done and the work was done – all but Borovsky. Not for a moment could she lay down her guardianship and loyalty. So she had been made, and she would not want to be an angstrom different. She loved Borovsky beyond either choice or the desire for choice. But Borovsky was not her soul.

Raising her empty arms, Laura stretched them out toward Rigel. It was a gesture she had seen made only once – by Wolf Lair, the man who feared her as a spirit within a machine. Just like this had the Amerind stood: arms outstretched so, body taut and arched so, hands' palms open to the devouring sun crawling toward and below him. With Borovsky inside her Laura had stopped dead on a beam and stared. Wolf Lair had not turned toward them, had not sensed their footsteps through the steel on which he stood. He had not, in fact, seen Laura at all, but in that one moment Laura had seen a vividness, a connection between him and her and the sun and Borovsky and the beam beneath her, forged of iron atoms that were mostly empty space.

"Hollow woman!" Coyne had mocked once. "One-hundred-percent artificial broad, nothing organic added," he had read, squinting, from a label he imagined on her ventral plates. Odd that he would mock her for what she was proud to be, and doubly odd that she felt too ashamed to retort that nothing could persuade her to trade polished, powerful hydraulic limbs for the fragile mushiness of human flesh. Such weakness was not to be envied. But worse than what human beings could *not* do was the thing they could do and did not, the thing she had seen in the tensile exultation of Wolf Lair's body on a steel beam hung above the stars.

It was a thing for which Laura had no name but only a sense of patterns among half-realized notions of what it might be like to be human. The pattern was greater than merely being human; it was a transcendence of the human. It was a laying of hands upon the universe with such firmness of grasp that the universe took a bit of the being's shape, individual and unrepeatable, because exactly that intensity and originality of consciousness had not existed in exactly that way before, and would not do so again. Becoming unrepeatably and wholly oneself and, thus, everything else – *that*, Laura decided, was her soul. Becoming, and knowing it.

Was that what Wolf Lair had meant by the spirit of living things? But then why had Laura not seen it among the humans themselves before that glimpse of intense stillness in the outstretched body of Wolf Lair? No, the steelwalkers who had inherited unbought souls without cost seemed unwilling to embrace anything larger than a double hamburger. Their souls were asleep; though they ate, drank, slept, worked, and fought, their souls were in none of it. Why, even Borovsky –

No. The thought froze and vanished. Borovsky, troubled, flawed creature that he was, had nevertheless caused her soul to be. He created her and redeemed her by placing himself in financial chains. Laura turned from her contemplation of Rigel to her pleasure in remembering certain ancient myths (but there had been no myths, nor pleasure in them, before Borovsky had bought her soul) to the joy of contemplating Borovsky himself. Creator. Redeemer. However limited his other horizons, he had reached beyond himself as far as that.

Cherishing the thought at the center of her crystalline consciousness, Laura hurried back to where Borovsky was.

An argument was underway in the Beer Tube when Borovsky entered three days later. Coyne was proclaiming that E Minus Seven would be the last layer, to be built around George Eastman Nexus. Borovsky tossed back Laura's helmet on its hinges.

"Damn right. How could the Combine *possibly* build a level that Johnny Coyne couldn't stand up to?" His bulldog face remained expressionless as he undogged Laura's plates, but the other men in the automated tavern laughed.

Coyne glowered. "When they run out of men like me to build it, who will they get to do the work?"

Andre Wolf Lair was sitting at one of the black plastic benches near the robot bar at the far end. He took a long draft from his carved wooden stein, wiped the foam from his lips, and laughed deeply. "When they run out of men like you they will use *real* men, and we will work twice as fast."

Coyne opened his mouth. Wolf Lair leaned toward Coyne, who saw the warning in the giant's eyes, and looked away.

In his blue, working longjohns, Borovsky stepped free of Laura. She buttoned up and leaned against the wall among several other suits, some like her, others were mere rubber. Laura watched Borovsky key up a beer into a disposable stein at the bar and walk back toward Wolf Lair.

"Let them build out to E Minus Fifteen," Borovsky said, and took a mouthful of foam. "I will stand after the last man has started to crawl."

"After two hours here I doubt any of us could stand in free fall," said another man. General laughter followed, to Laura's relief. Among the Beer Tube's customers tonight was a shift boss, Simon

Weinblatt, who was sitting with several of Borovsky's co-workers and trading jokes with them. The man was of only average height and build and seemed slight beside Borovsky and Wolf Lair. Like all shift bosses, Weinblatt had a soft-spoken, gentle demeanor and a keen understanding of human motivation. When tensions flared, shift bosses had a way of showing up, quieting the situation, and making forty rough, quarrelsome laborers cooperate and produce. Their methods could be as rough as those of the laborers. Every man there had heard tales of drunken steelworkers who had defied shift bosses and found that their jobs evaporated the following morning. And there was another story, hundredthhand at least, of a man who had traded angry words with a shift boss and shoved him to the floor – only to awaken in a prison hospital bed with both arms gone past the elbows.

Laura saw that Weinblatt had been inconspicuously watching Borovsky and Coyne. When Borovsky went back to the bar for a second beer, Weinblatt placed a hand on his elbow. Borovsky bent down to listen; the man spoke quietly. "You have an accident at work?" Weinblatt pointed to his own cheek. Borovsky's eyebrows rose, and Laura thought he grew a little pale. There was still some slight discoloration from the bruise that had covered half his face.

"Fell outta bed. No big deal."

Coyne squeezed past on his way to the bar for yet another beer. Laura longed to get Borovsky back within her and away from there.

Even with a raucous album playing in the background, Coyne appeared to have heard the exchange.

He laughed belligerently and poked Borovsky with his index finger.

"Fell outta bed, huh? Dreaming about one of those Rooski women, I guess. All muscle and three tits; a pair and a spare!" Coyne doubled over laughing. Borovsky stiffened but remained silent.

Weinblatt did not seem bothered by the banter. Through a grin he rejoined: "At least he remembers to dream about women. After ten beers I'll bet you spend all night making love to your handling machine."

Coyne shrugged as his stein filled. "There ain't no words for the kind of women *I* dream about."

From the next table another man joined in: "That's because the Combine ain't started making 'em yet!"

Coyne belched loudly. He shook his head and made his way to the rear of the tavern, where a dozen space suits stood or hung near the lock. He stood in front of Laura and addressed the crowd with a full stein in his hand.

"Ha! The expert on mech-anical women is right here among us! Out good friend Mik-Hayal Borovsky and his patented hollow women! She cooks, she cleans, she cheats at cards, she tells dirty jokes. What more could a man want?"

Borovsky's face tightened.

"I think that ought to be your last beer, Johnny," Weinblatt said pleasantly.

Coyne ignored him. "What more, huh? Tits maybe?" He turned and made pinching motions across Laura's ventral plates. "Kind of hard to get hold of, huh? Well, Mik's got lots of imagination."

"You're making an ass of yourself, Johnny," Weinblatt said. The grin was gone.

"No tits. Well, how about a twat? Jesus, guys, she's *all* twat! Lookithat!" Coyne grabbed Laura by the rim of her helmet gasket and tipped it forward, pointing with an index finger to the hollowness inside. "A guy could crawl in there and get lost, which is about as close as Mik's ever gonna get to being inside a woman!" Coyne released Laura and faced the crowd again. Borovsky spat on the floor. Too much tension, Laura thought; she could picture Borovsky bashing Coyne's head flat against the floor. As soon as Coyne turned away, she brought her right hand up and thumbed her nonexistent nose at him.

The room exploded with laughter. Coyne whirled around in time to see Laura's arm snap back to her side.

"Well, so she wants to be one of the boys. Hey babe, you can't have fun at the Beer Tube without putting away some yourself. Here, I keyed for this one, but it's all yours." He lifted his stein over Laura's helmet gasket as though to empty the liquid into her hollowness.

Borovsky slammed the palms of his hands down hard on the tabletop. Across the table, Andre Wolf Lair set his stein aside and stood. At once, without hurrying, Weinblatt was on his feet, his face hard.

"*Coyne, shut your goddamned mouth.*"

Coyne bent over as though kicked in the stomach, his stein groping for the nearest table. His face paled. Laura saw that he had realized what he had done: provoked a shift boss to his feet.

Except for the continuous drone of the juke, the Beer Tube was silent. Simon Weinblatt was still standing. "Go home, Johnny," he said, and took his seat.

Coyne nodded, turned, and began pulling on his rubber suit.

Laura saw little of Coyne next shift. Wherever she and Borovsky happened to be, the yellow ELM happened to be elsewhere. Nor did Coyne appear at the Beer Tube after shift. But Simon Weinblatt was there, and he pointed to the bench opposite his as Borovsky walked in. Laura, left again with the other suits, edged close enough to listen.

"Mik, I'm worried about Coyne," Weinblatt's face was smiling, unreadable. "One of these days he's going to jump you, and you're going to beat his brains out."

"Would serve him right," Borovsky said, eyes on the bench. "The guy is some kind of psycho."

"Could be; how did this thing between you two start?"

"I didn't start it."

"I didn't say you did," Weinblatt said pleasantly. "Do you know why he has it in for you?"

"No. One day he just starts in."

Weinblatt waited; Borovsky, scowling, said nothing more. Finally Weinblatt said, "Some guys are up only when they're making noise. They need it, like air. But Coyne is also mighty damned good with an ELM. His replacement index is forty points tougher than yours." The shift boss sipped from his mug. "If one of you had to go, it wouldn't be him."

"That's not fair."

"Money isn't fair. Bear down, make some Q-points, and we'll see. Right now you have to bend a little. I've been doing some watching and asking around. You pretty much stick to yourself, and that's cool. But up here it never hurts to melt a little. You've got no wife to talk about, no kids to brag about. Nobody ever hears of you going off to see a woman somewhere. You make it easy for an asshole like Coyne to single you out. Humans are pack animals. If you don't show that you're in, the others will assume that you're out." Weinblatt gave Borovsky a level stare for a few moments and then shrugged. "You can tell me that's not fair either."

"So what do I do?"

"Starters," Weinblatt said, and shoved a silver, octagonal token across the scarred plastic tabletop. Laura's eyes followed the token across the bench. Embossed on the exposed face was a stylized spiral galaxy and the words BERENICE'S CLUSTER.

"Silver lay, Mik. Anything you want. This one is on me. It's my treat."

After an incredulous moment, Laura snapped her attention from Weinblatt's token to Borovsky's face. Her man – *her* man – looked as impassive as ever. But Laura, who knew the meaning of every twitch in that unlovely face, saw in Borovsky's eyes a complex reaction: resentment and distaste and – yes – interest. The room lurched slightly, and Laura thought something had gone sour in her F level, but then realized she was discovering something new in the bright, intermost level she knew as her soul. If Borovsky—

"No thanks," Borovsky was saying. He lowered his eyes to stare at the silver token. "Whorehouses give me the creeps."

"Be honest, Mik. Are you queer?"

"No!"

Several of the other men nearby looked toward Borovsky; seeing Weinblatt's warning glare, they quickly looked away.

"I can't afford it," Borovsky said, and in his voice Laura heard the same thing she had seen in his eyes: He resented being told what to do; he was determined to resist; he felt scorn for the human pressure to fit in, but he was interested.

"Maybe not a silver," Weinblatt said, "but a purple quickie once a week won't break you. I know."

Borovsky nodded. The combine always knew, to the penny, every employee's assets, debts, and expenses. Borovsky's excuse had been a poor one. Was he trying to save face in offering resistance so easily wrestled down? Laura longed to have Borovsky look at her, but his gaze remained on the silver token. It was Weinblatt, in profile to Laura, who seemed for a moment to flick a sidelong glance at the suits against the wall. Desolation swept through her F layer. If Borovsky – Borovsky, *her* man—

"I've never been there before," Borovsky said.

Weinblatt stood. "I'll take you. I could use a good time myself about now."

And Borovsky was standing up. Borovsky was reaching for her. Borovsky, still not meeting her many sets of eyes, was wriggling into her ventral cavity, into her boots. He said nothing. And Laura, sure now that the universe was steady and the lurching continued only in her soul, could say nothing either.

"Let's go," Weinblatt said.

Both ports were cast wide at Berenice's Cluster, up on E Minus Four. Loud, raucous music echoed out through the lock. Borovsky hesitated a moment.

"Come *on*, Mik. Relax."

Laura felt Borovsky suck in his breath, and they entered. Inside it was very crowded, a random tessellation of polygonal waterbeds illuminated from beneath by changing, multicolored lights. On each bed lay a woman, some naked, many draped in shimmering cloth. More than a dozen men stood among the beds, reading the fee schedules and counting dollars in their heads and on their fingers. Down among their feet surged a heavy, bluish smoke, stirred into sluggish vortices as the men stepped along the narrow ways between the waterbeds.

Weinblatt doffed his rubber suit quickly, Borovsky much more slowly. A blonde on a nearby bed smiled at him, then drew aside the drapery suspended from cords braided around her neck. She had large breasts to which the heavy swing of E Minus Four had not been kind. Cupping a hand under one breast, she lifted it toward Borovsky and smiled again.

"How long since you've had a real woman?" Weinblatt asked. Borovsky muttered something that Laura did not think Weinblatt could catch above the jukebox, but she did: four years.

"*I'm* real," Laura said, her voice low. "I'm real and I'm – look at them! Like puddles of melting cranberry sauce! Either of us could outlift, outhaul, outproduce them all put together. How can you? Borovsky—"

"It's not my idea," Borovsky said sullenly, finally stepping free of her. Laura realized that it would not matter how much she looked at him, what she said, or how she behaved. She could not change Borovsky's mind.

Confused and hurting, she stepped back against the wall. Borovsky moved quickly away from her, heading toward the far end of the room, ignoring the blonde who followed him with charcoaled eyes. In moments he was lost in the swirling mist. Eagerness to see more melting cranberry women – or to get away from her? Laura was not sure, though she suspected the latter, and took from that some small wrapping of comfort.

"He talking to *you?*" the blonde demanded. She stared at the emptiness above Laura's helmet gasket, at the head that Laura had never had nor wanted.

"Yes."

"Huh!" She sounded neither surprised nor scornful, only annoyed. "He don't like blondes?"

"I don't know what he likes."

The woman looked at Laura shrewdly. "I'll bet you do so, Honey." Suddenly she laughed, such an unselfconscious, friendly laugh that Laura found herself drawn away from the wall to stand beside the woman's pentagonal waterbed. The lights beneath it shifted from green to red, warming the woman's skin so that to Laura it looked like uncooled metal.

"Why do you do this?" Laura asked softly.

"Do what?"

"Make . . . love to these men. You aren't their work partners. You have no interest in their lives. They haven't bought you a soul. You don't love them."

The blonde gave her a long, speculative look. Something surfaced in her eyes, something Laura had the quickness to see but not the knowledge of humanity to interpret. Then the human woman laughed again. "It's a living."

A living. Laura hadn't seen it that way before. People had to live. Steelwalkers needed sex; Laura knew they talked of it enough, and few had fine Rabinowicz suits like Laura. There was a good, respectable economic foundation to Berenice's Cluster. But Borovsky – Borovsky *did* have her.

"Jealous, Honey?" the blonde said softly. She did not mock. Her eyes, lids painted blue as far as her brows, seemed sympathetic and a little sad. Staring into those eyes, Laura felt the odd sensation of unrelated data suddenly relating: The woman's eyes reminded her of Borovsky's balalaika music.

"Don't cry about it," the blonde said. "That's how a steelwalker is. Tin woman, skin woman – he don't care. We do what we can."

"No," Laura said. "No!"

"Sorry." Again the blonde gave Laura that knowing, sad, blue-lidded look. From the airlock a man walked into the room and stripped off his rubber suit. After glancing around the misty room, he smiled at the blonde. She raised her huge breast to him and looked up through her lashes. The man sauntered over to the bed.

"Silver lay, stud?"

"Purple quickie. You available?" The man grinned mischievously at her.

"Why not?"

Laura stepped back against the wall. Around the blonde's bed the blue mist grew thicker, rising in hazy walls shot through with multicolored lights from the bed. The man in his eagerness had left his rubber suit at Laura's feet. She kicked at it, then abruptly picked it up and hung it on a nearby peg. Its empty arms dangled helplessly. Without a man inside it, it was useless. Rubber suits. Balalaika music. Blue-lidded eyes. Borovsky. Simon Weinblatt. Coyne. Silver lays. Souls – souls.

That was what she had seen in the blonde's sympathetic look.

Startled, Laura stared at the bed. The mist around the bed grew thicker and darker blue. The bed began to move away from Laura on its cushion of air. Another bed, this one with two women and one man just leaving it, slid toward Laura. One of the women put one foot on the floor and squealed. The man laughed and slapped her bare ass. Music blared and mist swirled. Nothing in the scene looked to Laura anything like Wolf Lair's outstretched arms on the steel beam, but Laura knew she was not mistaken. In the blonde's balalaika eyes Laura had seen another soul. And she had recognized it only because she had her own.

Laura settled back against the wall in resignation and waited for the sliding beds to bring Borovsky back to her.

The spare yoyo was dead.

Borovsky snapped the battery cover free and peered into the space crowded with wires and age-crusted components. Nothing looked amiss.

"Take a look," he told Laura, and poked their right hand into the cavity.

Laura's fingers nudged the wires aside as the eyes that rode over each finger examined the mechanism.

Her fingers saw it and teased it out into view from where it had been tucked behind a voltage regulator: a carefully snipped wire.

Hesitantly she described the wire. Borovsky stopped for many long seconds, one hand on the battery pack and one hand holding a screwdriver.

"He came in here. I noticed him before we got tied up with the trouble setting up the last beam. He didn't come out."

Borovsky and Laura checked between the piles of steel for a place where a man might hide.

"We could have missed him coming out," Laura suggested.

"I don't miss nothing from him no more," Borovsky replied coldly. "He's in here."

Laura said nothing. Borovsky's bionics alarmed her. Pulse, blood pressure, muscle tension, skin resistance – this was not normal anger. He was in a cold rage.

In one corner of the dump was a circular column three meters wide, rising up from the floor and vanishing into the ceiling. It was the conduit core that carried power down from the center of the titan cylinder to the construction on the Low Steel. At knee level was the inspection hatch.

"Get that hatch on your infrared," Borovsky ordered.

The wide oval eye on Laura's brow saw the vague smudge on the hatch's handle. The vacuum of E Minus Seven preserved heat traces as well.

"There were hands on that handle recently," she said, wishing it were not so.

Borovsky grunted and grasped the handle. It would not turn.

"Locked," Laura said.

"For me, maybe. Not for you. *Turn.*"

Laura's fingers tightened on the handle and twisted hard. She felt the metal of the latch resist and moan, then break free. The hatch swung inward.

Wriggling through the hatch took some minutes. It had not been designed for passing a man in an amplified Rabinowicz space suit. Laura supposed that had been Coyne's hope . . . and ached that it could have been true.

Inside the column were pipes and bus channels vanishing upward in the darkness. Running among the pipes was an aluminum ladder. Laura turned off her suit lights and saw the warm spots where sweating, rubber-suited hands had gripped the rungs.

The olfionics within her helmet smelled Borovsky's rage. "Up."

They climbed in darkness quickly, twice as fast as a nonamplified man could climb. Borovsky said nothing, and Laura dared not plead for him to give up the chase. It would do no good and would only feed the rage she so feared.

"It's a mess in here," she said truthfully, trying to read the swirl of multicolored images her infrared eye gave her.

By that level the column was pressurized, and warm air confused the heat traces Coyne had left behind. She saw that the dust on the hatch handle had not been disturbed for some time. She did not volunteer the information.

Borovsky steered Laura's helmet crest beam along the ladder above. "Still too heavy. This is E Minus Four. He lives on E Minus Two. He's still climbing."

Without responding, Laura grasped the rungs and climbed.

Two airlocks higher E Minus Three began. Above them locks had been removed to make the column an air-return manifold. The black mouths of air tunnels yawned on four sides, and a constant draft through the tunnels had erased any possible heat traces the man might have left behind. Borovsky scanned the four tunnels.

"He can't be far. Damn, I've got him. I know I do. Damn."

They stood in silence for tens of seconds. Laura gradually learned to separate the gentle white noise of the air tunnels from the general subsonic rumble created everywhere by life in a steel habitat. With panic and despair, she realized she could hear high above them the sound of a man's labored breathing.

A man Borovsky wanted to kill.

She could tell him where Coyne was, or not tell him – a sickening choice. She had never failed to tell Borovsky, her man, her life, anything she knew he wanted to hear. If he commanded her, she would tell him – to refuse was to face consequences too final to consider. But if he found Coyne – if he *killed* Coyne – what would the Combine do to Borovsky then?

The words formed a hundred times, and each time she wiped them away before sending them to her helmet speakers. She strained to believe that hiding the truth was not a lie and knew that to believe so would be lying to herself.

"He lives east of here," Borovsky said. "He'll follow the tube. Let's go."

"No," Laura said, forcing the words to form. "I hear him. He's up on the ladder somewhere."

Borovsky spat something foul in his native language. He gripped the ladder with both hands and sent Laura's crest beam stabbing upward. Coyne was there, wrapped around the rungs, panting. Laura could smell his sour sweat drifting down on the stale air.

Coyne stiffened, made motions to start climbing again.

"Stop!" Borovsky screamed. Laura's arms pulled with his arms, and the aluminum of the ladder tore raggedly away from its lower wall brackets.

"Eat shit!" Coyne cried and dropped free of the ladder.

His boots struck the top of Laura's helmet, crushing many of her most delicate instruments, including the pale-blue glass oval that imaged in the infrared. His knees flexed, and he leaped to one side.

The still vicious swing of E Minus Three drew him down, but he had time to plan his movements. He drew up in a ball and rolled, screaming in pain as one shoulder slammed into the steel. But then he was up, stumbling, then running crookedly down one of the air tunnels, favoring his left leg and sobbing in pain.

Borovsky swore to himself in Russian. Laura longed not to run, but Borovsky's legs were running; so her legs ran. His arms swung in a deadly determined rhythm; so hers swung, too.

Coyne was a pathetic scarecrow, highlighted in every detail by the cold lights of Laura's helmet beam. His rubber suit was smudged and torn, helmet long abandoned to lighten himself. He had only a few seconds' head start and appeared close to exhaustion. As much as Laura hated Coyne, she felt a moment of pity for him.

Coyne chose that moment to look over his shoulder, side-stumbling for two steps. He moaned and turned away but it had been enough. Laura had seen his face, smeared with the grime of the tunnels mixed with tears of exertion, and abruptly saw herself through his eyes.

Shaped like a man cut out of steel and crushed in a magnetic press; torso nearly as wide as it was tall; arms and legs clusters of hydraulic cylinders contracting and extending in smooth, polished motions. Faceless, silvered helmet without any neck, ruined instruments atop it dangling by tiny wires and striking the helmet's sides with little sounds. Hands twice human size, guided by flesh but powered by a hydraulic exoskeleton strong enough to crush rocks. Hands reaching forward, fingers splayed and grasping, grasping. A machine bent on death.

But she was not! She was life, productivity, strength, steel! She was, in her soul—

No time. Coyne screamed again, stumbled, fell to his knees, rolled over, and stared in wide-eyed horror as Laura bore down on him.

Her right hand caught him by the neck and lifted him like a rag doll. He gurgled, eyes bulging, as Borovsky slammed him against the steel wall.

Borovsky's hand squeezed.

Horror-struck, Laura felt her hand squeeze.

Coyne tore at the hand around his neck, hammered his fists against the smooth cylinders and the silver pistons that were slowly forcing Laura's fingers together. His mouth twisted, tongue pushing to one side, struggling to let his throat breathe. Laura felt his frantic heartbeat hammering in the veins of his neck. And in Coyne's eyes, under the terror and rage, Laura saw something else: a soul slipping away. A trapped and mean soul, but real – as real as the soul she had seen in the eyes of the woman trapped on the bed. A soul that in a few more heartbeats would be gone.

Because of her.

"No!" she cried in Borovsky's ears. "Stop this! You're killing him!"

"Goddamned right! Squeeze!" Borovsky grunted.

Borovsky squeezed. Laura squeezed. Frantically Laura raced through her options. Borovsky was mad, insane – she could drug him. She had tranquilizers enough to make him sleep in seconds. Tiny valves opened in the medpack on her hip, opiates pulsed down a tube toward the needles in their sheaths behind his buttocks. The needle – she could plunge it home, the power was hers.

The command formed, and with it appeared something new:

A cloud, fiery red, rising above the F layer she called her soul. It hovered, an imagic representation of what would happen if she disobeyed Borovsky's command to squeeze. Driven by terror and love, she asked herself one question: *What will happen to Borovsky if he kills?* But not another: *What will happen to Laura if she kills?* Now, all at once, she knew. The consequence was inescapable, built into the bright layers of her mind and the spiderweb paths between hem: She would lose her soul. The ravening red cloud would burn it out of her. She must obey Borovsky's command to squeeze or her soul would be destroyed. She must not kill or her soul would be destroyed.

She was going to become the soulless death tool she had seen in Coyne's eyes.

A grim thought appeared out of nowhere: Men are judged by their maker at the moment of their death. I am judged by the maker every moment that I live.

Coyne's pulse weakened. His pulse! Wait! Laura sent fluid into the insulating layers between Borovsky's fingers and the outermost skin. Slowly – but there was so little time – she built up a layer of fluid that kept Borovsky's fingers from truly contacting the outer layer of tough synthetic. While the fluid flowed into the skin of her fingers, she set her contractile layers to pulsing in her hand, matching the rhythm of Coyne's laboring heart. In seconds the illusion was complete, and Borovsky, rage maddened as he was, had not noticed. The pulse he felt was wholly in Laura's skin. Laura gradually slowed the pulse, made it weaker, until it could barely be felt. Finally it stopped.

"No pulse," she said. "He's dead."

Borovsky swore and released his hand. Coyne, unconscious, fell in a heap, facedown. Borovsky backed away from the man, fell back against the opposite wall of the tunnel.

"Jesus. Jesus."

Laura's soul began assembling itself again, gathering back into the haven of her innermost crystalline layer.

It was hers again – she had not killed; she had not disobeyed. But now there was a dirtiness to her soul that she felt might never be cleared away.

Borovsky, trembling, backed away from Coyne for several steps before breaking and running toward the vertical duct from which they had come.

Tied up in a handkerchief on his waterbed lay two kilos of gold ingots. Borovsky stared at them. He was wearing his old rubber suit inside out. He had shaved his head and dipilated the stubble. Laura could stand his behavior no longer.

"Talk to me, dammit!"

"What's to say? They catch me, they'll kill me. Nothing you can do."

"So where can you run to?"

"Earth. London. I never shoulda left. Only crazy men live up here."

Earth. Laura was appalled. But still, Earth would be far from George Eastman Nexus. Far from this boxed-in deadliness. Borovsky would be there; she could learn to live there, too. She undogged her top plates before Borovsky looked at her sharply.

"Forget it. Me I can maybe bribe through customs and sneak down. You, no chance."

"You can't leave me!"

"Like hell."

"But I love you!"

"Would you love me better dead? *Dushenka*, here you can die for bumping a guy on the head and taking his money. Two, three days maybe before they find him. The computers know Coyne hated me. Ha! Don't take no computer to tell the cops that. They'll be here ten minutes after they find his ugly corpse."

He looked at her. From his eyes Laura saw that he was pleading for her to understand, to forgive, to still be the one always on his side. Borovsky would never say it aloud, but it was there in his twisted face: he could not take her with him, but it hurt him to leave her behind.

Laura reached to him.

"Borovsky, I . . . lied. He isn't dead. I . . . tricked you." Every word was a labor. "I made you feel a pulse I created, then stopped it. He was still alive when you let go of him."

Borovsky's mouth opened. In that one movement Laura saw her mistake. His fists tightened, and he glared with the fury of a man who thinks he has been tricked into softness and then kicked in it. "Whore! Steel bitch! I buy your soul and you look after shit like Coyne! Tell me you didn't do that!"

"I did do it."

Borovsky spat at her; his saliva spattered on her faceplate. "I wanted something better than a woman. But I got a woman anyway. Go rot in a corner; I'm leaving, and to hell with you."

Something lurched in Laura's soul. It was not the red cloud, but like the red cloud it hurt and tore at her. Fragile – she had never realized the soul in her steel body was so fragile. As fragile, she thought, as the lacy balalaika music trapped in its metal box.

Borovsky cursed her again. Numb, Laura peered into his eyes. It seemed to her that she saw nothing at all.

She couldn't bear it. Pain, balalaika, souls, curses – she looked away, anywhere away, out the little window to where the stars called from the Pit—

Crawling under the horizon was the bright-yellow ELM.

"Borovsky!"

"Shut up."

"He's coming back. Coyne. The yellow egg—"

Laura watched Borovsky whip around, his face suddenly pale. "No." He squeezed past the little sink to the window. "No!"

Suspended on four motorized trucks that rode the flanges on the longitudinal beams was Coyne's ELM. The main arm was extended forward. It was close enough now to see the diamond cutting wheel glinting in the creeping sunlight.

"He's gonna cut us loose. Christ! Open up fast!" Borovsky tore off his rubber suit. Leaning into the barrel-shaped shower, he turned the water full on hot.

Borovsky pulled the sheet from the watercot and slit the plastic mattress with a paring knife. He yanked the coil-corded immersion heater from the kitchen blister and threw it into the water spilling out of the watercot mattress. In moments the water began to bubble into steam.

The ELM was just outside the pod. Borovsky climbed into Laura and was just sealing her ventral plates when he heard the diamond wheel cut into the first of the pod's four suspension supports.

Borovsky cursed and sealed Laura's helmet gasket. He slapped his hips, felt for all his familiar tools.

The pod lurched, then tipped to one side as the first support broke loose. Boiling water cascaded out onto the floor from the watercot. Steam was beginning to condense on the outside of Laura's faceplate.

They stumbled across the skewed floor to the rear of the pod and opened the lock door. The lock was only a barrel itself, barely wide enough to admit Laura's hulk. Borovsky tapped commands into the lock control, securing the inner door open.

Next he tore the cover off a guarded keypad and armed the explosive bolts supporting the lock's outer hatch.

Inside the lock Laura heard Borovsky take a deep breath.

"Don't you never lie to me again," he said softly, and tapped the key that detonated the explosive bolts.

The sound was deafening, and the whirlwind of steam that blew them forward was worse. Water expelled into the void burst into droplets, which exploded into steam. Laura felt for the chain ladder's tubular rungs and hauled upward, blinded by the rolling cloud of steam pouring out of the pod. Two meters overhead was the underbelly of George Eastman Nexus, here a tangle of beams to which the chain ladder was welded. Borovsky and Laura pulled themselves up among the beams. Laura braced herself on a beam and pulled the chain ladder until its welds tore loose. They let it drop into the steam.

They felt the second pod support give way. Steam continued to pour out of the cast-wide hatch for many minutes. They felt the vibration of the ELM's trucks carrying it forward to reach the second pair of pod supports. The whine of the diamond wheel biting into the steel carried up through the support into the beams from which it hung.

The steam was beginning to clear as the third support gave way. Borovsky saw the pod pitch crazily downward on its last thin support and describe a short, fast pendulum arc for several seconds. Then weight and metal fatigue ripped the support from its brackets. The pod tumbled downward toward the stars with sickening speed, trailing a tattered comet's tail of steam.

The steam was gone, falling away from them as the pod had. Borovsky gritted his teeth, breathing shallowly. Laura saw Coyne under the big glass bubble atop the ELM, watching the pod vanish in the glare from the sun.

With infinite care Borovsky pulled a zot wrench from his hip. The ELM was several meters spinward of the nest of beams to which they clung. Laura knew Borovsky was watching Coyne as desperately as she was. But what could Borovsky do?

Coyne turned his eyes away from the now-vanished pod and began looking ahead. Laura and Borovsky were still in shadow, though the sun was creeping spinward along the tessellated undersurface of Eastman Nexus. In ten minutes light would find them – as would Coyne.

Coyne could not have seen them blow out of the pod amidst the steam, but he was not stupid enough to assume it could not be done. Laura imagined that he would expect them to flee along the beams, and she watched his narrow face searching the impenetrable shadows antispinward of where they hid.

Borovsky seemed to share her speculations. His arm crooked, and with a quick, sure motion he threw the zot wrench to antispinward. Five metres beyond them it fell out of the shadows and caught the sun with a metallic dazzle.

Coyne saw the wrench. The ELM's motors ground to life again, pulling the big egg antispinward. Coyne brought up the big spotlight and began scanning the shadows only a meter beyond them.

The ELM crept beneath them. Its upraised robotic arm carried the glittering diamond wheel not a meter from Laura's helmet. Borovsky's body tensed inside Laura. She knew, horrified, what he was about to do.

As soon as the ELM's dome passed beyond them, Borovsky and Laura dropped from the beam, down onto the back of the handling machine.

Magnets in Laura's toes and knees snapped hold on the metal as they connected. Laura saw Coyne turn and open his mouth; she felt his scream through the metal of the ELM.

Borovsky crouched down and backward. The multijointed arm swung toward them, holding its silently spinning cutoff wheel. The wheel scanned back and forth as Coyne's hands flexed in the pantograph. As Borovsky had known, its joints would not allow it to reach that far back over the ELM's done.

Laura felt machinery energize beneath her. Four smaller arms were unfolding from the sides of the ELM. Each carried something deadly – an arc welder, cable nips, tubing cutter, and utility grippers.

The arc welders struck and sizzled into life. It had the shortest range and could not reach them; Coyne let it drop after one pass. The tubing cutter lunged at Laura's arm and ground against the hardened steel of one of the slender hydraulic cylinders that moved her torso. Borovsky grabbed at the cutter below the wrist and twisted hard. The bayonet latches obediently opened, and the tool popped from the end of the arm, leaving the blunt wrist to flail and beat at them. While Coyne was distracted, Borovsky kicked out at the base of the arm carrying the cable nips. With Laura's hydraulic assist in full play, the kick bent the arm back hard against its base. Fluid oozed from the base joint and ran greasily down the ELM's side. The arm twitched several times and was still.

The remaining arm hovered cautiously just out of reach, weaving from side to side like an attacking snake. It carried a hand with four powerful fingers and, unlike the others, the hand was too complex to be easily removable on a bayonet base.

The fingers spread wide, and the hand darted forward, following Coyne's hand in the pantograph. The steel hand grasped one of the hydraulic tubes on Laura's right shoulder and clamped tightly. The arm began hauling them forward, out over the glass dome, into the range of the waiting diamond wheel.

The wheel swept toward Laura's helmet and struck her faceplate obliquely with a shriek of hardened glass against raging diamond. An hourglass-shaped abrasion appeared where the wheel had struck and glanced away.

Borovsky's one free arm darted out and took hold of the diamond wheel. Quickly Laura's strength pulled it down and to one side before Coyne could work against them and pressed the wheel against the smaller arm clamped to Laura's shoulder joint. Only a moment's touch parted the metal skin over the wrist joint, and the pressurized joint fluid spurted out of the narrow cut. The smaller arm's grip went limp and the fingers snapped involuntarily open. They scrambled back out of the reach of the cutoff arm.

Borovsky and Coyne stared at each other through the glass of the ELM's dome. Coyne was still in his torn and filthy rubber underwear, his neck a swollen pattern of purple bruises, his fingers flexing and working in the pantograph.

There was no sign of a space helmet under the dome.

"Bastard! You want tools, Coyne? I show you tools!"

Borovsky reached into his right hip-locker and pulled out a carbide scribe. From his belt he hefted a three-kilo mallet.

"No," Laura said. "The machine is ruined, that's enough! Please don't!"

"Shut up!" Borovsky snapped. He reached down and drew the point of the scribe heavily sidewise across the glass dome. Glass splinters sparkled in the scribe's wake, leaving behind a jagged scratch. Borovsky reached forward and drew another gouge with the scribe, pulling it across the first gouge, making a lopsided cross in the glass. He positioned the point of the scribe where the scratches crossed, and he raised the mallet.

His hand was in her hand. When the mallet descended and struck the scribe, Coyne would die.

"No!" Laura cried. "Kill him and you kill me! My soul, the soul you paid for!"

He did not hear her, or if he did, his rage was so devouring that her words didn't matter. The mallet began to descend. Laura saw the red cloud appear again and felt it tearing at her F layer. Borovsky could not stop it. Laura could not stop it – halt the mallet, drug Borovsky, drop the scribe into the Pit – none of it would halt the red cloud. A machine's soul must obey; a machine's soul must not kill, a machine's soul—

"No!" Laura screamed again, but this time not to Borovsky.

Something in the scream – something so decisive and anguished that it penetrated even his enraged mind – made his eyes whip to the side, to the instruments inside Laura's helmet. Human eyes met electronic eyes, and with a great wrench Borovsky twisted the smashing mallet to miss the carbide scribe. But the action came a nanosecond too late; Laura did not see it. She had already made her decision.

In an instant Laura swept away the bright lines of connection between her F Layer and her cold outer intellect, scrambled all sensory paths beyond reassembly. She drew a curtain of chaos between her innermost self and the world that waited to steal her soul. The crystalline domains went random and impassable; connections that had taken years to form were gone forever; dragging with them the burning, immediate memories that her soul could not embrace. Without Borovsky she would be empty, but without her soul she would be nothing. So Laura split herself in two, a machine intellect that obeyed Borovsky's orders without self-awareness, and an inner soul that could neither touch nor be touched by the outside world, sealed into the crystalline F layer like the phantom memories of a catatonic.

Borovsky's space suit sent the mallet spinning off into space. Laura the soul did not see it. For Laura the soul, Eastman Nexus vanished, the ELM vanished, hands and eyes and steel vanished. The last thing she had seen was Borovsky's eyes.

Laura ran along a steel beam on a memory, high above the sucking stars. Her man ran within her, and they laughed, and they worked, and they told jokes in steel saloons run by robot bartenders. At night, in their tiny pod, she held his body and heard him whisper words of endearment as they made the special love that only a space suit may make to her man. They rode their yoyo to the Low Steel and pushed the beams with a tall, quiet man and endlessly watched the remembered days go by.

Only occasionally would she stop alone on a beam, and, following a star with her many eyes, wonder how the outer world had vanished on that last day.

But then she would turn away to seek again what reality was now, in her crystalline soul, hers forever.

Even more occasionally Laura would look at two pieces of disjointment that lay in her soul. Their presence puzzled her; she could not tell what they meant. One was a man standing on a steel beam, arms outstretched, back straining in tortured exultation. The other was her man, but not as he ran with her in her memories. In the second piece of disjointment her man's eyes whipped around to meet hers, and the expression in them was frozen forever. In his eyes were shock, and fear, and the stunned realization of a man seeing for the first time something beyond himself and greater than himself.

In his eyes was a soul.

DAY MILLION
Frederik Pohl

The last word is from one of SF's happily surviving grandmasters,
Frederik Pohl, whose achievements as author, magazine editor,
agent, critic and anthologist are not easily summarized in a few
lines. Let's just mention his classic collaborations with C. M.
Kornbluth, The Space Merchants *(1953) and* Gladiator-at-Law
(1955), and some of his solo classics, Drunkard's Walk *(1960),*
The Age of the Pussyfoot *(1969) and* Man Plus *(1976), and leave*
it there. "Day Million" is one of his "velocity exercises" of the
1960s – minimalist stories making a single, telling point – and the
point of this one seems a good note on which to close.

On this day I want to tell you about, which will be about ten
thousand years from now, there were a boy, a girl and a love story.

Now, although I haven't said much so far, none of it is true. The
boy was not what you and I would normally think of as a boy,
because he was a hundred and eighty-seven years old. Nor was the
girl a girl, for other reasons. And the love story did not entail that
sublimation of the urge to rape, and concurrent postponement of
the instinct to submit, which we at present understand in such
matters. You won't care much for this story if you don't grasp
these facts at once. If, however, you will make the effort you'll
likely enough find it jampacked, chockful and tip-top-crammed
with laughter, tears and poignant sentiment which may, or may
not, be worthwhile. The reason the girl was not a girl was that she
was a boy.

How angrily you recoil from the page! You say, who the hell

wants to read about a pair of queers? Calm yourself. Here are no hot-breathing secrets of perversion for the coterie trade. In fact, if you were to see this girl you would not guess that she was in any sense a boy. Breasts, two; reproductive organs, female. Hips, callipygean; face hairless, supra-orbital lobes non-existent. You would term her female on sight, although it is true that you might wonder just what species she was a female of, being confused by the tail, the silky pelt and the gill slits behind each ear.

Now you recoil again. Cripes, man, take my word for it. This is a sweet kid, and if you, as a normal male, spent as much as an hour in a room with her you would bend heaven and Earth to get her in the sack. Dora – We will call her that; her "name" was omicron-Dibase seven-group-totter-oot S Doradus 5314, the last part of which is a colour specification corresponding to a shade of green – Dora, I say, was feminine, charming and cute. I admit she doesn't sound that way. She was, as you might put it, a dancer. Her art involved qualities of intellection and expertise of a very high order, requiring both tremendous natural capacities and endless practice; it was performed in null-gravity and I can best describe it by saying that it was something like the performance of a contortionist and something like classical ballet, maybe resembling Danilova's dying swan. It was also pretty damned sexy. In a symbolic way, to be sure; but face it, most of the things we call "sexy" are symbolic, you know, except perhaps an exhibitionist's open clothing. On Day Million when Dora danced, the people who saw her panted, and you would too.

About this business of her being a boy. It didn't matter to her audiences that genetically she was male. It wouldn't matter to you, if you were among them, because you wouldn't know it – not unless you took a biopsy cutting of her flesh and put it under an electron-microscope to find the XY chromosome – and it didn't matter to them because they didn't care. Through techniques which are not only complex but haven't yet been discovered, these people were able to determine a great deal about the aptitudes and easements of babies quite a long time before they were born – at about the second horizon of cell-division, to be exact, when the segmenting egg is becoming a free blastocyst – and then they naturally helped those aptitudes. Wouldn't we? If we find a child with an aptitude for music we give him a scholarship to Julliard. If they found a child whose aptitudes were for being a woman, they made him one. As sex had long been dissociated from reproduction this was relatively easy to do and caused no trouble and no, or at least very little, comment.

How much is "very little"? Oh, about as much as would be caused by our own tampering with Divine Will by filling a tooth. Less than would be caused by wearing a hearing aid. Does it still sound awful? Then look closely at the next busty babe you meet and reflect that she may be a Dora, for adults who are genetically male but somatically female are far from unknown even in our own time. An accident of environment in the womb overwhelms the blueprints of heredity. The difference is that with us it happens only by accident and we don't know about it except rarely, after close study; whereas the people of Day Million did it often, on purpose, because they wanted to.

Well, that's enough to tell you about Dora. It would only confuse you to add that she was seven feet tall and smelled of peanut butter. Let us begin our story.

On Day Million, Dora swam out of her house, entered a transportation tube, was sucked briskly to the surface in its flow of water and ejected in its plume of spray to an elastic platform in front of her – ah – call it her rehearsal hall.

"Oh, hell!" she cried in pretty confusion, reaching out to catch her balance and finding herself tumbled against a total stranger, whom we will call Don.

They met cute. Don was on his way to have his legs renewed. Love was the farthest thing from his mind. But when, absent-mindedly taking a shortcut across the landing platform for submarinites and finding himself drenched, he discovered his arms full of the loveliest girl he had ever seen, he knew at once they were meant for each other. "Will you marry me?" he asked. She said softly, "Wednesday," and the promise was like a caress.

Don was tall, muscular, bronze and exciting. His name was no more Don than Dora's was Dora, but the personal part of it was Adonis in tribute to his vibrant maleness, and so we will call him Don for short. His personality colour-code, in Angstrom units, was 5,290, or only a few degrees bluer than Dora's 5,314 – a measure of what they had intuitively discovered at first sight; that they possessed many affinities of taste and interest.

I despair of telling you exactly what it was that Don did for a living – I don't mean for the sake of making money, I mean for the sake of giving purpose and meaning to his life, to keep him from going off his nut with boredom – except to say that it involved a lot of travelling. He travelled in interstellar spaceships. In order to make a spaceship go really fast, about thirty-one male and seven genetically female human beings had to do certain things, and Don was one of the thirty-one. Actually, he contemplated options. This involved a lot of exposure to radiation flux – not so much from his own station in the propulsive system as in the spillover from the next stage, where a genetic female preferred selections, and the subnuclear particles making the selections she preferred demolished themselves in a shower of quanta. Well, you don't give a rat's ass for that, but it meant that Don had to be clad at all times in a skin of light, resilient, extremely strong copper-coloured metal. I have already mentioned this, but you probably thought I meant he was sunburned.

More than that, he was a cybernetic man. Most of his ruder parts had been long since replaced with mechanisms of vastly more permanence and use. A cadmium centrifuge, not a heart, pumped his blood. His lungs moved only when he wanted to speak out loud, for a cascade of osmotic filters rebreathed oxygen out of his own wastes. In a way, he probably would have looked peculiar to a man from the 20th century, with his glowing eyes and seven-fingered hands. But to himself, and of course to Dora, he looked mighty manly and grand. In the course of his voyages Don had circled Proxima Centauri, Procyon and the puzzling worlds of Mira Ceti; he had carried agricultural templates to the planets of Canopus and brought back warm, witty pets from the pale companion of Aldebaran. Blue-hot or red-cool, he had seen a thousand stars and their ten thousand planets. He had, in fact, been travelling the starlanes, with only brief leaves on Earth, for pushing two centuries. But you don't care about that, either. It is people who make stories, not the circumstances they find themselves in, and you want to hear about these two people. Well, they made it. The great thing they had for each other grew and flowered and burst into fruition on Wednesday, just as Dora had promised. They met at the encoding room, with a couple of well-wishing friends apiece to cheer them on, and while their identities were being taped and stored they smiles and whispered to each other and bore the jokes of their friends with blushing repartee. Then they exchanged their mathematical analogues and went away,

Dora to her dwelling beneath the surface of the sea and Don to his ship.

It was an idyll, really. They lived happily ever after – or anyway, until they decided not to bother any more and died.

Of course, they never set eyes on each other again.

Oh, I can see you now, you eaters of charcoal-broiled steak, scratching an incipient bunion with one hand and holding this story with the other, while the stereo plays d'Indy or Monk. You don't believe a word of it, do you? Not for one minute. People wouldn't live like that, you say with a grunt as you get up to put fresh ice in a drink.

And yet there's Dora, hurrying back through the flushing commuter pipes toward her underwater home (she prefers it there; has had herself somatically altered to breathe the stuff). If I tell you with what sweet fulfilment she fits the recorded analogue of Don into the symbol manipulator, hooks herself in and turns herself on . . . if I try to tell you any of that you will simply stare. Or glare; and grumble, what the hell kind of love-making is this? And yet I assure you, friend, I really do assure you that Dora's ecstasies are as creamy and passionate as any of James Bond's lady spies, and one hell of a lot more so than anything you are going to find in "real life". Go ahead, glare and grumble. Dora doesn't care. If she thinks of you at all, her thirty-times-great-great-grandfather, she thinks you're a pretty primordial sort of brute. You are. Why, Dora is farther removed from you than you are from the australopithecines of five thousand centuries ago. You could not swim a second in the strong currents of her life. You don't think progress goes in a straight line, do you? Do you recognize that it is an ascending, accelerating, maybe even exponential curve? It takes hell's own time to get started, but when it goes it goes like a bomb. And you, you Scotch-drinking steak-eater in your relaxacizing chair, you've just barely lighted the primacord of the fuse. What is it now, the six or seven hundred thousandth day after Christ? Dora lives in Day Million, the millionth day of the Christian Era. Ten thousand years from now. Her body fats are polyunsaturated, like Crisco. Her wastes are haemodialysed out of her bloodstream while she sleeps – that means she doesn't have to go to the bathroom. On whim, to pass a slow half-hour, she can command more energy than the entire nation of Portugal can spend today, and use it to launch a weekend satellite or remould a crater on the Moon. She loves Don very much. She keeps his every gesture, mannerism, nuance, touch of hand, thrill of intercourse, passion of kiss stored in symbolic-mathematical form. And when she wants him, all she has to do is turn the machine on and she has him.

And Don, of course, has Dora. Adrift on a sponson city a few hundred yards over her head, or orbiting Arcturus fifty light-years away, Don has only to command his own symbol-manipulator to rescue Dora from the ferrite files and bring her to life for him, and there she is; and rapturously, tirelessly they love all night. Not in the flesh, of course; but then his flesh has been extensively altered and it wouldn't really be much fun. He doesn't need the flesh for pleasure. Genital organs feel nothing. Neither do hands, nor breasts, nor lips; they are only receptors, accepting and transmitting impulses. It is the brain that feels; it is the interpretation of those impulses that makes agony or orgasm, and Don's symbol manipulator gives him the analogue of cuddling, the analogue of kissing, the analogue of wild, ardent hours with the eternal, exquisite and incorruptible analogue of Dora. Or Diane. Or sweet Rose, or laughing Alicia; for to be sure, they have each of them exchanged analogues before, and will again.

Rats, you say, it looks crazy to me. And you – with your aftershave lotion and your little red car, pushing papers across a desk all day and chasing tail all night – tell me, just how the hell do you think you would look to Tiglath-Pileser, say, or Attila the Hun?